THE CLIVEDEN SET

By the same author

The Gentile Zionists
'Baffy': The Diaries of Blanche Dugdale
Vansittart: Study of a Diplomat
Lewis Namier and Zionism
Chaim Weizmann: A Biography
Churchill: An Unruly Life

THE CLIVEDEN SET

Portrait of an Exclusive Fraternity

Norman Rose

JONATHAN CAPE
LONDON

Published by Jonathan Cape 2000

2 4 6 8 10 9 7 5 3 1

First published in Great Britain in 2000 by
Jonathan Cape
Random House, 20 Vauxhall Bridge Road,
London SW1V 2SA

Random House Australia (Pty) Limited
20 Alfred Street, Milsons Point, Sydney,
New South Wales 2061, Australia

Random House New Zealand Limited
18 Poland Road, Glenfield,
Auckland 10, New Zealand

Random House (Pty) Limited
Endulini, 5A Jubilee Road, Parktown 2193, South Africa

The Random House Group Limited Reg. No. 954009
www.randomhouse.co.uk

A CIP catalogue record for this book
is available from the British Library

ISBN 0–224–06093–7

Papers used by Random House are natural,
recyclable products made from wood grown in sustainable forests;
the manufacturing processes conform to the environmental
regulations of the country of origin.

Typeset by Deltatype Ltd, Birkenhead, Merseyside
Printed and bound in Great Britain by
Mackays of Chatham PLC

For Inbal and Amit

Contents

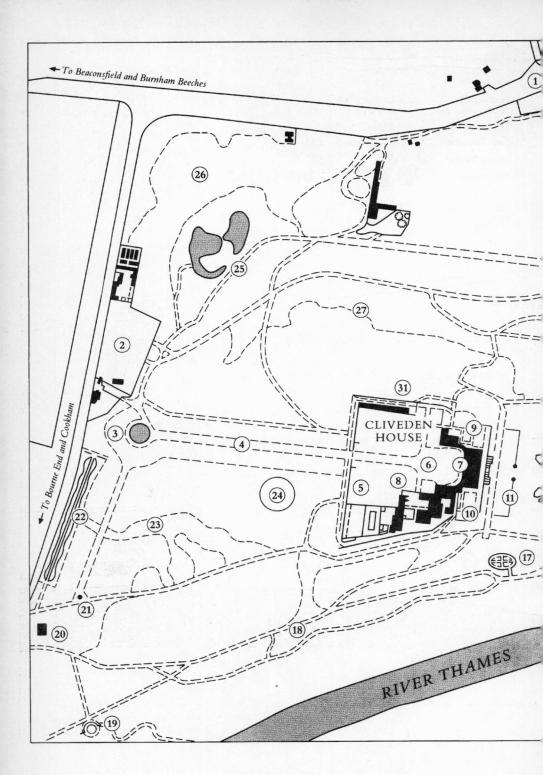

To Beaconsfield and Burnham Beeches

To Bourne End and Cookham

CLIVEDEN HOUSE

RIVER THAMES

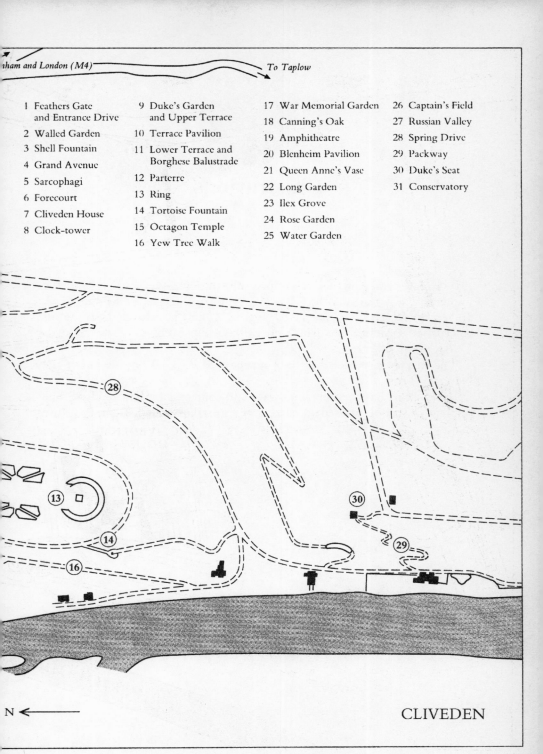

ham and London (M4) ───────────────→ To Taplow

1 Feathers Gate
   and Entrance Drive
2 Walled Garden
3 Shell Fountain
4 Grand Avenue
5 Sarcophagi
6 Forecourt
7 Cliveden House
8 Clock-tower

9 Duke's Garden
   and Upper Terrace
10 Terrace Pavilion
11 Lower Terrace and
   Borghese Balustrade
12 Parterre
13 Ring
14 Tortoise Fountain
15 Octagon Temple
16 Yew Tree Walk

17 War Memorial Garden
18 Canning's Oak
19 Amphitheatre
20 Blenheim Pavilion
21 Queen Anne's Vase
22 Long Garden
23 Ilex Grove
24 Rose Garden
25 Water Garden

26 Captain's Field
27 Russian Valley
28 Spring Drive
29 Packway
30 Duke's Seat
31 Conservatory

N ←──────

CLIVEDEN

Illustrations

For kind permission to reproduce illustrations the author and the publishers wish to thank the following: Country Life Picture Library (1, 2, 4); Hulton Getty (3, 5, 6, 8, 10, 12–16); The Royal Institute of International Affairs, Chatham House (9); Group Archives Service, Lloyds TSB Group (11).

The map of Cliveden has been reproduced by kind permission of the National Trust.

Every effort has been made to trace and contact copyright holders. The publishers will be pleased to correct any mistakes or omissions in future editions.

Prologue

In October 1921, Lloyd George spoke to Lord Riddell, publisher of the *News of the World*, of

> a very powerful combination – in its way perhaps the most powerful in the country. Each member of the Group brings to its deliberations certain definite and important qualities, and behind the scenes they have much power and influence.[1]

Jan Christian Smuts, soldier, philosopher and South African prime minister, added that 'the Group's' words were studied 'by nearly everyone who determines public policy or originates public opinion'.[2] On one occasion, Sir Maurice Hankey, Secretary to the Cabinet, himself a puller of many strings, placed them 'among the most influential' of the 'political congeries' operating in London during the Great War. He named names and venues (not all of them entirely accurate).

> They dine every Monday usually at the house of Major Waldorf Astor MP, Sir Edward Carson, or [F. S.] Oliver. Milner is the real leader of this group, which includes Amery, Philip Kerr, and the editor of *The Times* Geoffrey Robinson, as well as the various young men associated with the [group].[3]

Repeatedly described as 'a ginger group', 'a junta', 'a camarilla', 'a cabal', an 'inner circle', it was esteemed for its judgements, which were considered 'careful, weighty, and responsible', even 'indispensable'. Here indeed were 'the great and the good', persons of 'light and leading'. Together they formed 'God's Truth Ltd', a company whose decrees were invariably 'Olympian'.[4]

'God's Truth Ltd' attracted other charges, however. Called by some 'a deadly secret committee', it was held to be 'a clique which encourages every centrifugal force in the British Empire'. Others considered that its existence ensured that Britain would become 'permanently second-rate intellectually among the nations'. The *Morning Post* regarded it as 'a phalanx or palace guard of idealists, who could be trusted by a sort of spiritual perversion to take a line injurious to British interests on every question'.[5] Joseph Caillaux, a French prime minister, saw it as 'a group of Oxford men, highly placed in British affairs', conspiring to restore 'the tottering power of the caste to which they belong and the strengthening of the supremacy of Great Britain in the world'. By 'gazing too intently at the stars', thought Sir Robert Laird Borden, the Canadian statesman, they occasionally 'fall into a ditch or stumble over a low-lying wall'.[6] Although well-meaning, their influence was 'poisonous', 'a disaster to our way of life'. Forever 'pontificating', or engaged 'in deliberate sabotage' of the League of Nations and collective security, they were fobbed off as 'highbrow noodles'.[7]

What was the true nature of this controversial fraternity? Were its promoters prophetic visionaries or interfering busybodies? Its origins date from the period of reconstruction in South Africa immediately after the Boer War. Lord Milner, the high commissioner, had conscripted a band of young men just down from Oxford, mainly from New College, to aid him in the formidable task of rebuilding the war-torn country. He explained his purpose to a colleague.

> I mean to have young men. There will be a regular rumpus and a lot of talk about boys and Oxford and jobs and all that . . . Well I value brains and character more than experience. First class men of experience are not to be got. Nothing one could offer would tempt them to give up what they have . . . No! I shall not be here for very long but when I go I mean to leave behind me young men with plenty of work in them . . .[8]

Known collectively as the *Kindergarten*, a term of derision coined by Sir William Marriott, a former Judge Advocate-General, who liked neither Milner nor his 'young men', the group proudly adopted the nickname, elevating membership to its distinguished circle as a mark of special distinction.

The *Kinder* were instrumental in guiding Milner, and his successor, Lord Selborne, towards a process that culminated eventually in the Union of South Africa. The creation of the Union spawned other ingenious ideas. They began to think in terms of union or federation or close cooperation – opinions were divided – between the mother country and the Dominions, the idea being to establish a bloc sufficiently powerful to ensure that Great Britain retained its status as a great power. Drawing on the racial theories of Cecil Rhodes and Milner, they envisaged also an Anglo-Saxon brotherhood, involving close ties between the United States and the British

Empire – or Commonwealth, as it was later defined by one of them. And finally, as the ultimate panacea for a troubled international system, the most dedicated of the *Kinder* floated a master plan for world government, a blueprint that would inaugurate an era of eternal peace.

After the Union the *Kindergarten* broke up. A few remained in South Africa, but most drifted back to England. In London, they continued their tradition of conducting Moots to deliberate upon diverse imperial problems.* In 1910 they founded the Round Table movement, with branches in South Africa, Canada, Newfoundland, Australia and New Zealand. In November of that year the first issue of their quarterly review, *The Round Table*, appeared. Disseminating information and informed comment on imperial and international affairs that would be 'entirely free from the bias of local political issues', the journal swiftly established its reputation as an authoritative, if somewhat opinionated, voice on these matters. Although the review operated within a regular editorial framework, the Moot – like the *Kindergarten* – was a more informal affair. It occupied no official position, nor did it benefit from a constitution. None of this hindered its activities. A self-appointed pressure-group, its members, as if by divine right, spiced their colloquiums with a rare kind of intellectual conceit. Its mission, by way of persuading those that mattered, was to stimulate a movement to promote 'the closer union of the British Empire'.[9] These Moots, held either at its London headquarters or at other select venues, characterized the group's activities for decades to come.

Attracting new adherents, this resolute team broadened the scope of its pursuits. It was influential in founding and running the British (later Royal) Institute of International Affairs, originally planned as one of a number of similar institutes to be set up throughout the world. This network, it was anticipated, would act as 'a telephone exchange between the few hundred men in each country who administer foreign affairs and create public opinion on the subject'.[10] Within its walls, the Institute would conduct postgraduate-like 'study and research', bridging the gap between 'men of theory' and 'men of action'. More popularly known as Chatham House,† the Institute's wider purpose, yet again, was to educate opinion, to sort out the tangled relationship between Britain and the outside world. It defined opinion in the narrowest sense of the word, aiming its erudite missives mainly at the members of 'London's clubland'. 'Permeated by the

---

* From early Middle English, the word *moot* implies an encounter, a meeting, or an assembly of people. It was widely assumed that the moots held by Anglo-Saxon freemen showed the first stirrings of popular government.

† Located at 10 St James's Square, London, the one-time residence of William Pitt, 1st Earl of Chatham, the house was donated to the Institute by a Canadian couple, the Leonards. Inaugurated as the British Institute of International Affairs in July 1920, it received its Royal Charter in 1925.

semi-conspiratorial neo-Platonism of nineteenth-century Oxford', they saw themselves as sublime elitists enlightening other, less discerning, members of the same magic circle.[11] And indeed Oxford figured large in their endeavours, for many of them, apart from being graduates of the University, were Fellows of All Souls College, or were welcome guests in its Senior Common Room.

Who were they, these would-be inspirers of leading opinion? The lists of those associated with these fraternities, from the *Kindergarten* to Oxford High Tables, are long and varied. They included many prominent politicians, businessmen, academics, authors, journalists, and members of the landed gentry.[12] But some names reappear time and again with intriguing regularity: Philip Kerr (later Lord Lothian), a distinguished public servant and Liberal politician of independent means and impeccable aristocratic lineage; Robert (later Lord) Brand, a hard-headed international investment banker; Geoffrey Dawson (né Robinson), a Yorkshire squire and editor of *The Times*; Lionel Curtis, a Fellow of All Souls, driven by an inner force to champion elusive causes; Waldorf, 2nd Viscount Astor, an American-born multimillionaire, the owner of Cliveden, and by association his wife Nancy, by birth a Virginian belle, and the first woman MP to take her seat in the House of Commons, who together acted as hosts to a political-literary-academic salon at their estate at Cliveden or at their London mansion at 4 St James's Square.

By the mid-late 1930s these last names were catapulted into unexpected, and certainly uncalled-for, notoriety. They had been identified by a maverick Communist journalist, Claud Cockburn, as the core members of a cabal that sought to manipulate British foreign policy, and at crucial times even to determine it. 'This shadow cabinet' conspired, he claimed, to procure a humiliating, dishonourable settlement with Nazi Germany. It had loaded and pointed a 'One-Way Gun' aimed at central and eastern Europe, in particular at the Soviet Union, where Hitler would be given a free hand secure in the knowledge that Germany's position in the West had been guaranteed. And it did so, Cockburn stressed, to uphold its own narrow class interests. He named it the 'Cliveden Set'.

This piece of startling information caught fire with astonishing speed. The catchphrase 'the Cliveden Set' reverberated around the world. Journals from Singapore to New York to Buenos Aires picked it up and elaborated upon the sensation, crowning Nancy Astor as 'Queen of the Set' who reigned at the 'Schloss Cliveden'. Cliveden weekend house parties, where the cream of English society – whether prime ministers or literary lions like George Bernard Shaw, or mysterious adventurers such as T. E. Lawrence (of Arabia) – was regularly entertained, had been for some time a feature of contemporary gossip columns. Claud Cockburn's latest revelation added a new and sinister dimension to these gatherings.

The 'Set' widened. The popular press, at times throwing all caution to the wind, drew up an imposing list. It now included John Jacob Astor V, who, together with his brother Waldorf, owned controlling interests in the *Observer* and *The Times*. The Astor family interest in Parliament alone aroused intense suspicion. Five in the Commons, three in the Lords, they constituted a genuine family lobby.* Other conspirators were named: Thomas Jones (T.J.), one-time deputy secretary to the cabinet and the intimate of prime ministers; Edward Grigg, journalist, Conservative politician, and colonial proconsul; James Garvin, editor of the *Observer*; Lord Londonderry, a former Secretary of State for Air, widely known for his pro-German views; Henry 'Chips' Channon, a dedicated socialite and ardent government supporter; Sir Montague Norman, governor of the Bank of England; Sir Henri Deterding, director-general of Royal Dutch Petroleum. Prominent Cabinet ministers such as Lord Halifax, Sir Samuel Hoare, Sir John Simon and Sir Thomas Inskip were also included. Even Charles Lindbergh, the American aviator, whose wildly exaggerated reports of the Luftwaffe's destructive power received wide currency at the time, was nominated for membership. The list of abettors was, apparently, never-ending. 'The Cliveden Baronage', to use the *Tribune*'s nomenclature, was a veritable 'Who's Who' of passé aristocrats, great landlords, captains of industry and finance, influential journalists, slippery politicians, pretentious academics and over-mighty civil servants. According to the *Washington Post*, it constituted 'the real centre of British foreign policy', menacing and challenging 'the constitutional structure of British Democracy'.[13] Together with their hangers-on, they would use any means, however devious, even traitorous, to maintain the privileges of their decaying class.

Here was a classic conspiracy theory, appealing, compelling, perhaps comforting to the uninitiated. Its historical truth is another matter. No hard evidence has yet come to light to sustain this fanciful interpretation. But this does not resolve the quandary, it merely makes it more intriguing. For when does a 'Set' become a Cockburn-like 'Set'?[14] What is abundantly clear is that the cadre, the nucleus of the so-called 'Set' – Lothian, Dawson, Brand, Curtis and the Astors – formed a close-knit band, on intimate terms with each other for most of their adult life. Here indeed was a consortium of like-minded people, actively engaged in public life, close to the inner circles of power, intimate with Cabinet ministers, and who met

* It embraced: Lady Astor, MP for Plymouth; John Jacob Astor V, MP for Dover; William Waldorf Astor, Lord and Lady Astor's son, MP for East Fulham; Lord (James) Willoughby de Eresby, son-in-law of Lord and Lady Astor, MP for Rutland; and Ronald Tree, MP for Harborough, who had married the eldest daughter of Nancy Astor's brother-in-law. In the Lords sat Viscount Astor; the Earl of Ancaster, James Willoughby's father; and the Earl of Minto, John Jacob's brother-in-law.

periodically at Cliveden or at 4 St James's Square (or occasionally at other venues). Nor can there be any doubt that, broadly speaking, they supported – with one notable exception – the government's attempts to reach an agreement with Hitler's Germany, or that their opinions, propagated with vigour, were condemned by many as embarrassingly pro-German. The high drama masking their activities sprang from their distinguished pedigrees, their network of social and political contacts, and the glamorous settings in which they concocted their so-called plots.

Today, the 'Set' would be categorized as an establishment group *par excellence*. Henry Fairlie, a prominent English journalist, first gave common currency to this emotive term when he charged that the spies Guy Burgess and Donald MacLean, who had defected to Moscow, had been protected from exposure by the 'Establishment'. By this he did not refer only to the visible 'centres of official power', but to 'the whole matrix of official and social relations within which power is exercised'. Holding down key jobs or maintaining positions of influence in the country's affairs, these establishment figures are 'disinterested and high-minded, steeped in classical learning', with the added advantage that 'they keep their hands out of the till'. But more crucially, 'they meet each other frequently at lunch and at dinner and appear on the same guest lists on grand occasions, both state and private'. Political power, influence, leverage in England, he expounded, 'cannot be understood unless it is recognized that it is exercised socially'. Not only do they 'run their own shows', they have 'box seats for all the rest'.[15]

The 'Cliveden Set' falls neatly into these categories. Its pedigree impeccable, its social standing beyond reproach, its persuasive powers permeated the clubs and institutions of London, the Senior Common Rooms of Oxbridge colleges, the so-called quality press, in particular its correspondence columns, and the great country houses of England. Concerned almost exclusively with imperial and foreign affairs, it carried on as a disparate, irregular 'ginger group'. Soliciting 'a revolution by dinner-party',[16] it operated within, not against or outside, the parameters of conventional political behaviour. It did not challenge the government, but sought to brace its resolve, to guide it in ways that accorded with its own preconceived opinions. It was plainly a part of what has been identified as 'the foreign-policy-making elite' of Britain.[17] And the members of the 'Cliveden Set' were, so to speak, among its most prominent paid-up members.

No binding majority decisions were taken when the 'Set' met around the dinner table or on the terrace at Cliveden.* Differences of opinion, of

---

* Unlike the Round Table circle, with whom it was closely associated, the 'Set' boasted neither a long-term political programme nor an organized structure. The link was solely in

emphasis, frequently emerged. And, as so often happens, the more influential or the more motivated of them – or those with more time on their hands – made the running. Leading members of the 'Set' made no secret of their views, nor did they veil their efforts to promote them. On the contrary, they drummed up the widest possible publicity, at times staging theatrical gestures that were designed to catch the public eye. The 'Set' now emerges in its authentic guise, as a kind of self-appointed, unstructured think-tank. Regarding itself as an intellectual powerhouse, it did not hesitate to provide a rationale for the government's all too often controversial foreign policies. Although it could not be accurately described as 'a second Foreign Office', its members often appeared to behave as an amateur, part-time diplomatic corps, entertaining ambassadors or flying off to Germany to sound out Hitler and his cohorts about the chances of a European settlement. The professionals at the Foreign Office registered strong disapproval. 'Not a very safe intermediary,' ruled Sir Robert Vansittart, permanent head of the Office, about Lord Lothian, a power-broker among the dilettantes.[18]

Much has been written and spoken about this exclusive fraternity. It has been the subject of speculation and gossip, and also of much misrepresentation. Forever associated with Cliveden, the 'Set' regularly gathered there during the inter-war years, when the traditional country-house weekend still flourished, in an atmosphere that has been described as 'partly a luxurious holiday, partly a seminar, partly a retreat'.[19] In its elegant, palatial surroundings they ruminated, speculated, intrigued and – so their detractors claimed – plotted. So Cliveden itself, this imposing stately home, plays a leading role in their story.

the personalities involved. The 'Set', as described in the narrative, refers exclusively to the names mentioned on p. 4, those identified time and again by the press as its core members. With the exception of Nancy Astor (an honorary associate), all were Round Tablers as well as participants in the 'Set's' more high-profile practices. The 'Set' never sought this catchy designation. It brought them no satisfaction, nor did it add to their prestige. Quite the contrary, they believed, rightly, that it damaged their reputations. But they were stuck with it. And so, for better or worse, are we.

CHAPTER I

Cliveden

In 1538, the antiquary John Leland, exploring the stretch of 'the Tamise' between Cookham and Boulter's Lock (to the north-west of Maidenhead), described it as 'cliffy ground hanging over' the river with some 'Busshis growing on it'. Often rising to a height of one hundred and fifty feet, its chalk cliffs dominate this reach of the Thames and lend their character to the site first known as Cliefden, or as it is recognized today, Cliveden. Divided by a small valley that dips steeply towards the river, its heights afford the most spectacular views of the surrounding countryside, likened by Garibaldi to the 'mighty river prospects' of South America.[1] Indeed, the magnificent views it offers provides the most convincing *raison d'être* for building a great house at this point.

But it was not the only reason. Only five miles from Windsor Castle and twenty from Westminster, situated conveniently on the banks of the Thames, Cliveden was readily accessible to the centres of political power. Even in the seventeenth century it was possible to lunch in London and dine at Cliveden. Doubtless it was a combination of these factors that first induced George Villiers, 2nd Duke of Buckingham, to begin building in the late 1660s a palatial home for himself – although, apparently, he was also moved by an urge to impress his latest mistress, Anna Brudenell, Countess of Shrewsbury, one of the great court beauties of her day. The pile that emerged remained as a monument to Buckingham's grandiose fancies, a queer blend of the Orangery at Versailles and the famous terraces above the Seine at Saint-Germain.

The 2nd Duke's flamboyant character expressed itself in numerous other enterprises. 'Politician, diplomat, poet, playwright, amateur chemist, gambler, adulterer, and murderer', his scandalous behaviour never ceased to titillate Restoration England. His most notorious exploit occurred at the end of 1667 when he ran through and killed the Earl of Shrewsbury, the unfortunate husband of his mistress, in a duel at Barne Elmes, near Putney – a drama recorded in the Duke's Garden at Cliveden where the visitor will observe a pattern of flints shaped as a rapier, dated 1688, laid out on the lawn. Buckingham's licentiousness was matched only by his political wheeling and dealing. In the long run, it brought him little benefit. Regarded as corrupt, debauched and irresponsible, a reputation buttressed by his inclination for brawling, he was finally dismissed by Charles II and retired to his estates, stripped of all political influence. Thrown by his horse, he died in April 1687, mourned as a 'chymist, fiddler, statesman and buffoon' who was 'always in the wrong'.

After Buckingham's death the house passed into the hands of Lord George Hamilton (later created Earl of Orkney). A distinguished soldier and a friend of William of Orange, he had served with distinction as Marlborough's second-in-command at Blenheim. His wife, Elizabeth Villiers, was a kinswoman of the late Duke. Famously ugly – Elizabeth was reputed to 'squint like a dragon' – she was also, according to the highest authorities, exceptionally astute and sharp-witted. Politicians of the day found Elizabeth 'extreamly medling' in affairs of state, classifying her as a political intriguer of the first order. Orkney was of a quieter disposition. He turned his attention to improving the neglected house and gardens. What emerged was a considerable extension of the parterre and the landscaping of the Thames view of the house. A Yew Tree Walk now led down to the river, while to its north the wooded river slope was 'cutt out very agreeably in walks and *vistas*', to include also an amphitheatre. Orkney also enhanced the approaches to Cliveden. He widened the Grand Avenue, bordering it by two smaller avenues, that now led from the forecourt of the house to a *rond-point*, from which sprang other radiating walks and drives. Orkney had achieved much. Visitors wandering through the grounds today can still enjoy many of his improvements.

On Orkney's death, the estate was leased by Frederick Louis, Prince of Wales, son of George II. Frequently lampooned as 'Poor Fred', the Prince desperately sought to assert himself, searching for that elusive role in great affairs that so often eludes heirs to the throne. He quickly became a focus for oppositionist intrigue against the hated Sir Robert Walpole, the King's chief minister. Banned from the court, forbidden contact with foreign ambassadors, he received the ultimate slight when his father refused him command of the army against the Jacobite insurrection of 1745. Frederick Louis paid back his parents by cruelly caricaturing them in the *Histoire du Prince Titi*, a spoof that he either wrote or inspired.

Frustrated in London and Windsor, the Prince enjoyed Cliveden as a place for relaxation. Surrounded by his cronies, he amused himself in a routine of pleasure – cards, cricket, house games, or simply drinking at the Three Feathers inn (still in business as the Feathers inn). A cellist in his own right, Frederick Louis combined his love of music with a stab at his political tormentors. On 1 August 1740 he commanded that the first performance of *The Masque of Alfred* – a story of the 'Patriot-King-in Waiting' – be given in Cliveden's amphitheatre.* Owing to a heavy downpour the audience withdrew to the relative comfort of the house to listen to the remainder of the show. Wet and befuddled they might have been, but they must have been profoundly moved when they heard the stirring chorus,

> When Britain first, at Heaven's command,
> Arose from out the azure main,
> This was the charter of the land,
> And guardian angels sung this strain:
> 'Rule Britannia, rule the waves;
> Britons never will be slaves.'

It was somehow prophetic that the most patriotic ode in British music should first have been performed at Cliveden.

By the mid-nineteenth century Cliveden was in the possession of the 2nd Duke of Sutherland, purchased for the sum of £24,850, with an additional £9,566 for effects. It had been gutted twice by fire, the last occasion in 1849. This was a major calamity, but the Sutherlands (or Leveson-Gowers, pronounced 'Looson-Gores') were a family of formidable means, having amassed an immense fortune by what Disraeli called its 'talent for absorbing heiresses'. Sutherland employed one of the most notable architects of the day, Sir Charles Barry – then engaged on creating (to much criticism) his masterpiece, the Houses of Parliament – to remodel Cliveden. Seen today, Barry's Cliveden embodies a rewarding 'synthesis of English Palladian architecture with the Roman Cinquecento'. On its seventeenth-century raised terrace now stands an arcaded ground floor supporting a heavy balustraded cornice. On either side, Barry refurbished the curving colonnaded corridors that led into the wings of the house, where extra accommodation was provided to cater for additional guests when the main house was full. Above the first floor he erected another two storeys, tucked in neatly towards the centre and decorated with Ionic pilasters. Topped by a heavy parapet lined with heavy urns that concealed the roof, intended also as a viewing platform, the exterior of this imposing edifice was rendered in Roman cement (a mixture of slaked lime and volcanic ash) on a base of brick, its embellishments being expressed in moulded terracotta.

Seen from its garden front, Cliveden's pleasing symmetry cannot fail to impress the viewer, its southern outlook meticulously bisected by a double stone stairway descending in both directions from the terrace to the

* *The Masque of Alfred*, lyrics by the poets James Thomson and David Mallet, assisted by the Prince's secretary, George, 1st Lord Lyttleton, and music by Thomas Arne.

gardens and walks. There was one typical Victorian flourish. Gladstone, a close friend of Sutherland, composed a series of Latin inscriptions, embedded in a deep frieze just below the upper parapet, that glorified Buckingham, the founder of Cliveden, Sutherland, its benefactor and restorer, and its brilliant architect, Sir Charles Barry. Later a group of picturesque brick, half-timbered and tile-hung cottages, together with a boathouse, were added to the estate. Adorning the banks of this beautiful stretch of the Thames, they provide a setting that manifestly evokes scenes from the world of Jerome K. Jerome's *Three Men in a Boat*. By 1861, one other structure had been completed. Standing to the west side of the forecourt, an imposing campanile rose to a height of one hundred feet. Disguised as a clock tower, it in fact contains 17,000 gallons of water, pumped up from an artesian well on the other side of the Thames, a practical as well as attractive storage system designed to supply the needs of the house.

Harriet, the 2nd Duke's Duchess, was considered 'daringly radical' for an aristocrat. Under her careful guidance, Cliveden acquired a well-deserved reputation as a prominent Liberal salon. Distinguished visitors from all walks of life were always on hand. Alfred Tennyson, the poet laureate, Sir Joseph Paxton, gardener and architect, Carlo Marochetti, a titled Italian sculptor patronized by the British royal family, a varied assortment of Whig grandees, and, of course, the Gladstones. Even Queen Victoria stayed there during the summer of 1866.

But Harriet's most sensational catch was the Italian revolutionary leader Giuseppe Garibaldi, who arrived in London on his controversial visit in April 1864. His appearance caused a tremendous brouhaha. Not only a hero to the masses, he was also lionized by London society. Garibaldi retired to Cliveden to recuperate from this rapturous welcome. He planted a tree (it still stands in the Ilex Grove by the Clock Tower), admired the vistas of the Thames, lent his name to 'the Garibaldi room', and even, most daringly, smoked a cigar in Harriet's boudoir. Queen Victoria recorded her displeasure at these 'follies'. Harriet, the Queen's Mistress of the Robes, remained resolute, clearly heartbroken at the thought of her favourite leaving Cliveden. 'Although I cannot expect that the company of a woman who is no longer young [she was fifty-eight] can satisfy you,' she wrote to Garibaldi, 'nevertheless I shall try to divert your attention from other women who possess the blessings of youth and good health.'

Despite Victoria's censure, this seductive combination of high-flown political gossip and intriguing companions, set in the most opulent of surroundings, proved to be irresistible. Lucy Cavendish, Gladstone's niece, commented after one visit: 'The perfect taste, refinement, and luxury of the place almost oppresses me. When one lives in Paradise, how· hard it must be to ascend in heart and mind to Heaven.'

On the Dowager Duchess Harriet's death in 1868, Cliveden was purchased by her son-in-law, Hugh Lupus, Earl Grosvenor (created 1st Duke of Westminster in 1874). Although addicted to hunting and racing, Hugh Lupus had wider interests than these traditional pursuits. Deeply involved in national politics as he was, Gladstone thought him a 'selfish aristocrat' who had destroyed his proposed parliamentary reform bill of 1866. Throughout the 1870s, when not politicking in London, Westminster spent much of his time at Cliveden. But his main building energies were focused elsewhere, on his principal country residence, Eaton Hall, situated on the Cheshire–Flint border. By comparison, Westminster made only marginal renovations at Cliveden. Naturally, he added new stables. But he also reordered the Grand Avenue, the imposing approach to the house. His one major improvement was to combine Barry's two drawing rooms on the south front to form a spacious whole, while also allowing easier access to the terrace and gardens. Otherwise, apart from overhauling its heating system, he hardly touched the interior of Cliveden.

By the early 1890s Westminster was anxious to rid himself of Cliveden. He was quite adequately housed. Eaton Hall in Cheshire and Grosvenor House in Park Lane alone provided him with the splendid accommodation that his station demanded. Cliveden was never high on his order of priorities. In June 1893 he sold the property (reputedly for $1.25 million) to William Waldorf Astor, an American multimillionaire who had finally decided to settle in England. Saddened by the news, Queen Victoria mourned for her 'Dear beautiful Cliveden', now in the possession of an alien breed. 'It is grievous to think of it falling into these hands,' she lamented. Cliveden was to remain the home of the Astor family for the coming three generations.

Already saddled with a reputation as a centre of political intrigue, Cliveden, as run by the Astors, would do much to improve on its well-merited image.

If Westminster was probably the wealthiest man in England, the present near owner of Cliveden, William Waldorf Astor, was surely one of the richest men in the world. A scion of the Astor dynasty, his fortune had been founded by his great-grandfather, John Jacob Astor. Born in the village of Waldorf, just south of Heidelberg, John Jacob had left his home at the age of sixteen to spend four years in London, working for his brother making musical instruments, flutes, clarinets and oboes. Having acquired a working knowledge of English, he then crossed the Atlantic to the newly created United States, travelling steerage at a cost of £5. After an arduous journey of four months, he arrived in Baltimore at the end of

March 1784. In New York he first set up a musical emporium with stock he had brought with him from London. A steady, respectable business, it proved to be too humdrum for this bustling entrepreneur. Seeking more profitable callings, he began dealing in furs. Lack of ready capital forced him into occasional partnerships with more established furriers. But John Jacob was of too independent a spirit to tie himself to others. He took to travelling up the Hudson river to negotiate the sale of pelts from the Iroquois and other skin trappers. Annual trips to Montreal yielded him rewarding deals with the powerful North West Company. His business enterprises spread westwards. Within twenty years, he had a monopoly of the lucrative fur business throughout North America, the trading posts of his American and the Pacific Fur Companies spanning the entire continent. From the eastern seaboard, he exported his furs to Europe, an insatiable and remunerative market. On the North-West Pacific coast, at the mouth of the Columbia river, he founded the town of Astoria, an entrepot for trade with the Far East. From here his merchant ships crossed over to China, carrying back tea, silk and spices, netting him even more fabulous profits. The revenues mounted, seemingly without limit.[2]

Gradually John Jacob switched the focus of his business affairs. By the mid-1830s he had closed down his fur companies and had withdrawn from the China trade. Now a person of considerable substance – his sobriquet was simply 'the richest man in America' – he extended his business interests to banking (he had already helped to establish the Second Bank of the United States), insurance, government bonds, acquiring land in upper state New York and Canada, and even, briefly, speculating in railroads. But more than anything, he began to buy up chunks of Manhattan real estate. Astor holdings stretched from the Battery to Harlem, along Park Avenue and Broadway, but in particular they were to be found in the area bounded by the Hudson river, the northern extent of Central Park, Fifth Avenue and 42nd Street. He developed properties, apartment houses and office blocks. In 1836 he opened the doors of the Park Hotel (later, Astor House) at 223 Broadway, with its eighteen shops, three hundred bedrooms and seventeen bathrooms, to the delight of New York's upper crust and its more prosperous visitors. Three years later he decided upon a great civic enterprise, setting aside funds to launch the foundation of the New York Public Library. Despite this dabbling in philanthropy, his reputation as a cold-blooded landlord and avaricious plutocrat preceded him, and would continue to dog his heirs. Yet whatever slurs he incurred, by the time of his death at the age of eighty-five, John Jacob was readily acknowledged as the greatest moneyspinner of his day, enjoying an annual income of about $2 million a year. The founder of the first great American fortune, his wealth was rumoured to be second only to the Rothschilds.*

* As most of John Jacob's means were entangled in real estate deals, estimates regarding

John Jacob's successors have been widely considered to have lacked his audacity and verve. Perhaps, it was also whispered, they had perfected the gift of serendipity to a fine art. Or perhaps, to be more generous, they felt instinctively that he had guided them in the right direction. At any rate, they distanced themselves from the scramble to control the American economy through risk-growth enterprises. Not for them the wheeling and dealing of the Vanderbilts and Carnegies. Instead, the Astors concentrated on buying up New York City. William Backhouse, John Jacob's son, developed over seven hundred properties throughout the city – stores, offices, apartment houses, hotels, restaurants. His son, John Jacob III, ended his career as the largest private owner of real estate in New York. As New York prospered, so too did the Astors.

William Waldorf, John Jacob III's heir, now owner of Cliveden, realized his share of the fortune in 1890 when he came into his inheritance of $100,000,000 (approximately $2.8 billion by today's reckoning).* William Waldorf was something of a maverick in Astor circles, his temperament poised precariously between convention and idiosyncrasy. Since infancy he had showed signs of a remoteness and lack of communication with others, characteristics that were to blossom in later life. An only child, he was brought up in a forbidding atmosphere – no whistling, no games on Sunday; instead his routine was tempered with mastering texts of an improving quality. Although he took a law degree at Columbia, he was privately educated, never subject to the rough and tumble of school life. As befitted a solitary adolescent, he was an avid reader, attracted to the historical romances of Walter Scott or James Fenimore Cooper, but also fascinated by the biographies of ruthless despots like Napoleon Bonaparte or the Borgias. Enthralled by the delights of the chessboard, he developed into an exceptionally proficient player, usually travelling with a pocket set, and able to play blindfolded. Chess's

his personal fortune varied widely. His executors put it at a modest $8 million; gossip columnists were less restrained, calculating it at an astonishing $150 million. It is now generally held that it was close to $30 million – about $900 million at today's reckoning. A fortune of such epic quality gave rise to equally epic tales about its origins. The most notorious of them had John Jacob, or one of his agents, unearthing Captain Kidd's legendary treasure hoard on an island off the coast of New England, the island, naturally, being the property of another prominent, though unidentified, American family. From there this fantastic windfall of gold and assorted jewels was secreted to London where it was sold for a fabulous sum to a firm of goldsmiths. In this way, one pirate – Astor – had illegally profited from the criminal gains of another – Kidd. Although this yarn had long since been exposed as a hoax, such was its fascination that in 1936, Sir Robert Bruce Lockhart, author, journalist and diarist, was asked in all seriousness by Faber whether he would redraft this modern version of *Treasure Island*.

* One source (Derek Wilson, 108) puts his inheritance as high as $170 million. Since it is impossible to be precise about these figures, the lower sum has been preferred – still astronomical by any standard.

'axioms', he later wrote, 'are a fixed star of methodical procedure'.[3] Order, precision and punctuality were traits that William Waldorf refined to the point of obsessiveness.

Reserved and somewhat strait-laced, William Waldorf could have found little in common with other members of his immediate family. His uncle William, although he maintained the Astor reputation as a thrusting landlord, had also gained a name for himself as a playboy, spending much of his time aboard his yacht, *Nourmahal* ('Light of the Harem'), the most luxurious in the world, where, to the gratification of the press, unspeakable orgies were said to take place. With his imperious aunt Caroline, who reigned over New York's elite, carefully monitoring the Four Hundred couples deemed worthy enough to be admitted to her ballroom, he had even less in common. Out of touch with the spirit that animated New York society life, William Waldorf decided to go into local politics on a Republican ticket, suddenly conscious of his civic duty to serve those who had kindly underwritten his privileged position. But he was no populist. Faithful to his elitist upbringing, he aimed to clip the wings of the parvenu 'robber barons' and their crooked officials, squalid, vulgar creatures who debased public life, and to restore political power to where it belonged: in the hands of an enlightened oligarchy, those few honoured and honourable patrician families who intuitively had the best interests of the masses at heart.

For someone of his fastidious tastes, William Waldorf could not have chosen a worse time to break into public life. Corruption was rife. Assorted gangs of con-artists and fixers openly manipulated the ballot, particularly at the municipal and state level. New York itself had recently fallen victim to the excesses of 'Boss' Tweed – of the notorious Tammany Hall ring – who in 1873 had been jailed (where he later died) for having systematically plundered the City's treasury of sums estimated at anywhere between $70,000,000 to $200,000,000.[4] Still, William Waldorf fought his way into the New York State legislature at Albany, and from there advanced to a seat in the state senate. In 1880 he was nominated as the Republican candidate for New York's seventh congressional district, losing by the narrow margin of 165 votes. Almost immediately he was asked to run again, this time for the seventeenth district, a wealthier area; but once again he was beaten.

These campaigns were conspicuously grubby affairs. Although, as anticipated, William Waldorf spread his dollars around liberally, his campaign style was judged to be condescending, even arrogant. One commentator noted that when he shook hands with his constituents he kept his gloves on. Press notices were cruel. Gleefully identified as a 'slum landlord', his name and reputation were vilified without mercy. Nor would he fight back. Too proud, too remote from the democratic process, too disgusted at the chicanery, he refused to sink to the level of a street-brawler. Instead, he cut himself off from 'those trained vulgarians'. Exposed to the rancour of 'the tobacco-spitting' press, he determined to remove himself from its glare, cultivating a visible distaste for any kind of publicity. For a man of William Waldorf's renown, this was a self-defeating attitude. Unable to escape public scrutiny, his antipathy towards unsought-for attention intensified.

One consequence of these humiliations was to set in motion a scheme that would allow William Waldorf a respite from the hurly-burly of American life. Alluded to as 'the English plan', it was hoped that he would eventually find his niche in the more genteel, sophisticated setting of late Victorian England. William's father, John Jacob III, a committed Anglophile who, unfortunately, had had to refuse the ambassadorship to the Court of St James, was agreeable to the idea. But then, unexpectedly, Chester Alan Arthur (twenty-first President of the United States) offered William the post of Minister to Rome. What were to be his duties, he asked the Secretary of State. 'Go and enjoy yourself, my dear boy; have a good time!' – cogent advice that he was to keep in mind. Later in life, he wrote appreciatively of the founder of the dynasty, John Jacob I: 'I am glad that my great-grandfather was a successful trader, because in all ages trade has led the way to Civilization.' In Rome, he found 'Civilization'.

William Waldorf arrived in Rome in 1882. In his grandson's words, it was here that he began 'to weave into his life a pattern of formalistic behaviour which fell somewhere between that of a Roman emperor and his idea of an English medieval baron'; and, one might safely add, that of a Renaissance prince. He drew, painted, sculpted in the classical style – one of his statues, 'The Wounded Amazon', stands awkwardly today in the Rose Garden at Cliveden – and wrote two historical novels, *Valentino* (1884), a diligent refashioning of the life of Cesare Borgia, and *Sforza, A Story of Milan* (1886), neither of which caused a great stir. But first and foremost, he became a collector – and a collector on a grand scale; a polished version of the stereotype American millionaire ransacking Europe of its cultural treasures. He took his hobby seriously, consulting experts, sketching Renaissance palaces and ancient ruins, itemizing the *objets d'art* that took his fancy. Paintings by Murillo and Holbein, Clouet and Mabuse, early illustrated prayer books, medieval weaponry and armour, and particularly Roman marbles, were among his many acquisitions. From the Villa Borghese he purchased a splendid stone balustrade, carved for Cardinal Scipione Borghese in 1618–19. Almost two hundred metres long, and set off by fountains and statues, it was shipped to Cliveden and reassembled on the Lower Terrace, providing a magnificent approach to the Parterre. In this relaxed, civilized manner, William Waldorf whiled away the remainder of his tenure as Minister in Rome.

By the early 1890s William Waldorf had decided to implement his 'English plan'. 'America is good enough for a man who has to make a livelihood,' he later recollected, 'though why travelled people of independent means should remain there more than a week is not readily to be comprehended.'* What, then, could be more natural than to revert to his European heritage. In 1893, he bought Cliveden, leased 18 Carlton House Terrace as his London residence, and erected a baronial office block, Astor House, on the Victoria Embankment to serve as his business headquarters. Ten years later he acquired Hever Castle in Kent, including its surrounding 640 acres. A moated manor house dating from Norman times, romantically associated with the courtship of Anne Boleyn by Henry VIII (its corridors were said to be haunted by the ill-fated queen), its restoration took four years at an approximate cost of $10 million. At times, its rebuilding bordered on the fantastic. He sank an artificial lake, designed a maze, laid out an Italian Garden complete with a Roman bath, loggia, grottoes and a colonnaded piazza (all modelled on the Gallery of a Thousand Fountains at the Villa d'Este, Tivoli), and planted an Anne Boleyn Garden, its yew hedges pruned in the shape of Tudor chessmen. Inside his castle, where he resided alone, he installed mock doors and hidden passageways. It was said that he slept with two revolvers by his bed to ward off any intruder. Such was his passion for privacy that for his guests he erected, beyond the moat, a rambling sham Tudor village that cunningly concealed their living quarters, access into his castle being permitted only by way of a covered bridge over the moat. Here was a more dignified version in the Kent countryside of Hearst's wonderland at San Simeon.

An epicure with wine, and both a gourmand and a gourmet with food, William Waldorf entertained frequently. But, as it was noted, his musical soirees and weekend parties lacked the *joie de vivre* that usually accompanies such occasions. Highly organized, well-regulated affairs, 'Guests were told exactly when to arrive; and when they arrived they were greeted by a secretary (or by his daughter, Pauline) who showed them to their rooms and told them where, and at what time, they would assemble before meals. The rest of the weekend ran according to a schedule, short periods set aside for walking, driving, resting, eating, and finally sleep.' Timing was all-important: not to be a second early, or a second late. This imperious behaviour must have seriously alarmed William Waldorf's guests.

Although he craved to be accepted into English society, William Waldorf went about it in a most contrary manner. Apart from his

* This controversial supposition, subject to the most acerbic comments in the American press, was proposed by William Waldorf when he became a British subject in 1899.

idiosyncrasies, considered excessive even by the standards of English eccentrics, he seemed determined to antagonize, socially at least, those few who made or broke any *arriviste* who aspired to infiltrate the gilded circle. He feuded with Westminster, who had carelessly forgotten his family's visitors' book at Cliveden, perversely refusing to return the duke's possession. More provocatively, he painted his horse-drawn carriages in the same colour – chocolate brown – that had, until then, been reserved almost exclusively for the royal family. Nor did the life style of his king, Edward VII, appeal to his withdrawn personality. 'I have never shown myself subservient,' he haughtily proclaimed, 'which his intimates of the smart set, the South African crowd and his Jew friends always are.' As for the king's latest mistress, Mrs Keppel, she was no more than 'a public strumpet', so William Waldorf noted delicately, and 'When I speak of her relations with the King it is only fair to add what all the world knows, that the King has been physically impotent for more than twenty years.' (William Waldorf was not above a little philandering himself. In 1909 he embarked upon an *amitié amoureuse* with Lady Sackville – Vita Sackville-West's mother – at nearby Knole.)[5] No doubt, a garbled version of his charges eventually reached Edward's ears. For a man who desperately wanted, indeed needed, some form of public recognition, perhaps a knighthood or a peerage, these indiscretions reveal a self-destructive urge, an inability to compromise, not the most fitting attributes for someone who aspired to a life of public distinction.

On the other hand, William Waldorf was among the first of a string of multimillionaires who sought to make their mark by running newspapers to suit their purpose. In 1892 he bought the *Pall Mall Gazette*. A Liberal journal that had firmly backed Gladstone on Home Rule for Ireland, William Waldorf steered it into the Unionist camp. When his editor, Harry Cust, declined to publish his articles, having judged them too artistic for a political journal, William Waldorf launched the *Pall Mall Magazine*, a more highbrow literary periodical. So, eventually, he found an outlook for such pieces as 'The Vengeance of Poseidon' or 'The Wraith of Cliveden's Reach', titles that betray his somewhat high-flown literary style. Still, the *Magazine* attracted contributions from some of the foremost literary names of the day, among them H. G. Wells, Rudyard Kipling, James Barrie, Laurence Housman and Walter de la Mare.

In 1911 William Waldorf acquired the *Observer*, Britain's oldest Sunday newspaper, from Lord Northcliffe, a deal that was hatched by his eldest son, Waldorf, who four years later assumed control of the journal. With the *Observer* came its editor, James Louis Garvin. 'Garve', who agreed to take over the *Gazette* as well, was probably the most influential journalist of his time. Self-educated, well versed in French, German and Spanish, familiar with European literature and history, he had secured his present position by application, energy and talent. Combining dependable news coverage with stimulating treatment of the arts, he had initiated a new pattern of Sunday journalism, turning the languishing *Observer* into 'a fiery force', rescuing it from financial ruin. While resolutely upholding his editorial independence, Garvin held robust Unionist views, views that at times did not square with those of the Astors. Under his stewardship, the *Observer* took a hard line on tariff reform, encouraged the Lords to throw out Lloyd George's 'People's Budget' and to reject the Parliament Bill, spotlighted the German peril, and pressed for an alliance with Russia. Over Ireland, the most divisive political issue of the day, Garvin's vision of imperial union led him to propose a federation of the British Isles, a solution also recommended by Waldorf and his Round Table friends.

By now William Waldorf could assert that aspects of his 'English plan' had been accomplished relatively smoothly. This did not signify the abandonment of his New York interests. But more and more they took on the character of a hobby – a highly rewarding one, of course – rather than a vocation. On the site of his father's old mansion, on the corner of Fifth Avenue and 33rd Street, he erected the Waldorf Hotel. A staggering financial success – grossing four and a half million dollars in its first year – it had the added advantage of persuading his feisty aunt Caroline, whose house occupied the adjoining lot, to move further up Fifth Avenue, to a more sumptuous residence opposite the Metropolitan Museum of Art where the ballroom could hold six hundred couples! (The Waldorf was so profitable that it induced William's cousin, John Jacob IV, Caroline's son, to found an even grander hotel, the Astoria, on the site of his mother's former house. Sound business sense survived this gamesmanship. The two cousins agreed to a merger, creating the celebrated Waldorf Astoria, its fifteen hundred bedrooms entitling it to the accolade 'the world's grandest hotel'.)* And so William Waldorf went on, developing mid–Manhattan mainly in the area just south of Central Park, a building spate that culminated in the opening of the plush Astor and Apthorp apartment blocks off Broadway and 75th. These enterprises added to his fortune, but did not improve his reputation. Less popular in America than ever before, he found himself hailed no longer as 'a slum landord' but as 'an absentee slum landlord'.

William Waldorf's real interests, however, remained centred on England, his 'English plan' still unfulfilled in one crucial respect. Having placed himself at the service of the Unionist party, subscribing heavily to its funds, revealing himself as a diehard over parliamentary reform and Ulster, he felt the time had arrived to receive his due. Sir Herbert Praed,

* The hotel survived on Fifth Avenue and 33rd Street until 1931, when it was torn down to make way for the Empire State Building.

chairman of the Association of Conservative Clubs, put William's dilemma to his party leader, Andrew Bonar Law.

> In addition to the large sums he has given me for the Party Fund, he has contributed most generously to oppose Communism and in other ways . . . He is in favour of fighting the Radicals on every feasible opportunity . . . I know he thinks he has been neglected by the Party and that his efforts have not been recognized . . . He thinks Balfour might have put forward his name for a peerage.[6]

Bonar Law listened carefully but reacted coolly to this lobbying. William Waldorf's ambition was not to be realized until 1916. But his long-sought elevation to the peerage, the culmination of determined petitioning abetted by the dispensation of plentiful largesse to party coffers and various charities, was to have profound consequences for the Astors.

William Waldorf lived at Cliveden for thirteen years. Beset by loneliness – his wife Mary ('Mamie') had died in 1894 at the age of thirty-six – and increasingly remote from his children* – he was said to have instructed rather than educated them – he retreated more and more into his shell. 'Cliveden', recorded his grandson Michael, 'was a court with governesses, tutors, secretaries and servants in attendance, ruled over with a majestic sense of justice by a lonely aristocrat who was obsessed by highly personal notions about convention.' Yet it could also be said that Cliveden benefited from this state of affairs. Much of William's time and energy was expended in renovating his newly acquired property. Typically, one of his first improvements was to erect a perimeter wall, topped by cut glass, cutting off his estate from the outside world. Local suspicions were fuelled. 'Waldorf by name and walled-off by nature,' was his neighbours' verdict.

Secure in his solitude, William Waldorf demolished Westminster's bizarre remodelling of the east wing in the Flemish Renaissance style, and restored it to its original Palladian design by Barry. To house his armour, musical instruments and works of art in an appropriate setting he needed extra space and the right atmosphere. This was largely achieved by creating a magnificent Great Hall on the north side, the walls adorned by three of the 'Art of War' tapestries,† extra oak panelling, and Corinthian

---

* He had four children, Waldorf (b. 1879); Pauline (b. 1880); John Jacob V (b. 1886); and Gwendolyn (b. 1893), who died shortly before her ninth birthday of acute heart disease.

† The 'Art of War' tapestries commemorate Marlborough's campaigns during the War of the Spanish Succession. Marlborough had six sets – each of eight scenes – made up for his generals. Lord Orkney, the second owner of Cliveden, who served as Marlborough's second-in-command at Blenheim, received one of them but it was generally assumed to have been destroyed in one of the fires. William Waldorf chanced upon three of the tapestries in Paris in the early 1890s and brought them to Cliveden, unaware at the time of their historical connection with his new home.

columns and pilasters, its floor laid with Minton tiles. At the far right of the Hall he put in a new staircase carved in wood, its newels sculpted to represent historical figures associated with Cliveden. At the other end, he installed a fine, intricately cut stone fireplace, dating from the early sixteenth century, and thought to have originated from the chateau of Arnay-le-Duc in Burgundy. The bedrooms were redecorated by the Parisian firm of Allard, as were the rooms overlooking the gardens. Of these, the French dining room was of particular architectural merit. Its rococo wainscotting and overdoors, coloured in a soft green, its marble chimney-piece, and parts of its plasterwork cove and ceiling, decorated with water and oil-gilded artwork, came from the Château d'Asnières, rumoured to have once been the hunting lodge of Louis XV's mistress, Madame de Pompadour, whose bust dignifies its mantelpiece at Cliveden. William Waldorf himself ordered the furniture and mirrors, painstakingly designed to suit the style of the room, placing in the centre of these imposing surroundings a huge, rectangular mahogany table, easily capable of seating a dinner party of thirty guests.

Whatever guests were invited were housed in the east wing, which could accommodate some forty visitors. The Astor family occupied the first floor of the main house, with the day and night nurseries situated on the storey above them. In the basement were located those facilities necessary for the smooth running of the house: the kitchens; the servants' hall; the brushing-rooms, where the guests' clothes were cleaned and pressed; the china room; the silver safe; the butler's pantry, where the silver was washed in teak sinks before being polished; and the wine cellar. Along the length of the basements were miniature railway lines, ensuring that the food arrived from the kitchens via the dummy-waiters on to the guests' plates still hot. House staff were accommodated in the west wing, together with the offices of the estate. The number of servants varied, but at the height of Cliveden's fame it included: a steward-butler, a valet, an under-butler, three footmen and a hallboy; a housekeeper, four housemaids, four laundry maids and two ladies' maids; and for the kitchens, a chef, three kitchenmaids and a scullery maid. Apart from these necessities, a telephonist, a night watchman, a house carpenter, odd-job-men and dailies were also retained. The stables – developed into a first-class stud-farm by Waldorf, William's son – employed twelve stablemen. There were also about 700 acres of gardens and woodland on both banks of the Thames to look after, a task that employed up to fifty gardeners.[7]

William Waldorf did much to beautify Cliveden. He conceived an Italian garden near the Octagon Temple, laid out the Long Garden along the northern perimeter of the estate, constructed a Pagoda (now the centrepiece of the Water Garden), and devised a maze (that no longer exists). But more than anything, the gardens provided a grand setting for his statuary. Apart from the Borghese balustrade, William had brought with him Roman sarcophagi and classical and Renaissance sculptures that he had acquired from other Italian and French collections. Nor were contemporary works excluded. At the circular entrance to the Grand Avenue, he erected the ornate Shell Fountain of Love (*c.* 1897), commanding the approach to the house.

In May 1906, William Waldorf abandoned all this and retired to Hever Castle. His eldest son had just married. And in an act of high-minded generosity, he bestowed, as his principal wedding present, Cliveden and all it contained upon Waldorf and his new bride, Nancy Shaw (née Langhorne), a divorced lady from Virginia, America.

CHAPTER 2

Waldorf and Nancy

Waldorf Astor was born in New York on 19 May 1879 – by chance, the same birthday as his future wife, Nancy. As befitted the heir of a family of legendary wealth, Waldorf's earliest years were spent in the closeted world of nurseries and nannies. Whatever parental warmth penetrated his tiny domain undoubtedly emanated from his mother, Mary Dahlgren (née Paul), known more familiarly as 'Mamie'. His father, William Waldorf, by temperament withdrawn and stern, was in any case wholly wrapped up in his fruitless efforts to break into politics. 'Mamie', who came from a well-established Philadelphian family, was far more outgoing by nature. Socially acceptable, she attracted friends easily, exhibiting most of the social graces that William Waldorf lacked.

Three years after his son's birth, William Waldorf, by now thoroughly disenchanted with Tammany Hall-style politics, took his family off to Rome, where he assumed his new duties as United States Minister and set about acquiring the substance of a European, and particularly Italian, culture. This satisfactory state of affairs ended in 1885, when his Republican patrons were replaced by a Democratic administration. Forced back to New York, William Waldorf was more than ever determined to put his 'English plan' into operation. By October 1890 he had settled his family, and servants, in St Thomas's Hotel, near Berkeley Square, London.

Waldorf was immediately despatched to a preparatory school to begin his English education, a suitable start for the son of a wealthy father determined to carve out his niche in English high society. He arrived with a thorough grounding in languages, having been tutored in French, Italian and Latin. It was from this point on that Waldorf's English upbringing began – though technically he remained a foreigner until his father was naturalized in 1899. According to most evidence, life in late Victorian boarding schools in England was a gloomy affair, more an exercise in what passed for character training than in developing scholarly aptitudes. Classics, a smattering of mathematics, geography and history, a heavy emphasis on sports and religion, and a rigid, often brutal, disciplinary regime were the usual fare, tempered only, if at all, by the disposition of the headmaster. Its most celebrated advocate, Dr Thomas Arnold of Rugby, put it plainly: 'What we look for here is, first, religious and moral principles; secondly, gentlemanly conduct; thirdly, intellectual ability.' Waldorf never found fault with this phase of his life. Perhaps he adapted easily, or perhaps, by nature, he was not given to complain. Once, however, he did mention his

> embarrassment at arriving at a crowded school in which everyone seemed to know each other, in a strange country, talking English like an American, French like a Frenchman (a lapse not easily forgiven by English schoolboys), and Latin like a Latin.[1]

In 1893, Waldorf passed with high grades into Eton, where he boarded at the house of Mr A. C. Ainger, a classics scholar who was among the authors of *The Eton Latin Grammar*. Waldorf's house was run in the traditional fashion, based on the fag-system. 'A fag's life', it was said, 'depended very much on the temper of [his] fagmaster'; there was no appeal from his fury. Unleashed, it could drive its victim into a mood of deep despair. On the other hand, an imaginative fagmaster could make life far more congenial 'with an occasional egg or the end of a pot of cream, or a sausage for Sunday breakfast'. Every day in the dining room at lunch and supper, the boys were allowed as much beer as they could consume, while on Sundays, at lunch, they were offered the choice between a glass of port or sherry, solemnly handed round by the presiding butler.*[2]

Over this system ruled Edmund Warre, an outstanding example of the scholar–athlete then so much in vogue. Following the recommendations of a Royal Commission of February 1864, the College had begun to implement a number of sweeping changes in its curriculum and management, in particular those placing the teaching of science, mathematics and modern languages on a proper footing. Warre took up these proposals with marked enthusiasm. Self-confident, possessor of a deep, vibrant voice and considerable rhetorical powers, he combined a nobility of appearance with a devastating temper – 'I have seen no one so grand in anger,' recalled one of his pupils. Warre would sail into a classroom 'with his head thrown back and crunching stride, with flowing gown and very broad silk band round his middle . . . hardly mortal in his bigness', leaving

---

* Edward Frederick Lindley Wood (created Lord Irwin, 1925, succeeded as 3rd Viscount Halifax, 1934), the author of these afterthoughts, was an exact contemporary of Waldorf's at Eton, and later became a member of Waldorf's political-social circle. Halifax pursued a distinguished career as Conservative MP for Ripon, 1910–34, including various Cabinet appointments; Viceroy of India, 1926–31; Foreign Secretary, 1938–40; ambassador in Washington, 1941–6.

an awesome impression on his charges.[3] This certainly must have been how Waldorf saw Warre, leaning motionless 'over the big raised desk at the end of Upper School', gazing dourly before him at his captive audience.

Waldorf seldom came into direct contact with this legendary figure, whom he would eye, like most of his contemporaries, from a guarded distance. His day-to-day routine was spent with his tutors and house-master. But the new reforms worked to his advantage. For though Waldorf was of scientific bent, his main strength was in foreign languages. His reward came in 1897 when he won the prestigious Prince Consort's French prize, a much sought-after honour. Waldorf was equally active outside the classroom. Elected Captain of his House, he also contributed to, and helped edit, the *Eton College Chronicle*, and for some time acted as treasurer of the fashionable Eton Society, more commonly known as 'Pop', a self-nominating club of about twenty-five collegians that occupied itself with literary activities, debates and readings. Generally credited with setting the social standards of the College, its members adopted a flamboyant style of dress all their own, gaudy waistcoats being their crowning achievement. A keen oarsman, or a 'wet bob', Waldorf was chosen Captain of the Boats towards the end of his spell at Eton. As the historian of the College notes: 'Great, in the estimation of Eton boys, are the Keepers of the Field and of the Wall, greater still is the Captain of the Cricket Eleven, but greatest of all is the Captain of the Boats ... recognized [as the] leader of the School.'[4] All in all, Waldorf could look back on a distinguished school career.

A year after Waldorf entered Eton his mother died. The birth of her daughter Gwendolyn had left Mamie considerably weakened. Most of her time was spent at Cliveden, resting. Whether her complaint was physical or nervous remains unclear. But throughout 1894 her condition deteriorated. By December, peritonitis had set in, a condition soon diagnosed as terminal. Shortly before Christmas she died, aged only thirty-six. Introspective as he was by nature, his wife's untimely death aggravated William Waldorf's tendency to self-communion, his behaviour rising to new levels of eccentricity. Waldorf was then fifteen years old. His relations with his father had never been demonstrably affectionate. Lacking the human touch, more remote and unpredictable than ever, William Waldorf now forced their relationship on to even more business-like terms.

In one respect at least, Waldorf lived up to his father's expectations. His achievements at Eton could not have failed to bring pleasure into William Waldorf's cheerless existence. At the same time, young Waldorf was developing those traits that most of his contemporaries would unfailingly comment upon. By nature 'a man of classical rather than romantic mould, a respecter of institutions rather than a rebel', he was widely seen as unassuming, serious, conscientious, scrupulous, somewhat prudish – 'his occasional jokes, practical by definition, were strictly of a conventional sort'.[5] There was a pitfall here. His innate modesty could easily lean towards a self-denying mode, depriving him of the prizes that his ability and industry would otherwise have warranted. At Eton he also absorbed the conventional values and tastes of the class and generation to which he now belonged. In particular, he cultivated a sense of public service, to his mind the self-evident function of wealth and privileged position. Patronizing though it might now sound, Waldorf developed a social conscience in regard to those less fortunate than he. 'You are lucky enough to be rich,' he once lectured to his sons; 'that gives you a profound responsibility towards all those who are not so lucky.'[6]

There was another aspect to Waldorf's 'social conscience'. This was the heyday of British imperialism. But recent confrontations with France at Fashoda on the Upper Nile, with Germany in South Africa (where the Boer War was shortly to break out), and with Russia on the North-West Frontier or in the Far East, conveyed the strong impression that it was an imperialism under siege. Such challenges sparked off feelings of intense patriotism. The literature of the period, though jingoistic to the modern ear, perfectly reflects these sentiments. Henry John Newbolt, an old Cliftonian, dubbed the 'poet laureate of High Imperialism', secured his literary reputation with a volume of ballads, *Admirals All* (1897), in which his celebrated poem, 'Vitaï Lampada', appeared, its most memorable verse reading:

> The sand of the desert is sodden red, –
> Red with the wreck of a square that broke; –
> The Gatling's jammed and the Colonel dead,
> And the regiment blind with dust and smoke.
> The river of death has brimmed his banks,
> And England's far, and Honour a name,
> But the voice of a schoolboy rallies the ranks,
> 'Play up! play up! and play the game!'

The public schools of England, with their emphasis on character-building and public service, could not be immune to this kind of special pleading. Loyalty to the school, to Queen, country and Empire, the all-pervasive team spirit, with God justifying every move, and looking back to a nostalgic, golden past all blended into a heady brew. They were the holders, the bearers, of a sacred trust. The Reverend James Edward Welldon (later Bishop of Calcutta), headmaster at Harrow, could not have been more explicit:

An English headmaster, as he looks to the future of his pupils, will not forget that they are to be the citizens of the greatest Empire under heaven . . . he will inspire them with faith in the divinely ordered mission of their country and their race; he will impress upon their young minds . . . that the great principles . . . of truth, liberty, equality, and religion – are the principles which they must carry into the world

Winston Churchill, who as a schoolboy had heard Welldon's sermons, and who never failed to be stirred by the raw patriotism of the Harrow School Songs, later recollected 'Listening to . . . those tales of great deeds and of great men and wondering with intensity how I could ever do something for my country'.[7]

Much the same spirit animated Eton. Yearly, on the Fourth of June (Founder's Day), when much thought was given to theatricals and speechifying, the most topical, rousing, not to say violently chauvinistic, recitations would be heard. Choice selections from Kipling's 'The Old Issue', 'The White Man's Burden', 'The English Flag/The Flag of England', Tennyson's 'Hands All Round', and the American poet R. C. Rodgers' 'To the Race' were rapturously received. The *Eton College Chronicle* noted 'the splendid devotion to the mother country and the pride of race which thrills through the spirited verses [of "To the Race"]'. A graduate of this system later wrote that 'I think we believed in our hearts . . . that the creation of the British Empire was the best thing that ever happened to mankind.'[8] Waldorf would not have quarrelled with these sentiments. And these themes came to play a crucial role in his life, as they did in that of his intimates.

In 1899 Waldorf arrived at New College, Oxford. Founded in 1379 by William of Wykeham, who thought its task was to produce 'men of great learning, fruitful to the church of God and to the king and realm', New College flaunted its position as an enduring bastion of male supremacy, as Dean Burgon had made clear when censuring the opposite sex. Despite his stern ruling, the College was not lacking in a sense of humour. One epitaph, commemorating an ill-starred New College organist, read: 'Here lies one blown out of breath,/Who lived a merry life and dy'd a merry death.' It was also – and remains – a singularly attractive college, boasting what has been judged 'the most perfect of the Oxford gardens'. Entered by way of splendid wrought-iron gates, it is bounded by a stretch of the old city wall and edged by wide herbaceous borders from where it descends to 'big. rolling lawns and some glorious chestnuts, and in the very heart of it all, covered with trees and thick grass, stands a carefully untended eighteenth-century mound'.[9]

Waldorf must have been moved by the grandeur of New College, but apparently its academic distinction failed to stimulate him. Whether he had peaked early, or whether he simply neglected his studies, the upshot was that Waldorf took a fourth-class honours degree in history, the lowest category the University offers. However, he shone in other fields. He began to pass himself off as a young 'blood' – although his temperament belied this image – and as an aspiring athlete, a figure more in touch with his ambitions. As he had strained his heart rowing, he was compelled to give up the sport at which he had excelled. But he more than made up for it by his equestrian and fencing skills, representing the University at polo, steeplechasing and sabres. He also raced point-to-point, hunted with the Bicester, and was Master of the Drag Hounds. For social diversion he spent much time at the fashionable, and boisterous, Bullingdon Club, the haunt of the wealthy hunting set. To what extent he enjoyed its rowdy activities, it is difficult to judge. He did what was expected of him. He conformed. So far, Waldorf's career reflected the pattern of his generation and class, honouring its values without question.

If Waldorf made any special friends at New College, they have yet to be identified. But between his gentlemanly pursuits, he must, occasionally, have met those members of the College who were later to champion the same political values and to move in the same social circles as himself, members of the *Kindergarten* and the Round Table coterie, including in particular Philip Kerr and Robert Brand.

What kind of young man was Waldorf when he came down from Oxford at the age of twenty-three? No one could, or would, accuse him of being pushy. Conventional, modest, serious, conscientious were the most common descriptions heard. Did he lack drive? Certainly, there was no compelling need for him to make his way in society; he had a ready-made world, affluent and bounteous, to fall back on. And it was initially this path that Waldorf chose to follow, indistinguishable from that of any other gentleman of leisure, fortune and social standing. He travelled, he hunted, he shot. He took up winter sports in Switzerland with particular enthusiasm. But more than anything he indulged his passion for horses. While still at Oxford, he bought the thoroughbred mare *Conjure* for £100, laying the foundations for one of the most successful racing stables in England. Over the years, Waldorf's stable won eleven classic races and secured over two hundred other wins; only the Derby eluded him.[10]

Diligent as ever, Waldorf's concern to perfect his stud farm led him to undertake veterinary studies in order to master the anatomy of the horse. One thing led to another. Mendelian theories of heredity, the science of genetics, experiments in cross-fertilization, all excited Waldorf's curiosity. He studied these concepts in earnest, his library reflecting his commitment. Much of his public life was to be devoted to improving agricultural practice. Eventually, he published four impressive books on the subject, *Land and Life* (1932), *The Planning of Agriculture* (1933), *British Agriculture* (1938), and *Mixed Farming and Muddled Thinking* (1946).

All this lay in the future. For the moment, Waldorf followed his calling as a country squire. Yet he was not entirely lacking in ambition. It is clear that he wanted to make something of his life but his course was perhaps more difficult than that of many of his contemporaries. No privation drove him forward to seek a livelihood: all depended on self-discipline and free choice. He toyed with the idea of entering Parliament, not as a vocation but as a part-time pursuit appropriate to his station as a scion of the landed gentry. This dormant ambition may have been inherited from his father, before the latter's outlook on life had soured. Waldorf would embrace his inheritance rationally, in a manner free of his father's eccentricities and unpredictability. Given his privileged upbringing, it was inevitable that some would consider his endeavours patronizing, but this did not make his goodwill any the less valid. Devoid of any strain of radicalism, he would observe the man-in-the-street and sympathize with his situation, if from afar. For the time being, however, he merely played with these options. It only needed someone – or something – of dramatic impact to bring to the surface Waldorf's latent desire to enter public life.

In some ways Waldorf personified the cliché of the lonely, unhappy millionaire. With whom could he debate his future? He had no confidants. His mother had died; his siblings were preoccupied: Gwendolyn was a child; John Jacob V, seven years younger, was still at Eton; Pauline, although closer in age, was too busy attending to their father. As to William Waldorf, his complex temperament made their relations uneasy. It is difficult to imagine Waldorf ever fully confiding in his father. Waldorf's declining health was also a cause for alarm. Already suffering from a weak heart, he later developed signs of tuberculosis. His doctors prescribed rest. Banned from strenuous activity, veering between normal health and physical exhaustion, he would spend several months of every year abroad, recovering his strength in a more agreeable climate. However, when in good health Waldorf could surprise. A keen dancer, he revolutionized the waltz. Until his intervention waltzers had spun continuously in the same direction, getting giddier and giddier. In 1915, Waldorf imported from Paris the 'daring reverse', an audacious step that brought stability to the waltz in London ballrooms.[11]

Passion was not a feature of Waldorf's make-up. No philanderer, he has left no history of conquests. His one recorded affair has about it an air of fairy-tale romance, with no hint of eroticism. It concerned Queen Marie of Rumania, a granddaughter of Queen Victoria – her father was Alfred, Duke of Edinburgh, later of Saxe-Coburg. William Waldorf had had dealings with the Rumanian court since his days as a diplomat at Rome. They deepened after Marie married Prince Ferdinand in 1893, a man she barely knew and who in any case was enamoured of another woman. The Astors would visit Bucharest; Marie would come to Cliveden. She formed a special attachment to the family, and especially with Waldorf who was only four years her junior.[12] They met now and then, and exchanged letters. It was a relationship without a future. It did not peter out, but it was put on a proper footing when Waldorf met Nancy Witcher Shaw.

Waldorf and Nancy first met on a transatlantic liner crossing from New York to Southampton in December 1905. Nancy was returning to England, where she planned to spend another season riding to hounds in Leicestershire. She was certainly not hunting husbands. One of her English hosts had chided her: 'I suppose you have come over here to get one of our husbands,' to which Nancy had tartly responded: 'If you knew the trouble I've had gettin' rid of mine, you'd know I don't want yours.'[13] Her first marriage had been a disaster. When she first became aware of Waldorf's interest, she put him off. 'Perhaps' she would meet him, then 'perhaps' not. Waldorf persisted. Nancy soon yielded, after discovering that he was 'very good-looking' and possessed 'immense courtesy and very great personal charm'. Their courtship persisted throughout the winter, Waldorf an anxious wooer, Nancy still hesitating. Before she could finally commit herself, Nancy had to dissolve a relationship she had formed with a certain Lord Revelstoke, a scion of the Baring banking house. Although Revelstoke was rich, powerful, cultured, a great dandy and gourmet who cut a leading figure in London society, he was also taciturn by temperament, lacking in humour and, in truth, somewhat dull. By March Nancy was ready to announce her engagement to Waldorf. One obstacle remained. However, the Bishop of London readily waived in her favour the Anglican Church's ban on the remarriage of divorced persons. Two months later Waldorf and Nancy were married at All Souls Church, Langham Place.[14]

William Waldorf, the bridegroom's father, did not attend the ceremony, pleading 'poor health'. A 'diplomatic cold'? On the surface, he might have been expected to have preferred an English lady of aristocratic birth, instead of Nancy, a daughter of the country he had rejected. But in fact they got along well, and William Waldorf was generous to a fault in his marriage settlement. As a personal wedding gift, he gave Nancy a glorious tiara containing the Sanci diamond (now in the Louvre), a fifty-five-carat jewel that had, at various times, belonged to Charles the Bold, to Queen Henrietta Maria (wife of Charles I) and to Louis XIV. For the couple, he made over Cliveden, the house, its contents and the estate, together with a huge endowment – running into several millions – for its upkeep and to maintain them in their allotted station in life.

Although William Waldorf would have shuddered at the thought, he had, unwittingly, set in motion a process that would turn topsy-turvy the staid, sedate, conventional Cliveden that he had created. It would also galvanize Waldorf, still the reserved, cautious intellectual, and provide him with the necessary incentive to follow his public calling.

Variously described as 'a grasshopper', a 'Chinese cracker', a 'charming Columbine' or 'a Gnat', Nancy conformed effortlessly to these nicknames. Restless physically and intellectually – she could never 'think consecutively for sixty seconds', said George Bernard Shaw, who knew her well[15] – her presence invariably threatened something out of the ordinary, a dramatic gesture, a sensational revelation, a shocking turn of phrase. Diminutive of stature – at five foot two inches – slender of build and of fair complexion, she had aquiline features set off by a firm chin, a strong, finely shaped nose, blue eyes and a high forehead. Although she was short and neat in appearance, Nancy's challenging, not to say aggressive, postures left her adversaries with the impression of a taller, more magisterial figure, one imbued with vitality and strength of purpose. Her vivacity was enhanced by her enthusiasm for physical activities, riding, swimming, squash, tennis, golf, but also her rare talent for mimicry, and her delight in performing high jinks, still executing at seventy the cartwheels that had first astonished Edwardian drawing rooms.[16]

Nancy was born at Danville, Virginia (where a street is named after her), the fifth surviving child of Chiswell Dabney and Nancy Witcher Langhorne (née Keene). They raised a large family: Keene, Elizabeth (Lizzie), Irene, Harry, Phyllis, William (Buck) and Nora, twenty years separating the eldest from the youngest. (There were three other children, but they had died in infancy, before Nancy was born.) The second eldest sister, Irene, a famous southern belle, achieved everlasting fame as the original 'Gibson Girl', that symbolic American beauty, poised, swan-necked, full-bosomed, with a wasp waist and a proud and beguiling look. But of all her siblings, Nancy felt the closest affinity to Phyllis. Almost the same age, they regarded one another with open affection, an attachment that was strengthened when Phyllis came to live in England, after her first marriage had broken down, and married an old Oxford friend of Waldorf's, Robert Brand.

Nancy's mother was of Irish stock, but her father 'Chillie' (pronounced 'Shillie'), was raised in the South. No southern aristocrat, he nevertheless enjoyed the privileges that a moderately prosperous Virginian landowning family could offer. At the age of seventeen he had fought for the Confederacy in its war against the Union. Terrible in its destruction, the Civil War had ruined also Chillie's prospects. 'I had nothing but a wife, two children, a ragged seat to my pants and a barrel of whiskey,' he recalled.[17] But he was nothing if not resilient. At times he worked as a night watchman, and later as a travelling salesman, scraping together a living, before he made his mark as a tobacco auctioneer, a calling that stabilized his fluctuating assets. But the years of Reconstruction presented other, more lucrative opportunities. Soon he was heavily, and profitably, involved in the great railway boom of the 1880s. His fortune now assured, he moved to the state capital, Richmond, and acquired Mirador, an attractive ante-bellum Virginian country house and estate some seventeen miles west of Charlottesville, lying within sight of the Blue Ridge Mountains.

It would be difficult to find two prospective fathers-in-law more disparate in character than Chillie, brazenly extrovert, and William Waldorf, so austere and reserved – although when they did finally meet, an encounter Waldorf dreaded, they got on surprisingly well. Chillie played poker with professional skill, drank hard, and chewed plug tobacco. Deadly accurate in his aim, he elevated the practice of spitting to a fine art. Even when attending church services he insisted on a cuspidor being placed within comfortable spitting distance. On one visit to London he caused a commotion when he was caught teaching the Duchess of Devonshire the techniques of this suspect skill. Edwin Lee, the legendary butler at Cliveden, recalled Chillie as a 'real tough American . . . [who] was very fond of a drink. He loved to make Egg Nog and Rum and got most of the guests tight . . .' Something of Chillie's homespun temperament, his spontaneity, perhaps naivety, rubbed off on Nancy. 'Even if she wasn't a lady, she was a great character,' noted Rose Harrison, Nancy's personal maid of long standing.[18]

There were significant differences, however. Affinity to alcohol was one. Throughout her life, Nancy dedicated herself to the temperance movement, never losing an opportunity to rail against the liquor trade. Often she took her crusade to absurd lengths, once insisting that England had lost the Ashes because its cricket team drank to excess, conveniently forgetting the well-publicized drinking habits of the Australians.[19] Nancy had learned from hard experience the hazards of strong drink. Chillie was a heavy drinker; so were two of her brothers, Harry and Keene, both of whom developed 'an overpowering attachment to the bottle', and both of whom died young of tuberculosis after having made little of their lives. In later life Nancy was asked why she never drank. 'There was no need to,' she replied, 'I was quite cheerful enough without.'[20]

But it must have been the traumatic experiences of Nancy's first marriage that reinforced her opinions, not only about drink but also about other aspects of her personal life. At the age of seventeen she met Robert Gould Shaw II, the wealthy, good-looking, polo-playing offspring of an established Boston family.* Robert, on first sight, 'made up his mind' to

* By an accident of history, Robert Gould Shaw I had fought and died for the Union.

marry Nancy. For her part, Nancy was 'flattered and pleased to have made this spectacular conquest'. On the whole she remained true to her initial feelings, despite the fact that other, more ominous, sides of Shaw's character soon began to surface. There were well-founded rumours of his dissipated behaviour, bouts of drunkenness, even reports of mental instability in his family. These stories reached Chillie, who registered strong disapproval of the impending marriage. Nancy hesitated. But Robert's mother exerted extreme emotional blackmail, reading Nancy 'a terrible lecture . . . [that she] was breaking Bob's heart and ruining his life, and that he needed [her]'.[22] Robert's parents were perfectly aware of their son's failings, but they believed that Nancy, although young and inexperienced, would act as a brake on Robert's excesses. Nancy, surrendering to her genuine feelings of affection for him, capitulated. In October 1897, they were married at Mirador. She was eighteen years old.

The couple retired to Hot Springs, Arkansas. Two days later Nancy cut short the honeymoon and sought refuge with her family. It is impossible to say precisely what caused Nancy to take this drastic step – perhaps a drunken rage leading to blows, for Bob Shaw did acquire a record for wife-beating; or perhaps a violent, bawdy introduction to physical sex. At any rate, throughout her life Nancy displayed an aversion towards the sexual act. One friend likened her to Elizabeth I as 'sexually cold'. 'I can't even tolerate seeing two birds mating without wanting to separate them,' she often said. Even after her second marriage, she couldn't 'get used to sharing her bed with anyone'.[23] Whatever the reason, after a few days Chillie sent Nancy back to her husband, urging her to persevere.

And so began four desolate years of marriage. Far from improving, the situation worsened. Shaw's drinking teetered towards alcoholism. He also began to deceive Nancy with other women. Desperate, she left Shaw on at least one other occasion. They parted finally in 1901, clearly incompatible, but not before a son, Robert (Bobby) Gould Shaw III, was born. Although her friends advised her to seek a divorce – there were, after all, more than adequate reasons – Nancy preferred, on religious grounds, to opt for a deed of separation. Shortly afterwards, Shaw's parents pleaded with Nancy to divorce their son. To their horror they had discovered that he had entered into a bigamous marriage and was facing criminal proceedings. Nancy, reluctantly, agreed. By February 1903 the divorce proceedings were concluded. One condition was that Nancy acquire the custody of Bobby, who remained tied to his mother for the remainder of his life. For her part, Nancy displayed a blind devotion to him, even though he proved, in his own way, no less troublesome than his father.

Son of a prominent abolitionist family, and Commander of the 54th Massachusetts Infantry Regiment, he was shot through the heart as he led a frontal assault on Fort Wagner, which overlooked Charleston harbour, in July 1863.

Nancy returned to Mirador, a divorced woman with an infant child. At the end of that summer, another blow fell. Her mother, aged fifty-five, died. 'The light went out of my life,' Nancy remembered; 'I was ill for months in a wretched, nameless fashion.' Nancy attempted to step into her mother's shoes, to ensure the smooth running of the Mirador household; but without success. She and Chillie, two spirited characters, communicated better without the habitual frictions of day-to-day contact. Travel abroad was one escape. Immediately after her divorce, Nancy had visited England for the first time. 'I loved it,' she recalled. 'I had this strange feeling of having come home, rather than of having gone abroad.'[24] It was while sailing to England for her second visit that she first met Waldorf – and, after vacillating for a respectable period, finally consented to marry him.

Was this a genuine love-match? Surely not in the traditional meaning of the phrase. No doubt, Waldorf fell under the spell of Nancy's forceful, optimistic, outgoing personality. But nothing points to the fact that she was bowled over by Waldorf – perhaps the frightful accident of her first marriage inhibited her from doing so. Of course, Waldorf was handsome, courteous, and possessed an old-world charm. His social standing was impeccable; and he was also exceedingly wealthy – she often delighted her dinner guests by portraying herself as 'the woman who's spending the Astor millions'.[25] All the same, it would be wrong to assume that this was simply a marriage of convenience. Despite an obvious clash of temperaments – one extrovert, domineering, emotional, tending to see issues and people in terms of black and white; the other, reflective, intellectual, self-controlled, almost ascetic in outlook – they were, at heart, linked by a deep, intuitive mutual need. One contemporary observer has commented: 'Superficially their temperaments seemed widely divergent, but the deep religious conviction and the uncompromising sense of duty which they shared made their respective virtues complement one another rather than cancel each other out.'[26] This was certainly true for long periods of their life together. But it did not hold for ever. Moderation never came easily to Nancy. Towards the end of the marriage their relationship soured, as her lack of consideration and her egotism got the better of her. At this final stage she allowed her feminist views, now fully matured, to prevail over plain common sense. All too often she was heard saying, 'I married beneath me, all women do.'[27]

After a brief wedding trip to Paris and to Cortina in the southern Tyrol, Nancy and Waldorf returned to Cliveden. The mausoleum-like atmosphere of William Waldorf's creation held no appeal for Nancy. She was wont to repeat, 'The Astors have no taste,' or at least not her taste. Out went the 'splendid gloom'; in came 'books and chintz curtains and covers, and flowers'. Roman statues, busts and sarcophagi were removed elsewhere. The mosaic floor of the hall was replaced with a modern parquet covering. Above all, there were masses of flowers, flooding the house with light and colour. This was a talent that Nancy had mastered at Mirador. Visitors were invariably impressed with the 'festoons of green stuff'. Harold Nicolson enthused to Vita Sackville-West, accomplished gardeners both, on how 'superb' Cliveden looked. 'I have never seen such *ikkibani* [Japanese flower-arrangements, though in the Nicolson vernacular the term also denoted an ostentatious, slightly vulgar floral design] in my life. Great groups of delphiniums and tuberoses, great bowls of oleander.'[28] William Waldorf was less ecstatic. On his first visit to Cliveden to inspect the damage – Nancy, tactfully, kept to her bedroom to avoid any immediate confrontation – he wrote in typical style to a friend: 'The house has been somewhat altered in decoration and furniture and without objecting to these changes, it is no pleasure to me to see them.'[29] But no unbridgeable rift occurred between Nancy and her antisocial father-in-law. 'He and I always got on immensely well together,' Nancy recalled, 'although we had many passionate arguments.'[30]

Eventually the Astors acquired three other homes, apart from Cliveden. In London they were based at 4 St James's Square, an eighteenth-century town house situated in the north-east corner of the square. It was a magnificent residence, allowing them to entertain in grand style: two dining rooms large enough to seat forty guests, an enormous ballroom able to accommodate up to one thousand revellers, while at the top of the house was an added attraction, a squash court. Later, Nancy felt she also needed 'a cottage by the sea'. But Rest Harrow, near Sandwich, Kent, was no 'country cottage'. Containing fifteen bedrooms, with resident housekeeper and maid in charge, it boasted extensive gardens, a miniature golf course, a squash court, and sandpits to play in. Nancy often lent it to friends, including Lloyd George. These were delighted to discover that 'In the roof of the lounge there is a compass showing the direction of the wind, moving noiselessly in obedience to some vane outside. There is a fine model of a sailing ship in the drawing room, a complete set of Everyman's Library, a gramophone with [a surfeit of] fox trots . . . Upstairs are hot and cold seawater baths laid on.'[31]

When Waldorf eventually entered politics he bought a home in his constituency, the Sutton division of Plymouth. In Astor manner, they named it 'the lodging house'. In fact, it was a five-storeyed Victorian terraced house at 3 Elliot Terrace, on the Hoe overlooking the Sound, with ample room for guests and with the usual resident servants. (Ultimately, it was handed over to the city as the official residence for the Lord Mayor.) To these properties must also be added their holiday retreat, Tarbert Lodge, an estate on the isle of Jura in the Inner Hebrides. A renovated farmhouse, and comparatively spartan by Astor standards, it was used for deer stalking and fishing holidays.

But the charm of Cliveden ensured that it remained the Astors' principal home. In these early years they appear very domesticated. Children were born in steady succession: William (Bill) Waldorf III (1907), Phyllis (Nancy) (1909), David (1912), Michael (1916) and John Jacob (Jakie) VII (1918). Waldorf set up his stud farm and developed his interest in agricultural practice, while Nancy launched her reputation as one of England's foremost hostesses. Large weekend parties – Cliveden could accommodate up to forty guests – became a habitual entry on the social calendar. By modern standards the living conditions offered were somewhat primitive, belying Cliveden's appearance of opulent luxury. As there were no washbasins in any of the guest rooms, hot water in cans had to be carried to the rooms every morning. No lifts had been installed, so everything had to be hauled up and down the stairs – luggage, food, coal for fires and ashes from the grates (Cliveden consumed about 100 tons of coal a year). The domestic economy of Cliveden was highly 'labour-intensive'. These inconveniences were alleviated somewhat by the high quality of the domestic staff, supervised by the redoubtable Edwin Lee. Dressed in livery, the footmen, for example, projected an old-fashioned elegance with their yellow silk stockings, knee breeches, buckled shoes, and – if there were more than eight guests for dinner – powdered hair.[32]

Nancy added her own dimension to Cliveden's appeal. Devoid of affectation as she was, her sense of fun, her wit and banter, her spontaneity, lent to her social gatherings a novel character. Intent on being the life of the party, she coaxed others to follow suit. 'The moment she entered a room all was laughter and fun.' Party games always amused her (and one assumes also her guests) – musical chairs being a particular favourite. A consummate actress, she exploited her talents as a mimic on every occasion. Negro servants from her childhood, *nouveau riche* social climbers, insecure Jewish businessmen, horsey types who hunted in Leicestershire, or upper-crust English ladies, conventionally narrow of outlook, who suspected all things foreign and thought all Americans common and vulgar, were part of her repertoire. Margot, Countess of Oxford and Asquith, was a choice target. Equipped with a set of celluloid false teeth, Nancy would caricature Margot to the general delight of her audiences. Although there was a malicious element to her buffoonery, the popular verdict on her performances was 'Quite uncanny and terribly funny.'[33]

All this was a far cry from the austere regime favoured by William Waldorf for his weekends in the country. Nancy accounted for her success in the following manner.

There was lots to do at Cliveden. My guests would go off and amuse themselves or talk to people they wanted to, or read, ride, explore the grounds or play tennis. My rule was not to appear before lunch. I never interfered with them. That was how I got clever people like Arthur James Balfour to stay.[34]

In this way, a kind of 'Set' emerged at Cliveden in the years leading up to the First World War. Unstructured and unplanned, it just happened. 'Everyone was here . . . But I was never a lion hunter,' Nancy recalled, almost apologetically. Yet the lions came. The net was cast wide. It included expatriate American heiresses who had married impecunious English aristocrats: Consuelo Vanderbilt, 9th Duchess of Marlborough; Consuelo Yznaga de Valle, 8th Duchess of Manchester; Mary (May) Goelet – believed to be America's richest heiress – 8th Duchess of Roxburghe. Perhaps, unconsciously, Nancy was making her first move in what later became an avowed aim: the strengthening of Anglo–American understanding. Royalty followed. The Archduke Franz Ferdinand and his escort, the Countess Sophie, came to Cliveden shortly before they were assassinated in Sarajevo. Queen Marie of Rumania arrived in 1911, the first of many visits. Queen Victoria's third son, Prince Arthur, Duke of Connaught – 'the greatest gentleman', thought Nancy – was a regular guest. His brother, Edward VII, appeared less often. One occasion, however, gave rise to one of Nancy's most famous *bons mots* (though probably apocryphal). When invited by Edward to partner him in a game of bridge, Nancy refused, claiming that she never played cards, and by way of proof exclaiming, 'Why, I don't even know the difference between a King and a Knave.'

Leading politicians were also favoured. Lords Curzon, Cecil, Salisbury, Minto; or Balfour, Asquith and Lloyd George. Winston Churchill – with whom Nancy was to conduct a running feud for most of her political life – first came in May 1907. Nancy remembers him as sulking if placed 'next to a person he did not fancy'. Kitchener was another bothersome guest. An avid collector of *objets d'art*, he would praise items that took his fancy in the firm expectation of receiving them as gifts from his host. 'I won't give you anything,' Nancy bluntly told him, when she saw him eyeing her things.

Literary figures were encouraged, and faulted – Rudyard Kipling, recalled as 'dour' and 'poor company'; James Barrie, a 'spoiled' soul who had 'lost all his homely Scotch ways'; and John Buchan, indicted as 'guilty' of snobbery. But not Lytton Strachey, Nancy's 'Dear Author', whom she found 'excellent company, so droll and lively'. Other, less well-known, figures joined in. Relatives, close neighbours – particularly Julian and Gerald (Billy) Grenfell, the sons of Lord and Lady Desborough, owners of near-by Taplow Court – rising civil servants, anonymous Americans, enlightened social workers, religious do-gooders or unknown provincial journalists, were among those chosen. Her son David later recollected: 'She brought us up, not to admire celebrities, but people of worth, and to admire celebrities for their worth only.'[35]

It was at about this time, in 1908, that John Singer Sargent, the American artist, painted the portrait of her that now hangs in the Great Hall at Cliveden. Dressed in a flowing white gown, her decolletage turned discreetly away from the viewer, with hands tucked neatly behind her back and her head inclined knowingly to one side, she has that delicate 'fresh-air girl' look found in contemporary advertisements for a new brand of soap. A charming court portrait, it in no way catches Nancy's assertive, vibrant, possessive personality.

Hilaire Belloc, poet, essayist, historian, biographer, as well as Liberal, and later Independent, MP for Salford, was among Cliveden's most frequent visitors, and for a time a close friend of Nancy's. Yet for all his undoubted gifts, Belloc's character was seriously flawed. A zealous Catholic, moved by a deep vein of hysterical anti-Semitism, he allowed his bigotry conspicuous, and continuous, display. Nancy finally concluded that having two manias, 'against the Jews and the rich, I had to give him up at the end'. In fact, their break came over religious differences. By then Nancy had become an ardent Christian Scientist, and catching her trying to convert his daughters to her new-found faith and away from Catholicism, Belloc severed their relationship, denouncing her as a 'dangerous woman'.[36]

Whether Belloc planted in Nancy a chronic suspicion of Jews must remain an open question. At times, she certainly expressed herself in deplorable terms that carried a clear anti-Semitic ring. Did this signify genuine intolerance or was it merely another manifestation of Nancy's celebrated lack of tact? Most likely a mixture of both, depending upon the circumstances. She constantly greeted her brother-in-law Bob Brand – a director of Lazard Brothers – as a Jew, 'actual or honorary'. Brought up in a devout religious setting, Nancy must have been subject to the anti-Jewish strains that permeated much of western Christian civilization. Upper-class English society was not immune from these prejudices. It was not the paranoid, murderous anti-Semitism of Continental Europe, but a more genteel variety, insidious in its own right because of its sophisticated veneer. As Harold Nicolson noted, after the Holocaust, 'The Jewish capacity for self-destruction is really illimitable,' adding, in a revealing turn of phrase: 'Although I loathe anti-semitism, I do dislike Jews.' Given Nancy's innate flair for blunt speaking and role-playing, this most subtle of distinctions eluded her, particularly when she felt under pressure from prying journalists.[37]

But what eventually came to consume Nancy was not so much the supposed Jewish menace as the so–called Catholic threat. Her hardline anti-Catholicism smacked of genuine bigotry. To her mind the Papacy stood at the centre of a sinister conspiracy. Rooted in superstition, totalitarian in outlook, it regimented men's minds, dictating what people should think and how they should conduct their lives. All this was an affront to her own finely developed sense of independence of thought and expression. Maligning Catholics as 'Red Cherries' or 'Roman Candles', she came to abhor them. Edwin Lee was instructed never to employ Catholics. A friend was admonished for allowing her daughter to become a Catholic nun. And when her youngest son, Jakie, dared to marry a Catholic, Ana (Chiquita) Inez Carcano, daughter of the Argentinian ambassador, she refused to attend the wedding ceremony, and made certain that Waldorf joined in the boycott.[38]

For good or ill, such attitudes were a sign of the central role that religion played in Nancy's life. In part, this sprang from her upbringing at Mirador, a household of strong Protestant persuasion that was steeped in a 'deep religious faith'. Initially, she had refused to divorce Robert Shaw on religious grounds, marriage being a sacred bond. (Throughout her public career she continued to oppose divorce, despite her opponents gleefully pointing out the contradiction between her stated position and her personal example.) Although now happily remarried, during these years Nancy was plagued by ill health. Suffering from what her doctors diagnosed as nervous disorders, she spent much her life as a semi-invalid, resting, often bedridden. No spa or cure helped her. Is this what God wants, Nancy asked. Had God 'made sickness' to turn His children 'into useless self-centred people who became a burden to themselves and everyone else'? She long pondered this question. Her own Church, unable to provide that source of inner strength that she craved, offered no persuasive answer. 'An unrequited passion for religion' remained, a search for a particular source of inspiration, 'something outside herself on which she could lean and something that would in turn respond to her inward vision of life'. Eventually, in the spring of 1914, Nancy found it in Mary Baker Eddy's Christian Scientist Church. Upon reading its seminal work, *Science and Health*, Nancy underwent a genuine spiritual revelation:

> I read the first chapter on Prayer. It was just like the conversion of St Paul. Here I found the answer to all my questions . . . If I was spiritual I would not have to suffer in the flesh, I learned. It was like a new beginning for me. My life really was made over.[39]

By stumbling upon Christian Science, Nancy had designed her own godly Do-It-Yourself-Kit. It taught her that a true believer, a genuinely spiritual person devoted to daily prayer and study, would be rewarded with perfect health of body and mind. Bad thoughts were toxic: if you thought you had cancer, then you will have cancer. This attitude held enormous appeal for Nancy, particularly as it seemed to work. From her conversion – or as a result of her conversion, as Nancy preferred to put it – her nervous afflictions were relegated to the past. 'Her faith had made her whole,' she concluded. Her commitment to Christian Science was intuitive, emotional rather than intellectual – a trait that distinguished her behaviour at large. Protestant and nonconformist in character, it allowed Nancy's prudish inclinations to surface whenever challenged, an aspect of her new-found belief that strongly appealed to her.

Nancy believed passionately in Christian Science – even though later experience induced her to moderate her enthusiasm – often riding rough-shod over the feelings of others in an attempt to impose her views. She was a fervent proselytizer. Her dearest friend, Philip Kerr, a lapsed Catholic, fell to her special pleading. So, eventually, did Waldorf. Her children were subjected to a process of 'intense religious indoctrination', though in the end it proved counter-productive owing to the intransigence of its advocate. Nor did chance visitors to Cliveden escape Nancy's missionary zeal. All too often Bibles would turn up on the arms of their chairs, innocently marked with passages thought relevant to Mrs Eddy's doctrines.[40]

Nancy denounced Catholicism for its dogma and arrogance of opinion. But her fixation on Christian Science left her open to the same charge. Did she ever fully understand its tenets? Not according to the Christian Science practitioners who every so often were brought to Cliveden. They detected 'a certain originality of approach' – it was said that Philip Kerr provided Nancy with intellectual backing. 'Mary Baker Eddy, if she had met your mother, would have taken off and jumped over the clock tower,' one seasoned Christian Scientist told Nancy's son Michael. An irreverent thought later crossed Michael's mind: 'With or without a broomstick?' – a remark forgivable in the light of the extreme religiosity he remembered from his childhood at Cliveden. For apart from churchgoing twice a week, several hours a day were devoted to studying the Bible and religious manuals, notably *Science and Health*, and silent prayer.[41] Michael and his siblings may well have agreed with Mark Twain's judgement that it was all 'Eddygush'.*

There is no evidence that at this stage Nancy was particularly interested in politics. Only one subject continually fired her imagination. Proud of her

---

* 'Eddygush'? Certainly! But by the time of Nancy's conversion the Christian Science Church, founded in Boston in 1879, could boast over a million believers. It had also made Mrs Eddy – dubbed as '*the* monumental hysteric' – the richest woman in America.

Virginian birth, she displayed an exceptional loyalty to the Confederate cause. Winston Churchill, who insisted on calling her 'a Yankee' whenever they quarrelled, which was often, was sharply informed, 'Your mother was a Yankee – I am a Virginian.'[42] Neither would her most devoted, her most charitable friends have judged her an intellectual. One highbrow acquaintance, Alfred Leslie Rowse, historian, poet, and a Fellow of All Souls, perhaps holding the extreme view, 'never took seriously anything Nancy thought, about politics or religion'.[43] Although curious about many things, she did not possess an inquiring mind. Nor was she well read – except in the Bible and *The Times*, a family publication 'which I have to read'. Something of a chatterbox, given to flights of fancy and rash outbursts, she found it difficult to hold her tongue. By temperament, she held the strongest of opinions, always robustly expressed, regardless of the audience. 'Nothing pleased her more than a punch-up,' confirmed one contemporary. 'She bored in, flinging jabs and combination punches, got hit but never threw in the towel.' Outspoken to the point of tactlessness, her disorderly mind skipped effortlessly from topic to topic, concealing little. 'Yes, we *heard* you listening,' her critics duly noted.[44] These were not the most auspicious traits for a serious politician in the making. One factor worked to her advantage. Perched on the top of the social pecking order, Nancy was moved by a lively sense of duty. Like Waldorf, she felt a burden of obligation towards those less fortunate than she. Paternalistic? Undoubtedly; but genuine none the less. For the moment, however, none of this counted. During these years Nancy was content to organize her houses, plan her weekends and enjoy her role as a society hostess.

Rather it was Waldorf's sense of duty that gave the initial impetus for the Astors to move into politics. Waldorf did not approve of his father's aloof and idiosyncratic outlook on life. 'He [Waldorf] wanted to succeed in a life of public service and make amends, as he saw it, for his father's negligence in this respect. He felt particularly keenly that he owed this to the country of his father's adoption.'[45] At first, ill health prevented him from realizing his goal. Forced to spend much time abroad recuperating his strength, there was no possibility of his pursuing an active political life. Instead, at his own pace, he rode, shot and hunted, developed his stud farm, ran his estates, and deepened his knowledge in scientific agricultural methods. This led naturally to an interest in public health, no doubt also prompted by his own history of tuberculosis. Such was his concern at the ill-effects of contaminated milk that whenever he went on family holidays he took with him, in a special carriage attached to the end of the train, a cow – and cowman – to provide fresh milk for the children at stations along the way.[46] Later, these social matters found vigorous expression in his public career.

Waldorf's sedate life as a country gentleman soon came to an end. Adopted as Conservative candidate for the Sutton division of Plymouth, he was duly elected to Parliament in the elections of December 1910, having failed at a previous attempt. Although both great parties had returned the same number of MPs, 272, the Liberals remained in power, dependent on Labour and particularly Irish Nationalist support. Waldorf plunged into a period of acute confrontational politics. The controversy over Lloyd George's 'People's Budget', the battle over the Parliament Bill of 1911, and not least the perennial question of Ulster, had generated a turbulent atmosphere that threatened to undermine the constitutional structure of the country.

One factor that both complicated and eased Waldorf's career was the family's acquisition of the *Observer* in 1911, with Garvin as editor. Waldorf was the moving spirit behind this purchase. Although his father, having put up the money, was the legal owner, his prolonged absences abroad left Waldorf effectively in charge – four years later he was to take over the *Observer* in fact. Newspaper proprietors were thought to wield considerable political clout. And there can be no doubt that owning two newspapers – the other being the *Pall Mall Gazette* – enhanced Waldorf's standing in Conservative circles. But Garvin was no tool of the Astors. Holding staunch Conservative views, he jealously preserved his editorial independence. Disagreements were inevitable, both with William Waldorf, who often took an outright reactionary line, and with Waldorf, who inclined to a more liberal approach. On the whole, however, this particular proprietor–editor relationship – always by definition prickly affairs – proved fruitful; at any rate, it lasted until 1942, when differences over wartime policy brought it to an end.

Waldorf made an impressive opening to his parliamentary career. His maiden speech, on 1 March 1911, was 'well received', wrote Churchill to King George V. Two months later Churchill, himself a distinguished parliamentary performer, felt able to add:

> The best speech yesterday was made by young Mr Waldorf Astor, who confined himself to the provisions affecting the cure & prevention of tuberculosis, from wh he has at one time been a sufferer. The knowledge and distinction of the speech and the pleasant manner of the delivery won great praise from all sides & quarters of the House.'[47]

Waldorf concentrated on those topics he knew best: agriculture, health, social reform, imperial affairs, relations with the United States. Of independent mind, in December 1911 he defied the Tory whip and voted in favour of Lloyd George's revolutionary National Insurance Bill, a package deal that included health and unemployment benefits. Active on government health committees, he promoted a group of like-minded Conservatives that formulated progressive policies over a wide range of social and economic issues, proposals that were eventually published in *The Health of the People – A New National Policy* (1916), in some ways a harbinger of the much acclaimed Beveridge Report of the Second World War. In a very real sense, Waldorf's activities helped to prepare the ground for the subsequent establishment of the Ministry of Health in 1919.

Waldorf was not simply a multimillionaire do-gooder, an idealist remote from the cut and thrust of backroom politics. If necessary, he would not shrink from exploiting his social position to his own advantage. At the height of the parliamentary crisis over the Parliament Bill, he was drawn into the activities of the so-called Halsbury Club, named after the 87-year-old ex-Lord Chancellor who led a 'no surrender' charge against the Bill. The Club was not only a refuge for Tory diehards; many young Conservative MPs joined in, alarmed at Balfour's timid handling of the crisis. This was a difficult situation for Waldorf who was on friendly terms with Balfour, a frequent visitor to Cliveden. But he was clearly influenced by Milner – Waldorf's idol – and Garvin, both of whom were solid Halsburyites. Intended as a ginger group, the Club was designed to shore up the vacillating Balfour, not necessarily to topple him, although this was the ultimate result. Waldorf, for one, was not entirely satisfied with this outcome. Not only had Balfour gone, but his successor, Andrew Bonar Law, a Glasgow iron-merchant, a more staid and sober figure than the aristocratic, intellectually stimulating Balfour, did not fit Waldorf's image of a Conservative leader. This would not be the last such cabal that Waldorf would be involved in.

Despite Waldorf's faultless background of wealth and property, he must have appeared to party hacks as something of a Conservative maverick. Over Ulster he rejected the extreme Unionist view of no compromise, favouring instead the federal-type option upheld by his Round Table friends. And as he held advanced ideas on social reform – including the highly contentious issue of votes for women – he was perceived by them as upholding, indeed disseminating, dangerous radical tendencies. More than anything else his intimate association with Lloyd George tended to confirm this image. His support of Lloyd George's Insurance Bill in the teeth of vigorous Conservative opposition was a case in point. 'If science and religion have failed to stem the tide of disease and sorrow,' he said, endorsing the Bill, 'it is now the duty of the State to act.'

The Astors' relationship with Lloyd George deepened. He would often unwind at the Astors' house, Rest Harrow, near Sandwich. At Cliveden he was always welcome. A story is told of how he would sit by the fire in the Great Hall singing Welsh songs, accompanied by Nancy's sister, Nora, on the ukulele. In retrospect, Lloyd George appears very much as Waldorf's patron, nudging him up the political ladder. Later, Nancy herself admitted that 'Waldorf was at heart a Liberal'. With the passing of years, the perception of the Astors as Conservative misfits sharpened. Representing conventional Conservative opinion, David Alexander Lindsay, an ex-Conservative minister and art connoisseur, remarked: 'He [Waldorf] is not *persona grata* to our House [of Lords] – lectures us too much, and his wife annoys us by coming to the bar and disturbing us by her loud talk.'[48]

From about 1910 some of Waldorf's acquaintances from his Oxford days began to attend Cliveden more regularly. They had gradually moved back to England from South Africa, cloaked in collective distinction as Milner's *Kindergarten*.[49] In London, they had founded the quarterly review *The Round Table*, had set up a formal organization, and had begun to establish a network of kindred groups throughout the white Dominions. Waldorf now joined the 'Tabloids', as his sister-in-law Phyllis persisted in calling them. As these were strictly male bastions, Nancy was excluded, formally at least, from their Moots. But by virtue of her hosting the Round Tablers whenever they congregated at Cliveden, her presence was felt in other ways. One Tabloid declared that she exerted 'a profound effect' upon them, almost as though she breathed into their stuffy world a puff of earthly realism.

> There was also an innate and irresistible force inside her, a sort of 'power' engine, something that enabled her and indeed forced her to cut her way through life, something that compelled her to try to reform the world, and even to make the universe do what she wanted . . . Reason was not a weapon she cared to use much, if at all, but she certainly had a very powerful intuition, which worked like a flash. She liked our society because she was full of desire to do things in the world.[50]

What they meant by doing 'things in the world' was primarily to sustain the Anglo-Saxon fraternity. Dedicated to an intimate partnership between the Dominions and Britain, perhaps federation or even union, and a strengthening of the Anglo-American connections, they aimed in this way to preserve Britain's distinctive role in international affairs. And what of Europe? As regards 'the Latins' and others, an air of disdainful superiority prevailed. Waldorf, typifying the Little Englander views of his peers, wrote to Nancy after one infuriating session of the League of Nations in Geneva: 'All in all, I am inclined . . . to agree with that person who said that you leave the white race when you cross the Channel.'[51] Nancy would not have quarrelled with Waldorf's attitude. Nor would other members of the group, though they might have phrased it differently. Their outlook came to represent wide and influential sections of British opinion. They never ceased to promote their views. Among the most prominent of these budding opinion-makers, who were also among the most frequent guests at Cliveden, were Philip Kerr, Lionel Curtis, Geoffrey Dawson and Robert Brand.

CHAPTER 3

The Kinder

Oxford remained the common meeting ground of the *Kinder*. They absorbed its traditions, its values, its culture and mores. It could also be argued that they fell victim to its myths. But however these factors are juggled, Oxford fashioned their perspective on life.

The city of Oxford in the 1890s radiated a tranquil atmosphere, relaxed, composed, self-assured. Undergraduates arriving at the railway station would either call a hansom cab or take a horse-drawn bus to convey them to their colleges. No cars clogged the High or George Street. William Morris still ran his bicycle shop in James Street. The city was compact, self-sufficient. Marston, Wolvercote, Headington, Iffley lay well beyond the town's borders. London was readily accessible by train, but there was much less toing and froing. Industrial strife or economic discord scarcely penetrated its precincts. Poised, secure, frozen in its splendid past – 'Tory' Oxford ranged against 'Whig' Cambridge – the city was dominated by its University – *Universitas Oxoniensis* – which bestowed upon it a privileged status. Not only did it send three members to Parliament – one from the City, two from the University – it was also home to an episcopal see, the chapel of Christ Church serving as the cathedral of Oxford.

This appealing combination of town and gown could have a lasting effect on impressionable undergraduates. John Buchan remembered his first day in Oxford.

> [The] streets, when I arrived late from the North, were deep in snow ... I felt as though I had slipped through some chink in the veil of the past and become a medieval student. Most vividly I recollect walking in the late afternoon in Merton Street and Holywell and looking at snow-laden gables which had scarcely altered since the Middle Ages. In that hour Oxford claimed me and her bonds have never been loosed.[1]

Leo Amery recalled his days at Oxford as being 'almost entirely monastic', and John Buchan wrote to his son that his days at Oxford were 'spent peacefully in an enclave like a monastery'. In 1884, Dean Burgon, the chaplain at New College, reminded the opposite sex of its true standing in society: 'Inferior to us God made you, and inferior to the end of time you will remain.' It was only in the 1880s that Oxford dons – with the exceptions of heads of houses and professors – were allowed to marry, a breakthrough that led to the sprawl of North Oxford. Having graduated from the Christian masculinity of their public schools, approximately two thousand undergraduates took shelter among the cloisters of Oxford. The monastic image stuck, despite the studied scepticism of some of the makers of Oxford. 'My dear child,' Benjamin Jowett, the legendary Master of Balliol, told Margot Asquith, 'you must believe in God despite what the clergy tell you.'

New College proved the focal point for the *Kinder*, a veritable breeding ground for membership of the *Kindergarten* and its offshoot, the Round Table circle. Other colleges intruded – Balliol, Christ Church or Magdalen – but none could match New College's unique contribution. The list is impressive: Lionel Curtis; Philip Kerr (later Lord Lothian); Robert Henry (Lord) Brand, in time to become Waldorf's brother-in-law; Edward William Macleay Grigg (later Lord Altrincham), imperial administrator and Conservative politician; and Dougal Orme Malcolm, styled as a scholar and imperialist.

This tally of graduates from New College can easily be expanded. Why New College? Why did it become the focal point in recruiting the *Kinder*? For one thing, it was a classic example of how the old-boy network operated. One chum drew in another. Of the nine original members of the *Kindergarten*, seven were from New College. Apart from Curtis, Kerr and Brand, John Frederick (Peter) Perry, Lionel Hichens, John Dove and Richard Feetham were New College men, and they were joined by Geoffrey (Robinson) Dawson of Magdalen – recruited by his long-time friend, Perry – and Patrick Duncan, of Edinburgh University and Balliol. Among the founding Round Tablers may also be included Alfred Eckhard Zimmern, George Lillie Craik, Hugh Wyndham and Reginald Coupland, all from New College; and of course Waldorf Astor. Later, many of this in-group were elected to Fellowships at All Souls, considered by many as the ultimate accolade of academic excellence. The Oxford link was jealously preserved. Whenever they met, even in the seclusion of their clubs or the privacy of their homes, they must have sniffed the rarefied atmosphere of Oxford common rooms. They created an enchanted world of their own, one that they never entirely abandoned, or wished to.

Another compelling reason was the forceful personality of Lord Milner, a Fellow of the College. It was only natural that he should seek out his 'young men' from among its members; as he did, purposefully. The *Kinder* regarded Milner with awe. Impressed by his charisma, they set him up as an icon. This was somewhat ironic as Milner has been described as 'hardly English'. Although he was a Balliol man – he took a Double First and won four University scholarships – his critics pointed out that he had been born – his mother being English, his father half-German – in Hesse-Darmstadt and educated at the *Gymnasium* at Tübingen. From this background, apparently, he had imbibed the Teutonic qualities he now promoted, those of order and discipline, method and precision. Autocrat that he was, Milner's political philosophy was widely bracketed with racism – 'British Race – Patriotism,' he would proclaim, and authoritarianism, as he poured scorn on 'that mob at Westminster', or contemplated treason over Ulster, claiming it would be 'an uprising of unshakeable principle and devoted patriotism – of loyalty to Empire and the Flag'.* He was an unyielding negotiator. Clemenceau said of him: 'If Milner does not agree with you, he closes his eyes like a lizard and you can do nothing with him.' Perhaps this is what happened at the abortive Bloemfontein conference with President Kruger of the Transvaal (himself no trimmer), a clash of impenetrable minds that sparked off the Boer War. Having won the war, Milner worked for unity between the Boers and the British, but very much on his own terms. As he said to Churchill: 'My formula for South Africa is very simply: 2/5 Boers and 3/5th Britishers – Peace, Progress and Fusion. 3/5ths Boers and 2/5ths Britishers – Stagnation and Eternal Discord.'

Yet Milner was clearly a man of enviable talents. 'He was a formidable young man,' it was noted, 'and became a formidable old one.' Although Lloyd George sensed that Milner had 'no political nostril', he insisted that Milner join his War Cabinet. Still, for all his flair, for all his ability to inspire, Milner was more of an outstanding public servant than a first-rate politician. This did not deter his devotees, none more so than the *Kinder*, from pushing him forward, claiming for him the highest office, particularly when the country was faced with a national emergency. But Milner waited in vain for the call – perhaps fortunately for him, for if nothing else he died with his reputation intact.[2]

Lord Curzon, that other great imperial proconsul and one of Oxford's brightest stars – despite having attained only a second-class degree – once listed Oxford's order of priorities. It ought, he believed, to be 'a focus of culture, a school of character, and a nursery of thought'.[3] Jowett slightly reversed this sequence, though his formula was designed to bring about a

---

* Milner's ideas on race and Empire, if put to the test, were a certain recipe for disaster. Based on his premise 'British Race – Patriotism', he ruled that 'the only real and permanent tie of Empire is race'. Without this racial glue, he maintained, it would be 'impossible permanently to retain any great white community in political connection with the mother country' (quoted in May, 25–6). This theory was unlikely to appeal to Québecois or Afrikaners, to say nothing of the Indians or the Irish.

similar result. Balliol – to his mind synonymous with Oxford – stands for 'brain-power and worldly influence'. One of the formative influences on late Victorian Britain, Jowett – at times fetchingly ingenuous, at others ruthless – earnestly reflected the spirit of the age. 'A cherubic, shrill-voiced, fresh-faced little man', apparently incapable of small talk, though he would swiftly put down gauche undergraduates or disagreeable colleagues with a caustic remark, Jowett was dedicated to producing a ruling elite: he wished 'to inoculate England' with Balliol alumni.

The study of Greek, it was said, would not 'only enable [Oxford undergraduates] to read the scriptures in the original, but also qualify them for positions of considerable emolument'. The sciences, if not taboo, were frowned upon. Steeped in the classics, Oxford men were encouraged to think that 'they rule the world'.[4] Locked into their own closeted world, they formed a vintage social and intellectual freemasonary, a brilliant host of movers-and-shakers whose influence was at its peak in the years before the First World War. By the mid-1960s it had produced twenty-two prime ministers, ten viceroys, hundreds of Cabinet ministers and bishops, numerous senior servants, and a multitude of empire builders. One of the most prominent of them, Cecil Rhodes, who saw Oxford as 'the energizing force of Empire' and whose legacy was to figure prominently in the *Kinder*'s careers, was awarded an honorary DCL (Doctor of Civil Law) in 1899. Perhaps they even heard the Public Orator allude pointedly to the fiasco of the Jameson Raid, an excessive exercise in imperial skulduggery. 'Ah! let not excessive love of country drive to rashness, and do not resort more than is proper to alliances, stratagems and plots!'[5]

This was the Oxford that greeted Lionel Curtis, Waldorf Astor, Geoffrey Robinson (later Dawson), the Hon. Robert Brand and Philip Kerr when they arrived, strangers to each other, in the 1890s. Like many others they were delighted at what they found. No doubt they would have identified with Matthew Arnold reflecting on 'that sweet City with her dreaming spires'. But Arnold also noted another Oxford, one

> so venerable, so lovely, so unravaged by the fierce intellectual life of our century, so serene! . . . whispering from her towers the last enchantments of the Middle Age . . . Home of lost causes, and forsaken beliefs, and unpopular names, and impossible loyalties!'[6]

Philip

'My heart yearns over Philip,' wrote Lionel Curtis to Robert Brand – like Curtis, one of Kerr's closest friends – in January 1910. 'He has so nearly all the qualities needed for the fulfilment of a great purpose and I am wondering whether he will develop the stability of character necessary unless all his other gifts are to be thrown away.' The problem, as Curtis saw it, was that Philip 'flitted too fast . . . to gather honey'. Too easily bored intellectually, he craved the 'excitement of change', skipping to other, seemingly more profound issues, when he should have been concentrating on the matter in hand. Striving for all-round excellence, given to optimism and prone to wishful thinking, he flinched from appearing dull in the eyes of his contemporaries. So despite his erudite ways, many observers detected a shallow, superficial dimension to his character, even 'an element of instability'. 'Airy and viewy', judged Brand, harping on Philip's 'uncritical' appraisals of 'men and of the real character of the international problems of countries of which he had no personal knowledge'.[7]

This is a harsh criticism of someone who aspired to influence public opinion and to guide governments in imperial and foreign affairs. From what did it stem? It was said that Philip sought in all things the revealed truth. As an adolescent he had questioned his Catholic upbringing, to the point of renunciation. For the remainder of his life his prime concern lay in determining 'where the point of truth in Christian teaching lay'. A timeless quest, it produced in him an inner emptiness that for all his native intelligence left him emotionally incomplete. 'His feelings, every part of him, became involved in the process of living in the context of a religion.'[8] Unable to cast aside his own religious unease, he sought to redress the balance by an excessive concern for high moral standards, not only for himself but also for others. Unfortunately, international affairs in the first half of the twentieth century were dominated by demagogic rabble-rousers whose ruthless, bullying ways were foreign to Philip's cosier perception of world politics. He spent his life pursuing an absolute of spiritual fulfilment along with some form of international golden age. Neither aim was attainable. In the final reckoning, the vacuum in his personal and public life remained unfilled.

On the surface, none of this hindered his public career. At its zenith he served with distinction Britain's two great war leaders, earning their genuine esteem, though in varying proportions: from Lloyd George, high praise indeed, 'a young man of conspicuous ability who was especially knowledgeable on all Imperial and on foreign affairs'; from Churchill, a somewhat grudging admission that 'I had at last come to like Philip, after years of prejudice.'[9] It was Philip's flawless aristocratic background that furnished him with the credentials necessary to enter these circles. Born in April 1882, Philip Henry Kerr was the eldest son of Major-General Lord Ralph Kerr, third son of the 7th Marquess of Lothian, and Lady Anne Fitzalan-Howard, daughter of the 14th Duke of Norfolk. Although not in direct line, Philip succeeded eventually to the marquessate in 1930. It

brought him great estates and a cluster of titles. Along the border country
in Scotland he came to own Ferniehirst Castle, Newbattle Abbey and
Monteviot House; in Norfolk, he took possession of Blickling Hall.
Formerly belonging to the Hobart and Boleyn families, it had passed, by
marriage, to the Kerrs. A magnificent Jacobean pile, built of rose-red brick
and stone and islanded by a grassy moat, it stood in an estate of 4,500 acres
that included terraced gardens and a deer park. In the 1930s Philip would
do much entertaining here: hosting parties; conducting Moots; arranging
international symposiums.

Both the Kerrs and the Howards were ardent Catholic families. (Indeed,
the Howards, apart from retaining the premier English dukedom, could
claim with justification to be England's leading Catholic family: its
fortunes, dating back to the late thirteenth century, had prospered despite
the upheavals of the Reformation and the so-called 'Glorious Revolution'.)
At the age of ten Philip was sent to the Roman Catholic Oratory School at
Edgbaston, where he spent the next eight years. He imbibed deeply of its
spiritual life. His sister Cecil recalls that as a boy Philip was 'distinctly
pious'. Should he take holy orders? Unable to decide, Philip knew only
that he 'wanted to serve God in the way he has chosen for me'. But which
way? Although he felt drawn to 'the monkish ideal', the signposts he
encountered on his way pointed in different directions.

In this troubled state of mind Philip went up to New College, Oxford,
in 1900. Despite his personal ordeals, he adjusted readily to university life.
Modestly companionable, physically attractive – one admirer compared
him to 'a Greek God' – he affected a careless style of dress usually crowned
by an untidy mop of hair. Regarded by his contemporaries as 'rather
austere', Philip did not seek out intimate friendships, male or female. A
member of the Union and a musical club, he read papers and debated at
the (Catholic) Newman Society. He enjoyed most sports. Said to have 'a
wrist of iron', he played an impressive set of tennis and excelled at golf –
realizing eventually a plus two handicap. At College his tutor was the
historian (later Liberal politician) H. A. L. Fisher, to whom he remained
'eternally grateful . . . for having opened the doors to the intellectual life'.
Industrious and of keen intelligence, Philip took a first-class degree in
modern history in the summer of 1904, failing, however, to gain an All
Souls fellowship the following October.

For all these accomplishments, Philip's inner doubts persisted. But the
balance now began to tilt away from Catholicism. He discovered George
Bernard Shaw. 'New vistas' opened before him, he was wont to recall, as
his faith began to crumble before Shaw's trenchant criticism of contemporary social and political evils.* Some years would pass before he would

---

* Which of Shaw's works so influenced him? Kerr never specified. But by the time he

entirely abandon the Roman Church – though not before he had gone into retreat in a Roman Catholic institution, consulted Gandhi, and investigated the attractions of Buddhism. But by the time he arrived in South Africa in January 1905 it was obvious to his associates that he was no longer an ardent, practising Catholic.

Philip began his public career as private secretary to Sir Arthur Lawley, Lieutenant Governor of the Transvaal. Lawley had served under Lord Ralph Kerr, so that by a combination of parental leverage and Oxford contacts, principally John Buchan (who had served on Milner's staff), Philip's appointment was secured. He was twenty-three years of age. If he expected to plunge immediately into the great task of the reconstruction of South Africa after the Boer War, he was to be disappointed. At first, his duties were undefined and less than onerous. But by April, all that had changed. From Johannesburg came a message from Robert Brand, a New College acquaintance. Brand had been appointed by Milner to act as secretary of the Inter-Colonial Council of the Transvaal and Orange River Colony. Milner attached great importance to the Council's work. Charged with authority over the railways and police of the two colonies, he regarded it as the first essential stage in the final union of the provinces. When Brand asked for Philip as his assistant, Milner readily agreed. In this way, Philip joined that band of young men known as the *Kindergarten*. Unlike them, he never worked directly under the great man himself, for Milner left South Africa a week after Philip joined Brand's staff. But like them, he came to idolize Milner, cherishing him as a father-figure, or as he put it, 'a Roman of the Augustan Age'. Largely responsible for cultivating the 'Religio Milneriana' that bewitched so many of their class, the *Kinder* absorbed from Milner, if only by degree, something of his elitism, his suspicion of the democratic process, and his spurious conception of an 'Anglo–Saxon brotherhood' fuelled by the singular mission it would play in international life.

Philip had found his niche. His work was challenging; the company he kept stimulating. Not lacking in humour, he impressed those around him with his industry, his quick and perceptive grasp of issues. Although at times he could be 'viewy', not to say dogmatic, he demonstrated an equable disposition: he rarely lost his temper, even when crossed in debate. He inhabited an almost exclusively male set. In June 1906 he moved into a house owned by a colleague, Richard Feetham, together with Bob Brand and George Craik. Known as 'Moot House', it was situated on the outskirts of Johannesburg, looking out over the veldt and eucalyptus woods

went up to Oxford, Shaw, one of the founders of the Fabian Society, had published *An Unsocial Socialist* (1897) and edited *Fabian Essays in Socialism* (1889); in particular, he had revised his *Plays Pleasant and Unpleasant* (1898).

to the Magaliesberg mountains some forty miles to the north-west. It was here that the *Kindergarten* would often gather at weekends. By day they would help in the restoration of the house; the evenings were spent discussing the loftiest of issues: the future of the Union, of the British Empire, of the Anglo-Saxon race. 'We literally go on for hours until we have both reached the most extraordinary conclusions and opinions,' remembered Brand after one session. This loose framework of like-minded young men stood at the centre of Philip's social and intellectual life. He rounded off its key members; the others were Lionel Curtis, Dougie Malcolm, Richard Feetham, John Dove, Robert Brand, Lionel Hichens, Patrick Duncan, J. F. (Peter) Perry, Geoffrey Robinson (Dawson) and Hugh Wyndham (later Lord Leconfield). 'I have really been tremendously lucky,' Philip disclosed to his father, 'I have too been very happy in every way.'[10]

Philip's days were full, working on average from '9–1, 2–7, and 9–11.30'. Two of his reports were of particular significance. One dealt with railway tariffs. Apparently a dry topic, Philip enlivened it with a persuasive political message. Unless the colonies united, he argued, and an all-South African railway system would be a first, positive step, the country would slip back into internecine strife. He next drew up a memorandum – 200 pages of text, 400 of evidence – for the Transvaal Indigency Commission. It was 'most wearing work', and it touched upon the most sensitive of all topics: race relations. Philip rejected 'the pernicious theory' that equated the white man with skilled labour and the black man with the drudgery of menial work. 'Poverty will remain, and will grow worse so long as the white man continues to regard manual labour as beneath him.' Once again, he deliberately broadened his terms of reference. Not only the Transvaal, but 'South Africa as a whole must change its habits and ideas', he concluded. 'This beautiful child was . . . leading us by the nose,' wrote Lionel Curtis – who had been a member of the Commission – after Philip's death. If Philip knew the way, there was little dissent from those being led. The Report, unanimously signed, was hailed as 'a milestone in the study of the colour question'.[11]

By now Philip's official work in the colonies was coming to an end. The Inter-Colonial Council wound up its activities in June 1908. That autumn, a constitutional convention met at Durban to discuss the nuts and bolts of representative government. Older ideas of federation were brushed aside in favour of union. Inspired by Curtis, a Closer Union Association was lauched to promote the cause. In this changing climate, Philip's future was uncertain. Although he contemplated a political career in England, he hesitated, put off by the lack of an adequate private income to support one. Instead, his friends, particularly Brand and Curtis, came to his rescue. They suggested that he become editor of *The State*, another of Curtis's brainwaves, a new monthly review to be issued in English and Dutch. Originally intended to promote 'Federation in every way', it became in effect the organ of the Closer Union societies, promulgating 'the growth of a South African nationalism'. (In retrospect this was ironic, as both Philip and Curtis came later to regard national sovereignty as the root of international evil.) Philip and *The State* went on to foster the concept of a more closely-knit Empire. It would be 'a confederation of great white self-governing communities, each free to deal with its own internal affairs, but uniting for certain common objects'. What objects? To formulate a common political strategy; to coordinate their economic and financial affairs; and, no less crucial, to collaborate in matters of imperial defence, an issue of paramount importance in view of the growing German colonial and naval threat. Nor had overt Japanese ambitions escaped the notice of these young imperialists. These topics were to occupy Philip for the remainder of his career.

At the end of June 1909 Philip, accompanied by Brand, sailed for home. The South African Act, granting self-governing dominion status under the Crown, came into effect the following May. Philip's editorship of *The State* was of short duration; only seven issues were brought out under his management. But he had gained invaluable practical and journalistic experience in the running of a review. A skilled draughtsman, an efficient administrator, and now a proficient journalist, he had acquired useful qualities upon which to build a public career. His list of contacts had also expanded. On leaves in London he had moved among Unionist politicians, among them the former prime minister, Arthur James Balfour. Hoping 'to disabuse him of any narrow British views', Philip found Balfour's interest in matters South African 'largely speculative and academic'. His South African connections were more forthcoming. He came to know the leaders of the young Dominion well: Louis Botha, its first prime minister, and particularly Jan Christian Smuts, who was destined to secure an international reputation as a soldier and statesman. At first, Smuts – a Cambridge man – remained wary of the *Kindergarten*, a clique of self-important young Oxford men in too much of a hurry. 'We are ruled by the finest flower of Varsity scholarship,' he remarked sardonically, 'these estimable advocates of federation . . . [who] damn everything they touch.' 'He longs to be an autocrat,' answered back the *Kindergarten*, 'and rule without annoying ifs and buts.'[12] Later, their opinions of each other softened, and from the First World War Smuts and Philip cooperated closely, sharing a common outlook on the post-war settlement.

In September 1909, Milner presided over a weekend Moot at Lord Anglesey's estate, Plas Newydd, sessions taking place on the golf course and in the cricket pavilion. Philip took part in these, together with other members of the *Kindergarten*, particularly Curtis and Brand. Present also was Frederick Scott Oliver, whose interpretative biography, *Alexander Hamilton: An Essay on American Union* (1906), had, so Curtis claimed, first inspired the *Kinder* in the virtues of union. Here were laid the foundations of the Round Table movement. Based in London, an overseas network of kindred groups would be set up, each with its own review. To propagate the movement's aim of organic union of the Empire – the alternative, or so Curtis held, being disintegration – a quarterly journal, *The Round Table*, would be founded. Thus a balance would be struck between the Dominions and London. It was proposed that Philip should act as secretary of the organization at an annual salary of £1,000, and also edit the quarterly for an additional £600. But first a delegation to include Philip, Curtis and William Marris – a member of the London Moot – would be sent to Canada on a fact-finding mission. How would the foremost of the Dominions respond to their ideas?

Not too well, was Philip's general conclusion. Struck by the growing strength of dominion nationalism, he recognized the 'obvious disadvantages [to Canada] in the surrender of autonomy entailed in the creation of any Empire organization'. He saw no immediate reason why Canada should drift away from the United Kingdom, 'but for the life of me I can't see why it should want to get any closer'. Above all, there was the gravitational pull of America. What could Britain offer that 'the United States can't offer just as well'? Serious differences emerged with Curtis on these points. Curtis had no ready answer to Philip's scepticism other than that burning faith in his mission would carry him through, dragging the doubters along behind him. Elevating organic union to the status of a sacred icon did not please Philip. The British Empire 'is a noble thing', he wrote, 'but not fit to be a God ... I cannot worship at its shrine alone'. Although in some ways the Canadian trip clarified matters, in others it left Philip 'rather at sixes and sevens'.[13]

These disagreements, of emphasis more than of principle, were put down to a clash of temperaments – Curtis, single-minded to the point of dogmatism, pressing for immediate action to force the issue of union; Philip, of a more academic bent, struggling to maintain a balance between the two sides of any question, political or personal. For all their differences they remained firm friends, the most consistent of the ideologues of the movement. Referred to as Castor and Pollux, their relationship in Curtis's words was like that of two blades of a pair of scissors, briskly cutting up the opposition when working in accord.[14]

Philip was still unsure whether or not to go into politics. In April 1910 he turned down a safe Unionist seat. It was his decision. But Curtis helped him reach it, arguing that his talents would be more constructively employed by working full-time for the Round Table movement. This was a mark of Curtis's will-power and high-pressure salesmanship – or equally of Philip's malleability. By now the Moot had agreed upon a programme: to form an imperial government, constitutionally responsible to all the electors of the Empire, that would also conduct defence and foreign policies.[15] Philip took up his new duties. That November he published his first major article. Entitled 'Anglo-German Rivalry', its theme was clear but deeply pessimistic. The antagonism between the two powers – 'the central fact in the international situation to-day' – was depicted as a clash between two diametrically opposed political cultures – one based on respect for individual liberty and the rule of law; the other worshipping at the altar of the state, even to the point of resorting to war as an instrument of policy. Whereas British policy was based on 'enlightened self-interest', Germany's was in thrall to the Bismarkian-Prussian tradition of 'egoistic power'. 'Rattling the sabre' and striving after 'world dominion', demanding colonies and engaged in building a great navy, German policy was categorized as arrogant, aggressive, expansionist. Fearful of the effective union of the British Empire, the 'overwhelming majority of Germans regard war with England as inevitable'.

How to deter this Germany, bent on 'national aggrandizement'? Not through a universal peace movement, that child of 'far-sighted enthusiasts' but which 'falls deaf on German ears'. Nor by an internal revolt leading to the growth of 'true democracy' in Germany, a totally unrealistic option in its prevailing political climate. Nor had Philip any faith in the Triple Entente, that imprecise diplomatic arrangement that linked Britain with France and Russia. Would it, could it guarantee that one side would intervene to rescue the other from a belligerent Germany? What remained? 'Only one policy . . . to maintain such a counterpoise to the Germanic powers, as will make it impossible for Germany to achieve her ambitions by force.' Here was a cry for upholding the balance of power, for sustaining Britain's naval superiority, for fostering a common imperial defence strategy. One point was incontestable: Britain 'cannot take the risk of trusting to the benevolence of Germany'.

Other international problems troubled Philip, more remote but no less grave. In the Far East, Japan threatened. So far the Anglo-Japanese alliance of 1902 had held, but it was up for review again in 1915. By now a major regional power, Japan made no secret of its imperial ambitions. The probability of a conflict with Japan – already highly resentful of the restrictive immigration policies of Australia and Canada (and the United States) – could not be entirely ruled out. This brought the problem back to Europe, for how could Britain defend effectively the far reaches of the Empire if the mother country was menaced by a rampant Germany?

These issues absorbed Philip for the rest of his life, in particular the challenge of Germany. During the inter-war years he saw Germany, defeated and humiliated, in a different light, as an underdog, and was willing to meet its demands half-way – some said far more than half-way. Experience taught him otherwise. He came full circle. The last article he wrote for *The Round Table*, in June 1939, repeated the theme of his first: to find 'a counterpoise' or, as he now called it, a 'Grand Alliance', to stave off German aggression. And as before, his prognosis was gloomy, foreseeing little alternative to open conflict.[16]

From the autumn of 1911 Philip embarked upon a series of overseas trips that took him to Europe, the Near East, India, the Far East and the North American continent. There was a sound reason for these excursions. Although he wrote extensively about foreign and imperial affairs, he had little first-hand experience of these regions. He knew South Africa well, but he knew little of his neighbours in Europe, despite his pinpointing the German peril, and was fluent in no language other than English. For all its internationalism, Philip's outlook was beset by a kind of parochialism, limited to the horizons of the Anglo-Saxon world.

But Philip was also in need of a respite for personal reasons. His first, perhaps only, love affair had petered out owing to differences in religion.* This ordeal was compounded by the tensions of work – pressures that had been building up since his time in South Africa. Plagued by lingering colds, suffering from a slight deafness, he could no longer concentrate for long periods. 'In a state of complete mental coma', he put his condition down to 'brain-fag',[17] a polite way of saying that he was experiencing a nervous breakdown. Unable to commit himself to a lasting personal relationship, and tormented by profound religious doubts, he seemed to be seeking his own private martyrdom.

If that was Philip's intention, he caught a first glimpse of it in the company of Nancy Astor. Waldorf and Philip had been contemporaries at New College. In 1909, they had renewed their acquaintance at Hatfield House. On Philip's return to London their friendship grew, particularly after Waldorf joined the Round Table group and Cliveden became a regular venue for its Moots. Nancy too was undergoing a spiritual upheaval. Whenever they met, at St Moritz or Biarritz, Rest Harrow or Cliveden, they comforted each other. In April 1914, Philip became seriously ill: a burst appendix had led to peritonitis. The operation, in those days a dangerous procedure, was successful, and Philip spent the next few weeks recuperating at Rest Harrow. Introduced to them by Nancy, Philip was already familiar with Mary Baker Eddy's teachings. Studying afresh *Science and Health*, he wondered whether its message had

* This affair has long been veiled in discretion. However, the lady in question was Lady Beatrice ('Mima') Cecil, daughter of the 4th Marquess of Salisbury. Devoutly Anglican, the powerful Cecils no doubt perceived a union with a Roman Catholic as a fate from which there was no salvation. Lady Anne, an ardent Catholic, would have drawn a similar conclusion.

not contributed to his timely recovery. Like Nancy, who had undergone a similar experience, he too was convinced: 'Christian Science', he determined, 'was manifestly the religion that Jesus of Nazareth taught.' From that moment he never wavered from his decision.

Christian Science brought Philip spiritual relief. It also unlocked the door to his world outlook. He admitted it. 'I am increasingly convinced that Christian Science is the real key to all our problems, political and economic, no less than personal . . . So far as I am concerned Christian Science will have the first claim on my time and activities.' But, he assured an anxious Curtis, 'it will make me a more valuable rather than a less valuable coadjutor in any R[ound] T[able] work that may be undertaken'.[18] For Philip, belief in a true religion and the implementation of an ethically based politics were two sides of the same coin. His new religion bestowed upon him not only an inner strength and energy, it also endowed him with a heightened sense of public duty and respect for the rule of law, of concern for the welfare of mankind. Broader conclusions could be drawn. If on a personal level one attained individual salvation by subordinating one's will to an omnipotent authority, so an international golden age would arise only when national sovereign states yielded their prerogatives to a centralized world government. Whatever its feasibility, this concept remained a constant in Philip's thinking.

His conversion showed in other ways. He seemed more settled, more stable, more at ease with himself. 'He is the most Christ-like man I have ever known, and he seems to shed his personality around and radiate happiness,' noted Frances Stevenson, Lloyd George's secretary and mistress. Otherwise, Philip's life continued much as usual; a bachelor-like existence peopled by his Round Table cronies. He shared lodgings at Cumberland Mansions with Bob Brand, John Dove and Lionel Hichens, while at weekends he would perhaps set off to Cliveden for Moots and other relaxations. His relationship with Nancy Astor deepened. Most observers thought he was in love with her. 'There was an affinity between Philip and my mother,' wrote Michael Astor, 'love on his side, and something deeper than friendship and less passionate than love on hers.' It was an intimate, but yet an innocent and platonic, association. Did a flash of physical desire ever pass between them? Apparently, on one occasion. But nothing happened. They knelt on opposite sides of the bed and prayed until their fleeting passion had cooled. 'Now, Nancy, you know what men have to put up with,' Philip apologized. Many years later, in her old age, Nancy 'Thank[ed] God' that 'I never fell in love with Philip.'[19]

It was a lasting and rewarding friendship, fulfilling a real need for both of them. Nancy, certainly, placed a high premium on their relationship. She would sign her letters to him – perhaps in jest, perhaps not – 'Your devoted and affectionate slave'.[20] But it was no less satisfying for Philip.

More and more he came to act as her spiritual adviser and political mentor, no doubt using her as a sounding board to reinforce his own beliefs. But of no less significance, for Philip – as indeed for all of the tabloids – Nancy personified a fetching spontaneity and *joie de vivre* that their own earnest lives often lacked. And how did Waldorf respond to Philip being placed forever on a pedestal by his wife? Reticent to the last, he left no record of his reaction.

Philip remained editor of *The Round Table* until 1916. Financially guaranteed by Sir Abe Bailey, a South African mining millionaire close to the *Kindergarten*, its circulation peaked at 4,500 per quarter, including overseas sales. It soon established a sound reputation. Claiming the title of 'A Quarterly Review of the Politics of the British Empire', it was particularly authoritative on imperial affairs. It was also unashamedly elitist. 'We are out to propagate our views among the best people,' asserted Philip. With some, it succeeded. Walter Page, the American ambassador to London, thought it 'the best review, I dare say, in the world'. Others, Garvin, for example, were more cutting in their tributes about 'the "Round Table" lot'.[21] Philip contributed twenty-four articles to the journal during this period, only one on a domestic issue. He was a fluent writer, if somewhat dull in style, confessing frankly that those catchy turns of phrase, so often necessary to brighten up a stodgy subject, usually eluded him.

When war broke out in August 1914 Philip, then thirty-two, did not volunteer for army service, though he felt 'inclined to do something active'. In any case, he was still physically run-down; and even more disturbing, his 'brain-fag' persisted. Persuaded that he could make a greater contribution to the war effort as editor of *The Round Table*, he remained at his desk at 175 Piccadilly, the offices of the movement, until he was summoned to higher duties by Lloyd George in 1916.

Lionel

Lionel George Curtis eventually attained what many consider to be the most prestigious honour that the academic world has to offer: a Fellowship at All Souls College, Oxford. Yet those who were placed to know considered him 'a third-rate academic', though they hastily conditioned their ruling, 'but he was a doer!'[22] This judgement encapsulated his life.

Lionel was born in March 1872 at The Outwoods near Derby, the youngest of four children of the Reverend George James Curtis, and his wife, Francis Carr. The family soon moved to Coddington, Herefordshire, a hamlet overlooking the Welsh hills, where his father served as rector. Later Lionel transferred his birthplace to this more romantic, literary setting, one that conjured up images of John Masefield and *Piers Plowman*. With modest private means at their disposal, and buttressed by their prosperous middle-class backgrounds, the Curtises ran a gentlemanly household, complete with a valet–cum–gardener, maids, and at times a tutor for the children. The Reverend Curtis adhered to a new teaching, preaching the virtues of the authority of the scriptures and of personal conversion, of awareness of sin and of salvation by faith in the Atonement. An evangelical preacher, his sermons 'about Hell-fire', it was said, made the young Lionel quake. Something of his father's evangelical passion must have rubbed off on Lionel. In later life, many of Lionel's friends and colleagues would similarly quake before his sermons, when, seemingly impervious to criticism, he impressed upon them his panaceas for resolving the problems of the British Empire or for bringing international anarchy to an end.

From the Rectory at Coddington Lionel went on to Haileybury. Founded by the East India Company, Haileybury radiated a strong imperial bias, particularly playing upon its Anglo–Indian connections. Again, these were themes that were to assume a key role in Lionel's later career. At ease in his new environment, one year winning the English poetry prize, he cheerfully reported home that his time was 'filled up in as jolly a way as possible. I am having a most delightful time altogether.' Notwithstanding his delight at what Haileybury had to offer, his performance in the classroom or on the playing fields was not especially distinguished, a trend that continued when he went up to New College, Oxford, in 1891. Hard pressed with his studies, his spelling chancy, he took third-class degrees in Classical Honour Mods (1893) and *Literae Humaniores* (1895). 'I spend my life panting to keep up with the firsts,' he later confessed.[23]

Lionel's talents were expressed in other ways. An activist in the Christian Social Union, he spent two long vacations wandering the byways of Kent and Sussex masquerading as a down-and-out, determined to discover at first hand the truth about the evils of chronic poverty. One evening, desperate for lodgings, clad in rags and speaking with a simulated accent, he approached an unsuspecting curate to help him out. 'I'm studying social questions and look too big a blackguard for the pubs to take me in,' he explained. 'Will you give me a recommendation?' By chance, Oxford connections resolved his predicament. The curate turned out to be a Trinity man who also happened to be a student of social questions as well as a member of the local branch of the Christian Social Union. Lionel breathed more easily: 'I have indeed fallen among the brethren.'[24] He was already revealing those gifts of character, an acute social conscience, a sense of the dramatic, infinite persistence and an iron will, that were to guide him, often into deep waters, in his later career.

The curate from Trinity College, who had fortuitously come to his rescue, symbolized another thread in Lionel's life. Oxford, New College in particular, was to provide him with the contacts, ties and friendships that were to serve him well at decisive points in his career. At Evensong in New College Chapel he first saw the tall figure of Lionel ('Nel') Hichens. 'It was love at first sight,' Lionel remarked innocently. His vision materialized into a lifelong friendship, based firmly upon mutual admiration.[25] But Hichens only headed the list of those other New College and Oxford men with whom Lionel was to be closely associated.[26] Throughout his professional and personal life he was to be cocooned by this Oxford fraternity.

Lionel came down from Oxford at a loose end. At first, he took up voluntary social work in London's East End. Later, he replaced Leo Amery as part-time secretary to Leonard Courtney, Liberal MP, journalist, professor of political economy, and, ironically, a hard-line Free Trader and a vehement anti-imperialist.[27] Later, on Courtney's recommendation, he served as private secretary to Lord Welby, chairman of the London County Council. In these capacities, Lionel gained his first insights into the world of local government and high politics. Still seeking a regular vocation, he began to read law and to dine at the Inner Temple. Called finally to the Bar in 1902, he abandoned his new profession almost as soon as he had qualified. More glittering opportunities beckoned. The South African war was in progress, initially not to Britain's advantage, and like many young men Lionel sought adventure, to be 'doing something'. When the opportunity arose he volunteered, together with his friends 'Nel' Hichens and Max Balfour, to serve in the Cyclists Section of the City Imperial Volunteers. Was he also thinking, perhaps, in terms of staving off the Boer threat to the integrity of the Empire? There is no evidence for this. These worthy ideals came later. At the time, he was more concerned with swotting up Baden-Powell's *Reconnaissance and Scouting*.

Lionel saw some fighting. With his fellow cyclists he rode into Pretoria to take part in the liberation of the capital of the Boer Republic. Immediately afterwards he returned to England to clear up some family business. But by October 1900 he was back in South Africa, still with no firm plans, but with a warm recommendation to Milner who by then was recruiting his young men. Lionel was taken on as assistant to John Frederick (Peter) Perry, a New College contemporary, who had been appointed as Milner's Imperial Secretary.* As Perry soon fell ill, Lionel

---

* John Frederick (Peter) Perry (1873–1935). At this stage, Perry was one of the more influential of the *Kinder*, as his position as Milner's Imperial Secretary indicated. A graduate of Magdalen and New College (where he took a second in Greats) and a Fellow of All Souls, he entered the Colonial Office. Recruited by Milner in 1900, Perry in turn recruited many others. He served as Imperial Secretary to the administration until 1910, and from 1910–11 he acted as Secretary to the Rand Native Labour Association. On his return to England, his

was appointed acting private secretary on Milner's staff – a remarkable, though unforeseen, promotion. In this manner, now placed at the hub of great affairs, he came to know and admire Milner. Lionel pleased his new chief, who in turn quickly recognized his abilities. 'I think he will make a name for himself over here,' reported Milner.[28] Milner was not mistaken. The nine years Lionel spent in South Africa were, from his point of view, a conspicuous success story. As Town Clerk for Johannesburg he practically refounded the city, revamping its system of municipal government: its Council was remodelled, its boundaries were expanded, its revenues reorganized, and more efficient public services were provided for its citizens. As Assistant Colonial Secretary of the Transvaal for Local Government, and later as a member of the Transvaal Legislative Council, he was given an opportunity to broaden his interests and to hone his abilities in a wider sphere.

Part of the secret of Lionel's success was that he worked, not without some friction, within the loose, yet jealously guarded, framework of the *Kindergarten*. They were still meeting at Moot House, whose culinary attractions were now improved by the presence of a French chef. Lionel himself was busy 'laying an Egg' – *Kinder* parlance for an impending project – on the future of South Africa: it would prove to be the seminal testing ground for the group's development. His own ideas were fairly straightforward. Most of the *Kinder*, Lionel being no exception, were heavily influenced by Frederick Oliver's recently published biography of the American federalist Alexander Hamilton. Oliver, a chairman of Debenham and Freebody, unheard-of by the *Kinder* – though later he was to join the Round Table circle – had made out an incisive case for federalism based on the successful American example. Here was an inspired message, the breakthrough the *Kinder* sought, and, to their astonishment, from the pen of 'an unknown linen-draper'.[29] Lionel tailored Oliver's arguments to suit the needs of the four South African colonies, which, like the American territories, had been riven by civil strife and armed confrontation with the Crown. In one sense Lionel was marching in tune with British policy, for federation in South Africa had been its half-spoken aim for many years. After all, it had worked in Canada and Australia, models that also engrossed the *Kinder*. The immediate problem was to make it workable in the wake of the tension generated by the Boer War.

career took a different turn. Apparently, Bob Brand found him a job representing Lazard Bros. in Canada. Far removed from London, he chose to distance himself from Round Table affairs. In 1915 he was seconded to the Imperial Munitions Board based in Ottawa: he spent the remainder of his career in Canada, involved in banking and business. In 1932, he returned to England. But Perry's death three years later went unnoticed by *The Round Table*.

To validate his case Lionel travelled the colonies on a fact-finding mission, gathering data for his 'Egg'. Satisfied with the statistics he had gathered, he went ahead and composed his thesis for federation. As was his habit, one wholly in keeping with the character of the *Kindergarten*, he exposed its contents to the general opinion of the Moot. Few of the band would take at face value Lionel's blueprints for posterity. In an atmosphere of 'great secrecy' his study was subjected to intense criticism – 'mauling', in Kerr's preferred phrase.[30] Patrick Duncan's authority,* Brand's calmness of mind, Kerr's analytical skills, Dougie Malcolm's subtlety of thought and Hichens's rich administrative experience combined to exert decisive restraints on Lionel's wilder historical and theoretical assumptions. Lord Selborne, the High Commissioner, under whose name the memorandum was eventually published in July 1907, cut it down to respectable political proportions, but generously awarded Lionel the 'main credit' for its appearance.

This was just the beginning. These years saw Lionel's first appearance as the envoy for organic union. His energy and enthusiasm knew no bounds, sweeping up all who came into contact with him. Abe Bailey, the multimillionaire, was mobilized into providing the financial muscle for his projects. 'Closer Union' societies and the monthly journal *The State* – edited by fellow *Kind* Kerr – were set up, all designed to propagate the cause. Lionel was tireless, rushing from meeting to meeting to sustain the momentum. He laid another 'Egg', *The Government of South Africa* (1908), a Moot product in name, its inspiration derived wholly from Lionel. By February 1909 the National Convention, convened at Durban to discuss the relationship between the four provinces, reported in favour of the Union of South Africa. Lionel's 'Egg' had finally been hatched.

Lionel's years in South Africa had been a watershed in his career. Aged twenty-eight on arrival, he still had no fixed purpose in life. Half-hearted for the law, not clever enough for medicine, unfit for the cut and thrust of politics, without journalistic experience, he could not continue indefinitely his voluntary social work or remain for ever a private secretary to veteran politicians. All this now changed. His South African experiences begat a metamorphosis. He hit upon a mission in life, one perfectly fashioned to suit his gifts. He became the foremost advocate of 'organic union', first of South Africa, then of the British Empire, and ultimately of the world. He

* Patrick Duncan (1870–1943) was born in Banffshire and educated at Edinburgh University and Balliol College, Oxford, graduating with a first in Greats. Considered to be the *doyen* of the group, he worked under Milner in the Inland Revenue Department and as Colonial Treasurer to the Transvaal, later as Colonial Secretary. Unlike most of the *Kinder*, Duncan remained in South Africa, following a distinguished career at the Bar and in politics, usually as an ally of Smuts. His final office was as Governer-General of South Africa.

pursued these visions out of a deep sense of public duty, often to the despair of his friends. For, like so many ideologues, he could be a crashing bore. 'Can't anyone tell him to shut up?' whispered one exasperated dinner guest, echoing the general opinion around the table. But Lionel boomed on, 'noble and unbowed'.[31] Earnest, decisive, vigorous, tenacious, self-absorbed, he was dubbed by his friends the 'Prophet'. And for the remainder of his life Lionel pursued this calling, as an inspired revealer of a higher truth.*

This was to be the pattern of Lionel's future life: wandering the world or lobbying at home, preaching, proselytizing, pamphleteering; and, of course, marketing many other 'Eggs'. He brimmed over with self-confidence, not to say arrogance. It was noted that 'lack of familiarity with a subject never prevented Curtis from holding forth about it'.[32] Did he ever see two sides of a question? If so, he rarely gave notice of it. Perhaps a source of weakness for a scholar, for a 'Prophet' it bolstered his self-imposed role of guide and mentor. Tightly blinkered, he stormed his visionary castle, all too often leaving his companions, groggy from his verbal assaults, stranded behind. This may have shown strength of character but he paid a heavy price for his iron determination. Seeking forever to persuade, he acquired a reputation as a 'Bumptious Boy', a 'South African bore' or 'a sea-green incorruptible'. 'I know of no other man with so big a furnace in his belly,' wrote Kerr to Brand. 'It is so fierce that the fumes overwhelm his brain at times . . . scorch[ing] all whom he encounters', but, he added charitably, 'hound[ing] them to greater thoughts and greater deeds'. Kerr, though often critical, stood out as one of Lionel's more dedicated collaborators, their disagreements stemming from his more academic turn of mind, though also from his somewhat erratic temperament. Towards the end of his life Lionel was forced to admit the painful burden he had imposed upon his closest colleagues. 'My best friends are doomed to wear me like a hair shirt,' he confessed.[33]

The South Africa Act of May 1910 symbolized a brilliant triumph for the *Kindergarten*. From it sprang the mystique that would encompass this honourable, responsible pressure group, that canvassed, worked behind the scenes, strove to manipulate the decision-makers – all from the purest of motives and for the most righteous of goals. Veiled in anonymity – the most anonymous of all being Lionel, who shunned all publicity for himself – they were content to work in obscurity for the common good. A pleasing

---

* Lionel was often compared with the prophet Isaiah, the counsellor of kings. Principled, unflinching in the face of disaster, convinced of the ultimate triumph of right, Isaiah preached that following the fall of the savage Assyrian empire – that personified a biblical form of international anarchy – God would establish a general peace, create a new beginning for the world, and in his mercy set up a universal empire to be governed from Jerusalem.

theory, it proved alluring to an impressionable public. But to a marked degree it seduced the *Kinder* themselves, in particular Lionel, the acknowledged wheeler-dealer of the group. Victims of their own propaganda, they were inevitably reinforced in their convictions by their first sensational success. As the years passed, their glamour wearing thin, they would come to regard with increasing nostalgia their South African coup.

But were the *Kinder* in any case pushing at an open door? Would the Union have come about anyway, without their intense, at times hysterical, lobbying? British policy was already receptive to the idea. So, too, were the Boers. Their leaders, Botha and Smuts, were already committed, confident that in the long run they would dominate the Union. But they would move at their own pace. Early in his career, Smuts had declared:

> No policy in any Colony or State is sound which does not recognize, and frame its measures as much as possible in accordance with, the fact that South Africa is one, that consisting as it does of separate parts, it yet forms one commercial and moral unity. This is the corner stone of South African politics.

He looked further, to the 'deliverance of the whole of South Africa and the Union of our people into a great nation from Table Bay to the Equator'. Of course, it was highly convenient to discover a group of enthusiastic young Englishmen as allies; and 'Slim' Janny – an epithet that alluded to Smuts's reputation as a 'trimmer' and double-dealer – took full advantage of their appearance on the scene, exploiting their zeal, working particularly well with the more sober-minded Brand and Duncan. No doubt, the *Kinder* fulfilled an important task in softening up opinion in the colonies, notably among the British settlers. But in retrospect it was a marginal role. The leading players in this story were already in position centre-stage.[34]

His task completed, Lionel returned to England in June 1909 determined to apply his accomplishments in South Africa in a wider field. He elaborated his ideas to his closed circle. The options he presented were stark. 'Some definite business arrangement' must be reached in imperial, foreign and defence policies, or the Empire 'must break up'. In short, he aimed to readjust the balance of forces within the Empire – as he said, to give it 'a dominion perspective'. 'Britain', he laid down, 'is not the Commonwealth but merely a part of it.' To realize this aim it was necessary to come to grips with colonial nationalism, in the long run injurious to imperial unity, and to allow its legitimate aspirations to find expression within the framework of a reconstructed Empire based on 'organic union'. In this way, a more viable and influential body would take its place in the international community, one able to compete with those emerging giants, the United States and Germany. At the Anglesey meeting, where it was noted that Lionel did 'most of the talking', these ideas were consolidated, and an organizational framework instituted to put them into effect.[35]

One decision of the Anglesey conference was to send Lionel (accompanied by Kerr and Marris) on a fact-finding mission to Canada; or, to quote Lionel, to engage in 'Imperial Eggboiling'. In Canada this self-appointed commission of inquiry came face to face with widespread dominion nationalism. Sir Wilfred Laurier, the Canadian premier, was a firm opponent of any concept of Imperial Federation. He stood resolutely for the right of self-government for Canada and its sister Dominions, anticipating full-blown nationhood in the future.

Kerr quickly realized the consequences of these sentiments. 'If you forced Canada to choose now between Imperial Federation and independence, I think she would take independence.' There was also the alarming prospect of an American takeover, with Britain standing by helplessly. Reluctantly, he decided that 'an Empire egg – the pistol policy – is impossible'. If Lionel forced it to a conclusion, he wrote to Brand, it 'would be almost certain to break up the Empire'. Such was Kerr's anxiety at Lionel's recklessness that he toyed with severing his connection 'with the whole business'. Nor was Kerr alone among the *Kinder* in his scepticism. Even their master, Lord Milner, had concluded that the political climate in London 'was rotten from the Imperial point of view', adding another problematic dimension to Lionel's crusade.[36]

These home truths made little impact upon Lionel. On the contrary, they fuelled his determination to carry through his scheme. And it is a mark of his dogged enthusiasm, of the almost mesmeric hold that he exerted over his associates, that he succeeded – at least on paper – in pulling them along behind him. On his return from Canada he clarified his thoughts in the so-called *Green Memorandum*. As he saw it now, the greatest danger to the Empire was Germany: its enormous economic power, its unlimited political ambition, its declared policy of *Weltpolitik*, all of which, he speculated, was a function of its federative system. As it was inconceivable to stand aside and do nothing, he proposed 'An Alternative', the organic union of the Empire governed by an Imperial Parliament. Consisting of two houses – an elected lower chamber, balanced by an upper chamber of peers – it would control defence and foreign policy. It would also have the power to impose taxes, or 'we shall not be establishing a Government at all, but only a conference of separate States'. In domestic affairs a degree of autonomy would be conceded: social measures, economic policy, local tariffs would be left to the discretion of the Dominions and the mother country, in these matters awarded the same status. As for enlightening public opinion, that was the task of the Round Table groups: 'a few quiet but determined men in each of the States concerned, may accomplish much by patient and concerted inquiry'.[37]

Whatever Lionel's fixation, his scheme was seriously flawed, particularly the notion that in the long run it was somehow possible to fob off the Dominions with anything less than genuine independence. Naturally, this did not deter him. At the Imperial Conference of 1911 Joseph Ward, the New Zealand prime minister, floated a proposal for an Imperial Parliament, prompted, it was widely rumoured, by Lionel. It was unceremoniously shot down. The combination of Wilfred Laurier and Louis Botha, the most committed opponents of union, proved too powerful. 'The Conference is going quite well,' Botha cheerfully reported to Smuts. 'We have destroyed root and branch the proposal for an Imperial Council of State or Parliament.'[38] Of course, for Lionel this was a setback not a defeat, merely a stimulus to increase the pressure of his activity.

His efforts never slackened: at Moots, on dominion tours, he spared no effort to enlighten the ignorant and reassure the sceptics. Meanwhile, he lived on a slender private income, augmented by a grant from the Rhodes Trust or whatever the Round Table group could afford to pay for his work on its behalf. In 1912, Lionel, sponsored by Milner, was appointed to the Beit lectureship in colonial history at Oxford. Here he could bring into full play his gifts of persuasion, his need to instruct the uninitiated. By all accounts he was an imaginative teacher, the intensity of his inner conviction inspiring his students, instilling in them an awareness of the imperial factor as he saw it. When guest lecturers, ministers or high-ranking colonial officials came and 'talked of the Empire, the undergraduates, who knew better and called it "the Commonwealth of Nations", would draw in their breath sharply, as if an infinitive had been split'.[39]

Oxford proved to be a fertile base for Lionel's projects. His strategy was simple: 'the way to spread an idea was to capture the elite and convert them and they ... would spread the idea'. For this purpose the Ralegh Club – otherwise known as 'one of Lionel's stunts' – was founded, a fruitful meeting ground to thrash out imperial problems. At its annual dinners politicians of the front rank would be invited to speak, Milner and Churchill among them. Rhodes scholars, budding imperial statesmen, young Oxford dons – Keith Feiling, Lewis Namier, Alfred Zimmern, Reginald Coupland – were drawn into its net. For a brief period it toasted not 'the Empire of the Bretaignes' but 'the British Commonwealth'. Yet impatient to spread his word further afield, Lionel carried his message to university study groups and to Workers Educational Association meetings around the country. The scope and intensity of his activities must have been overwhelming. Eventually his professor, the retiring Hugh Egerton, wryly commented that he felt like 'a country rector with the prophet Isaiah as his curate'.[40]

Oxford was congenial to Lionel for other reasons: it brought him closer to his friends at Cliveden. By this time, most of his fellow *Kinder* had returned to England, the Round Table movement now providing an organized framework for their public activities. As its Moots were often held in the agreeable environment of Cliveden, it was inevitable that Lionel, its live wire, would soon be invited. He first came in August 1911 and fell immediately under Nancy's spell. Nancy had a liberating effect upon Lionel. He frankly admitted to being 'self-centred', to existing 'in an atmosphere of unpopularity especially among women'. Nancy polished up his social graces. He grated less. (In 1920, Nancy was even instrumental in smoothing his path towards marriage.)[41] All this was an added bonus. But the main purpose of his Cliveden weekends can best be illustrated when, one evening, he chanced to be on the Upper Terrace and saw Bob Brand and Winston Churchill strolling on the lawn below, engaged in a lively discussion on the Irish question. He joined them. The Irish situation was critical. With the Ulster Loyalists ranged against the Irish Nationalists, a full-scale civil war threatened. Nothing would have pleased the 'tabloids' more than to broker a deal between the conflicting parties along federal lines – a repeat performance of their South African triumph. Home Rule was the declared Irish policy of the Liberal Government, of which Churchill, as First Lord of the Admiralty, was a prominent minister. Most of the Moot were for federation; certainly Lionel was – and Churchill had been voicing similar sentiments, even if in less categorical tones. But Churchill proved wary of being drawn. 'In private conversation he [Churchill] tries on speeches like a man trying on ties in his bedroom to see how he would look in them,' Lionel sadly decided.[42]

Nevertheless, this encounter with Churchill was not wholly a failure. By inviting him – together with Bob Brand and Edward Grigg – to cruise on the *Enchantress*, the Admiralty's beautifully appointed 3,800-ton steam yacht, Churchill, a coming man in politics, enabled Lionel to take his lobbying into the highest political circles. Not that Lionel counted on Churchill. 'I haven't any hopes of Winston . . . [and] I feel like a toad for thinking this and accepting his hospitality but in our job if one was only friendly with people whom one entirely respected we should not get much further.'[43] Even the wayward Churchill would eventually prove useful. And as was quite obvious, in the coming years, Lionel, the 'doer', would have great need of politicians, however fickle.

Robin

One observer, summing up the career of (George) Geoffrey Dawson, identified him – not with tongue in cheek – as the 'Secretary General of the twentieth-century Establishment'.[44] This was not intended as a slur. After all, he had served *The Times* for thirty-two years of his life, twenty-six as editor. High-minded, self-effacing, hard-working, acutely conscious of his own moral rectitude and intellectual superiority, Dawson appears as the epitome of the virtuous, selfless, public-spirited civil servant.

He was born Geoffrey Robinson at Skipton-on-Craven in the West Riding of Yorkshire in October 1874. His father, George Robinson, a freemason and a devout churchman, was a prominent figure in civic affairs. An ardent supporter of the Volunteer movement,* he served as a governor to three local schools. By profession a banker, he married Mary Perfect of Langcliffe Hall, near Settle, the daughter of another banker. Mary was descended from the Dawsons, a family of landed gentry that could trace its origins back to the mid-sixteenth century.† The Robinsons lived in a large house, 'Overdale', on the road from Skipton to Bolton Abbey. Related to the Dawsons at Langcliffe Hall and to the Barretts at Skipton Castle, the family led a sedate social life typical of the time, entertaining themselves with garden parties, archery, croquet, the gentlemen appearing in top hats and frock coats, the ladies in flowing gowns with pinched waists and bustles.

Geoffrey was brought up in a manner wholly consonant with his background as a scion of the Yorkshire squirearchy. He enjoyed the outdoor life; attended steeplechases and point-to-points, and even took up golf, which he admitted to playing 'shockingly'. In time he became a keen shot, whenever duty allowed an enthusiastic participant, in the ritual slaughter of the 'Glorious Twelfth'. But in particular he delighted in taking long walks across the fells and dales, a habit he practised until his final years.

Geoffrey's early education began at home, under the tuition of his mother and a string of competent governesses. At the age of nine he progressed to Aysgarth, a local preparatory school of high reputation. Its well-known headmaster, the Reverend Clement Hales, was a no-nonsense teacher. 'What are you gaping at? Do something about it!' he would urge his pupils. Geoffrey soon gave evidence of high promise. Disciplined, conscientious, keenly intelligent, he had no difficulty in winning a

---

* The so-called 'Sunday Soldiers', about 160,000 in number, whose eye-catching weekend demonstrations embued the Victorians with a sense of security.

† The Dawsons could trace their lineage back to Christopher Dawson who first purchased property in Wensleydale in 1531. Other estates were soon acquired: the manor of Halton Gill, and Langcliffe Hall, by a judicious marriage settlement. In 1860, Langcliffe Hall was purchased by another branch of the Dawsons. Eventually, it came into the possession of William Mosely (Perfect) Dawson, Geoffrey's uncle, and his mother's brother. The inheritance then passed to Geoffrey's aunt, Elizabeth, William's sister. Upon her death in 1917, these holdings were bequeathed to Geoffrey, who then assumed by Royal Licence the name and arms of the Dawson squiredom. The Langcliffe estate was an extensive one, stretching for miles across the Yorkshire moors from Settle to Halton Gill.

scholarship to Eton. As a Colleger, Robin's* particular talents found expression not on the playing fields but in the classroom. His achievements were impressive. Prizes in Latin, Divinity and History, as well as the Strafford Shakespeare medal, were among the more conspicuous of his successes. His tutor, Edward Imprey – with whom he maintained a lifelong friendship – forecast a promising career for him. These accomplishments led the way to a demyship at Magdalen College, Oxford. In his *Memoirs*, Edward Gibbon, himself a Magdalen scholar, had painted a vivid portrait of 'the narrow, lazy and oppressive spirit' of Oxford, complaining of the 'idle and unprofitable' time he had spent at Magdalen. Future generations of scholars also regarded Magdalen in terms of 'a college where hard reading was not generally appreciated'. If so, Robin must have stood out, for once again he shone academically, graduating with first classes in Classical Moderations (1895) and in *Literae Humaniores* (1897). But in a sense his Oxford career had only just begun, for the following year he was elected to an Examination Fellowship at All Souls. 'Rather splendid isn't it?' he wrote to his mother. 'I feel supremely happy.'[45]

Oxford remained 'splendid' for him until his last years. As he later recorded, his election to All Souls remained the crowning distinction of his private life, a lasting tribute to his temperament and scholarship. Co-founded by Henry Chichele, Archbishop of Canterbury, and Henry VI in 1438, the College was designed in part to offer prayers 'for the souls of Henry V and those other nobles and faithful subjects' who had perished in the long French wars. Generally regarded as the most prestigious of the Oxford colleges, it has always claimed a unique status in the University, for although it plays a part in the University's teaching programme it has no undergraduates.† Its Fellows devote their time to research. Those who do leave the College, to enter the professions or public life, retain their Fellowship for a seven-year period, after which they become *quondams*, or sometime Fellows, excluded from conducting College business but entitled to enjoy its hospitality for the remainder of their lives. As one happy *quondam* remarked: it is a foundation 'in which academic and world-wide interests of every kind were blended in intimate informal association'.[46]

Most Fellows came to regard All Souls as their spiritual home. Robin was no exception. For a brief period, in the early 1920s, he served as its Estates Bursar; and a decade later he might even have been elected Warden, had he not made known that his duties lay elsewhere. The

* It was at Eton that his friends began to address him as Robin – some said because he looked like a robin, but more probably it was an abbreviation of his surname.

† All Souls has recently begun to accept a limited number of graduate students, joining the six other graduate colleges at Oxford: St Antony's, Nuffield, Wolfson, Linacre, St Cross and Green.

ambience generated at College gatherings must have been well-nigh irresistible. Here was a rare mix of highly placed politicians, distinguished jurists, top-flight journalists, prominent businessmen, influential civil servants and leading academics, meeting in the most congenial surroundings, their expertise on display, the dominant topic of conversation being inevitably 'politics in the widest sense'. Weekends at All Souls were Moots of a different kind, of a gilt-edged variety. As an outsider observed, its Fellows 'have an extraordinarily rich and deep common fund of information and intelligence which they are always pooling at their dinners – and they make a point of dining together a great many times a year'. He continued: 'they have taken upon themselves no less a task than that of forming an unofficial committee for running, or helping to run, the destinies of the British Empire', a judgement confirmed by an insider, A. L. Rowse, who witnessed the goings-on in the Smoking Room at All Souls at first hand.[47]

One of the attractions of All Souls was that it gave the chosen few the sense of belonging to a distinguished, select and ancient fraternity. Three years after his election, Robin described to his mother the archaic ceremony of the 'Feast of the Sacred Bird', celebrated once every hundred years. Led by the Lord Mallard (in fact, Cosmo Gordon Lang, the future Archbishop of Canterbury),* the Fellows of the College, holding high the mallard in effigy, scoured the College grounds and buildings in search of the 'Sacred Bird', chanting as they went, 'Ho the blood of King Edward!', their strained voices echoing across Radcliffe Square. 'You would have laughed to see grave professors & canons & arch-deacons & undersecretaries . . . scrambling around the pinnacles.' Not content with this bizarre ritual, the Fellows, secure in their Common Room, and well out of range of strangers' ears, honoured the 'swapping mallard' in risible verse:

> Then let us sing and dance a galliard
> To the remembrance of the mallard.
> And as the mallard goes in pool,
> Let's dabble, duck and dive in bowl.
> Ho the blood of King Edward, by the blood of King Edward
> It was a swapping swapping mallard.

But even in places geographically remote from All Souls it was impossible to escape its culture. In 1907, in South Africa, Leo Amery, another Fellow, captured a festive moment. 'Of many cheerful evenings the most joyous I can recall is an All Souls' Gaudy, celebrated in

---

* The mallard was the emblem of the College, and rumour had it that it was the 'swapping mallard' that first indicated the site of All Souls. As has been mischievously pointed out, it is a species of duck that instinctively flocks together.

Johannesburg *super flumina Babylonis*, by Robinson, Peter Perry, Brand, and myself standing on the seat of the Cape cart and chanting Homer.'[48]

Robin felt very much a part of this clubbable, self-absorbed, and inbred world. Indeed, it might be said that he never left it, for his life was to be bounded by All Souls, the Travellers' Club and the Athenaeum, Grillon's dining club, the Round Table and its Moots, Printing House Square, Cliveden and the great houses of England, offset by secluded holidays on the Yorkshire fells.

Robin's scholarly record at Oxford certainly marked him out for an academic career, had he desired it. Instead, he opted for the civil service. Perhaps there was something of the 'doer' also in him. After passing its competitive examination, he entered the General Post Office, serving in its telegraph section. But the routine of the GPO failed to stir Robin's imagination. He sought excitement elsewhere. Eventually, he found it at the Colonial Office. It was March 1899. The South African question was coming to the boil, and Robin, as chance would have it, was placed at the very epicentre of these matters. He received the Uitlanders' Great Petition to Queen Victoria, listing their many grievances. He studied the gloomy day-to-day reports from South Africa, forecasting confrontation, relaxing from his exacting office work with uplifting doses of Kipling, or James Bryce's *Impressions of South Africa*, or Baden-Powell's *Matabele Campaign*.

Seven months later the Boer War broke out. As hostilities dragged on, his abilities came to the notice of Joseph Chamberlain, the Colonial Secretary. Chamberlain was then at the height of his power and influence and arguably the most forceful personality in the government. He appointed Robin as his assistant private secretary. This was promotion on a grand scale. But when Milner visited London in May 1901, greater adventures beckoned. Robin was a close friend of Milner's Imperial Secretary, Peter Perry, and through his good offices was already lobbying vigorously to be included on Milner's staff. As Milner was now engaged in recruiting his young men, and Robin was engaged in vetting the candidates, these objectives harmonized. On 24 September he recorded in his diary that Milner was pressing Chamberlain 'to let me go out as Private Secretary for a year at £1,000'.[49] Chamberlain gave his consent, and Robin joined the nucleus of the *Kindergarten* – Patrick Duncan, Lionel Curtis, Hugh Wyndham and Perry – in South Africa as Milner's Secretary for Municipal Affairs. In the event, Robin was to spend the next nine years in South Africa, in some ways the most significant period of his life. He was twenty-seven years old.

The following May, the Boer War came to an official conclusion: the period of reconstruction had begun. Robin was soon hard at work at Milner's headquarters near Johannesburg, mainly 'writing memoranda and despatches on every conceivable subject', as he explained to his mother.

Although far too polite to be publicly at odds with his clientele, he thought the Johannesburg Municipality a 'rather ill-assorted and cantankerous crew'. And, if he found his clerical work tedious, he gave no sign of it. There were other compensations, however. The range of his social contacts widened. In 1904 Robin first met Edward Wood (later Viscount Halifax), then on a grand tour of the Empire. Intellectually and politically in tune with each other, he and Wood, who was also a Fellow of All Souls (and would eventually be appointed Neville Chamberlain's Foreign Secretary), became firm friends, an intimacy strengthened by their standing as neighbouring Yorkshire landowners. He was also on familiar terms with Lionel Curtis and Basil Blackwood with whom he shared Bixley Lodge, a one-storeyed cottage surrounded by trees that enjoyed 'a glorious view' of the forts at Pretoria. As a member of the Rand Club, he took what pleasures Johannesburg society had to offer. After a week of 'solid work', he would unwind with 'a good game of Polo . . . a grand game that can cram a whole week's exercise into fifty minutes'. Or else, in like-minded company, he would explore the veldt, spotting an 'eagle's nest and many strange parti-coloured birds', discovering caves and rivers and other topographical delights, all uncannily reminiscent 'of *King Solomon's Mines*'.[50]

Robin was a leading member of the *Kindergarten*. Fully involved in the drafting and redrafting of its seminal document, the Selborne memorandum, he was a regular visitor to Moot House and, together with Curtis, Kerr and Brand, took an active part in composing and promulgating its visionary messages. Although Milner had already left South Africa, his protégés had been strategically placed to fulfil his policies. Stirred by the righteousness of his message, they were careful never to stray too far from their master's views. At any rate, Robin showed no signs of nonconformism. Towards one of the most divisive issues of the day, whether or not to import Chinese labourers to work the mines of the Rand, he stuck closely to his chief's attitude. Milner saw this question as the key to his entire South African policy, confident that it would revive the economy of the war-weary country.[51] Robin agreed. But 'indentured labour', as it was ingenuously promoted, aroused the greatest commotion: in England, it was denounced by the Liberals and trade unionists as indistinguishable from 'slavery', their revulsion magnified by reports of illegal floggings and 'unnatural sexual practices' in the 'slave compounds'; in South Africa, it was no less fiercely challenged by Botha and Smuts. In a series of letters home, Robin dismissed this criticism as an 'immense amount of rubbish', justifying the controversial policy on the grounds that it would bring about a more efficient division of labour, as Chinese 'coolies' would release 'an immense quantity of niggers for agriculture etc., which they much prefer . . . [keeping] the yellow men for unskilled labour pure and simple . . . [and thereby securing] a great increase of skilled white labour in the mines'. After all the fuss, he found the arrival of the first '300 live pigtails' most 'amusing', noting that they seemed to be a 'docile and phlegmatic people . . . [although] very zealous about their work'. As to their working underground, rumour had it that 'the Northern Chinese is all right, but not the Southern who is a fat and timid creature'.[52]

In March 1905 Robin resigned from government service and moved into the offices of the *Johannesburg Star* as its editor at a salary of £2,000 a year. Although he had developed a deft hand at drafting memoranda, he had had no previous journalistic experience. Nor had he ever given any indication that he had considered journalism as a career. Put simply, Robin had been jobbed into the post by Milner to perform a particular task. Milner, about to leave South Africa, was troubled at what the future might hold. Anxious that his political inheritance should not be frittered away, he was wont to place his young men in positions of authority from where they could sway opinion. He acted from experience, for as a young man he had begun his career on the staff of the *Pall Mall Gazette*, and he never shrank from exploiting the press to advance his ideas. Shortly before his departure, Milner settled Robin's appointment with Lionel Phillips, a former Jameson 'raider' who had been captured, sentenced to death and subsequently released. Now resuscitated as a Transvaal mining magnate, he also held the controlling interest in the *Star*.[53] Similarly, Milner later stimulated Curtis's interest in acquiring the *State* to promote his aims, though, unlike Robin, Curtis needed little prodding.

Immediately after Robin's nomination as editor of the *Star*, he returned to England for a holiday. Visits to Yorkshire and Oxford took up much of his time, but he was mainly concerned to learn the rudiments of his new trade. He was not short of contacts on Fleet Street. He lunched with Leo Maxse of the *National Review*, an old friend and a convinced imperialist. He saw H. A. Gwynne of the *Standard* and Fabian Ware of the *Morning Post*. Long sessions were spent at Printing House Square, holding discussions with Valentine Chirol, head of *The Times*' Foreign Department, and William F. Monypenny of its editorial staff. Later, at a house party, he met Moberley Bell, the manager of *The Times*. This was a serious endeavour to master the nuts and bolts of editing a major newspaper. Before Robin left England he spent an evening with his ex-chief. Since his return, one observer noted, Milner had 'grown grim and (perhaps temporarily) bitter'. To his intense disgust he had found a country riddled with 'Little Englandism'. Yet against this depressing background his own imperial vision shone more brightly than ever. Certain of his purpose, Milner held that only by fulfilling his programme would the well-being of the nation be secured, an assessment he certainly passed on to his protégé.[54]

Already the editor of an influential colonial newspaper, Robin soon found his responsibilities expanding, first as South African correspondent of the *Daily Telegraph*, later of *The Times*, a post brokered by Amery. Robin was launched upon his long and distinguished journalistic career. He had not planned it; it had been foisted upon him. But what kind of journalism would he practise? Would it accord with the principle laid down by one of his employers, *The Times*, that the 'securing and presentation of news was the proper business of a newspaper'; or, phrased differently, that 'it was a newspaper first and not a journal of opinion'? Or was Robin too certain in his views, too committed to statecraft itself, to follow the counsel of John Thadeus Delane, a celebrated nineteenth-century editor of *The Times*? 'We cannot admit', said Delane, 'that its [a newspaper's] purpose is to share the labours of statesmanship or that it is bound by the same limitations, the same duties, the same liabilities as that of Ministers of the Crown.'[55] For Robin, the line between the 'securing and presentation of news' and sharing 'the labours of statesmanship' was a thin one. He crossed it often. In the 1930s, this dilemma would reappear in far graver circumstances.

In any case, Robin had been conscripted as editor of the *Star* to advance a clear-cut cause: Milner's 'Credo'.*[56] In July 1925, two months after Milner's death, *The Times* – now under Robin's stewardship – published its definitive text. 'I am a British (indeed primarily an English) Nationalist,' Milner claimed. His imperialism, he expounded, sprang from 'the destiny of the English race' that has known how 'to strike fresh roots in distant parts'. His patriotism, he clarified, knows 'only racial limits'. 'It is not the soul of England, dear as it is to me, which is essential to arouse my patriotism,' Milner went on, 'but the speech, the tradition, the spiritual heritage, the principles, the aspirations of the British race.' Milner recognized that the 'United Kingdom is no longer the power in the world it once was', but Britain's crumbling status as a great power could now be underwritten by 'the British Dominions', for they 'are not only self-supporting. They are more nearly self-sufficient than any other political entity . . . if they can be kept an entity.' 'The British State must follow the race,' Milner cried, for 'we cannot afford to part with so much of our best blood.'[57]

This was a stirring message. In the initial context of South Africa, its immediate aim was to ensure the Union of the provinces. And the *Star*'s mission under Robin's management was to soften local public opinion in favour of this scheme. But, as Milner and his circle consistently argued,

---

* The 'Credo', described by *The Times* as 'the conscious political faith of the best and most thoughtful patriots of the Empire', enjoyed wide coverage in its columns. Dawson later had it published as a pamphlet under the imprint of his newspaper.

this would only be the first step towards a federal plan for the Empire as a whole. In this way, a British-controlled, self-governing South Africa would emerge as another bastion of imperial power that, when allied with the other Dominions, would preserve, even enhance, Britain's international standing. This pleasant vision proved to be short-lived. The new South Africa eventually became a source of imperial discord, a dissident, sectarian voice, a force for disintegration not union.

Robin took easily to his new craft. Imperturbable, level-headed, undemonstrative, incisive in thought, his literary style reflected the man: lucid, relaxed, devoid of affectation, though now and then he would be struck by a flash of inspiration and turn a memorable phrase. He dealt with other people's 'copy' in much the same way: swiftly, economically, never shirking from amending an awkward article to make it fit for the printed page.

At the same time, Robin remained tied to the polemical side of his newspaper work. The *Star* preached federation, calling for the eventual unity of the Empire. Prolific in his output, Robin composed 209 leading articles in his first year as editor, no mean achievement. Hard-working, one evening he spent five hours 'digesting the Federal 'Egg' for publication'. Criticism spurred him on to greater effort. Pleased with the *Star*'s progress, he appreciated that 'it was annoying a good many people who deserve to be annoyed', and who were bound to respond by sending him 'several typewritten sheets of abuse'. Undeterred, Robin stepped up the campaign, producing an effective blend of exposition and advocacy. At home, Milner read the *Star* with satisfaction. 'If I make no comment on your proceedings,' he wrote, 'it is simply because I am almost invariably in complete agreement.'[58] For Robin, high praise indeed.

But the *Star*'s influence could only be limited, whatever its pretensions. Robin sought a wider audience. Together with Milner and Amery – though never a member of the *Kindergarten*, Amery was close to them in outlook as well as being a committed Milnerite – he floated the idea of an Imperial Press Service; its purpose to make 'a serious effort to pull the Empire together'. Nothing came of this project, although an Empire Press Conference did convene in June 1909.[59] Of more consequence, *The Times* had swung round to the *Kindergarten* point of view. Robin, of course, now acted as its South African correspondent. Amery, his co-Milnerite, had an even longer-standing connection with *The Times*. And in 1908 Edward Grigg, of similar views, returned to work for the paper, responsible for its imperial section.*[60]

---

* Of Edward William Macleay Grigg (1879–1955), a scholar at Winchester and New College, it was written that 'the true key to his life was his almost fanatical devotion to the Empire'. He joined the staff of *The Times* in 1903, as secretary to its editor, George Buckle; supported Joseph Chamberlain's imperial preference campaign; joined the London Moot

If in late Victorian times *The Times* took 'little pleasure in "painting the map red" ', and certainly did not envisage 'any plan of imperial federation', by the early years of the twentieth century 'it foresaw that British civilization, prosperity and power, firmly established in the four corners of the earth, would justify itself in its capacity as a guarantor of peace'. It now upheld the cause of 'the organic union of the Empire and the creation of an Imperial foreign policy'. As it said – was this Robin's voice? – in a famous leader of April 1914, 'the Empire cannot act at all, unless it acts as one', claiming that 'the only ultimate alternative to its [the Empire's] disruption' was 'a truly organic union'.[61] This was pure Milnerism. The conversion of *The Times* furnished the new imperialism with a mouthpiece of flawless credentials, for it was widely – though wrongly – assumed that 'The Thunderer' was a more sophisticated variation of the 'official mind' of government.

In June 1908 Robin dined at the Northcliffes'. It was his first meeting with the so-called 'creator of popular modern journalism', who, three months earlier, had secured control of *The Times* for the price of £320,000. Two weeks later he was invited to spend the weekend at Sutton Place, Northcliffe's Tudor mansion near Guildford. Northcliffe was impressed. 'You have seen me walking with the future editor of *The Times*,' he informed an associate. In one sense there was a frank meeting of minds, for Northcliffe, like Robin, was 'a genuine Imperialist'. But there was another side to Northcliffe. Offbeat, unpredictable, ruthless, autocratic – as a young man he had tried on Napoleon's hat at Fontainebleau and, as he expected, found that it fitted – he initially regarded *The Times* as 'a hobby', as a rich man's plaything. But it could never be just that. Crippled by financial losses, by dissension among the minority shareholders, and by an outdated constitution, he had paid hard cash for a derelict property. As such, it presented a challenge. Northcliffe's phenomenal success as a newspaper proprietor spurred him on. Eager to prove that he was not merely an irresponsible publisher of sensational halfpenny dailies, impatient to beat the 'establishment' at their own game and on their home ground, Northcliffe was no less conscious of the political dividends that would accrue to him if *The Times* yielded to his will.

Northcliffe knew that only he could provide the expert guidance to turn *The Times* around, to drag it, protesting, into the twentieth century. Only he could teach it the ABC of modern journalism – how necessary it was to

and became joint editor of *The Round Table*, 1913–14. Although not one of the original *Kinder*, he was a regular and welcome member of the Round Table group, though often holding dissident views. Later he pursued a distinguished career in the colonial service and politics, first as a National Liberal, then a National Conservative. Created Baron Altrincham, 1945.

use the telephone, for example. This implied thinning out the 'Old Gang' – 'Monks' or 'Black Friars', in Northcliffe's parlance – at Printing House Square.* Yet despite his firm resolve, he failed in the long run to make *The Times* into 'his personal organ'. 'Explain, simplify, clarify,' he was wont to say, but the 'Black Friars', who realized that 'they were utterly powerless to save the fabric of the paper without him', were equally determined not to permit him 'to destroy the essential quality of the paper'. Perhaps he intended to use Robin as his tool. If so, that never quite happened. In fact, it might be said that when the inevitable crisis broke, Robin joined the 'Monks'.[62]

All this lay in the future. Meanwhile, Robin had to return to South Africa, where he continued the *Star*'s missionary work on behalf of Union. By May 1910 that particular campaign had been brought to a successful conclusion. Unlike others of the *Kinder*, such as Patrick Duncan and Richard Feetham, Robin had no intention of pursuing a career in South Africa. Instead, he followed Curtis, Kerr and Brand back to England, celebrating that Christmas with his family at Langcliffe. Robin lost no time in renewing contact with his Round Table friends. A founding member of the London Moot, he spent leisurely and interesting weekends at Cliveden or Hatfield, pondering in communion the future of the British Empire. However, he still had to earn a living. His success as a journalist in South Africa, not to say his newly acquired standing with Northcliffe, opened the doors at Printing House Square. In February 1911, he joined the editorial staff of *The Times*, to work in the Foreign and Imperial Department. He performed extremely well. His editing skills were widely admired, particularly his treatment of the Coronation of George V and of the menacing railway strike that summer. Conscientious, sound, energetic, was he also representative of the new blood that Northcliffe had been clamouring for? Northcliffe certainly believed so. Although Robin had been taken on for a trial period – a normal procedure – the prospect of the highest position had been broadly hinted at. Actively abetted by Amery and George Earle Buckle, the incumbent editor (and also a Fellow of All Souls), Northcliffe, backed by the Walter family – who had founded *The Times* and still retained a substantial interest in it – finally found in Robin's favour. He was appointed editor of *The Times* in September 1912.

At the age of thirty-eight, Robin had succeeded to the most prestigious post in British journalism. 'Our task is great & worthy,' Northcliffe told him. 'If we get the barnacle-covered whale off the rocks & safely into deep water while we are comparatively young we may be able to keep it there until we discover others who can carry on the work.'[63] Robin carried 'on

* Blackfriars, where Printing House Square is located, took its name from the Dominican 'Black Friars' who first established themselves in this corner of the city in 1276.

the work', more or less without interruption, for the next thirty years. At first, their partnership worked famously, at least from Northcliffe's point of view. The layout of the paper was revamped and, to make it more competitive, the price was cut by half to one penny a copy. As such, it was a phenomenal success. Its circulation rose dramatically from 47,000 – when Robin took over – to an average 145,000 by the spring of 1914.[64] But the 'ideological' struggle over its character, its soul, remained unresolved. Who would determine its content, style and outlook? Who would safeguard the continuity and tradition of *The Times*?

Described as the 'greatest figure who ever strode down Fleet Street' – a thoroughfare that did not include Printing House Square, either physically or spiritually – Northcliffe, whose megalomania eventually destroyed his judgement, had grown rich and powerful by humouring the common taste. Careless of history, remote from English political tradition, 'his mind was finally occupied with distribution and means of attaining publicity'.[65] And as he always knew best, editors were considered to be little more than his instruments. This was not Robin's style. He was neither careless of history nor remote from English political tradition. Quite the contrary. Alive to the past and conscious of his new dignity, Robin entered upon his editorial responsibilities with his mind already cast. In any case, in a very real sense he had already chosen Milner as his 'Chief Editor'.

If his friends – Curtis, Kerr and Brand – could claim to be high-minded Liberals, Robin could claim with equal boldness to be a high-minded Unionist. He was close to Bonar Law, the Conservative leader, as later he was to be on intimate terms with Stanley Baldwin and Neville Chamberlain. He had no time for the 'poisonous' Liberal administration, dealers in 'rotten radical opinion', and those other gangs of 'rotters' that were out to thwart Milner's aims. He was all for 'slaying the Philistines' when the right time arrived. Over Ireland, the most contentious issue in British politics, he decided firmly in favour of Ulster's right to opt out of Home Rule. Unlike his Moot colleagues, particularly Curtis and Brand, who were busy shuttling between the two parties pressing the case for federation, Robin thought that Edward Carson had played his cards 'exceedingly well', going so far as to lend his tacit support to the Ulster leader's 'armed rebels'. As both Carson and Bonar Law were openly inciting insurrection, this was to adopt an extreme view, even if expressed in Robin's usual reserved style.

Was Robin taking his cue, yet again, from Milner, an ardent Ulsterite who never disguised his belligerent views, and who, according to his biographer, 'seemed to look forward to a clash of arms'? In a tantalizing phrase, Robin wrote to his correspondent in Dublin that as he upheld 'the exclusion of Ulster, I am not sure that a Nationalist revolt against compromise is not the best thing to hope for'.[66] Whatever he meant, he certainly planned to kill the Home Rule Bill of 1911 while preserving

Ulster's historic links with Westminster. War interrupted this agenda, postponing its implementation until the settlement of 1921.

It would not be accurate to claim, as many have, that Robin was ignorant of European politics. The complex system of Continental alliances and agreements, in particular the German danger, alarmed him, as it did all the Round Tablers. But his priorities were clear. European affairs were allowed to intrude only insofar as they touched upon the more vital interests of the Empire. Imperial unity was the key. If it was preserved and expanded, Britain's place among the great powers was guaranteed; if neglected and disregarded, Britain would sink to the rank of a second-rate power. Robin, together with the other 'Tabloids', embellished this grand imperial design to include another motif: cooperation among the English-speaking peoples. In effect, to nurture Anglo-American relations, or at least not to allow them to wither away. This factor would assume special significance in times of crisis or international tension.*[67]

Robin had first learned this world outlook in South Africa at the feet of Milner. He never abandoned it.

Bob

'Are you an Honourable?' Nancy Astor suddenly asked him. Puzzled, he replied immediately, 'Yes.' 'I am astounded,' she retorted; 'I thought you were absolutely middle class.'[68] Nothing could have been wider of the mark. The Honourable Robert Henry Brand – whose grandfather had been a Speaker of the House of Commons – was the fourth son of Henry Robert Brand, 2nd Viscount Hampden and 24th Baron Dacre, a former Liberal MP and Governor of New South Wales, and Susan Henrietta, daughter of Lord George Henry Cavendish, niece to the 7th Duke of Devonshire. In one respect, however, Nancy Astor might be excused her *faux pas*. Bespectacled, of rotund countenance, sporting a neat walrus moustache, wearing an old-fashioned cravat, possessed of a gentle voice and a self-deprecating manner, Bob Brand projected the image of a mild, if competent, provincial bank manager. Again, nothing could have been further from the truth. All who came into close contact with him quickly realized that before them stood a man of considerable ability. Known as the 'coolest head', 'the best brain' among the *Kinder*, he was thought by Smuts to be 'the most outstanding member of a very able team'.[69]

Bob Brand was born in Kensington, London, in October 1878. Little is

---

* It had a definite effect on Robin's attitude towards the Irish question. As the First World War progressed, and as he became more conscious of the strength of the Irish lobby in America, so he modified his attitude towards Irish nationalism.

known about his early life, but it would be safe to assume that nurses, governesses, tutors, stately homes and London mansions, and travel abroad, fashioned his childhood. He was raised at the family's large country estate, The Hoo, near Hitchen, Hertfordshire. One of a family of nine – though two of his brothers died young – he was brought up in a free-thinking atmosphere, somewhat at odds with the usual picture of a late Victorian household, his parents allowing their brood 'entire freedom to think any thoughts we wanted to'.[70] No doubt, there were everyday family tensions, but the impression remains that his early years passed in a composed and tolerant setting.

Bob gathered that his father 'was an agnostic'. His mother, he remembered, held strong religious views, but she did not press them on her children, though they went dutifully to chapel every Sunday morning. As Bob's father owned a couple of 'livings', he thought, perhaps, that one or two of his sons should become clergymen, but more as a means of providing a livelihood than of fulfilling any deep religious commitment. This dull prospect held no appeal to his offspring, and he did not press the issue. Instead, Bob's brothers all became soldiers and sailors. As for Bob, his intellectual precociousness led his parents to believe that his future lay in an academic career. Bob was quite willing, not from any burning ambition but because it would leave him enough free time to play his favourite game, fives. This plan too never quite worked out – although in his later career he certainly projected an air of academic detachment.

At the age of eight, Bob was sent to a respectable preparatory school near Reigate, Surrey. Here he spent the next six years, before going on to Marlborough College in 1892. Lying between the White Horse Hills and the Vale of Pewsey, Wiltshire, Marlborough had been founded in 1843, with the sons of clergymen in mind, and had soon acquired a lasting reputation for being 'violent, athletic and philistine'. On Guy Fawkes Night 1851, to the sound of fireworks and gunpowder explosions, a 'revolution' broke out, the rebels seizing the school for a week in protest against a merciless regime notorious for its vicious thrashing, its overcrowding and its starvation diet. Some student privileges were recouped, though as one old boy recalled as late as the 1920s, 'The upper classes were *not* pampered. We were treated with the ferocity of a concentration camp.' John Betjeman, another sensitive Marlburian, remembered 'The dread of beatings! Dread of being late! And, greatest dread of all, the dread of games!'[71] At Marlborough, as at most public schools, team games were encouraged as part of an elaborate ritual to develop 'character'. The recipe for success: '*Vigour* and *fiery dash* with *good temper* and *perseverance*'. No doubt Bob also underwent these rites, though whether with enthusiasm or reluctance remains a matter of guesswork. Academically, Divinity and Classical studies were cultivated; modern languages, history, geography, English literature, to say nothing of the sciences, little regarded. 'I assure you', reported the *Marlburian* with confidence in 1887, 'that not one of ten boys ... could tell me in what country Birmingham is.'[72] The competitive spirit, the imperial ethos, the God-fearing academic, mainly classical, training – which often found expression in a blend of scholarly arrogance and conventional good manners – were all part of the intellectual baggage that Bob carried with him to New College in 1898.

At New College, 'Old home of essays, gowns and lecture lists',[73] his horizons broadened. He read modern history, eventually obtaining a first-class degree. One dominant influence must have been H. A. L. Fisher, the history tutor at New College. Fisher – who later successfully combined academic life with active politics – was the leading liberal historian of his generation. Unlike some of his more obsessive colleagues, he failed to discern in history 'a plot, a rhythm, a predetermined pattern', but saw 'only one emergency following upon another as wave follows upon wave'. Take into account 'the play of the contingent and the unforeseen', he warned. This was sound advice for those who contemplated a public career – not that the *Kinder* always heeded it. But as has been pointed out, Fisher gave his pupils, among them Bob and his friends, Lionel Curtis, Philip Kerr and Waldorf Astor, 'an insight into humane statesmanship'.[74] In 1901, on completing his degree, Bob sat successfully for a Fellowship at All Souls, rounding off his Oxford career with another splendid accomplishment.

Had he wished it, Bob could have chosen the life of an academic. There can be little doubt that he possessed the necessary dedication, self-discipline and intellectual ability. But his practical turn of mind, coupled with the liberal imperialist traditions of his family, drew him in another direction: he too, ultimately, was 'a doer'. For a young man of his background and inclination the South African imbroglio would provide the perfect opportunity to realize his ambitions. Viscount Hampden took advantage of his connections in government to intervene on his son's behalf. His lobbying was augmented by that of Peter Perry, the first of the *Kinder* to arrive in South Africa, a close friend of Bob's from New College and All Souls, who had also recruited Dawson. Bob arrived in Johannesburg late in 1902. His job was to mother Milner's creation, the Inter-Colonial Council of the two Boer Republics, the Transvaal and Orange River Colony.

Composed of appointed and non-official representatives, the Council applied itself to the day-to-day chores of running South Africa after the war, particularly the reorganization of the railway systems and the policing of the two colonies. Apart from the administrative benefits it brought, Milner saw the Council's tasks as having a broader role. It would, he hoped, 'open a wider political horizon, [and] create a South African habit of mind, as distinct from a colonial one'. The aim was to create a spirit of cooperation, a sense of common purpose, as the first vital step towards a unified political entity. This, then, was no calm bureaucratic backwater. Issues of paramount importance were at stake. Milner moved with caution, first appointing Bob as the Council's assistant secretary, then its acting secretary, and finally, in March 1904, as its permanent secretary. Bob proved himself beyond expectations. Only twenty-six, he had made his mark as a first-class civil servant, running a complex network of committees in the most trying of circumstances. But Bob was not only a gifted administrator, he also had the knack of delegating authority to able assistants: Lionel Hichens as treasurer of the Council, and Philip Kerr to take charge of the railways. Milner was entirely satisfied. On handing over to his successor, Selborne, he wrote that Bob Brand was 'a fellow of real ability, who has this particular business at his fingers end. You can safely lean on him, for he has not only a great mastery of all the rather complicated details, but a good grasp of the general policy.'[75]

Like all the *Kinder*, Bob came to admire and respect his chief. He lauded the 'nobility' and 'dignity' of Milner's character, 'the innate simplicity, integrity, and charm of his mind'. Here were the 'qualities of a statesman' not 'a party politician'. Straight, single-minded, embarrassingly outspoken, Milner would 'pursue his ideals with the most undeviating firmness, regardless of any consequences to himself'. But what must have appealed to Bob – and to his friends – more than anything else was Milner's inclination to treat 'the young as if he wanted and appreciated their help', allowing them 'great latitude' in their work. Admiring Milner did not blind Bob to lapses in his judgement. When he felt his master's decrees were ill-advised, he said so. At first, he opposed Milner's key policy of importing Chinese labour – though he later accepted it reluctantly as a temporary expedient. Bob was already displaying that independence of thought that compelled him to challenge conventional wisdoms and to voice unfashionable views, often at variance with his closest colleagues. Bob's idealism was no less pronounced than that of his friends, but it was rooted in a more practical, hard-headed approach to contentious issues. He was opposed to 'all sorts of metaphysics, bad or good', judged John Buchan,* while another observer concluded that 'Brand seems to me more of a man of the

---

* John Buchan (1875–1940): novelist, biographer, Conservative MP; as Lord Tweedsmuir, Governor-General of Canada, 1935–40. On Amery's recommendation, Buchan served as Milner's private secretary from 1901–3, describing his chief as 'Plato's philosopher-turned-king'. In this capacity, he came to know well the members of the *Kindergarten*. But Buchan was never counted among their number; nor was he a member of the London Moot, nor did he write for *The Round Table*.

world than any of them, Curtis included; he is not so much of the apostle type. He has more savoir faire and yet is most charming.'[76]

Bob described himself at this time as 'a very weedy seedy young man'. Together with Richard Feetham and John Dove and Philip Kerr, he was a founding member of Moot House. It was he who introduced the temptations of fine French cuisine to bolster its cerebral attractions. This must have boosted the *Kinder*'s image in the eyes of their less-favoured compatriots, for Johannesburg in those early years reminded many of a sprawling, rough-and-ready mining camp. Every morning Bob would ride down from Moot House on his 'Basuto pony' and stable it behind Milner's office in town.

Trekking in northern Transvaal was one way of compensating for an otherwise sedentary life, although it could lead to unforeseen complications. Camping in a narrow valley, the *Kinder* went off to bathe at a near-by lake leaving one of their number, 'an abnormally sensitive character' (Philip Kerr?), who was feeling ill, behind. They exploited this opportunity to gossip about their sick friend, dissecting his character, laying bare his failings. On their return he looked up at them 'with a sickly smile', remarking on the 'extraordinary acoustic properties' of the area, assuring them that he had heard 'every word' uttered against him. Although their intimacy was strong enough to transcend these mishaps, intellectual small talk at this level undoubtedly scarred their relationships.[77]

Earnest and unsophisticated, the *Kinder* prospered as hard-working bachelors. In Johannesburg or Pretoria, there was little female society. But so preoccupied was Bob with his daily work and the exhilarating nightly discussions at Moot House – reaching such 'extraordinary conclusions and opinions' – that he could tell his mother disarmingly that 'bachelordom has great merits about it'. The 'hard Colonial' type of girl that he did meet was not to his liking. But when he went picnicking and fishing with 'two charming young (English) ladies', so 'nice and unaffected', he detected 'something very attractive about English girls. They are generally so natural and simple.' 'I expect it is dangerous to come home,' he confided again to his mother.[78] It was. Once home, Bob – by now an agnostic – fell for Philip Kerr's sister, Margaret, a devout Catholic and a member of England's leading Catholic family, the Howards. Will you take the Catholic faith, his bride-to-be asked. I will not, Bob replied, and the romance faded away after a year. Bob did not marry until 1917, at the relatively late age of thirty-nine.

Immersed in his work, stimulated by the challenge of his mission and the quality of the company he kept, Bob quickly concluded that at Moot House were gathered a cluster of 'first class brains'. As he reported home, they lived in 'a state of perpetual intellectual excitement'. At the time, he was engaged in cutting and polishing one of Curtis's papers (eventually the

Selborne memorandum), unable to swallow the 'Prophet's' apocalyptic forecast of either 'unity or disintegration'. Bob proved to be Curtis's fiercest critic, though in the friendliest manner. A 'most generous and unselfish fellow', Bob thought, a 'natural Communist'. But he needed gentle handling 'by some of his cold calm critical and unimaginative friends', for 'ideas crowd upon him and grow like mushrooms to maturity in a night, the next morning being treated as facts with a lot of other little mushroom facts surrounding them'. Nevertheless, Bob was firm for Union. He had heard with much admiration Milner's farewell peroration at Johannesburg in 1905, a clarion call for union 'to an Empire State in which Great Britain and South Africa would be partners'. 'There is no middle course,' Bob proclaimed.[79]

Bob's work did not end with the Selborne memorandum. As secretary to the powerful Transvaal delegation to the National Constitutional Convention, he became a key figure in composing the new South African constitution, bringing to bear on it his rigorous intellect and practical bent. Working behind the scenes, but always in close touch with Smuts, his main contribution was to advocate the benefits of proportional representation. 'I think I may say that proportional representation is my child,' Bob reported, arguing that it would reduce racial tension.[80] (By this he did not mean between the white and black populations – a problem that had barely penetrated the consciousness of most of the *Kinder* – but between the Boers and the British.) In September 1908, he told the readers of the *Cape Times* that it would result in 'not only the softening of the sharp line between town and country but also the mitigation of the asperity of racial conflicts'. Smuts was convinced. But this brave idea never worked out. At the last moment, the electoral calculations of the Cape Government blocked Bob's initiative. Despite this setback, the Convention, in February 1909, approved a constitution that owed much to Bob's creative draughtsmanship.[81]

Towards the end of his life Bob recognized that the Union would in any case have come about, 'because South African geography and conditions in general [made] it imperative'.[82] This should not detract from his achievement. At the time, the Union was a genuine step forward, with real potential for conciliation, even though in the long run it served fundamentalist Boer interests. One factor remained beyond anyone's control. Contrary to expectation, there never materialized a demographic swing in favour of those of British stock, even after the Boers' defeat. After a brief flurry, the wave of British emigration soon levelled out. North America and Australasia proved to be more attractive prospects than South Africa.

Unlike most of his contemporaries, Bob realized that the constitution he had done so much to fashion was lacking in one essential respect: it virtually ignored the black problem. This reflected an entrenched state of mind. Curtis, for example, the ideologue of the group, held at this time racial ideas that have been described as 'a conventional amalgam of prejudice, bad history, half-baked Darwinism, and spurious geography'; even as late as 1970, *The Round Table*, in its Diamond Jubilee number, lamented that Curtis 'had never really been sympathetic to the claims of black Africans'.[83]

Bob was more alive to the realities of the situation. A whole chapter of his book, *The Union of South Africa* (1909), was devoted to 'The Natives' and their place, or lack of it, in the new South Africa. At Westminster, this issue had come in for severe criticism. Balfour, typically, described the problem as being one of 'the most extraordinary difficulty and complexity', without 'parallel in the memory and experience of mankind'. Others, led by Keir Hardie, were less restrained, condemning the constitution as 'illiberal, unjust, pernicious, and retrograde'. Bob recognized the fundamental truth of these charges. All other problems 'are of minor importance', he wrote, 'when compared with the black shadow of the native problem . . . a matter of life and death to the inhabitants of South Africa'. Failure to resolve it would bring unmitigated 'disaster'. Self-government, in its present context, was 'a mockery' of the real thing. He damned the misguided policy of 'simple repression', of 'complete segregation', favoured by so many whites. 'If the black man sinks,' he argued, 'he will inevitably drag the white man with him . . . By raising in their breasts a sense of wrong the white man will be merely digging his own grave.' But given the racial prejudice endemic among a majority of the whites, Bob saw no immediate solution. He could only advise 'the utmost caution' when amending the system. For him, however, it was abundantly clear that in a society where the white man considered himself a member of a superior race, and where the black man was outlawed to the margins of society, 'extreme democracy will never thrive'.[84]

Bob's immediate tasks now over, he sailed for home that June, accompanied by Kerr, confident that he would return to continue his work on behalf of a united South Africa and a strengthened British Empire. As chance would have it, his plan to return permanently to South Africa never materialized. A bout of influenza caused him to miss his boat, and while waiting for the next he was introduced to Robert (later Lord) Kindersley, a prominent City figure, who persuaded him to join Lazard Brothers, the merchant bankers. Lazard's was then undergoing a structural reorganization, a process that allowed ample scope for an ambitious, able man. Bob accepted the offer. In this accidental way began an association that lasted for fifty years, Bob climbing steadily up the executive ladder, ending his career as managing director of Lazard's.

In *Lombard Street* (1873) Walter Bagehot wrote that the London banker aired 'a charmed value' since he represented 'a certain union of pecuniary sagacity and educated refinement which was scarcely to be found in any other part of society'. Banking, he thought, was 'a watchful but not a laborious trade', and a banker, 'even in a large business, can feel pretty sure that all his transactions are sound, and yet have much spare time' which he can readily devote 'to other pursuits'. Bagehot spoke from experience. But this engaging portrait of the gentleman banker fitted Bob only up to a point. In the years to come international banking became much more complex and demanding than in Bagehot's more leisurely days – a trend that Bob mastered fully. Even so, Bob found time for 'other pursuits', chiefly as an adviser to governments (and to his friends' portfolios), or as a member of specialist committees. He also sat on the board of various banks, of *The Times* Publishing Company, and the General Advisory Council of the BBC. Elected president of the Royal Economic Society, his interests extended to the Oxford Historic Buildings Fund. And, of course, his activities as an active Round Tabler never lapsed.

Secure in his new job, Bob set up a bachelor apartment at Cumberland Mansions, in Marylebone. Shortly afterwards, other *Kinder* – Kerr, John Dove and Lionel Hichens – joined him, forming a menage that survived until Bob's marriage.[85] Three months after his return from South Africa, Bob and his friends gathered at Plas Newydd, Anglesey, where he played a leading role in the crucial meeting that gave birth to the Round Table movement. Bob continued his calling as Curtis's most sophisticated critic, though never to the point of causing a break between them. He was certainly opposed, as was Kerr, to 'the Prophet's' pistol-like policy of forcing an Empire 'egg' down the throats of the Dominions. Impatient as ever, Curtis had returned from Canada full of complaints against the short-sighted dominion politicians who had obstructed his path. Unable to grasp the dangers that great power discord presented to the Empire, imprisoned by their own parochial considerations, they had failed to grasp the true nature of his 'new imperialism'.

It was to resolve some of these issues, to devise an acceptable form of organic union for the Empire, that Bob, Curtis, Kerr and Lord Robert Cecil met in November 1910. Four months of deliberations led to a considerable overhaul of Curtis's initial scheme.[86] His idea of a two-tiered parliament, designed to safeguard the Dominions from British dominance, was dropped. Instead, a single chamber institution was proposed, conferring a definite advantage on the British representatives. Nor would there be a peripatetic assembly, as Curtis had originally planned. Probably at Bob's urging, the right of direct taxation was stressed. The parameters of authority of this novel imperial creation were not precisely defined, but, as the group resolved, it 'ought to have power to do anything' in wartime. This was a far-reaching concession to dominion independence. It was also a sensible compromise with the new imperial reality as Kerr – who had kept Bob fully informed – and Curtis had encountered it during their recent tour of Canada. Canada, with good reason, was considered by the Round Tablers to be the test case. By 1914, it was estimated that thirty-five Round Table groups were spread across Canada, fully active and numbering three hundred 'men of influence'; similar groups were at work in South Africa, Australia, New Zealand and India.[87]

Bob was not always at odds with Curtis. Whatever differences emerged were usually resolved amicably enough, as befitted fraternal Round Tablers. Over the Irish question they were at one, busily campaigning in favour of a federal solution. Here Bob was on firm ground, as his father, an ex-governor of New South Wales, had been involved in the federation of the Australian colonies in 1900. 'As to what federalism precisely entails' was left (perhaps deliberately) vague. Certainly it included a measure of Home Rule for Ireland, but also for Scotland and Wales, in order to achieve a loose internal balance of forces. Broadly speaking, this style of devolution envisaged that, beneath the British parliament, there should be 'provincial assemblies entrusted with purely local concerns of the areas they represent', imperial affairs remaining the business of Westminster alone. This lukewarm formula was unlikely to appeal to vigorous-minded nationalists, but for Bob and the *Kinder* 'it was quite clear that the federal idea has come to stay'.[88]

Bob had known Waldorf Astor since their days together at New College. Nancy he had first encountered in the pages of the *Tatler*, and had been most impressed. 'Well,' he thought, 'Waldorf anyhow has done pretty well for himself.' Finally invited to Cliveden (and to Rest Harrow), they now met for the first time. As Bob eventually married Phyllis Brooks (née Langhorne), Nancy's favourite sister, their relationship developed into an extremely close one, though one not lacking in tension. Overwhelmed by her 'startling combination of great beauty, extreme frankness and friendliness, brilliant wit, tremendous energy and dashing initiative', Bob was profoundly impressed by Nancy, as were all the *Kinder*. But he was not blind to her 'uncanny instinct' to wound her acquaintances, to divine 'one's weak or sore spot and sometimes to rub it hard'. Beneath the gaiety and elegance lay a vein of cruelty. Later experience taught him that Nancy's 'reflective power was not so strong as her instinct'. 'Reason', he settled, 'was not her strongest point.' But whatever her faults, Bob – like his friends – fell easy victim to her charm. In the summer of 1913, together with Philip Kerr, he joined Waldorf and Nancy in Biarritz, where the Astors had taken a villa for a month. They went on to tour Provence, ending their holiday at the Ritz Hotel in Paris. Bob, hurrying back to London on business, went into Nancy's sitting room to say goodbye. She approached him directly. 'Are you in love with me?' she asked. 'Yes,' Bob replied without hesitation, knowing full well that all she desired was to add another 'unwanted scalp' to her collection.[89]

On one point Bob and Nancy profoundly disagreed. Her uncompromising religious beliefs held no appeal to his sceptical mind. Nancy had first dallied with an American movement called 'New Thought' before committing herself to Christian Science. Bob acquired one of its pamphlets, entitled *Dollars Want Me*. Put briefly, its thesis was that if you only thought about dollars enough, they would somehow come rolling in – a seductive thought, but one unlikely to excite a hard-headed banker. Christian Science worked on the same principle. If only you believed passionately enough in Mrs Eddy's teachings, you would emerge healthy and sound in body and soul. Bob would have none of it; and neither would Phyllis. He chaffed Nancy endlessly about her faith. 'Anti-Christ,' Nancy retaliated, deploring the pernicious influence Bob held over her beloved sister. Here there was no meeting of minds. As Bob said, although they both looked out over the same landscape, they saw the 'scenery' from different perspectives. There was to be a political fallout from this spiritual parting of the ways. Bob later acknowledged that his opinions on political or other subjects did not carry anything like the same weight with Nancy or Waldorf as those of Philip Kerr – or even Geoffrey Dawson and Lionel Curtis. In 'foreign politics', Bob once noted, 'you would be likely to hear a good many surprising and unverified assumptions' from Nancy. This was unfortunate, as Bob consistently showed during the prolonged foreign policy crisis of the thirties that his judgement was far sounder than that of his friends.[90]

More and more the 'other pursuits' that Bagehot had spoken of were tailored to suit Bob's banking expertise. The articles he began to write for *The Round Table* hardly strayed from matters of high finance. Realistic as ever, and on the supposition that 'Germany declared war on us', he acutely observed that 'at present one is almost entitled to suspect that just as the War Office will train the Territorials, so the Treasury hopes to acquire a knowledge of its [wartime] duties, after and not before war has broken out'. Once war had broken out in August 1914, he was not among the majority who held it would be of short duration, and certainly not because of financial constraints. 'All history goes to show that actual want of money or financial distress has seldom brought a war to an end.' 'So long as a Government has a printing-press, it can always make money,' he pointed out, a fact brought home in a very practical manner later on in the war.[91]

Bob did not see active service during the war. A weak heart prevented him from enlisting in August 1914. But the following September he was conscripted by Lloyd George, then Minister of Munitions, for the kind of war work for which he was eminently suited. Confronted by an acute crisis in the supply of shells, Lloyd George sent Bob to Canada to streamline the haphazard purchasing arrangements there. In Ottawa, Bob was instrumental in setting up the Imperial Munitions Board. Now a member of the Board, he acted as its permanent liaison officer in London. By the end of the war the IMB had acquired sixty million shells, at a total expenditure of £240 million. This kind of operation called for financial diplomacy and administrative ability of the highest order. It was the first of Bob's government appointments.

CHAPTER 4

War Games – and Peacemaking

On 4 August 1914 Britain found itself at war, ranged together with France and Russia against the Central Powers, Germany and Austro-Hungary, in a bloody armed struggle that would drag on until November 1918. Until the very last moment the Cabinet had been undecided how to act. Lloyd George was the key figure – as he was later to become to the future of the Round Tablers. No less convinced of Germany's aggressive intentions than his more hot-blooded associates such as Churchill, he was determined to act, but only when absolutely certain that he could swing the Cabinet behind him. The German invasion of Belgium brought the prevarication to an abrupt end, and with it collapsed the anti-war party, as Lloyd George suspected it would. His patience, his finely tuned political antennae ensured that Asquith brought his government, his party, and the country united into war.*

None of our Round Tablers volunteered for active service. Kerr, aged thirty-two, the youngest of the group, was clearly unfit to serve in the armed forces. Still recovering from his nervous breakdown, and soon to complain of yet more 'brain-fag', he soldiered on as editor of *The Round Table*. Although inclined 'to do something active', he eventually saw that it was right 'to keep on working on the far-sighted line for the present'. Waldorf Astor was excused on grounds of ill health: a strained heart and a tubercular condition. He was also at times incapacitated by crippling attacks of rheumatism – Brand once observed him having to be carried into 4 St James's Square.

Despite his delicate health, Waldorf insisted on enlisting for some kind

---

* Two ministers, John Morley, Lord President of the Council and Gladstone's biographer, and John Burns, formerly an active trade unionist but now President of the Board of Trade, resigned promptly from the Cabinet. Two others, John Simon, Attorney-General, and Lord Beauchamp, First Commissioner of Works, tendered their resignations but retracted immediately. All this had a marginal effect on the stability of the government.

of service. He went to the War Office and badgered the Quartermaster-General, Sir John Cowans, to employ him. Awarded the rank of major, he was put in charge of monitoring army waste, a thankless task that he performed with his usual diligence. Still active in his Plymouth constituency, attending to his parliamentary duties, he had little spare time for his pre-war social diversions, racing and grand parties. Nancy cooperated fully. Cliveden was put on a war footing. Vegetable gardens replaced flower beds and decorative shrubbery. Rooms were shut down. Most of the male servants went off to fight. In the winter of 1914–15, the Astors' repeated offer to exploit Cliveden's facilities as a hospital was taken up by the Canadian army. The large covered tennis court and bowling alley was adapted, holding, eventually, six hundred beds, complete with operating theatres. By the end of the war some twenty-four thousand casualties were treated there, or so Nancy estimated.[1]

Brand too was prone to ill health. Working hard for seven years in South Africa at a high altitude, which he confessed did not suit him, had left its mark. Susceptible to various ailments and with a weak constitution, he was consigned to his desk at Lazard Brothers. Gradually, however, he too was drawn into government service, called upon to deal with some of the financial aspects of the war. Dawson, of course, as editor of *The Times*, was placed at the very centre of events. It could be – and was – argued that his job, by definition, constituted essential war work. The eldest of the group, Lionel Curtis, aged forty-two – too old to venture gamely into the trenches – was of the same opinion regarding his own wartime duties. Unlike Kerr, who swung from one extreme to another, and who thought that *The Round Table* would go bust on the outbreak of war, Curtis harboured no doubts as to where his responsibilities lay. *The Round Table* had to continue: it was A1 priority war work, necessary 'to ram home' to the Dominions, and to all others who would listen, the lesson of federation, even union, particularly at times of crisis. Indefatigably energetic, Curtis produced *The Commonwealth of Nations* (1916) and *The Problem of the Commonwealth* (1916), works that advocated the restructuring of the Empire. Yet, in time, he too found himself involved in government work, formulating policy on Indian and Irish affairs. For all that, Curtis agonized, troubled at the soft life he was leading. Still based in Oxford, he inaugurated a strict domestic regime of self-denial, identifying with the long-suffering troops at the front. He was also heard quoting, wistfully, the stirring words of Shakespeare's Henry V: 'And gentlemen in England now a-bed / Shall think themselves accursed they were not here, / And hold their manhoods cheap whiles any speaks / That fought with us upon Saint Crispin's day.'[2]

Of the group, only Dawson could be classified as a true-blue Conservative. Curtis, Brand and Kerr considered themselves Liberals, naturally of the highest-minded variety. Waldorf Astor, although he sat in the Commons in the Conservative interest, was viewed by the party functionaries as a strange bird. In their eyes, his abiding attachment to social reform – that led him on occasion to defy the party whip – bracketed him, if not with the despised socialists, then certainly with those who held subversive liberal ideas. Because of his great wealth and impregnable social position, he was regarded as something of a maverick, by some even as a renegade. Certainly, he looked more to Lloyd George – now perceived as the coming man – for inspiration and leadership than he did to his own party chief, Bonar Law. This was true of the group as a whole. Even the more suspicious Dawson, hard-liner that he was, recognized Lloyd George's great qualities, particularly now that Asquith's were visibly failing. An 'interesting, impulsive, human, rather tricky creature', he thought him.[3] That the *Kinder* should form a Lloyd George admiration society had its ironic twist, given Lloyd George's record of opposition to the Boer War.

In these circumstances, it was pretty much business as usual. Moots convened and *The Round Table* continued to appear. Kerr, its editor (until December 1916), contributed eighteen wartime articles, Brand six, and Curtis, still inventively expounding on paper the commonwealth theme, only two. Dawson had *The Times* as a mouthpiece – though his capricious chief, Northcliffe, often stymied his path. *The Round Table* was intended to express, more or less, a collective point of view. Current topics were aired. First, the need to crush imperial Germany, to erase the 'Prussian Spirit', the '*kultur* of militarism'. The choice was clear: or world democracy or blind 'worship of the state-idea'. Once German militarism had been eradicated, the security of the world would be ensured, not by high-sounding conferences, but by 'practical safeguards' to preserve what was termed 'the Public Right', 'the liberties of the civilized world'. The discredited, illusory balance of power, based on egotistic national expediency, was out; 'a Concert of Nations' (a League of Nations?), with a settled constitution but without legislative, executive or military powers, dedicated to maintain the 'rights of all nations', was in. On one point *The Round Table* was crystal clear: a just peace could not entail the 'mutilation or permanent coercion of Germany by political or military or economic means'. This 'new and better Concert' had to embrace all peoples, including a rehabilitated Germany.

'Organic union of the world' was not neglected. In fact, according to the Round Tablers it was already 'in sight'. Not war, but 'the destruction of liberty', was the supreme evil in human affairs. A commonwealth, 'a world state', based on 'justice and liberty to all' was pictured as 'a cure for war'. Here the journal was elaborating upon Curtis's hazy theories of commonwealth, the ultimate foundation of which was 'fidelity to conscience – to justice, love and truth'. And what of the British Empire? It was marked out as 'the perfect example of the eventual world common-wealth'. In this context, *The Round Table* called upon the white Dominions to share in the formulation of policy. For practical reasons, the Dominions would not be able to share in the final stage of the peace negotiations. But prior consultations, within the framework of an extraordinary Imperial Conference, were considered to be imperative. These were familiar themes, and were to become even more so. There was one jarring note in this essentially optimistic assessment: the ambivalent role of the United States, oblivious to its duty 'to vanquish international tyranny'. Here was 'a failure of duty towards humanity'.[4]

From the group's point of view, the formation of Asquith's coalition government in May 1915 was a step in the right direction. They shared the general disquietude at his noticeably casual handling of the war. As Asquith was reconstructing his government, a weekend party gathered at Cliveden. Garvin, editor of the Astors' paper, the *Observer*, was present, but came away unhappy at the table-talk and uneasy about his personal position. As he had dared to defend Churchill, the main casualty of the crisis – and never one of Cliveden's favourites – he presumed that Waldorf, no doubt prompted by his friends, would wish to sack him. Churchill heard from Garvin: 'Just now they are all for Lloyd George . . . There is something more in all this than I can understand.'[5] In fact, there was very little to understand. 'Tricky creature' though he might be, Lloyd George, energetic and fertile of ideas, had long been identified by the friends as a potential war leader of genuine stature. There was, however, one conspicuous fly in this ointment. The preferment of Lloyd George failed to compensate for the exclusion of Milner.

Dawson had long thought that 'his old friend and chief, Milner', was 'the best man to conduct the war'. Even before the government reconstruction, the Conservative press, led by *The Times* and the *Observer*, had been singing Milner's praises. When Milner was passed over, Dawson opened to him the columns of *The Times*. Now the celebrated imperial proconsul, who claimed to stand above parochial party interests, was able to express his views on the running of the war – reflecting those of his Clivedenite allies – to the only audience that counted. 'The spirit of the nation is excellent,' Milner ruled, 'It simply needs firm leadership' – an obvious dig at the newly renovated Cabinet. Going further, he put in unambiguous terms the case for conscription, a most controversial and divisive issue. Dawson now played the go-between, bringing together his master and Lloyd George, generally recognized as Asquith's main rival. Both men were united in favouring conscription, as were many others, particularly Unionists: their aim now was to hustle the government into adopting it. Milner had written that 'The State ought not to be obliged to tout for fighting men'. 'Conscription was the only way,' Lloyd George agreed. Eventually, this kind of high-powered pressure paid off. Seeking a consensus, Asquith's initial response, typically, was to dilly-dally. But by the beginning of 1916 the first Military Service Act was passed, ending voluntary recruitment. Here was an encouraging omen for the Milnerites, indicating a fruitful partnership with Lloyd George.[6]

From January 1916 a small group of Milner's cronies began to dine together every Monday. The nucleus of the group included Milner himself, Dawson, Waldorf Astor, Leo Amery, F. S. Oliver (renowned for his biting, sarcastic wit) and Sir Edward Carson (the militant Ulster leader, currently serving as Asquith's Attorney-General). Usually, they were joined by Philip Kerr, Sir Leander Starr Jameson (the famous 'raider'), General Sir Henry Wilson (another militant Ulsterite and a compulsive political intriguer), and the most significant catch of all, Lloyd George. Amery took the initiative in convening this cabal. As a rule, it met at his home in Lord North Street or at Waldorf's mansion in St James's Square, or, less often, at Milner's house. In one form or another, this caucus continued its socializing until the end of the war.

Its dinner conversations revolved around what measures were needed to effect a more forceful, vigorous conduct of the war. Asquith's methods of running the war were derided as 'paralytic'. Nor was his Conservative partner, the unassuming Bonar Law, lacking a forceful personality, viewed in a more positive light. Wilson, as usual, expressed the general mood in the most violent terms. He wrote to Milner: 'You know my opinion of Squiff [i.e. Asquith]; he is a callous cynical blackguard – and a liar – who is mentally & physically incapable of action – an extinct volcano.' In other words, it was imperative '[to] get rid of Squiff as a first preliminary to any sort of action'. Once Asquith had been shunted off into nowhere, it would be possible to raise Lloyd George and Milner to positions of pre-eminence. Already reshuffling the government, jobs were mapped out for Kerr, as Under-Secretary for the Colonies, and Brand, as Financial Secretary to the Treasury. There was no consensus as to who should replace Asquith. Lloyd George, given his political standing, was obviously the front-runner. But there can be little doubt that Dawson, Waldorf Astor and Kerr would have plumped for Milner.

Sometimes the enthusiasm of these back-seat drivers ran away with their judgement. Certainly, Dawson and Waldorf Astor, usually the most cautious of men, came very close to overstepping the mark. In April 1916, they met Christopher Addison, Lloyd George's parliamentary under-secretary. Lloyd George should resign, they advised, force a crisis and seek a government reconstruction to bring back Milner as prime minister. Addison derisively dismissed this 'utterly absurd' proposal out of hand, describing Milner – no doubt, to their horror – as a 'second rate windbag'. Despite this superfluous, but potentially damaging, exchange, Lloyd George strengthened his contacts with the Astor–Dawson group, laying the foundation for a fruitful political alliance. But who was using whom?

Here were men of great influence united in a common cause. Carson, assertive, holding passionately held views, led the Unionist War Committee, a powerful group in the Commons. Milner, disillusioned with the cut and thrust of everyday party strife, sat in the Lords, a remote, Olympian figure, but one looked up to by many with a reverence akin to that reserved for a deity. Joined with them was that 'dynamic force' Lloyd George, ambitious, exceptionally able, manipulative, a past master in the art of expediency. Between them, they also controlled two great quality newspapers. Dawson was blatantly running *The Times* in the Milner interest. Nor, on this issue, was he held back by his boss, Northcliffe, who also happened to be fed up with Asquith's dilatory ways. As for the *Observer*, Waldorf had assumed control of it in February 1915, together with the *Pall Mall Gazette*. Still under the authoritative editorship of Garvin, it too adopted an anti-Asquith line no less hostile than the rest.[7]

What effect did this dining club have on the change in government that eventually came about in December 1916 and that raised Lloyd George to the premiership? No doubt, absorbed by their idea of themselves as kingmakers, they exaggerated their influence. They certainly pulled as many strings as possible, both in public and in private. In particular, Dawson, drawing sustenance from this 'ginger-group', was hyperactive. Having had Milner's candidature for prime minister brushed aside so contemptuously, he now favoured Lloyd George, a far more credible contender. The important thing was to get rid of Asquith, or at least to neutralize him. At the beginning of December, as the crisis broke, Dawson spent the weekend at Cliveden. Working late into Saturday night, he drafted a leader for *The Times*. Entitled 'Weak Methods and Weak Men', it appeared on 4 December. It generated a minor sensation. Trenchantly anti-Asquith and emphatically pro-Lloyd George, it excluded Asquith from any 'small War Council' on the grounds that '[his] qualities are fitted better, as they are fond of saying, "to preserve the unity of the nation" (though we have never doubted its unity) than to force the pace of a War Council'. Asquith would be foisted upon the public as a mere figurehead; or as he himself put it, as 'an irresponsible spectator of the War'.[8] Publicly humiliated, Asquith exploited the leader as an excuse to wriggle out of an earlier compromise with Lloyd George. Two days later, Lloyd George formed his government.

But it would be rash to allow the cabal, even the persistent Dawson, the decisive voice in this affair. They were little more than supporting players, waiting for the principal actors to speak their lines. Of more consequence was Asquith's illusory sense of confidence in his right to rule. Blind to his vulnerable position, he manoeuvred himself out of office. But no less crucial was Lloyd George's sense of timing. A past master at exploiting changing circumstances to his advantage, he knew instinctively when to hang back and when to strike. As so often, he called the final shot.

What is abundantly clear is that with Lloyd George as prime minister, and Milner and Carson occupying high office (the former a member of the inner War Cabinet, the latter at the Admiralty), the path was open for Milner's young men to take up their more humble roles. As one commentator dramatically put it, 'They were like hounds round a kill, after a long chase.' The lobbyists went to work: Oliver prodded Milner who prompted Lloyd George who, in any case on the lookout for new blood, responded readily to this canvassing. First to be appointed was Leo Amery – not quite one of the *Kinder* but as close to them as made little difference – who was posted to the War Cabinet Secretariat as an assistant to Hankey. This was not to Hankey's liking who considered Amery 'a scheming little fellow' whose 'connection with *The Times* would make it possible for him to oust me'.[9] In the event, Amery proved to be a loyal colleague; his sights were set on higher things.

All the 'friends' eventually found their niche. Philip Kerr, as private secretary to Lloyd George, now moved in the highest circles. His influence, which has sometimes been exaggerated, not least by himself, was nevertheless considerable, though as one colleague observed, 'Kerr pumps things into him [Lloyd George] and he seems to agree and then he goes and does the opposite.' 'You hate and love him in turns,' responded Kerr.* At the same time Waldorf Astor joined Lloyd George's personal aides, housed in the so-called 'Garden Suburb', a number of wooden huts erected in the garden of 10 Downing Street – an institution that gave the Prime Minister's critics a visible target for their ridicule and disdain. Astor served first as Lloyd George's parliamentary private secretary, and later, encouraged – some said, pushed – by Nancy, progressed to junior appointments at the Ministries of Food and Health.[10]

Brand's talents had long attracted Lloyd George's attention. As a result of the shell crisis of 1915, he had sent Brand to Ottawa as a member of the Imperial Munitions Board to sort out the chaotic purchasing arrangements there, a task Brand had fulfilled to high praise. With Lloyd George's rise to power, Brand was promoted and sent to Washington as deputy chairman to Northcliffe's British Mission, where he remained until 1919. While in America he wedded Phyllis (Langhorne) Brooks, Nancy's sister. They had

---

* The best-known anecdote regarding Kerr's alleged influence was told by Balfour. Had Lloyd George read a certain memorandum? he once asked Kerr. 'I don't think so,' came back the reply, 'but I have.' 'Not quite the same thing, is it, Philip – yet?' countered Balfour mildly. (Quoted in Blanche E.C. Dugdale, *Arthur James Balfour*, 1939, ii, 200.)

first become acquainted in 1912. After five years of courtship, chiefly by correspondence, they married. As Phyllis playfully put it: 'It was your oily letters that did the trick.' Dana Gibson, the artist, who had married the stunning Irene Langhorne – and immortalized her as the original 'Gibson Girl' – alerted Brand: 'Bob, we fellows who have married Langhorne sisters have got to pull together. We are all in the same boat; it's quite a job.'[11] By all accounts, it was a love match, brought to a cruel end by Phyllis's untimely death as a result of a riding accident in 1937. Brand, now related by marriage to the Astors, was linked even more closely to Cliveden.

Curtis too was preoccupied with grave affairs of state, but of a kind most congenial to his mind. He was in far-off Delhi, at the invitation of the governor of the United Provinces who had invited him to act as a behind-the-scenes adviser to constitutional changes then in the pipeline. This was a long-standing concern of the Moot and the Round Tablers. Curtis's ideas called for a measure of decentralization, a more carefully defined division of authority between the centre and the periphery, something corresponding to the relationship between English county councils and Westminster. At the provincial level, twin authorities would be set up, deriving their powers from elected legislatures. The first, the elected assembly, would act as a responsible government; the second, an advisory council to the Governor, staffed by Indians, would regulate topics still ostensibly reserved for central control. In this way, certain functions – education, health services, public works, sanitary works, agricultural and industrial development – would be transferred to these bodies, and more would follow as experience was gained; other matters – foreign and security affairs – would remain at the discretion of Delhi and Westminster.

This was 'dyarchy', Curtis's brainchild. It was not greeted with unreserved enthusiasm. Detractors saw it as a 'peculiar notion' promoted by 'a globe-trotting doctrinaire with a positive mania for constitution-mongering', whose fixations had 'produced the weakest form of government that human ingenuity ever devised'. This was unfair. 'Dyarchy' was certainly a clumsy conception, but it did signify a modest step forward to eventual Indian self-rule. The Montagu–Chelmsford reforms (of July 1918), which set this process in motion, also grew partly out of Curtis's ideas. Still, the element of patronage remained. As his biographer concluded, Curtis remained barely conscious of that vital force, 'Indian populist nationalism', or of the spirit that fostered it. And the same could equally be said of his awareness of dominion nationalism.[12]

One point should not have escaped Curtis's notice, or that of his friends. The case for 'organic union' was rapidly crumbling. The first blow had been struck at the Imperial Conference of 1911, when, according to Botha, the proposal for an Imperial Parliament – instigated by Curtis – had been 'destroyed root and branch'. Worse was to follow. The war was the great catalyst. Having sacrificed their manhood at Gallipoli or Flanders to preserve the British Empire, the Dominions would maintain the Empire but in their own way, one that would allow them the greatest freedom of manoeuvre in imperial matters within the loosest of frameworks. At the Imperial War Conference in 1917 Smuts drafted resolution IX. It called for 'full recognition of the Dominions as autonomous nations of an Imperial Commonwealth', and recognized 'the right of the Dominions and India to an adequate voice in foreign policy ... with continuous consultation in all important matters of common Imperial concern'. 'Autonomous nations'? How to interpret in practice this suggestive phrase? This was not quite the *coup de grâce* to imperial union, but it was as close to it as made little difference. Perhaps deliberately, Curtis closed his mind to these disagreeable implications. At any rate, he continued along his chosen path to the very end. When Smuts elected to discuss the consequences of the Conference with a group of Round Tablers, Curtis discovered to his astonishment that Kerr and Brand voiced no principled objections to Smuts's ideas. Curtis would long agonize about how to keep his less committed colleagues in line?*[13]

In October 1919, with the death of the 1st Viscount (William Waldorf) Astor, Waldorf succeeded to the title. He had dreaded this moment. When William Waldorf had been raised to the peerage in the New Year honours list of 1916, Waldorf and Nancy had protested furiously. A violent family quarrel ensued. In anger, William Waldorf rewrote his will. Trust funds of some $20 million were set up for his grandsons – prompting Nancy's tart comment that she found herself in 'the unique position of being Mother to four millionaires' – while a further $50 million were to be divided between Waldorf and his brother, John Jacob V. William Waldorf refused to see his eldest son again.[14] Having finally achieved his ambition of a peerage, William Waldorf appeared only twice in the House of Lords, once in 1916, when he took his seat, and again in 1917, after being created a Viscount.

The Astors had remonstrated fiercely at the prospect of becoming peers. The ageing William Waldorf had not consulted them about taking this step, although the peerage would affect them more than him. Nancy, perhaps in a fit of inverted snobbery, was fond of repeating that it was

---

* This process reached its logical conclusion with the Statute of Westminster, 1931, that proclaimed that Britain and the five white Dominions were to be recognized as 'autonomous communities within the British Empire, equal in status, in no way subordinate to one another ... though united by a common allegiance to the Crown and freely associated as members of the British Commonwealth of Nations'.

100 · The Cliveden Set

absurd and demeaning for them, as Americans by birth, to have a title. 'To be Mr Astor in New York meant something, because the Astors had long been prominent there. But to be Lord Astor meant nothing at all.' The title was 'bought – and paid for', she stressed to anyone who would listen. 'Let's abolish titles altogether,' she would scandalously propose, 'or else sell them to anyone stupid enough to want to buy one.' Still, Nancy came to relish this honour and all that it entailed, even though she would flaunt her displeasure from so-called egalitarian principles.

Nor could it seriously be claimed that a peerage would irreparably damage Waldorf's political career. Although he (and Nancy) maintained that 'real politics' were made in the House of Commons, Waldorf's ambition was carefully reined in. Mindful of his own limitations, Waldorf never aspired to the top job. In any case, a place in Cabinet could easily be squared with a seat in the House of Lords – as many subsequent examples have shown. Reluctantly, Waldorf reconciled himself to his fate, after having failed to get a motion passed in the House that would 'empower His Majesty to accept a surrender of any Peerage'. In this compliant manner, he faded from the public eye, content to manage his wife's burgeoning political career, attending the House of Lords only when he thought it necessary. Later, Waldorf would play a central role at Chatham House and in running Plymouth's local politics, claiming that this kind of work was more worthwhile and stimulating than participating in the ritualistic performances of the House of Lords. Was he being unduly modest? Did he lack sufficient ambition? Or, plagued by ill health, was he simply too tired? No doubt, it was a combination of all these factors.

Nancy took his place in his constituency, nominated initially as a stop-gap candidate until conditions enabled Waldorf to return. These conditions never materialized. In this roundabout way, Nancy was launched on a prolonged and eye-catching political career. Already active and popular in the constituency as Waldorf's consort, she was returned for the Sutton Division of Plymouth at the end of November 1919 with a comfortable majority of 5,200 votes, having gained the support of the temperance lobby. The following day, Nancy and Waldorf returned to Clivedon. At the Fountain of Love, in front of the house, they were welcomed by their cheering retainers. Climbing into a Victorian carriage, the newly elected MP and her consort were pulled slowly up the drive to the entrance of the house, past the bonfires lit for this grand occasion.

On 1 December, at 3.30 in the afternoon, wearing an impeccably cut black coat and skirt with a white silk blouse open at the neck, and a 'Tudor', a three-cornered, brimless black hat, she entered the Chamber of the House. Watched by her family in the Distinguished Strangers Gallery, she was introduced to the House by Lloyd George and Arthur Balfour, the former the incumbent prime minister, the latter an ex-prime minister.

After some uncertain shuffling at the Bar by her sponsors, they all advanced towards the Speaker, bowing, almost in unison, the traditional three times at Nancy's whispered command. Lloyd George recalled the scene.

> [Nancy] talked all the way up the floor of the House. This he and Balfour found most embarrassing, as it is against the rules to talk on the floor of the House. When she got to the table she almost forgot to sign the register owing to her anxiety to engage in conversation with Bonar Law. Then she wanted to have a chat with the Speaker.[15]

This was a truly historic occasion. Nancy was the first woman member elected to take her seat in the House of Commons (the Countess Markiewicz – Constance Gore-Booth – had been elected in December 1918, but as a Sinn Feiner, at the time incarcerated in Holloway prison, she denied any allegiance to the Crown and was therefore not sworn in). Nancy had to endure a great deal of inbuilt prejudice, not to say humiliation. Apart from the fact that the House lacked facilities for women – a boudoir and lavatory were hastily improvised – the more intractable members reacted testily, as though an exotic interloper had crashed the 'best club in town'. Viewed by them as a calamitous breach of tradition, her presence was greeted with remarks to the effect that 'a woman's place is in the home'. Women, perhaps, conceded one traditionalist, 'but Lady Astor is hardly the type'. Another reluctantly admitted that the new member was 'charming', adding if only 'she were English'. The last word, however, was voiced by Jack Jones, a broad-minded, plain-spoken Labour MP, to Nancy's manifest pleasure. 'We have plenty of old women in the House so I have no objection to having a young one.'[16]

With remarkable courage and persistence, with flair, elegance, wit and an exquisite appearance Nancy overcame these difficulties – though not the prejudices that fuelled them. It was as though she had waited for this moment, knowing it would come. Virtually overnight, Nancy became an international star, sought by the world press, basking in the ever-welcome publicity.

No one would ever accuse Nancy of being the most polished of parliamentarians. But her presence was always felt. She championed her causes with passion, although usually with a notable lack of tact. Her pet subject was temperance, the topic of her maiden speech. This was a courageous stand to take, defying not only the Tory brewers but also the prominent gin-makers of her own constituency, Plymouth. In 1923, Nancy introduced the Intoxicating Liquor Act, raising the age qualification for sale of alcoholic beverages to eighteen. It was a family affair, Nancy driving it through the Commons, Waldorf guiding it through the Lords. This was the highlight of her parliamentary career. For the rest, her main battles were fought to better the lot of women and children. Equal opportunity and pay in the civil service; the introduction of women police; raising the school leaving age to sixteen; juvenile courts to protect the young; cheap supplies of milk for children; play centres and clinics; slum clearance and modern housing; the protection of prostitutes from unlawful arrest; and the abolition of the death penalty were among the social issues she upheld. She also opposed extending grounds for divorce beyond adultery, claiming that it would weaken the 'spiritual idea of marriage'. A divorcee herself, this argument left her open to (baseless) accusations of hypocrisy, particularly from the pen of Horace Bottomley, publisher of *John Bull*, an unsavoury demagogue who was later convicted for fraud.

But probably the most impressive aspect of her public career was the nursery-school movement that she fostered. Thanks to her benevolence and initiative, a network of nurseries and trained teachers sprang up throughout England. In Plymouth too, free of parliamentary constraints, her resourcefulness bore fruit. Bankrolled by Astor money, the Lady Astor Housing Trust, to provide model working-class dwellings, was set up, as were the Astor Institute and the Virginia House Settlement, extensive recreational centres that included clubrooms, libraries, cinemas, gymnasiums, and that also catered for outdoor activities such as boating, camping and football. By any reckoning, these were substantial achievements.

Nancy was soon joined by other women MPs. In the elections of 1931, their number stood at fifteen, its highest for the inter-war period. Was she a feminist? Not in the contemporary meaning of the term. But she projected herself, by way of her combative personality and the causes she promoted, as a champion of women's rights. She called herself an 'ice-breaker'. At one time she agitated for a so-called 'Feminist Fourth Party'. An idea that cut across party lines, it held little appeal for the other women MPs, even though they insisted they were 'true believers'. No doubt they were also put off by Nancy's insistence on playing the role of mother-hen, and by her bossy way of browbeating them into agreement with her passionately held beliefs.

Although Nancy sat on the Conservative benches, she was by no means a machine-politician. At times, she proved a great embarrassment to the party whips. Like Waldorf, on social and economic matters she took an advanced stand. Waldorf prompted from the wings. Taking a back seat, he acted as Nancy's parliamentary chief of staff, seeking to guide her into calmer waters, to moderate her erratic behaviour, though not always with success. She possessed too mercurial a temperament to be disciplined. Harold Laski dubbed her 'the Pollyanna of Politics', and she acquired something of the status of the Commons Jester, providing amusement but not to be taken too seriously. On more than one occasion she was caught 'jumping around' in a 'frivolous way'. No rhetorician, Nancy was a great improviser. Heckling and manipulating hecklers were her forte. After one late-night session at the House she turned up finally at a dinner party at St James's Square very pleased with herself. 'I got in a wonderful interruption tonight,' she told her guests.[17]

While the Astors were manoeuvring to establish their new parliamentary status, their friends were in Paris as delegates to the Peace Conference. By now Curtis was well established as a professional *éminence grise*. In February 1918, he had returned from India. A year later he was in Paris, a member of the British League of Nations Section to the Conference. This post was congenial to his outlook. Still set on world government as the only certain means of eliminating war, he regarded the proposed League as an important staging-post towards this goal. Building on the experience of the Commonwealth, with the English-speaking peoples cast in a pioneering role, the League would constitute the kernel of Curtis's grandiose international order, leading, eventually, to the conduct of international affairs by 'frank conference instead of intrigue'. Anglo-American cooperation held the key. Weekending at Cliveden, Curtis and Kerr developed this theme. It would guarantee the peace, stabilize the post-war international system, and lay the basis for a central world authority. Curtis, his imagination now in full flight, even saw the United States as the 'last prodigal son that will some day return to the Commonwealth'. In this way, the essential unity of the English-speaking peoples would be preserved.[18]

None of this worked out. The Americans backed away from any firm obligation to participate in the new post-war international order. Nor were the Section members able to reach a consensus as to the final aim of the League. The 'Old Adam', that enigmatic, discredited figure of pre-1914 diplomatic practice, remained a vital force. How to reconcile total commitment to the League with the concept of national sovereignty – and this in an era where the principle of national self-determination was all the rage in international relations? Curtis left its discussions confused and disappointed. When he learned of a time-honoured Anglo-French deal to partition the African colonies, he sadly realized that 'the old pernicious idea of imperialism', of selfish national self-interest, was still very much alive. Frustrated, he suffered a nervous breakdown and withdrew to Morocco to convalesce.[19]

Curtis channelled his energies in other directions. On 30 May 1919 he convened a meeting at the Hotel Majestic for some thirty American and British delegates to the Peace Conference. After dinner, 'in a really admirable speech', he outlined his plan for an 'Anglo-American Institute of Foreign Affairs'. Its purpose: to enlighten public opinion by promoting research and discussion in foreign affairs. In this manner, Curtis would spread the cause of internationalism, relying on the Anglo-American experience. Further meetings were held: committees were appointed and a constitution drawn up. Curtis dominated these dealings. Meals at the Majestic became 'a happy hunting-ground where [he] would stalk and bag his game'. While the American aspect languished, the British side prospered. In July 1920 the British (later 'Royal') Institute of International Affairs was launched at a glittering affair held at the Astors' home in St James's Square. Orchestrated by Curtis, with Balfour as chief guest and Viscount (formerly, Sir Edward) Grey, Lord Robert Cecil and other leading statesmen present, the inaugural ceremony was endowed with widespread political backing. Two years later, the Institute moved into its permanent home at 10 St James's Square (previously the home of the 1st Earl of Chatham and William Gladstone), from where it still conducts its activities.

There could be no doubt who had nursed this project to fruition. Described as one of Curtis's 'major round-ups', he was 'the Founder' of Chatham House (the more familiar name of the Institute). He secured its finances, mainly, but not only, through the generosity of his multimillion-aire friend, Abe Bailey. 'Thank God, Chatham House is safe!' he reported to Leslie Rowse, 'I've got Abe Bailey to give it £150,000.' As its Honorary Secretary, he also monitored the appointments of its permanent staff. Nor were his Round Tabler friends forgotten. Kerr was closely involved as one of its advisers; Brand acted as its first Treasurer; while Waldorf Astor – another financial backer – chaired many of its study groups, and from 1935 to 1949 served as chairman of its Council. Spending so much time at Chatham House, supervising its day-to-day activities, worrying about its future, Curtis was allowed to keep a rough and ready *pied-à-terre* in its attic. Over the staircase at Chatham House hangs his portrait by Oswald Birley. Under it, the legend: 'Lionel Curtis, to whose inspiration Chatham House owes its existence.'[20]

Chatham House was Curtis's most lasting achievement. To this day it seeks to enlighten elite public opinion by fostering research and debate in international affairs. In 1921, however, while still securing the Institute's uncertain prospects, Curtis was co-opted as secretary to the British team negotiating an Irish treaty, joining other Round Tablers, Philip Kerr and Edward Grigg. His previous experience in South Africa and India in constitution-making, his proven powers of persuasion, equipped him with the necessary tools to explain and interpret the constitutional niceties of dominion status for Ireland. In December a treaty was signed granting dominion status to the newly created Irish Free State in the South; in the North, Ulster retained the Union with Westminster, but with its own parliament. Predictably, the treaty led to a fresh, and fiercer, outbreak of fighting. Stoked by the intractable nature of the problem, by the inability of the competing factions within the Republican – and Unionist – camp to compromise, a deadly civil war broke out in the South while violence escalated in the North. Cynics held Curtis partly responsible. Dubbing him an 'over-legalistic imperialist' or 'the hammer' of Irish nationalists, his detractors alleged that having established dyarchy in India he had created anarchy in Ireland. This was a specious charge. But there was something repellent in Curtis's certainty in the rectitude of his adopted causes which exposed him to such gibes. By the end of 1922, after Michael Collins's assassination and William Cosgrave's assumption of the office of President of the Irish Free State, Ireland settled down. Curtis remained as an adviser to the Colonial Office on Irish affairs for another two years.[21]

Curtis was still floating from job to job: in and out of the editorial offices of the *Round Table*, involved with the affairs of the Rhodes Trust, advising the Colonial Office, sustaining Chatham House. Apparently a dedicated part-timer, he eventually found a permanent niche at All Souls. Appointed a research fellow in 1921, he owed his position less to academic distinction than to the leverage of his friend Geoffrey Dawson, who at the time served as Estates Bursar of the College. Dawson wielded much clout. He backed Curtis's candidature – and T. E. Lawrence's – even though Warden Pember, more sceptical, regarded these 'Empire builders' with impassive suspicion.[22] Now holding an assured living, Curtis acquired Hales Croft, a rambling thatched house beside the Cher at Old Kidlington, from where he would commute to All Souls to conduct his multifarious pursuits.

Dawson had retired to the relative quiet of All Souls in November 1919. Ten months earlier he had resigned from *The Times*. His relations with Northcliffe had been deteriorating for some time. Northcliffe, after relinquishing his official wartime duties, had returned to Printing House Square confident that his would be the final voice in determining editorial policy. Moreover, it was widely suspected that he aimed at turning *The Times* into an upmarket appendage of his more earthy *Daily Mail*. To all this, Dawson was utterly opposed. Determined to retain his independence, Dawson rejected Northcliffe's habit of putting before him 'acid tests'. Undeterred, Northcliffe engineered a clash, warming to the task of driving Dawson into a corner. Either 'see eye to eye with me' or 'relinquish your position', he challenged Dawson. Other shadows passed between the two men. Northcliffe had no time for Dawson's intimates, Milner and Waldorf Astor – whom he particularly detested – declared supporters of Lloyd George, with whom, by now, he was in a state of open war. Shocked and angered at Lloyd George's recent landslide electoral victory, Northcliffe, by some quirk of his troubled mind, blamed Dawson for this supposed catastrophe. Nor were matters eased when it came to the notice of the distraught Northcliffe that his editor, usually the epitome of discretion, had been blackening his name over the dining table at Cliveden. 'A child in the hands of skilled intriguers', Northcliffe called him. Not prepared to serve as a cipher, Dawson resigned in February 1919.[23]

Dawson's resignation was eased by his having inherited his aunt's estates (and name) in 1917. Now a country gentleman of some stature, Dawson had acquired both status and a measure of financial independence. 'Robin', or so the wits in the *Times* office quipped, had changed into 'a Daw'. Soon installed at All Souls, he was also appointed, on Milner's recommendation, as secretary of the Rhodes Trust. After the stress of Northcliffe's regime at Printing House Square, Oxford must have seemed the calmest of backwaters. But Dawson's friends appeared determined to steer him into stormier waters. Philip Kerr, playing the all-powerful patron, was the chief lobbyist. He prompted Milner, then Colonial Secretary, to recommend that Dawson be appointed as his Permanent Under-Secretary. Dawson declined. Undeterred, Kerr proposed that Dawson succeed him in Lloyd George's secretariat; or failing that, perhaps he could be employed as permanent head of the Mandates Section at the Colonial Office? Dawson would not be enticed. The indefatigable Kerr kept pressing. But it was hardly likely that his final offer, that of political director of the *Daily Chronicle*, would tempt Dawson away from his retreat at All Souls.[24]

For most of these years Dawson devoted little time to public affairs (he left no diaries for 1919–20 and very few papers). Immediately after being manipulated out of his editorial chair, he had set off for Morocco, accompanied by Curtis, to recuperate for two or three months. At the same time his private life took a revolutionary turn. Hitherto regarded by his friends as 'a confirmed bachelor', he was in fact courting Cecilia Lawley, daughter of a Yorkshire landed family. On 14 June they were married at St Margaret's, Westminster. That November Dawson began his duties as Estates Bursar at All Souls. This crowded schedule temporarily pushed aside all other matters. But he had visited Paris for the opening sessions of the Peace Conference. His overall impression was one of indescribable chaos. 'All the world is here and most of his wives and my head aches with the number of people I've seen in the twenty-four hours since I arrived.' The Hotel Majestic, which housed the British delegation, had acquired, to his dismay, the ambience of 'a gigantic cinema show of eminent persons'. Despite the prevailing brouhaha, he was gladdened by one development: that the affairs of the League had been given first priority and were 'to be tackled in earnest'; if only the delegates would 'make a good job' of it.[25]

In August 1922, at the age of fifty-seven, Northcliffe died, broken physically and certifiably insane. *The Times* was put up for sale. Two months later Waldorf's younger brother, John Jacob Astor V – acting together with John Walter IV, scion of the paper's founding family – purchased a 95 per cent controlling interest in it for £1,580,000.[26] Dawson was not a party to these dealings, though naturally he was aware of what was afoot and was in close touch with his friends, Milner and Bob Brand among others, who were heavily involved. The current editor, Wickham Steed, was considered by the new proprietors as being too flamboyant and overbearing, and in particular too closely identified with Northcliffe, to continue in the editorial chair. A more accommodating personality was sought. John Astor took counsel with Brand. After settling on Dawson, Brand went on to clinch the deal. He dined with Dawson at All Souls, pressing his case into the small hours. 'Depressed', Dawson had spent 'a sleepless night'. Their exchange continued the following day. 'On a gorgeous afternoon', they took a long walk in University Parks, accompanied by Dougie Malcolm (one of the original *Kinder*, a Round Tabler, and a Fellow of All Souls), to persuade a hesitant Dawson to do his duty.

Eventually, Dawson yielded. He returned to *The Times*, but very much on his own terms. He drafted a memorandum that defined the guidelines of his second editorship. It gave him 'a "free hand" ', necessary, as he put it, for every editor 'worth his salt', and a prerequisite that would restore 'the reputation of [*The Times*'s] news columns for absolute accuracy and impartiality'. Having laid out the demarcation lines of authority between the editor, the managing director, and the owners, he insisted that no 'assistants or correspondents' be chosen except 'by his own choice or with his full approval'. As he would have to relinquish his directorship at New Consolidated Goldfields – and others in the offing – as well as his positions at Oxford, he expected his salary to compensate adequately for his loss of income. Finally, he trusted that 'an official motor' would be placed at his disposal, 'absolutely indispensable to his work'.

There was something in the nature of genteel *coup d'état* in this carefully phrased ultimatum. However, the owners accepted it. (Cliveden gossip irreverently had it that although 'Uncle John . . . owned *The Times* he probably did not read it'.) Letters of congratulations poured in, including one from Churchill: 'On every public ground I am very glad indeed for I feel that however much one may differ from "The Times", it will under you be conducted from the general standpoint of British interests rather than from the queer points of view which have governed it in recent years.' Dawson remained as editor until his retirement in 1941, by which time Churchill had been given cause to radically revise his opinion.[27]

Robert Brand, who had been the leading go-between in the Dawson affair – and later became a director of the Times Publishing Company – was by now a well-established merchant banker. Lord Robert Cecil, chairman of

the Supreme Economic Council, had brought him to the Paris Peace
Conference to act as his special adviser. Frustration dogged his every step.
Desperate, Bob appealed to America's better judgement. Frank Altschul,
an American financier, received his sombre message. Germany was
'destitute', in a state of imminent collapse. 'It was a question now of weeks
. . . and a collapse there means trouble everywhere else.' As Europe is
'destitute', everything 'depends on America . . . full of all the resources
Europe wants'. It was in the interests of all parties, he argued, to devise a
plan of mutual assistance. 'The whole future of the world depends upon
whether it is done and done quickly.' But he sensed that his plea, however
cogently argued, would go unheeded, its implementation blocked by the
appalling ignorance of Congress and the American people.[28]

Brand's most pressing task was to make sense of the vexed question of
Germany and reparations. Like his friend John Maynard Keynes, he found
it hard going. No matter how he grappled with the problem, he arrived at
the same conclusion: the reparation sums being aired at Paris – and those
that were finally agreed upon – were entirely 'fantastic' and would simply
destabilize the European – including the British – economy. Massive
indemnities, he pointed out, would only act as 'a forcing house to German
exports to the detriment of British trade'. But the British public and
Parliament had been 'misled by their betters' who, in their folly, had raised
false hopes by prescribing 'pledges which cannot possibly be fulfilled' – an
obvious dig at Lloyd George's opportunism. Early on Brand had cautioned
Cecil that any sum – he thought in terms of an overall £5,000,000,000,
without interest – should be linked to Germany's capacity to pay. Nor
could any money payments be expected from Germany for at least two to
three years. On the contrary, international aid would have to prime the
German pump. Ultimately, Brand asserted, any reparations settlement
would stand or fall on German goodwill – the dearest of all commodities.
But there was a wider significance. It was feared that the Germans would
exploit a vengeful reparations agreement 'to repudiate her undertakings'
under the treaty as a whole.[29]

These arguments made no visible impact at Paris. The well-meaning but
ineffectual Woodrow Wilson, 'a disillusioned evangelist', proved no match
for the formidable Georges Clemenceau. For Brand, as for Keynes,
Clemenceau dominated the Conference. There he sat, aged seventy-eight,
twice prime minister of France, 'the Tiger' to his countrymen, composed
in debate, radiating menace to his fellow delegates. Dressed in funereal
black, his hands, protected by lavender-coloured suede gloves, betraying
nothing, he presided over the Conference, often, it was noticed, with his
'ivory eyelids' closed. Set in his policy, Clemenceau conducted its
proceedings in a high-handed manner. '"Y-a-t-il d'objections? Non? . . .
Adopté." Like a machine gun.'[30] Having witnessed German aggression in

1870 and 1914, he was committed to guaranteeing French security, even if it meant Germany's ruin.

Much to Brand's chagrin, French policy after the Conference continued along Clemenceau's line. 'We cannot allow Poincaré to ruin Europe. If we do then Germany and Russia must inevitably join up.'[31] This was a constant fear: that French intransigence would destroy any hope of a stable European settlement. A wave of Francophobia swept up many influential people in public life in Britain, including the 'friends'. They had, as it were, transferred the theory of 'original sin' in international relations from Germany to France. Robert Vansittart, himself a passionate Francophile, put it accurately, if picturesquely. When he was about to go to Paris for the first time, a prim great-aunt of his threatened to cut him out of her will, and did.

> She thought Paris was a wicked place. The Victorian view was that the French practised all sorts of occult forms of sexual intercourse and were the wildest people on earth. The modern view was the same, only it had turned from the sexual to the political. If you went to Paris, you would catch some politico-venereal disease. They would infect you with their ideas and guarantees.[32]

Surprisingly, Nancy Astor, prudish in habit and speech, adopted a similar imagery. 'All Latin nations' were 'absolutely rotten', 'unprincipled, bibulous and immoral', she decided, overwhelmed by her own prejudices. Her bigotry was directed in particular against 'Roman Catholics'. France was both Latin and Catholic, so the French were a depraved and sinful nation. Bob Brand once overheard her saying, 'France is nothing but a big brothel.'[33]

These sentiments could only have been reinforced by Philip Kerr's experience at the Conference. As Lloyd George's private secretary, Kerr was close to the decision-makers. He had held conventional views regarding the causes of the war. In his mind, Germany was unquestionably the guilty party. To prevent another war he advised eradicating its '*kultur* of militarism' and destroying its 'political and military control over her neighbours'. This was to advocate the 'knock-out' blow in all but name. But he sought a tough, not vindictive peace. Germany, a 'criminal nation', should pay, but should not be treated 'as if it were the Sahara'. No stable peace could be based on 'the mutilation or permanent coercion of Germany by political or military or economic means'. Thinking of South Africa, he called for 'magnanimity'. Eventually, he believed, Germany would have to be included in 'the comity of nations'.[34]

Immediately after the treaty was signed in June 1919 he recognized that its 'broad justice' outweighed 'its minor defects'. What about the possibility of revision, he was asked. At a loss for a straight answer, he

countered, 'Which features of the Treaty do you think require modifica-
tion? . . . Certainly the Treaty is very stiff, but apart from the fundamental
question of reparation, I have always found it difficult to see where it could
really be revised.' He soon changed tack. Kerr's mind has been compared
to 'a weathervane', spinning around according to the weather. Bob Brand
noted that 'he was very impressionable . . . rather like a pendulum
swinging from time to time perhaps too far in one direction or another.'
Back in London, out of the hothouse atmosphere of Paris, Kerr soon
discovered that 'the present Treaty, indeed, is full of defects, and contains
countless temporary makeshifts'.[35]

What 'defects' had he in mind? Almost all can be traced to the hard-line
French. Nothing had changed. A year after the Conference Kerr wrote
them off. 'We are rapidly drifting into a crisis with the French, but the
French have played their cards so badly that they are practically isolated in
the world.'[36] Reparations were one bone of contention. No fixed amount
had been set at Paris, but the wildest figures were being bandied about –
also by some of the British experts. Kerr had no doubt that Germany
should pay, and pay heavily, for the havoc she had caused. But echoing
Brand's fears, he assumed that the preposterous, entirely impractical sums
being demanded would give Germany the 'incentive to repudiate her
undertakings in all parts of the peace'. This could well threaten the
territorial arrangements of the treaty. Although Kerr favoured national
self-determination – canonized in the Covenant of the League – he also
recognized that 'racial boundaries are nowhere exact in Europe'. In
particular, he identified the 'millions of German race which this settlement
cuts off from the central German state', the Germans stranded in an
independent Austria, in Poland and Danzig and the Sudetenland. Here
was fertile ground for disrupting 'the new framework of Europe'. To
overcome this danger he counted on the Covenant of the League. Article
19 made possible 'the progressive revision of treaties and international
agreements as circumstances require'. Kerr was an early advocate of the
League's role as an international policeman. During the war he had talked
'a lot of academic stuff about the League enforcing the peace', as Hankey
noted scornfully after one dinner conversation. Some months later, Kerr
put forward a scheme to revamp the Supreme War Council into a League
of Nations.[37] Now he came to see the League as the instrument 'for the
peaceable adjustment of disputes and the prevention of war'.

Why had the 'pendulum' swung so rapidly in so short a time? What was
troubling Kerr? Was he cracking under the strain, overripe for another
'brain-fag'? Observers at the Conference had already begun to comment on
his increasingly 'shrill' and 'unstable' behaviour. His predicament
stemmed from his duties as Lloyd George's favoured secretary. The Prime
Minister acknowledged his debt to Kerr, both on a personal and national

level. He had spoken of Kerr's 'brilliant work' and 'priceless help' at Paris, of how he was treated by all as 'a [very important] emissary to the Conference', and how difficult it would be 'to replace him'.[38] In November 1918, in an allied note to the German government, Kerr had determined 'that compensation will be made by Germany for all damage done to the civilian population of the Allies and their property by the aggression of Germany by land, by sea, and from the air'. This draft, written 'off his own bat', served as the basis for Article 231 of the treaty, the notorious war-guilt clause that eventually saddled Germany with a massive, unmanageable reparations account of £6,600 million, and that poisoned international relations until 1932 when Germany unilaterally cancelled the debt. The following June Kerr had composed, on behalf of the allies, his 'last note', an uncompromising refutation of the German observations on the draft treaty. Powerless to resist, Germany submitted, damning the Versailles settlement as a *Diktat*. In time Kerr came to judge this whole episode as criminal folly, one that he bitterly regretted. Tormented by his own complicity in this blunder, he was burdened by his Versailles guilt-complex even after.[39]

Kerr's growing frustration must have been compounded by the failure of his chief, Lloyd George, to persuade the allies, particularly the French, to moderate their attitude towards the peace with Germany. On the weekend of 22 March 1919 Lloyd George, with Philip Kerr, Maurice Hankey and Field Marshal Sir Henry Wilson, convened at Fontainebleau.* The party drafted 'Some Considerations for the Peace Conference'. Fearful 'that Germany may throw in her lot with Bolshevism', Lloyd George took a 'long-sighted' view, arguing for a more judicious, balanced settlement.

> You may strip Germany of her colonies, reduce her armaments to a mere police force and her navy to that of a fifth-rate power; all the same in the end if she feels that she has been unjustly treated in the peace of 1919 she will find means of exacting retribution from her conquerors.

In prophetic words, he repudiated the proposals to strip Germany of territories in central and eastern Europe. 'Masses of Germans clamouring for reunion with their native land . . . [must] lead sooner or later to a new war.' Clemenceau regarded this document as a prime example of 'British selfishness'. He sent back an icy response. Appease Germany, perhaps, but not at France's expense. Striking back, he recommended that Lloyd George should offer Germany 'colonial satisfaction, naval satisfaction, or satisfaction with regard to her commercial expansion'. On receipt of this

---

* It is often suggested that Smuts was also present, but this remains an open question.

pointed message, Lloyd George promptly withdrew the Fontainebleau memorandum.[40]

Soured by their first exposure to summit diplomacy, the 'friends' must have left Paris feeling dejected, let-down, an attitude common among many of the high-minded young participants at the Conference. Much of their disenchantment was targeted on the French. But anti-French sentiments implied pro-German sympathies, and the friends staggered under this intellectual burden until well into the 1930s. New dangers threatened everywhere: Soviet Russia; the Near East; the Far East – where Japanese ambitions were exhaustively itemized; central and eastern Europe. To ward off these hazards the greatest 'measure of responsibility' lay with France and the English-speaking peoples. Unless their alliance was preserved the world 'will inevitably drift back into anarchy and war'. France, unyielding and narrow-minded, had ruled itself out of this equation. But also regarding the commitments of the English-speaking peoples there were more question marks than answers.

For the Dominions, the Conference marked a key stage along the road to nationhood. Separately represented, they advanced their own interests rather than those of Britain. Nowhere was this more evident than in the behaviour of 'Billy' Hughes, Prime Minister of Australia, a 'puny raucous-voiced David . . . bidding defiance to the whole civilized world', claiming as his country's inheritance the former German Pacific colonies.[41] Nor had the British government done much to create a 'true Commonwealth', that is a Commonwealth in the spirit of the Round Tablers. The United States, a crucial factor in the 'friends'' world outlook, were an equal disappointment. For almost three years America had sat on the fence, jealously preserving its neutrality, a posture that had eroded the credibility of the 'special relationship' – akin to a religious faith for the Round Tablers – and that had plainly worked to the detriment of the western allies. America, *The Round Table* proclaimed, 'will have to abandon the dream of selfish isolation'. But would it? By now Wilson, whatever his good intentions, was a proven man of straw. Moreover, in the mid-term elections of November 1918 he had lost control of Congress, where a Republican, largely isolationist majority now set the tone. The prospects for greater American involvement in world affairs faded fast. Nor were they revived throughout the inter-war period. The United States, anchored in its 'selfish isolation', continued to disappoint.

How to preserve international sanity in this cheerless situation? Not, Kerr had written, 'by high-sounding conferences' or 'well-meaning agreements' intended to weaken or to disarm 'the policemen among the nations'. Even the League of Nations – which, given sufficient optimism, might have been interpreted as a first step towards world government – failed to satisfy the *Kinder*. Already, the spectacle of arrogant national self-interest was taking root. Kerr, at least, expressed grave reservations as to the organization's future role, holding that it would become 'discredited through its inability to live up to the expectations which have been formed of it'.[42] *Faute de mieux*, he was thrown back on old-style Concert of Europe diplomacy, solid treaties that would include 'practical safeguards for the liberties and rights of the civilized world'. (Unfortunately, the example he offered of the 1839 great power guarantee to Belgium was, in the circumstances, somewhat odd.) Their world outlook crumbling, the 'friends' international perspective had narrowed. From their point of view, the new world order had got off to a bad start.

CHAPTER 5

Back to Normality

On the last Sunday evening of February 1922, Lytton Strachey found himself stranded in a colossal traffic jam in St James's Square. It was 'pouring cats and dogs'. His taxi edged forward inch by inch, ever nearer the 'portals of bliss'. He had been invited to one of Lady Astor's 'hectic frenzies' to celebrate the occasion of Balfour's elevation to the Order of the Garter. 'A huge rout', eight hundred guests had been invited, from duchesses to the Stracheys. With studied condescension, Strachey rated the whole affair as 'a great bore', perhaps because – 'horror of horrors!' – Lloyd George, though bowing 'very politely', failed to recognize him, even if the prime minister's wife, 'an unparalleled frump', did. Fortunately, the guest of honour, Balfour, hiding behind his 'large demi-ghostly spectacles', made up for Lloyd George's lack of tact, considerably rewarding Strachey with the compliments he required.[1]

Dining at 4 St James's Square was always a grand occasion, its dining room reminding one guest of a spacious 'chapel vestry, all panelled', the table 'lit with candles and silver', the chairs placed too closely together – despite the footmen's complaints – because Nancy believed this would encourage more lively, intimate conversation. This was not to Churchill's liking: 'Thirty dishes served and no damn room to eat one,' he complained. But it was the splendid evening receptions at the Astors', the 'hectic frenzies', that caught the columnists' eye and that became a regular feature of the London scene. Joyce Grenfell, Nancy's niece, remembered how Waldorf Astor, moved not by snobbishness but by a self-imposed sense of obligation to act the 'Host of England', invited the delegates to the League of Nations, then gathered in London, to a grand party. They all attended, together with prominent British political and social figures. After dinner Nancy insisted that they play one of her favourite party games, musical chairs. Some complied, but others stood by, amused and smiling benignly, 'thinking, no doubt, that the English are mad, quite mad'. 'Baffy' Dugdale (Balfour's niece and biographer) observed this bizarre scene with mounting frustration. 'A number of people played . . . But neither von Hoesch nor Maisky [the German and Soviet ambassadors] so my hopes of seeing those two scrabbling for the last chair were not fulfilled.'[2]

Not all of these functions had a political slant. There were balls, often for a thousand people, the guests waltzing and polkaing until the small hours. Nancy, for ever the individualist, Paul Jones'd her way through the night. At dawn, the company would take their leave after an early breakfast of eggs and bacon and a champagne cup with lemonade. There were other extravaganzas, fancy-dress children's parties for the cream of London society. On one occasion the Princesses Elizabeth (dressed as a Dutch peasant) and Margaret (in a Kate Greenaway costume), who were so 'well brought up', chaperoned by two Queens, Mary and Marie of Yugoslavia, were the guests of honour. Upstairs, the dining room had been painstakingly converted into a country fair, with artificial grass on the floor. Stalls, draped in scarlet and white canvas, stood around displaying their wares – fruit and flowers, sweets, toys and fancy balloons. At one end of the room, a floodlit Punch and Judy theatre had been set up. In the ballroom a three-piece orchestra and a wandering minstrel with an accordion, attired as a gypsy, entertained the children. This spectacular production was followed by a 'tea of major proportions'.[3]

The Astors were firmly anchored at the centre of London social life, but there were other political-social-literary salons vying for precedence. One leading contender was Lady Emerald (Maud) Cunard, born in New York, and variously described as showing off a 'pretty wrinkled Watteau face' or 'looking like a third-dynasty mummy painted pink by amateurs' – not charges that could easily be levelled against Nancy. Sometimes Emerald's dinners went off splendidly, sometimes they were 'ghastly', a fact that must have pleased Lady Sybil Colefax, whose house at 19 Lord North Street was frequently referred to as 'Lions Corner House'. 'Bejewelled, eye-brow plucked, virtuous and wise', Sybil was not as well-to-do as Emerald and there came a time when she would discreetly bill her guests a few days after her parties – her so-called 'ordinaries'. These two hostesses were serious rivals, never more so than when seated around the same table. 'Emerald Cunard says that she has had a very nice letter from Grandi [the Italian ambassador to London]. "Have you also heard from him, Lady Colefax?" "Only by telegram," Sybil answers like a flash.'[4]

Neither Lady Colefax nor Lady Cunard were great favourites of Nancy. For one thing, both took Edward VIII's part in the abdication crisis. Nancy's puritanical turn of mind would not countenance philandering, even in a king. Her royal loyalties were reserved for the Duke and Duchess of York (later King George VI and Queen Elizabeth), earnest, dignified, symbolizing sound family values. When Nancy heard that the King had invited his mistress, Mrs Wallis Simpson, *and* Emerald Cunard for dinner, she became 'terribly indignant' at this scandalous lack of form. Emerald, in any case, was 'bad company', a 'dreadful person' and a 'disintegrating influence' – it was held that she had influenced Edward in his pro-Nazi leanings. Only 'the best Virginian families should be received at Court', Nancy hinted. After the Act of Abdication 'the Hostesses' were severely castigated by the Archbishop of Canterbury for their false role in this disastrous affair. Circumspectly, they backed away from their former idols. 'Ridiculous, I hardly knew Mrs Simpson,' declared Emerald. 'Rat Week', Edward's sympathizers noted, taking their cue from Osbert Sitwell's privately circulated satirical poem, 'Where are the friends of yesterday / That fawned on him / That flattered her? . . .'[5] This was not Nancy's way.

And neither, it must be assumed, was it Mrs Laura Corrigan's, the immensely wealthy American widow of a steel tycoon. Eccentric, snobbish and well-meaning, she threw the most lavish of private parties, amusing her guests with star cabaret turns and presenting them with expensive presents, gold Cartier lighters and the like. 'One must always be kind to the poor,' quipped Lady Cunard. 'It's only Mrs Corrigan who's kind to the rich.' A stickler for conventional etiquette, she was once heard shouting down the table, 'Who's the next ranking dook?' in an attempt to rectify her botched table-seating arrangements. Mrs Corrigan's odd habits flourished under the aegis of Edith ('Circe'),* Marchioness of Londonderry, reputedly the foremost political hostess of her day, and a match, in this respect at least, even for the Astors. The Londonderrys' annual reception for the opening of Parliament was regarded as a major event of the London season. 'Circe', sparkling with jewels, would stand at the top of the magnificent staircase at Londonderry House, attended by her husband 'Charlie' and the incumbent Prime Minister, to greet her guests, usually around 2,500 in number. Some found this opulence a trifle ostentatious, but few refused an invitation. Lord Birkenhead, in typical style, put it about that Londonderry was 'catering his way into the Cabinet'. Later, the Londonderrys were linked to the 'Cliveden Set', an assumption based simply upon their much flaunted pro-German tendencies, 'Charlie' being widely lampooned as 'the Londonderry Herr'. But the Astors were not enamoured of the Londonderrys. Nancy thought Edith a pernicious influence: 'bad company', in her vocabulary. Of course, they met socially,

---

* Circe, the famous sorceress of Greek legend, who by incantations and spells could change humans into beasts. Edith's nickname derived from her command over the so-called 'Ark', an exclusive dinner-party club that met periodically at Londonerry House, but only on condition that every guest adopted the name of a mythical or real creature. So, her husband took the form of 'Charlie the Cheetah'; Ramsay MacDonald, 'Hamish the Hart'; Balfour, 'Arthur the Albatross'; Churchill, 'Winston the Warlock'; Lady Astor, 'Nancy the Gnat'; and so on.

but the Londonderrys were not favoured guests at 4 St James's Square or at Cliveden.[6]

After the years of wartime austerity, Cliveden reverted to its more familiar routine. The house was fully reopened, the gardens restored, the weekend house parties resumed. Every Friday the household would be moved 'lock, stock, and barrel' from St James's Square to Cliveden, Nancy switching between her two types of party, her town and her country styles, the first more formal, the latter more relaxed, but both spiced with politics. Cliveden's domestic affairs ran smoothly, owing mainly to the efficiency of two dominant personalities, Rose Harrison, Nancy's personal maid, and Edwin Lee, the butler. Lee was a legendary figure. It was said, with justification, that just to have been trained by him 'was a reference in itself'. He supervised an inside staff of thirty-four – by 1928, the Astors were employing in all their homes 146 servants. Meticulous and circumspect, he managed a strict, but fair regime. Once, exasperated by Nancy's capricious conduct, he tendered his notice. Alert to the danger signal, Nancy counter-attacked. 'In that case, Lee, tell me where you're going because I'm coming with you.' Undone, Lee remained. He instilled in those under his charge a golden rule. If ever they were faced with an embarrassing scene between their employers, they should judiciously ignore it. 'Good servants', he said, 'at the sight of any emotion turn away from it and make an opportunity to absent themselves.'

Rose Harrison began her duties in 1929 and remained in service until Nancy's death in 1964. Over these years she experienced at first hand the vagaries of Nancy's volatile temperament. Born in the small village of Aldfield, Yorkshire, Rose had the qualities typically associated with the Yorkshire character: blunt, no-nonsense, plain-speaking. Not easily intimidated, she conducted many 'battle royals' with her 'lady', who dubbed her 'the sergeant-major'. 'Shut up, Rose,' was Nancy's usual way of terminating these ongoing tiffs. Suspicious and interfering, Nancy could also be 'sadistic and sarcastic', taking a positive enjoyment in 'goading' those who served her. A talented mimic, she would cruelly ape Rose's Yorkshire accent. Stinginess was another complaint voiced by Rose, odd as it might seem. After all, Nancy never tired of reminding all who would listen that it was *she* who was spending the fortune the Astors had accumulated. Still, she was delighted when Rose brought her cheap, but fashionable, dresses from Marks and Spencer, a far cry from her usual haunts in Grosvenor Street or Knightsbridge. Determined to get 'her money's worth' out of her servants, she balked at raising Rose's salary, finally relenting to add a paltry £5 a year. 'I never asked for another rise, and I never got one.'

'Black and white, that was Lady Astor,' Rose admitted, adding that there was 'much white'. As many have testified, there was also a generous streak to Nancy's nature, even if tempered by a touch of patronage. She would dispense five-pound notes to panhandlers, sign cheques for hundreds of pounds to hard-up friends, and rescue relatives in straitened circumstances. Rose – and not only Rose – benefited from her hand-me-downs. At Cliveden, she kept a special 'present room', stocked with sweaters, silk scarves and stockings, chiffon squares, linen handkerchiefs, ties, golf balls, diaries, toys, games, books, and 'lots of candy'.

Like any gifted actress, Nancy could turn on the charm when necessary, graciously yielding when she realized that she had overstepped the mark. Nancy paraded an unflagging zest for life. Whatever criticisms she invited, her company was never dull. Mercurial, arbitrary, wayward, she also generated a sense of fun, of gaiety, a spirit of excitement, even at times of danger. Nancy enjoyed travelling fast. On one occasion, driving recklessly down Constitution Hill in wintry conditions, her car went into a slide and almost decimated a Guards band that had chanced to stray into its path. Motorcycling with T. E. Lawrence was another distraction. She would jump on the pillion and they would speed off down the drive towards Shell Fountain 'in a cloud of dust', returning to pull up by the front entrance in a hair-raising skid. 'We did a hundred miles an hour,' Nancy shrieked. Waldorf just stalked away, furious.[7]

Nancy imposed her vivid character upon her weekend parties. She kept open house. Her guests spanned the widest spectrum of opinion and taste, refusing to conform to any rigid social-political mould. Much of her hospitality was directed to furthering the causes she promoted in Parliament. Much of it was devoted to meeting 'her betters', as she put it, people who were 'doing something interesting', whether in social or political affairs, the theatre or literature. She admired '"achievers" and took them seriously': and they responded readily to her invitations. Visitors varied. Anybody might be on the guest list – Henry Ford, the Queen of Rumania, Charlie Chaplin, Gandhi, Bernard Shaw, Arthur Balfour, a general or a Christian Scientist, relations, protégés, Round Tablers, Charles Lindbergh, American senators, 'and, if you were lucky indeed, one or more of the Langhorne sisters, the only beings on earth whom Nancy really regarded as equals'.

Naturally, at Cliveden weekends the talk was of 'politics all day and all night', at times to 'the bane' of some of the guests. Hankey recorded one such gathering in February 1920, attended by Lloyd George, Garvin, several MPs and 'a lot of silly women . . . who have no business in politics'. A 'dead tired' Lloyd George and Garvin had 'a terrific set-to about the Peace Treaty' that left Garvin 'badly worsted'. Desperately needing a rest, the Prime Minister departed. In his absence, Garvin and the Astors urged upon the company the 'nonsensical idea' that Lloyd George should resign and stage a comeback after six months. Hankey brought them back to earth by reminding them of Asquith's example.*[8]

Foreign politics predominated, the exchanges enriched by their informative, often polemical, quality, though regularly seasoned with diverting hearsay and small talk. 'After dinner a discussion starts on the future of England' – a perennial topic. 'Lothian says that democracy and Empire cannot go together ... The others join in. The main conclusion is that Parliament, though susceptible to dealing with politics, is hopeless at finance and economics.' Not all were happy with this pontificating, or with those who inspired it. An 'interfering termagant' was how 'Chips' Channon – a chronic socialite and gossip – described Nancy, warm-hearted only so long as 'she can patronize one'. Harold Nicolson, more serious, included her among those 'silly selfish hostesses ... [who] give the impression that foreign policy is decided in their own drawing-rooms' – a 'kindly' woman, Nicolson relented, yet inordinately 'foolish'. Spreading a subversive influence, she would wine and dine politicians, creating an atmosphere of authority and responsibility and grandeur, whereas in reality 'the whole thing is a mere flatulence of the spirit'.[9]

In winter, afternoon tea was taken in the Great Hall before the fire. In summer 'it was laid out with infinite detail, under a pavilion roof at the end of the broad terrace'. Tea? queried Walter Elliot, a regular guest, who went on to compare it to 'a Bedouin encampment. There was a table for tea, a table for cakes, a table for children, a table for grown-ups, and generally a nomadic group coming and going somewhere in the neighbourhood of Nancy herself. Cushions, papers, people, were mixed in a noble disarray.' At dinner, twenty people were considered a small gathering, forty a more normal party. Conversation was continual, free-ranging, unconventional in character: 'it was a debate, it was a riot, it was a tidal wave, in the midst of which small islets might be seen holding out determinedly in private talk till they too were borne away by the ever-rolling flood.'

Under Nancy's vigorous regime there would be no purposeless idling. On Saturdays Nancy would gird herself for exercise, tennis or golf, swimming or long walks, and would 'sally forth, after some high-pitched objurgations against those who remained clustered around the big hall fire, or reading in one of the rooms. "Why don't you all go out, what do you want to sit around here for? Go out! Go out! Look at the lovely day. Or at any rate go into one of my nice rooms, where I have the flowers. Sitting around here in the dark, all day long ... Go out – play tennis – go for a swim in the river. You can always read in London."' Tennis, always 'strenuous', was a favourite pastime, played on tropical evenings and even on rainy days when the players would retire to the covered court. Anthony

* Asquith had resigned as Prime Minister in December 1916; but he never came back.

Eden, a fine player, was a prominent figure on the court. His all-round game was impressive, prompting 'Baffy' Dugdale to remark, 'If only his politics were like some of his tennis strokes down the centre of the Court!' But Nancy, it might be said, was the Number One Seed. 'I played three sets of singles with Aunt N. and she won them all! She's jolly nearly sixty and is quite tireless,' Joyce Grenfell – thirty years younger – grumbled, after having been thrashed 6–2, 6–3, 6–0.[10]

'Cliveden was never more itself than in the dusk, on the high paved terrace outside its drawing-room windows. But one always looked for the fireflies, and listened for the grasshoppers – and the mosquitoes,' remembered Walter Elliot. Geoffrey Dawson recalled an 'immense party' including Neville Chamberlain, David Bowes-Lyon (brother-in-law to the future King George VI) and Philip Kerr sitting 'out on the terrace in the moonlight while Molly (Lady) Frey played the piano & others played bridge'. One 'delicious evening with wonderful moon', the guests gathered 'to see a play televised on a set got down for a trial'.[11]

Somehow or other Nancy's parties evolved, arranged themselves, separated, came together again, and then remarshalled for dinner. Indoor entertainment was never lacking. Charades, or more usually a few rounds of musical chairs, followed dinner. But the liveliest pastime was conversation, from a cosy *tête-à-tête* to more formal symposiums. Most enjoyed Nancy's style of orchestrating her parties. Some did not. Harold Nicolson travelled down to Cliveden on a gloomy autumnal day to find a cold and draughty house full of 'great sofas in vast cathedrals'. Little groups of people were standing around, bored, unsure what to do, wishing they were alone. Somehow, the party did not hang together. 'After dinner, in order to enliven the party, Lady Astor dons a Victorian hat and a pair of false teeth. It does not enliven the party.' Nicolson's captious eye detected 'a ghastly unreality' about Cliveden. 'Its beauty is purely scenic. I enjoy seeing it. But to own it, to live here, would be like living on the stage of the Scala theatre in Milan.' In the exclusive Nicolson vernacular, his experience must have been terribly 'bedint' (or vulgar, lacking in standards). Another visitor, Henry ('Chips') Channon, like Nancy an expatriate American, also felt '*désoeuvré* and bored' at Cliveden. 'There is nothing so out of date as a 1900 house, which Cliveden is, *en plein*.' One aspect of Cliveden pleased all, however. Its superb gardens and flower arrangements – glorious views and vistas set off by 'great groups of delphiniums and tuberoses, great bowers of oleander'.[12]

In retrospect, it was the sounds of Cliveden that most poignantly evoked its atmosphere – lawnmowers cutting the grass; the chimes of the clock tower; the whispering of swifts in the eaves, or the soft growls of the two Pekinese, 'Peeky' and 'Sue-Sue'. In the Great Hall, the log fire sputtered day and night. After dark, the night watchman made his rounds, from the cellars to the top landings, at every stage clocking in, moving with a slow, measured tread that made the floorboards creak. Early in the morning, the stable boys could be heard at work. Before first light, the housemaids would begin their day, scrubbing, scouring, dusting, working in haste, knowing that convention required they become invisible before the first guests appeared. At precisely nine o'clock Lee struck the gong. Reverberating like thunder it crashed to a climax, imperceptibly rolling and fading away, summoning the guests for breakfast. It signalled that their day had formally begun.

The Astors began their day earlier. It commenced with readings from the Bible and Mrs Eddy's magnum opus, *Science and Health*. Drafted into attending these doctrinal sessions, the children, lacking their parents' fervour, preferred Nancy's light-hearted, humorous ways of inculcating religion to Waldorf's sterner, more uncompromising methods. After 'doing the lesson', Nancy took her cold bath, performed her physical exercises, touching her toes or standing on her head, before moving on to her daily chores. She would arrange the day's menus with the chef, Monsieur Gilbert, issue instructions to Mrs Addison, the housekeeper, and consult with Lee. While Waldorf attended to his administrative duties, running the estate, Nancy, the busy parliamentarian, spent her mornings answering letters, drafting speeches, responding to petitions – usually seeking Waldorf's counsel in these matters – her paperwork constantly interrupted by the telephone. Cliveden-style house parties – almost a weekly occurrence – had also to be structured: guest lists drawn up, invitations despatched. Five o'clock tea, taken in the Great Hall, was generally considered one of the highlights of the day. Nancy would then read *Uncle Remus* stories to the children, acting out the different characters, reserving for each of them a distinct, authentic accent.

The estate's social life centred on its club and recreation rooms, located in the complex that had housed the Canadian war hospital. It boasted its own bar, billiard room, kitchen, stage and piano. There were also distractions on the river, good fishing, or punting and pleasure steamers by Boulter's Lock. On Saturdays, Cliveden's football or cricket teams defended its reputation from its neighbours and rivals. Lee, it was recalled, stood out, raffish in his whites and blue peaked cap. After the game, high tea would be served to all.

But the climax to the Cliveden season came at Christmas. Visitors, family and friends would be greeted by Lee and his footmen at the front entrance; but no less by the 'delicious Cliveden smell' that permeated the house, an incense-like aroma that emanated from scattered pots of humea (a plant, now rare, adorned by a feathery cascade of reddish-brown flowers). Once settled in their quarters, Nancy, dressed neatly in a sweater over a white silk shirt, a tweed skirt, golf socks and ghillie shoes, would commence her duties as hostess. By custom, the local bell-ringers and carol-singers would announce themselves and render their specialities, 'The Blue Bells of Scotland' or 'See Amid the Winter Snow'. On Christmas Day the festivities began in earnest, lasting from breakfast to midnight. The Great Hall was lavishly decorated. A sparkling Christmas tree stood at the foot of the oak staircase, festoons of evergreens and flowers scattered everywhere. It resembled 'Harrods or Selfridges', piles of presents littered over the chairs, sofas and carpets, or stacked on trays and baskets. Some presents were of special note – David Astor once received a live pony from his stepbrother, Bobby Shaw. The present-giving ceremony lasted until eleven o'clock, when those who felt so inclined trooped off to church. Lunch was served at one. The party, generally not less than thirty in number, ate at times in accordance with one of Nancy's quaint rulings: only one plate was to be used for all courses, a saving that would ease the work of the kitchen staff. In the afternoon there were walks in the grounds or team games on the lawn below the terrace, 'French and English' or 'Flags', Nancy adapting the rules to her fluctuating circumstances. After tea, all would assemble in the Library for some light entertainment, often with Ruth Draper, the American solo performer, parodying the plight of a Scottish immigrant on Ellis Island or the airs of a typical French dressmaker.

These scenes were preparations to the finale of the day, the traditional Christmas dinner – turkey, plum pudding, sweets, coffee and crackers – but in fancy dress. So began 'a characteristic Astorian evening of dance and song all jumbled up in a rollicking way', casual and frivolous. Most of the company would appear as run-of-the-mill Arabs, cowboys, apaches, pirates or gypsies. Not Nancy. She sought to catch the eye, striking poses, playing to the gallery, always theatrical, often melodramatic. Perhaps she would assume the role of 'a Virginian belle'; or of an immaculately attired *nouveau riche* huntsman, badgered by his imaginary wife, 'Rosie'; or, aided by her 'prop' plastic teeth, of an upper-crust English lady, snobbish, arrogant, condescending. Her take-off of a racing tout was a particular hit, however insensitive and indecorous. Miming the face of 'a low-caste Jew', she would strut around clad in an ill-fitting jacket, waistcoat, and black and white check trousers, field glasses slung over her shoulder, a small bowler hat stuck on her head, 'an extraordinary figure'. Charades would follow. The carpet was rolled up in the Library, the records turned on, to form an improvised stage for Nancy. Chattering incessantly, her timing perfect, her accents accurately pitched, she would flesh out her characters. The results were 'uproarious'.

At the estate Christmas dance, another fancy-dress affair but for the employees, Nancy would have been hard pressed to maintain her star billing. Rose's portrayal of 'Little Orphan Annie' triggered gasps of admiration. But it was Arthur Bushell, Waldorf's valet, who threw all caution to the wind. Cunningly made up as Nellie Wallace, wearing lorgnettes and a preposterous hat, he would conclude his wholly convincing sketch by brazenly displaying his 'green knickers with a Union Jack on the behind' to Nancy. Nancy was not amused: 'Arthur, you're disgusting.' At about midnight, the revellers retired to bed, but not before a hearty singsong, mainly of folk songs and spirituals, to banjo accompaniment.

There could be no doubt who was the driving force behind these fun and games. Nancy, it was said, presided over her balls and dinner parties and weekends like 'a blend between Juno at the seige of Troy, and one of the leading Valkyries caracoling over an appropriate battlefield'. She herself once said, in her southern accent, '"Ah' don' care. I'm a Virginian; I shoot to kill."' Bobby Shaw, watching his mother practise golf shots, put it more elegantly: 'This house is like a huge liner and that little woman is the rudder.'[13]

After his official involvement in the Indian and Irish settlements – where he could be said to have commanded tangible political influence – Lionel Curtis's public life shifted into a different gear. Now firmly based at All Souls and Chatham House, he volunteered his services whenever he deemed it necessary, reverting to his preferred role as an *éminence grise*, prodding, initiating, persuading, inspiring, consolidating his reputation as a guru among those who were fired by his visions of a New Commonwealth and World Union. A natural-born fidget, he would not willingly succumb to the lures of academic detachment. Instead, he went off campaigning – or 'stunting', as it was charitably called – to proselytize the unconverted.

Invited to give a series of lectures to the Williamstown Institute of Politics, Curtis spent the spring and summer of 1922 in the United States. Aided by Kerr, who was already in America, they sought to foster Anglo-American relations. Aspiring to forge a common world-policy, they argued in particular that both powers should now wield in concert the naval supremacy that had once been Britain's alone. They set out to establish a network of study groups to propagate these views. But the response was negligible. An aversion to foreign entanglements was deep-rooted in the United States, as was suspicion of machiavellian-like operators from Westminster embroiling the United States in matters contrary to American interests.

However, the lectures at Williamstown (later published as *The Prevention of War*) went down rather better. Tracing American history from the Covenant of the Pilgrim Fathers at Massachusetts Bay to the present Federation of the United States, it concluded that war, an ordained outcome of the 'anarchy of national sovereignties', could only be avoided by the establishment of a world Commonwealth, a community based on the ideals of freedom and liberty, the true goals of humanity. According to the *Boston Evening Transcript*, the final address, 'A Criterion of Values in International Affairs', received 'favourable and enthusiastic comment'. It was pure Curtis. Elaborating on the link between religion and politics, he argued that 'human intelligence guided by conscience' was the only real yardstick to adopt in the conduct of foreign relations. He then went on to outline the 'defect' of the British Empire. Governed from London and not subject to laws deriving from the common consent of all its peoples, it must either change from an Empire into an authentic Commonwealth, or perish. But he anticipated an even more apocalyptic outcome: should the Commonwealth collapse, 'the peace of the world would fall in unspeakable ruin'.

After America, it was the turn of tropical Africa. Safeguarding native rights, promoting industry and commerce among backward peoples, drawing up principles of trusteeship for Crown Colonies and Protectorates, or devising alternative measures of responsible government, were among the many causes that consumed Curtis. One of the founders of the Commonwealth Trust, he also set up a Chatham House African study-group, bodies whose aim was to provide answers for these problems. Curtis found it hard to impose his ideas. One key proposal, to transfer three southern African protectorates to the Union, was emphatically quashed. Other experts, better versed in African affairs than he, intervened. Margery Perham, then Reader in Colonial Government at Oxford and his chief adversary in this matter, although impressed by his 'splendid head' and 'almost mystical aura', also recalled her sense of *lèse-majesté* whenever she disagreed with him – which she often did. It proved to be Curtis's last African 'stunt'.

From Africa, Curtis descended upon the International Settlement in Shanghai. Here he spotted 'the central knot' in the Chinese imbroglio. Curtis would untangle it. How? By endowing the Settlement with the benefits of popular government, free speech and an independent press. In this manner, he sought to introduce the theories and practice of responsible government in China, while at the same time preserving British commercial interests. To advance these goals he mustered a parliamentary China lobby and manipulated his contacts in the Foreign Office. In fact, Curtis knew nothing about China. His romantic notions of Commonwealth harmony were far removed from the reality of China's infinitely complex problems. Most China pundits viewed his ideas as completely hare-brained. Bill Astor, the Astors' eldest son, who served as Curtis's secretary on his Pacific travels, reported on one speech that had traced Commonwealth doctrine from Aristotle and Moses to the League of Nations. 'No one could quite follow him in his flights,' Bill Astor revealed, 'but they were all profoundly impressed.' On another occasion, in Shanghai, Curtis pontificated: 'Can anyone dream, as I dream, of all nations knit in one robe for the infinite Mind and not rejoice that such stuff as China produces is in store for His loom?' Invoking the name of the Almighty was unlikely to appeal to the hard-headed merchants, mainly British and American, who dominated the Shanghai Municipal Council.

Curtis's 'stunting', in particular his preoccupation with China, upset some of the Round Tablers. Edward Grigg, one his severest critics, wrote of 'Lionel's . . . political religion called the Principle of Commonwealth'. Having 'failed magnificently' to implement his principle 'for the whole Empire', he was 'now busy evangelizing Gentiles all over the earth'. Grigg warned: 'If we do not bring *The Round Table* back to its imperial mission it will soon be nothing but a subsidiary and washy branch of the Institute of International Affairs.' Curtis was impervious to this kind of criticism. An indefatigable 'stunter', the challenge of unravelling his 'central knot' spurred him forward, regardless. This whole exercise was, as his biographer has put it, the *'reductio ad absurdum* of [his] constitution-mongering'. In the event, it was the Japanese conquest of Manchuria and the assault on Shanghai in February 1932 that put paid to Curtis's 'evangelizing'. He did, however, publish a monograph in which he disarmingly confessed that although he had previously 'taken no particular interest' in China, he now thought it 'a problem second in importance to no other'.

Curtis's quest for 'the infinite Mind' in international affairs may be seen as a reflection of his current work-in-progress, *Civitas Dei*, an attempt, by way of a vast historical sweep, to mirror on Earth the Kingdom of God: only by transcending the constraints of nationalism, by fostering the growth of *His* Commonwealth principles, would a new, and worthier, world order emerge. This project was to engage him until the late 1930s.[14]

While Curtis was bustling about Africa and the Far East, Bob Brand's reputation as an international banker prospered.[15] As managing director of Lazard Brothers, a director of Lloyds Bank and other companies, he cut a leading figure in the City, his expertise much in demand. His main concern was the reconstruction of Europe: how to revive its economy and ensure its financial stability, while, most important of all, assessing how the ramifications of these aims would affect the state of Britain? In September 1920 he was among the initiators of an international financial gathering convened in Brussels under the auspices of the League of Nations. Its chief purpose was to deal with questions of currency and rates of exchange. As vice-president of the conference, Brand strove to bring it to a successful outcome. His keynote speech was generously received. Congratulated by everyone, sought out by journalists, he was subject to 'a great deal of réclame'. But the conference eventually petered out, owing to the great powers' refusal to sanction any discussion about the vital issues of reparations and inter-allied war debts.

Two years later Smuts persuaded Brand to represent South Africa at the Genoa conference. Lloyd George's brainchild to cure Europe's economic malaise, it too ended in failure. All the outstanding stumbling-blocks remained in place: German reparations; war debts; the integration of the Soviet Union into the European economy. When, in August 1922, the British government proposed the so-called Balfour Note as a way out of the impasse, Brand hesitated. On the surface, it read as a magnanimous offer: an all-round cancellation of inter-allied debts, with the proviso that Britain would collect from her former allies only enough to pay its war debts to America. Brand thought the Note harmful, mainly because it would ultimately result in Germany 'increasing her exports against ourselves', damaging British economic recovery. But as the United States refused to underwrite this proposal, it remained a dead letter.

These issues sustained Brand's relationship with Keynes. In general, they were at one in their thinking about post-war reconstruction and Britain's place in it. Both men thought France bull-headed, both opposed a punitive reparations policy, and both would have preferred an unconditional cancellation of allied war debts. Both were also horrified at Baldwin's settlement of the American debt, yielding casually to Bank of England orthodoxy and United States pressure. Typically, Keynes was 'shocked', while Brand thought it 'unwise and unprofitable'. Though different in temperament, and mixing in different social circles – Keynes among the Bloomsberries, Brand among the Clivedenites – their professional friendship prospered. Always sympathetic, Brand, tough-minded and of practical bent, proved to be an ideal foil to Keynes's fertile genius. Together with Keynes, Brand was a regular member of the Tuesday Club, a cluster of select economists and bankers who dined monthly at the Café Royal to discuss post-war financial problems. 'Formidably clever on paper, but lacking in self-confidence', noted one participant of Brand. Brand was also invited to attend a seminar that Keynes ran for the Liberals, an industrial inquiry that convened at Churt, Lloyd George's country estate, or at King's College, Cambridge.

Brand was a traditional Liberal. Critical of Keynes's 'abandonment' of *laissez-faire*, he was far less interventionist in outlook. Favouring a free market economy, individual enterprise and the profit motive, he accorded government only a modest role in regulating the economy. When they disagreed, Keynes, on occasion, was not above heeding his advice. Over the return to the Gold Standard in 1925 they found no room for compromise. Keynes opposed it. Brand recognized the move as 'defective', but he preferred it to relying 'entirely on the skill and economic knowledge of bankers harassed by politicians'. One observer has noted that their relationship generated 'creative tension', a factor that animated the sessions of the powerful MacMillan Committee on Finance and Industry set up in November 1929. Keynes dominated its proceedings. Brand, as usual, was 'swayed' but not 'converted' by his brilliant expositions. As these were inevitably based on the experience of the 1920s, its recommendations, in any case cautious, were largely overtaken by the repercussions of the world economic crisis. Ironically perhaps for Brand, its Report, bearing Keynes's imprint, paved the way for a managed currency in the coming decades.

Throughout these years Brand was heavily involved in German affairs. He was a regular visitor to Germany. Periodically called upon to advise the German government in an official capacity, he also had Lazard's investments to protect. After the great crash of 1929 Brand was instrumental in setting up the *Stillhalteabkommen* (Standstill agreement), a mechanism designed to stabilize the Germany economy and in the process to lift the world economy out of depression. By it, merchant banks, including Lazard's, agreed to freeze withdrawals of the short-term loans they had made to Germany, hoping to redeem their investments at a later date. Brand moved in the highest circles, hobnobbing with ministers, senior government officials, and leading bankers. Naturally, his chief concern was professional. But more than any of the Cliveden circle he became familiar with the darker aspects of Germany's political culture, a fact that separated him from his less perceptive friends.

In the autumn of 1922 Brand was invited to join a commission of experts to advise on currency reform in Germany. Sacrificing a pheasant shoot for the sake of the German mark, he travelled to Berlin with Keynes, a co-member. Perhaps not unexpectedly, the arrival on the scene of a group of experts caused the mark to spin out of control. Brand found everything 'very difficult'. Currency problems were 'the devil. I often feel out my depth in them.' He wrote to Phyllis, 'All they [the Germans] hope is that we shall lend them money & we shan't.' Nor did the committee's work go smoothly. Keynes was one problem. Brand harboured no doubts as to 'his extraordinary cleverness'. But his quickness of mind, decoded as intellectual arrogance, stirred up opposition. Far too 'arbitrary & critical', and always wanting to 'rush everyone', he unsettled his colleagues with 'his completely formulated drafts'. Brand intervened, mediating between the warring factions. Eventually, together with Keynes, Gustav Cassel and Jeremiah Jenks (professors from the Universities of Stockholm and Columbia, New York), he signed the commission's majority report. It called for a two-year moratorium on reparations; a balanced budget;

rigorous retrenchment in government spending; and more ruthless techniques in the raising of taxes. Lord D'Abernon, the British ambassador at Berlin, praised it as 'the most important document' of its kind. Unfortunately, he added, 'Creditor and debtor – who agreed in nothing else – agreed in ignoring it.'

In any case, the report was soon overtaken by events. On 11 January 1923, French and Belgian troops occupied the Ruhr basin in an attempt to compel Germany – in default on coal and timber deliveries – to honour its reparations' commitments. This move had disastrous results. The German government urged passive resistance, an act that paralysed the German economy, led to hyperinflation and stimulated extremist political activity. Eventually, Europe as a whole was adversely affected. Britain distanced itself from the Franco–Belgian action, declaring it 'a sanction [un]authorized by the treaty'. The Round Tablers saw it as another telling example of French perversity. Nor, they claimed, was the British government entirely blameless. Its failure to check the French coup was tantamount to abandoning the high moral ground of the British Commonwealth. Brand quickly realized that the old reparations agreement, which in any case he thought 'indefensible', could no longer be revived. He feared that the occupation would lead to 'a prolonged and bitter struggle', a recharged Franco–German nationalist conflict, its outcome impossible to forecast. If, however, the French would regain their senses, would 'ultimately come back to the British view' and accept the principle of 'mediation', 'a satisfactory settlement' could yet be arranged.

Paradoxically, the intemperate French action led to the first substantial appeasements of Germany. Brand's anticipated 'mediation' finally materialized in the form of American and British intervention. New plans were agreed upon. Reparation payments were significantly scaled down and short-term loans, mainly American, were negotiated 'to prime the German pump', all to Germany's distinct advantage. Brand was in touch with the mediators. Unhappy with the French, he was equally aware that the Germans never missed an opportunity to raise 'every sort of difficulty'. Here was another justification to escape from perilous European entanglements back to the relative calm of Empire politics.

These considerations certainly prompted the 'friends' to query the Locarno agreements of 1925, rated by most contemporary commentators as a milestone in the pacification of Europe.* By now Kerr was a free agent,

* The centrepiece of the Locarno treaties, initialled in October 1925 and ratified the following December, was the Anglo-Italian guarantee confirming the inviolability of the German frontiers with France and Belgium, and including German obligations to honour the demilitarization of the Rhineland as set out in the Versailles treaty. Other aspects of the Pact related to arbitration conventions between Germany and Poland, Czechoslovakia, France and Belgium, augmented by French treaties of mutual assistance with Poland and

having resigned from Lloyd George's secretariat in 1921. He was still wrestling with his religious conscience. 'The only solution of our problems, economic & political, is in progress in morals and religion,' he wrote to Brand. 'Politics is really secondary . . . all the great leaders & teachers of mankind [unnamed in the text] have seen this, & have concentrated their efforts in the realm of ideas, rather than of practical politics.'[16] Still, he returned full-time to his duties as a Round Tabler, 'mooting', expounding on imperial affairs, travelling widely in the Dominions and the United States, a perk allowed him as secretary of the Rhodes Trust, a post he retained until 1939. He greeted the Locarno treaties with a piercing critique tempered by the faintest of praise. 'Pregnant with hope', they were also 'pregnant with danger, and even disaster, both for Europe and especially for the British Commonwealth'. Kerr thought the guarantee a most extraordinary act, overriding the traditional tenets of British foreign policy. More binding than any other previous commitment, it was an undertaking 'not to make peace but to go to war'. Conjuring up a domino–type effect, he feared that Britain, because of its pledges in the West, would be dragged into a needless war in eastern Europe.

And what of the Empire? By virtue of the ill-starred guarantee, Kerr presumed that its frontiers had been extended into the heart of Europe, a condition that would lead to 'immense difficulties both with the Dominions and the United States'. Here, in effect, was a 'tremendous blow' to the diplomatic unity of the British Commonwealth, of the English-speaking world. Smuts elaborated: Locarno had given added impetus to the 'natural and inevitable centrifugal tendencies at work in the Empire', it sowed the 'seeds of dissension and division'. Where would this ruinous process end, asked Kerr.

In Printing House Square, Geoffrey Dawson asked similar questions, in contrast to his foreign editor, Francis Williams, who believed that Locarno was an 'exceptional opportunity' that Britain 'should grasp . . . with both hands'. Suspicious of French intentions, uneasy at the thrust of German policy towards the Soviet Union – as seen by the Rapallo treaty and closer commercial and military arrangements between the two countries – Dawson hesitated. Apprehensive that the new settlement would lead Britain into unilateral action or would trap the Dominions into uncalled-for commitments, he feared the possible break-up of the Empire. He raised the most pertinent of questions: 'Are we a single unit for purposes of diplomacy? Or half a dozen separate units? How far can one nation commit its partners to the obligations which it has undertaken for itself?' Wholly bound to imperial harmony, Dawson protested at binding Britain, or the Empire, to enforcing blanket guarantees in Europe.[17]

Czechoslovakia. To cap the deal, Germany was scheduled to join the League of Nations.

Dawson and Kerr had posed questions of cardinal importance for the future of the Empire. Austen Chamberlain, the Foreign Secretary and one of the architects of the treaty, dispelled these speculations. Neither the Dominions nor India were bound by the treaty, he clarified. Nor, should an emergency arise, could Britain mark time in the hope that a joint Empire policy would eventually emerge: there would then be a need to act swiftly, even independently. But the decisive rebuttal was given at the Imperial Conference that convened in London in the autumn of 1926. Balfour's formula, accepted by the Conference (and given legal effect in the Statute of Westminster of 1931), recognized Britain and the Dominions as 'autonomous communities . . . equal in status, in no way subordinate one to another in any aspect of their domestic or external affairs, though united by a common allegiance to the Crown and freely associated as members of the British Commonwealth of Nations'. This was a far cry from the coordination of imperial policy, from the 'diplomatic unity' that Kerr and Dawson and their friends sought. But General Hertzog, Prime Minister of South Africa, left London entirely satisfied. Prior to the Conference, the very word 'imperial' avowedly stank in his nostrils. Now he deduced that 'the old Empire no longer existed'. The conception of it masquerading as a sort of super-State had been finally scotched. All that remained was 'a free alliance of England and the six Dominions cooperating as friends'. 'National freedom' for South Africa, and its sister Dominions, had finally been achieved.[18]

Curtis's vision of an Imperial Parliament was rapidly fading. Disheartened but unbowed, he persevered in his Commonwealth-building crusade, refusing to concede defeat. Kerr and Dawson were more flexible. While resisting all manifestations of nationalism that might weaken the Empire, Dawson thought it wise of the Conference not to have laid down an imperial constitution, an exercise that would surely have stretched the forbearance of its participants to breaking point. He viewed the Empire as a kind of League, its members bound together by long-standing historical, cultural, political and commercial interests, working together in a common cause. There was simply no point in defining precisely contentious issues such as the meaning of 'dominion status' or the consequences of the 'right of secession'. At this stage, he and Kerr were in general agreement – though Kerr's opinions were often suspect, particularly when under pressure from Curtis. Ever since his Canadian tour of 1909 Kerr had been sensitive to the claims of dominion nationalism. Provided there was true equality between the Dominions and Britain, and a genuine partnership emerged, he was content.[19]

But Locarno remained, menacing the cohesion of an already frail Empire. By focusing on Europe, it distracted attention away from imperial affairs, disrupting, for the 'friends', a hitherto sacred order of priorities.

Even *The Times* was suspected of trimming its views, perhaps as a result of Dawson's intimacy with Baldwin, the prime minister. At a weekend at Cliveden, the Astors, together with Kerr – who guided them in foreign affairs – and Tom Jones – then Deputy Secretary to the Cabinet – pounced upon Robert Barrington-Ward, Dawson's assistant editor, stressing 'the shortcomings' of his paper's editorial policy, charging it with being 'much too subservient to the Foreign Office . . . and conventional club view'. Austen Chamberlain, the Foreign Secretary, was rightly suspected of being a Francophile. Would his warm feelings for France drag Britain, and the Empire, into uncharted European conflicts? For Kerr and his friends, France was the bogeyman of Europe. There was an almost paranoid fear that scheming French politicians would embroil Britain in disputes at variance with its genuine interests. France, pronounced Kerr in November 1928, 'has no real belief in the possibility of European problems being settled peacefully, and is doing everything she can to get us into an entente which is really anti-German, though labelled "Locarno"'.[20] It was truly a case of *la perfide France*.

Nancy stayed in the public eye, unable or unwilling to avoid the spotlight. In Parliament, she maintained her reputation for 'bustin' loose at times'. Her battles on behalf of temperance, women's and children's rights and social issues persisted. Conducted with splendid panache, they often paid off. Foreign affairs were another matter. Whenever she ventured into this sphere 'you would be likely to hear a good many surprising and unverified assumptions'. Nancy possessed many essential qualities for a successful politician. Independent of spirit, an energetic, original electioneer, capable of a bruising work-rate, she ensured her campaigns were never dull. A natural speaker, she would punctuate her oratory with a down-to-earth common sense, her off-the-cuff wit sufficient to beat down most hecklers. But her failings were also much in evidence. Unsuited for patient investigation and enquiry, she was in too much of a hurry to study political questions in depth. Problems resolved themselves in terms of 'Right' or 'Wrong'. Resolute, she stuck to her convictions, however far-fetched. Impatient and lacking in guile, she reacted instinctively, not conceptually. By 'bustin' loose' and firing off her 'wonderful interruptions', so pleasing to herself, Nancy often infuriated as much as she amused. A mass of contradictions, she was marked down as 'a violently radical Conservative, a recklessly unladylike Lady, a Prohibitionist member of The Trade Party, and all sorts of contradictory things, including (on the authority of the late Speaker) the most turbulent member of the Party of Order'. Periodically, Waldorf would attempt to guide Nancy into calmer waters, but it was a risky business. As Bob Brand once jocularly, but pertinently, noted, they reacted to one another like 'a good animal trainer and a dangerous wild beast'.[21] Ultimately, all this worked against her, ruining her competence and reputation as a parliamentarian.

Nancy's egocentric behaviour, her domineering spirit, her will to possess, bolstered by a careless impetuosity, had its effect on her family circle. Demanding more than she was able to give, her personal relationships were preordained to be one-sided – with Waldorf certainly; but also with his brother John. Although they had signed 'peace terms', it was held that 'the only way they will be peaceful is not to see each other'. Her offspring were particularly susceptible to her managing instincts, their natural intimacy always likely to boil over into a crisis. 'All your children are cases of arrested development,' Jakie once told her. Nowhere was this more apparent than in Nancy's relationship with Bobby Shaw, her eldest son from her first marriage. For Nancy, Bobby stood on a different plane from the other Astor children. Wealthy, handsome, witty, charming, gifted with a sense of the dramatic, he was perfect copy for one of Evelyn Waugh's 'divine young things'. But he could not quite manage his relations with his overbearing mother. Part insider, part outsider at Cliveden, he fashioned a role for himself as its licensed clown, poking fun at everything in his contrived Cockney accent, from Christian Science to the pretensions of the great. He drifted along, with no set purpose in life. He took to drink, his room at Cliveden known as its 'speakeasy'. Also, in a more strait-laced age, he had to contend with his homosexuality. Unable to cope, he self-destructed. Forced to resign his commission in the Royal Horse Guards, the 'Blues' – whether from being caught in a homosexual act or from being drunk on duty, or both, is unclear – Bobby was picked up by the police in July 1931 and charged with soliciting. Sentenced, he served four months. The downward spiral continued. Drinking heavily, he sank into depression, Joyce Grenfell sadly noting how his conversation, once so sparkling, now 'pervades and fouls the atmosphere'. He developed suicidal tendencies. In 1966, two years after Nancy's death, he took his own life. Typically, Bobby wrote his own epitaph: 'I've had a very full, empty life.'[22]

Michael Astor remembered the Cliveden of his childhood as 'a place of lyrical beauty'. But behind its 'brilliant social façade' he came to see another world, one of 'moral abjuration', a world 'united uneasily by the voice of parental authority', a world he found 'increasingly stultifying', a world from which he was 'determined to escape'. If Bobby was an extreme case, all the Astor children, in their own way, reacted against these pressures, their paths smoothed by the financial independence bequeathed them by their grandfather. Bill, heir to the title and estate, took to a strained conformism, as 'a cultivated official . . . who comprehended the mysteries of family institutions, of ritual and rite';[23] David, to parading radical, left-wing tendencies, betraying, in Nancy's view, his class and position. Michael, with his artistic and literary leanings, opted for a bohemian lifestyle; Jakie, nicknamed 'Jokie', high-spirited and sharp of wit, took to out-clowning Nancy; and the only daughter, Nancy Phyllis Astor, 'Wissie', married out. All rejected Christian Science. Three of the brothers, Bill, Michael and Jakie, took their seats on the Conservative benches in the Commons, though none flourished politically. On the other hand, David's career as a distinguished journalist prospered. Eventually, he succeeded Garvin as editor of the *Observer*, an appointment that brought distinction to the paper but that thoroughly exasperated Nancy, its advanced views so much out of tune with her brand of conservatism.

Bobby's arrest was a traumatic experience for the Astors, particularly for Nancy. Hushed up in the press, it passed off without public scrutiny. Some days later, they left on a much publicized visit to the Soviet Union.[24] The party included their nineteen-year-old-son David; Lord Lothian (Kerr had succeeded as the 11th Marquess in March 1930); another Christian Scientist, Charles Tennant; and Maurice Hindus, an American Jewish author, the only one of the party who spoke Russian. Its star attraction, however, was the Astors' close friend George Bernard Shaw, a self-styled Communist. The trip had originated with an invitation to Shaw by the Soviets to celebrate his seventy-fifth birthday in Moscow. Charlotte, his wife, unable to accompany him for health reasons, arranged that some friends, the Astors, should chaperone him. Shaw readily fell in with the idea, perhaps, as has been suggested, because his mischievous spirit told him that such august company would shock and confound both the Soviets and left-wing observers the world over. 'Nancy, I do trust you,' Charlotte wrote.'You will take the right sort of care of him, & *not let him do too much*! It will be difficult: but if anyone can keep him in hand *you* can!' So, according to Churchill, began 'a merry harlequinade' featuring 'the World's most famous intellectual Clown and Pantaloon in one, and the charming Columbine of the capitalist pantomime'. Stalin, he noted cuttingly, pushed aside 'his morning's budget of death warrants, and *lettres de cachet*' to receive his guests 'with smiles of overflowing comradeship'.

It was at all times difficult to upstage Shaw: by second nature, he grabbed the limelight whenever possible. But Nancy, fusing the compassionate side of her nature with her intimidating outspokenness, was more than a match for him. Her head full 'of Bolshevik horrors', Nancy told her hosts: 'I am a Conservative. I am a Capitalist. I am opposed to Communism. I think you are all terrible.' When not 'mothering' Shaw, she was 'flirting' with Ionov, an official of the State Publishing House, who was attached to the delegation as its senior guide, trying to convert him to Christian Science; or else she would tease Anatoly Lunacharsky, a former

Commissar for Education, accusing all Soviet leaders of being 'aristocrats', a charge which did not 'wholly displease them'. She comforted a group of bare-footed women, conscripted labour working as railway navvies. In an impromptu speech, perched on the roof of a lorry, she 'stood right up for capitalism' to a crowd of factory workers, 'but made no converts'. She visited welfare centres for children and danced with young members of the Communist youth movement at a Pioneer Camp, later reprimanding Stalin that his wards were 'too clean, too perfectly drilled and managed'. She and Shaw had been canvassed by Dmitri Krynin (a Russian counter-revolutionary currently teaching at Yale University) to intervene with the Soviet authorities in the hope that they would permit his wife to join him in America. Shaw declined. But Nancy presented her petition 'on bended knee'. 'Most humbly I pray you in the name of humanity to save this suffering family.' Coldly indifferent to Nancy's plea, Litvinov answered: 'This matter is not within my jurisdiction.'

On 31 July Shaw was invited to meet Stalin at the Kremlin. Refusing to go alone, he insisted that the Astors and Lothian accompany him. The interview lasted two and half hours, with Litvinov and an interpreter also in attendance. Nancy, at least, was not overawed by the occasion. She went for a 'grim' Stalin – who stood there, clad in a dark tunic and black knee-length boots – 'like a steamroller', harping on the savagery of the Soviet regime and its regimented methods of education. She would not be intimidated. 'The attempt to abash and silence Lady Astor was about as successful as an effort by a fly to make head against a whirlwind,' recalled Shaw, not above adding a dramatic flourish of his own in his account of the encounter. 'How long do you think you will have to go on ruling by Tzarist methods?' Nancy demanded. The interpreter, naturally reluctant to translate so provocative a question, hesitated; but Shaw insisted. Stalin responded: 'What do you mean?' Nancy told him: no habeas corpus; exiling political dissidents to Siberia; the lack of freedom of expression and accepted democratic procedures. 'When peace comes we shall stop it,' Stalin promised, 'when we have achieved the full aims of our revolution,' reminding the audience of Cromwell's example and his treatment of the Irish. As for regimented education, he asked coolly when the English were going to stop beating their young as part of their education. Questioned by Waldorf about the enormous Soviet military establishment, Stalin retorted: 'The Poles have a large army and, anyhow, how do I know that Winston Churchill won't come back to power again?' His English guests assured him that there was no possibility whatsoever of the veteran anti-Bolshevik fighter making a political comeback. And with all respect to the Poles, surely the Red Army was not frightened of the Polish cavalry? Shaw 'scented the soldier and the ecclesiastic, certainly not the cobbler' in Stalin's performance. Waldorf noted: 'He has a clear rather kindly eye . . .

1. Approaching the Forecourt at Cliveden from the Shell Fountain down the Grand Avenue.

2. A view of Cliveden from the south-west corner of the parterre.

3. Nancy Astor relaxing at Cliveden.

4. The Great Hall. Note Sargent's portrait of Nancy over the sixteenth–century fireplace.

5. Waldorf Astor running his Cliveden estate.

6. 'Now look here . . .': Nancy Astor campaigning at the elections of November 1923.

7. The Kindergarten:
(*standing, left to right*) Robert Brand, Herbert Bauer, Lionel Hitchens; (*middle row*) Hugh Wyndham, Richard Feetham; Lionel Curtis, Patrick Duncan, J. F. Perry, Dougal Malcolm; (*front row*) John Dove, Philip Kerr, Geoffrey Robinson (Dawson).

8. Chatham House in committee: 'standing orders count'. Lionel Curtis second from right.

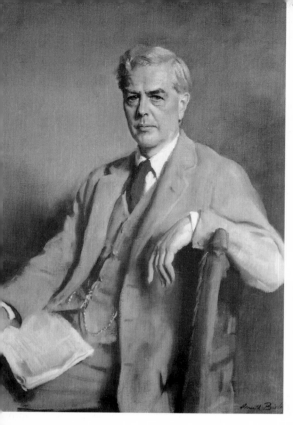

9. Lionel Curtis, 'The Prophet'.

10. Geoffrey Dawson (*left*) and Robert Barrington Ward of *The Times*, editing the news.

11. Robert Brand (*sitting on the right*), the international financier, aware of the darker aspects of Nazi culture.

12. Lord Lothian (Philip Kerr): the reawakening.

13. (*Left*) Lord Halifax, the Foreign Secretary. An honorary member of the 'Set' on his way to Geneva to settle foreign affairs.

14. (*Below left*) Jan Christian Smuts advising from afar.

15. (*Below right*) Lord Lothian (Philip Kerr) teeing off.

16. Claud and Patricia Cockburn, practising 'preventive journalism'.

17. 'The Shiver Sisters'. Dancers from left to right: J. Garvin of the *Observer*, Nancy Astor, Geoffrey Dawson of *The Times*, and Lord Lothian. Joseph Goebbels dictates the rhythm to the tune of German Foreign Policy.

[and] is supposed to owe his position to an iron will and to a close association with Lenin. He seemed shrewd rather than big mentally. He had quite a sense of humour and knew how to parry questions he did not wish to deal with.'

It has been suggested that Shaw's innate sense of theatricality had become 'a habit of mind'. It certainly appeared so. When questioned by a group of eager reporters about the meeting with Stalin, he carefully climbed the marble staircase at the Hotel Metropole, gazed down at the expectant crowd, crossed his arms, paused dramatically, and announced that 'Stalin has splendid black moustaches'. A knockabout performance, it left 'everyone seething'. As if by request, Shaw played to the Soviet gallery. He extolled the Five Year Plan, saw 'the realists in command of the philistines', discovered 'freedom of worship', and concluded that the Soviet Union was 'acting in the interests of civilization'. In Russia, he asserted, 'I have actually been convinced that the new Communist system is capable of leading mankind out of its present crisis, and saving it from complete anarchy and ruin.' Carried away by his own performance, his words swept him well beyond the bounds of good sense. 'I wish we had forced labour in England,' he frivolously noted, 'in which case we would not have 2,000,000 unemployed.'

Shaw's biographer has likened his subject's account of 'Touring in Russia' to a happy fantasy. Although impressed with aspects of their visit, neither the Astors nor Lothian succumbed to Shaw's make-believe world. Lothian was by no means ignorant of the workings of Soviet society and took every opportunity to ferret out further information. Through their journalistic contacts – in particular George Barnes, correspondent for the *New York Herald Tribune* in Moscow – the Astors knew something of the gruesome reality behind the carefully contrived scenes produced for their benefit. After one of Shaw's flightier speeches, Waldorf, low-key as usual, remarked on his 'bad effort'. Concerned with the nuts and bolts of the Soviet system, he pumped his hosts with shrewd questions about the mechanism of state-run industry, its financing, and the draconian experiments in collective farming which had recently been imposed.

On their return to Cliveden, the Astors suffered the worst of both worlds. Castigated by members of their own class as fellow-travellers and traitors, they won no friends on the left with their strictures against Stalin and his regime. This would be a familiar situation. In the coming years they – and their close friends – would be subject to cries of traitors and fellow-travellers from all quarters. Despite this invective, there could be no doubt of one thing. They instinctively distrusted all totalitarian regimes.

CHAPTER 6

Regional Distractions

Shortly after noon on 30 January 1933 Hitler emerged from the Chancellery in Berlin accompanied by the cheers of the expectant crowd. He had just been appointed Chancellor of Germany, the result of a shady backstairs intrigue with the 'Old Gang', a clique of time-serving generals and extreme nationalist politicians. Hitler, it was reckoned, could provide a stable parliamentary majority after the political chaos of recent years.* Tamed by the responsibilities of office, the Austrian upstart would be little more than a tool in the seasoned hands of this shabby crew – or so they reasoned.

Similar misconceptions were commonplace in Britain. The Nazis had begun to receive serious attention in the British press after their startling election successes of September 1930. Now the second party in the country, they had polled 6.4 million votes, gaining 107 seats in the Reichstag. For those weaned on liberal principles there was an inherent difficulty in grasping the true nature of Nazism, of its nihilistic spirit, its emphasis on spurious racial doctrines, its paranoiac anti-Semitism, its power structure. The failure to understand its subservience to the so-called *Führerprinzip* was crucial, as it conveniently separated the behaviour of the Leader from the actions of his followers, particular the unruly and brutal SA, Hitler's private army of street-thugs. Many pundits perceived Hitler as a legitimate, if uncouth, politician being pushed forward by extremist factions in his party. The *Observer* even portrayed him as being 'definitely Christian in his ideals' and anxious to renew his 'country's moral life'. Hinting at undue Jewish influence in Germany, the paper told its readers that Hitler's anti-Semitism was merely 'a blot' on his Christian principles. After a violent Nazi rally at Brunswick that left seventy wounded and three

* The November 1932 elections had left the Nazis as the single largest party in the Reichstag with 196 members, even though they had sustained a loss of 34 seats since the previous elections in July.

dead from SA-inspired street brawls, *The Times* saw fit to comment on this 'remarkable manifestation of organizing power, of discipline, of earnestness, and of confidence', noting Hitler's 'moderation and common sense' as he advanced towards his goal of ruling Germany.

Here, then, was a truly radical movement commanding mass support. And according to the Astor newspapers, the *Observer* and *The Times*, Hitler, 'of moderate outlook', was its 'megaphone', speaking up for the discontented, rallying 'honest and earnest elements' among the 'splendid young people of the German middle classes' to his cause. Moreover, Hitler's avowed goals in foreign policy were entirely defensible. That most favoured statesman of the Weimar Republic, Gustav Stresemann, had been no less concerned to overturn Versailles and restore to Germany its national pride by securing its rightful place as a great European power. These were valid aims, endorsed by the German people and wholly reasonable in the eyes of many foreign observers.

Given this perspective, was it not justifiable, and constitutionally proper, to include the Nazis in a coalition government? *The Times* advised its readers not to put 'too sinister an interpretation' on Nazi electoral gains. Even the liberal *Manchester Guardian*, although writing off Hitler as 'a ranting clown' who 'bangs the drum outside the Nazi circus', took heart from the responsible behaviour of Wilhelm Frick, the first Nazi to assume state office as Minister of the Interior of Thuringia, concluding that the Nazis were 'Ordinary Politicians When in Office'. *The Times* identified common ground between Chancellor Heinrich Brüning's policies and Hitler's ideas, assuming that no German cabinet could survive without the Nazis. But even a Nazi-dominated government, probably an object for 'ridicule' and 'irritation', and perhaps not bound by accepted norms of conduct, would not do 'any real harm'. Only days after Hitler's appointment, the paper hailed his 'sincerity' and 'personal magnetism'. But as he had yet to pass 'the real tests of a ruler', it would be a waste of time 'to speculate about the future of Germany' – or, it might be added, of Europe. 'Hitler', wrote two prominent intellectuals, was not 'yet generally thought of as an enemy; he seemed only an unpleasantly dynamic element in the world, ultimately manageable if the proper tactics were adopted.' But what were the proper tactics, they asked – a question that puzzled most onlookers.[1]

In one way, this qualified optimism about Germany and its future reflected a wider anxiety. Hit hard by the world economic crisis, with millions unemployed and industries at a standstill, most countries, even those firmly rooted in traditional democratic procedures, were seeking unorthodox solutions and spawning extremist movements. Everywhere serious doubts were raised as to whether the old system could survive the emergency. In Britain, Churchill, railing against the maladies of universal suffrage – the most fundamental characteristic of modern democracy – proposed bypassing Parliament by creating a new technocratic body, an 'Economic sub-Parliament' composed of impartial economic experts. Professional, specialist, authoritative, and immune from narrow partisan pressures, it would, by definition, arrive at 'dispassionate or disinterested decisions'. Here was elitism with a vengeance. No scenario was too extravagant to contemplate. Was, as many fantasized, Hitler little more than a Teutonic edition of Ramsay MacDonald? After all, MacDonald – vilified by the extreme left as a crypto-fascist – had split his party, shed its radical elements, and had emerged as the figurehead of a reactionary, Conservative-dominated National Government, his own revolutionary ardour 'killed by kindness', by the fatal embrace of the old ruling orders. By a convoluted leap of the imagination it was possible to transfer this setting to Germany, where Hitler had not seized power but had been constitutionally appointed, and where he too headed a Nationalist Government, sharing authority with the 'Old Gang'.[2]

Of course, not all observers of German politics subscribed to these sentiments. Some took a different line, recognizing the dangers a Nazi Germany posed to Britain and Europe. The most prominent politician to do so was Churchill. Only months after Hitler came to power, convinced that the German dictator would 'resort to armed force' at the first available opportunity, he predicted the 'renewal of a general European war'. But during the 1930s Churchill gained the reputation of an alarmist. His apocalyptic prophecies of impending disaster were listened to with mounting scepticism, caught out by the law of diminishing returns.

Several officials of the Foreign Office were equally perceptive. One outspoken authority was Sir Horace Rumbold, the British ambassador in Berlin from 1928 to 1933. In a series of despatches to London he accurately reported the true nature of the Nazi movement and Hitler's place in it. Hitler's dominance over his party was 'remarkable', he wrote. Its policy was his policy, not that of 'his wilder men'; his every order secured 'instant obedience'. As the Nazis tightened their grip on the country, Rumbold's forebodings deepened. In his well-known 'Mein Kampf' memorandum, he warned that the inner dynamics of Nazism would eventually lead to war. On the eve of his departure from Berlin, Rumbold categorized Hitler, Goering and Goebbels as 'notoriously pathological cases' driven by an 'aggressive nationalism'.

But it was Sir Robert Vansittart, Permanent Under-Secretary at the Foreign Office, who gave voice to the most violent anti-German views. Rumbold's reports were so much grist to his mill. More than any other official Vansittart nurtured the tenet of 'original German sin'. German policy, he summed up, was dedicated to destroying the post-war settlement. Not that he – or Rumbold, for that matter – was indifferent to the humiliations imposed on Germany by the Versailles treaty, of its 'penal provisions', or of the wisdom of revising certain of its clauses. Nor did he stint his criticism of the 'Latin Sisters', Italy and France, censuring strongly their self-serving and vindictive policies. But Vansittart realized at once that the appearance of Hitler, a 'half-mad and ridiculous demagogue', introduced an irrational and explosive factor into the European equation. 'The Nazis are coming,' he cried in January 1932, 'the old German spirit is abroad in plenty.' Immediately upon Hitler's rise to power he wrote of 'these wild men and killers' who, once rearmed, will 'loose off another European war'. In the meantime,

> it will endeavour to cog and lull so as better to eat the artichoke leaf by leaf. This is crude; but we are considering very crude people, who have few ideas in their noddles but brute force and militarism . . . This crude barbarism may of course change its ideas. I don't believe that it will.

Damning though his judgement was, Vansittart did not rule out negotiations with Nazi Germany. As he would argue later, diplomacy could not be conducted by saying 'No' to everything. But if any bargaining were to take place, it must be circumscribed by carefully defined guidelines.[3]

For Vansittart and Churchill, and those of similar outlook, the advent of Hitler fundamentally changed the ground rules. For the Astors, Dawson and Lothian and their following, the reverse was true. They continued to regard a Nazi Germany with much the same 'qualified optimism' they had conceded to the Nazi Party as it undermined the Weimar Republic, their perceptions lingering on well into the 1930s. Their priorities had already been set out by Dawson. His attitude to the German settlement is perfectly clear, and it reflected that of his inner circle. In December 1918, he had castigated Lloyd George's electoral mandate to go to Paris as 'disastrous and wholly unnecessary'. By championing a Carthaginian peace, Lloyd George had sacrificed his principles for sordid political gain, sullying 'his great career'. Dawson, on the other hand, intended to abide by his convictions. First, as an imperialist – this implied no Continental entanglements. A sound enough concept, yet he sensed that it was compromised by the flawed nature of the Versailles treaty. The settlement 'created risks': it invited German hostility. Of course, it could be imposed. But was it morally right to enforce a treaty that Dawson and Company thought indefensible from the outset? And what price would imperial unity have to pay for an interventionist European policy? These questions nagged at their collective conscience. When the French decided to coerce Germany and occupied the Ruhr, the ensuing crisis sharpened the agonizing choice between European obligations and imperial solidarity.

Dawson was outspoken. 'So long as the centre of international friction lies in Europe, London will always be overtaken by the final rush of events before Ottawa.'[4]

For the Dawson–Lothian–Astor circle, revision in the 1920s had come tardily and grudgingly, always overdue, forever lagging behind crises, never anticipating them. In this way they interpreted the rise of Hitler as no less – perhaps more – a function of inept, short-sighted and vengeful allied policies, than as a consequence of economic distress and political machinations in Germany. France – 'the main creator' of National Socialism – bore the heaviest responsibility. Hitler, they believed, was simply an extreme manifestation of German nationalism, conjured up by the victors who had misused a crushed and humiliated Germany. As Lothian told the Scottish Liberals in Edinburgh, Germany had been 'driven to National Socialism'. Dawson concurred. Agreeing with Brand as to the innate barbarity of the Nazi regime, he added, as a matter of course, that it was 'very largely the creation of ourselves and the French in the past'.[5] Here was the Versailles 'guilt complex' writ large. How to expunge it? One way surely was to remove the sting from legitimate German grievances. Logic dictated the compelling need for genuine treaty revision.

Focusing upon the German problem forced upon the 'friends' an awkward choice, though one largely of their own making: how to reconcile European commitment with imperial unity? Their self-imposed duty to sustain and strengthen the Anglo–American axis, that other bedrock of their world outlook, further complicated matters. For one thing, British policy-makers were readjusting their order of priorities. Previously, the Chiefs of Staff had calculated that the main danger to British interests lay in the Far East where they were threatened by Japan's onslaught on China. Now, in February 1934, the Defence Requirements Sub-Committee (DRC), a high-powered interdepartmental committee, concluded that Germany was 'the ultimate potential enemy against whom our "long range" defence policy has to be directed'. As for Japan, it proposed 'an ultimatum policy of accommodation . . . and an immediate policy of "showing a tooth"'. This switch in priorities was supported by leading politicians and civil servants – most notably Neville Chamberlain, then Chancellor of the Exchequer, Sir Samuel Hoare, Secretary of State for India, J. H. Thomas, Colonial Secretary, Sir Warren Fisher, Permanent Under-Secretary at the Treasury, and Sir Robert Vansittart. Ever since the Manchurian crisis of 1931 they had been 'bemoaning the loss of the Anglo-Japanese alliance'.[6]

There was a snag. An Anglo-Japanese rapprochement, almost by definition, would be at the expense of the American connection. This was a price the Japanese-oriented group were prepared to pay. There was some discussion as to the precise cost. Vansittart defined the predicament. He had impressed upon the DRC his hope that any improvement in Anglo-American relations would not be 'thrown away in order to run after the Japanese'. On the one hand, he realized the folly of antagonizing the Americans; on the other, he had no faith that they would ever act vigorously. How, then, to persuade, or coerce, Japan into adopting more pacific policies? Would the Americans ever take concrete measures to stave off a Far Eastern crisis? Recent Anglo-American naval talks had broken down in atmosphere of 'subdued bitterness', the British demand for seventy cruisers leaving the Americans 'appalled', a sure sign that they were blind to British global interests.

The advocates of refashioning the old Anglo-Japanese alliance poured scorn on the United States: left to their own devices, the Americans would never take a firm stand. In prescient mood, Chamberlain said: 'we ought to know by this time that USA will give us no undertaking to resist by force any action by Japan, short of an attack on Hawaii or Honolulu.' Fisher – of whom it was said that he 'hates' the Americans as much as Vansittart 'hates' the Germans – remarked: 'they [the Americans] are no use to us, but make use of us – to our detriment – vis-à-vis Japan'; Vansittart added: 'I still desire as much as ever, that we shall get on well with this untrustworthy race . . . [but] we shall never get very far; they will always let us down . . . In ageing I have lost my wind for running after the United States Government. It is a futile paper chase.'[7]

In this charged atmosphere an attempt was made to promote an Anglo-Japanese agreement. Neville Chamberlain positioned himself as the front runner in this enterprise. Backed by Fisher, and upheld by the conclusions of the DRC, he led a formidable pro-Japanese coalition. In August 1934 he drafted a paper that proposed 'making eyes at Japan'. A non-aggression pact, he suggested, would bolster imperial security, preserve the integrity of China, and restrain Japanese naval building. Justifying his initiative to Sir John Simon, the Foreign Secretary, he spoke of having reached 'one of those crucial points in history'.[8]

Lothian and his group, by independent reasoning, had arrived at the same crossroads, though they chose a different path. Any talk of rebuilding the Anglo-Japanese alliance set off their alarm systems. This policy – consistently resisted by Lothian – had been abandoned at Washington in 1922.* By preserving the American connection and strengthening imperial

---

* Summoned on American initiative, the Washington Conference met from November 1921 until February 1922. Nine powers were represented: Britain, the United States, Japan, China, France, Italy, Belgium, Holland and Portugal. In all, four treaties were concluded. The Anglo-Japanese alliance was brought to an end, replaced by a British–American–Japanese–French guarantee of each other's Pacific territories, with a proviso for joint consultation should their rights be threatened. The Conference also collectively guaranteed China's territorial independence, while Japan agreed to return Kiaochow to China by the Shantung

ties, the Washington agreements were regarded, in the words of Smuts, as 'the greatest step forward yet taken since the Peace on the road to a stable world order'. Why then destroy them? Rumours of an impending Anglo–Japanese rapprochement spurred Lothian on. He saw it as 'both a feeble and a delusive policy'. It would turn over the Far East to Japan, relegating Britain to a minor role in the region, dependent on Japan's good (but non-existent) offices. And it 'would, of course, inevitably split the Empire from top to bottom'.[9]

Lothian would have preferred extending the Washington arrangements. However, as he was well aware, with the militarists in Japan in the ascendancy the margins for compromise were narrow in the extreme; at the same time the stalled Anglo–American naval talks only compounded suspicion on both sides of the Atlantic. There were no pat solutions, as he himself had discovered in America that autumn. He had met the President. As was his wont, Roosevelt had hummed and hawed. But the gist of his cloudy phrases ruled out a joint activist policy. 'Rely on the fact that our ideals and interests [are] fundamentally the same,' he placated Lothian. This was most unsatisfactory. High-flown declarations hardly constituted a credible deterrent, even for Lothian. 'I doubt whether that is enough,' he eventually conceded. Still, despite all evidence to the contrary, he persisted in clinging to this flimsy straw. The Americans, Balfour had once speculated, bound to Britain by a common tradition and political culture, would always come in 'on the right side, late perhaps, but in time'. This was a calculated risk, but one that Lothian was prepared to take since it left him 'fundamentally optimistic'. He candidly admitted that he was not an expert on Asian affairs. But this did not inhibit him from resolving the Far Eastern crisis still shackled to his Atlanticist concepts. He was quite definite. Only Anglo–American cooperation, supported by the Dominions, would 'make the collective system or the Washington principles effective in the Pacific'. 'Together we can succeed; divided we are impotent.'[10]

Lothian worked hard towards this end from the summer of 1934. Perhaps, also, he took heart from a report in *The Times* that stressed Roosevelt's extreme displeasure at the possibility of an Anglo–Japanese deal, inferring that it would hurt American interests. Buoyed up, he told Vansittart that Roosevelt was like 'a tiger in the White House', who, if baited, 'would fight for us in the Far East'. This was highly fanciful, as Lothian well knew. In any case, Vansittart brushed aside Lothian's lively conjectures as nonsense. Not 'a tiger in the White House', but a rabbit in a 'hutch', he minuted. In November, Smuts arrived in London. Scheduled

treaty. Finally, a disarmament convention was signed pledging the signatories to a ten-year naval holiday during which no new capital ships were to be constructed, and establishing between Britain, the United States and Japan a ratio of 5:5:3 for capital ships.

to address St Andrews University on the occasion of his election as its Rector, he was persuaded – by Lothian and Curtis – to lecture also at Chatham House. He took as his theme cooperation between the British Commonwealth and the United States. Any other course, he claimed, 'would mean building our Commonwealth policy on quicksands, and placing the future of this group at the mercy of incalculable hazards'. The Astor papers were drafted into playing their part in this campaign. Lothian, a director of the *Observer*, published a centre-page article setting out his views on the Far Eastern situation, telling Garvin that Smuts saw 'the pro-Japanese and anti-American element all over the place "like a snake in the grass"'. At the same time, Dawson, by arrangement with Lothian, received the text of Smuts's speech and had it reprinted – together with a *Times* editorial – as a pamphlet: by January 1935, it had sold 37,867 copies.[11]

By late 1934 the attempt to obtain a concord with Japan had petered out. It was only natural that Lothian and Smuts and the Round Tablers should grab the credit for killing 'the pro-Japanese movement'. 'My Chatham House speech has served the purpose for which it was intended,' crowed Smuts. Lothian leaked to the Americans that even Neville Chamberlain was weakening. 'Japan could not be trusted,' he reported Chamberlain as saying, 'she was perhaps bluffing and . . . England and the United States must at the proper time take a common stand and call the bluff.' A firm 'common stand' was no less a bluff. As one authority has put it, American policy throughout the 1930s was exceptional in its 'passivity'.[12]

In fact, the initiative died a natural death. Powerful forces in the government were hesitant about coming to any accommodation with Japan. Ramsay MacDonald and a tentative Sir John Simon, backed by the Admiralty – and with Baldwin and Hankey occupying the middle ground – were more than a sufficient counterweight to the Chamberlain–Fisher combination. But probably the chief cause was the Japanese lack of response. Joseph Grew, the well-informed American ambassador in Tokyo, could point to 'no evidence' that 'definite negotiations' had taken place. Riding high on the crest of a hard-line nationalist wave, the Japanese saw no compelling reason to humour their imperial rivals, except on their own (unacceptable) terms. In December, Japan gave notice of its intention to withdraw from the Washington naval agreements. The Far Eastern crisis, muted for the moment, would flare up again in the summer of 1937.

Smuts brought this episode full circle. He impressed upon Lothian that 'It is not only Asia but Europe that should be tackled. We *must* prevent a Japanese-German combination which will be fatal. And this can only be done by ceasing to treat Germany as a pariah.' Lothian needed no persuasion. These sentiments accorded perfectly with his own hopes for drastic treaty revision in Europe.[13]

*

In December 1934, the same month that Japan resolved to quit the Washington agreements, there occurred at Ualual (Wal Wal), a remote watering spot in the Ogaden desert, an armed clash between Italian and Ethiopian troops, both sides incurring casualties. The parties reacted immediately, but pulled in opposite directions. Italy demanded substantial indemnities and a public apology; Ethiopia appealed for justice to the League of Nations, invoking its right under Article 11 of the Covenant to bring before the Council 'any circumstance . . . which threatens to disturb international peace'.

Attention now focused on 'the Ethiopian imbroglio'. Italy's hopes of building a greater Italian empire in East Africa – at Ethiopia's expense – were long-standing and well known, as was Mussolini's determination to fulfil them. The Wal Wal incident was seen as his first step, for although the Ethiopian-Italian Somaliland border had never been accurately demarcated, the wells lay at least fifty miles deep inside Ethiopian territory. Here was a model case of creeping annexation. For Britain, the threat was twofold. By 1934, Libya was firmly under Italy's control, Mussolini having brutally crushed the Senusi insurrection. It required little imagination to envisage Egypt and the Suez Canal yielding to an Italian pincer movement, the British position in the eastern Mediterranean and the Arab East falling victim to Mussolini's quest for empire.

This affair could not fail to be of vital concern to the 'friends'. Lothian put it bluntly on more than one occasion. Mussolini would exploit the first opportunity created by an international crisis 'to seize the Sudan, Egypt, the Suez Canal, Palestine and the Arabian hinterland as the beginning of a new Roman Empire'. Imperial communications would be cut; the unity of the Commonwealth would be put at risk. Mussolini would impose his primacy on these highly sensitive areas.[14]

Initially, Fascist Italy benefited from a considerable groundswell of sympathy, even admiration, among foreign observers, assiduously fostered by Mussolini's propaganda machine. 'Yes, I agree that Mussolini is most impressive,' conceded Dawson. 'No one can go there without being struck by what he has done,' and in justification he deployed that most hackneyed of clichés: 'The trains run and the streets are swept.' Dawson was not alone. Even Churchill felt free to refer to Mussolini as that 'Roman genius . . . the greatest lawgiver among men'. The Moot's collective mind was equally well-disposed. Some were even prepared to tolerate Mussolini's imperial ambitions, providing they could be channelled into distant waters, remote from British interests. At one time Lothian tended to play down Italy's martial spirit, electing to blame the primitive condition of Ethiopia, its feudal regime and unbridled slave trading as the main danger to peace.[15]

As the crisis developed, doubts began to creep in. Dawson warned of foreign adventures, 'the course of all dictators'. With the League playing a greater role, other questions, hedged since the peace settlement, re-emerged. For Lothian and Curtis the League, at its conception, was greeted as the first phase in that Manichean struggle between 'national sovereignty' and a 'new world order'. As the results of the Paris Peace Conference became apparent, their mood changed. The League emerged as a badly flawed body, its failings highlighted by Congress's refusal to ratify the Treaty and the Covenant. Was the Covenant an effective instrument in resolving international disputes, they asked: Should the League fail to live up to its high expectations, they warned that its credibility would be fatally damaged. As usual, Lothian put the general view. The United States, he explained, had opted out because it had grasped the true significance of the Covenant's purpose.* 'None of the democracies of the British Empire' had been as prescient. Had they shown the same foresight, they would have repudiated it 'at once', and would do so 'if put to the test'. There was an urgent need to remould the League, to tone down its obligations, to tailor its commitments to its capacity to implement them. Above all, it was necessary to ensure that America became a full partner in the League's activities.[16]

None of this happened. If anything, the situation grew progressively worse. After the illusory heyday of the Locarno period, the League fell into steady decline. Japan and Germany had quit the organization, losses only partially compensated by the admission of the Soviet Union. At any rate, three great powers were no longer subject to the League's rulings, a fact of international life that placed a formidable burden upon Britain and France. Having failed to make any impact during the Manchurian crisis, or even to intervene effectively during the so-called 'Chaco war' – a protracted border dispute between Bolivia and Paraguay that flared up on and off between 1928 and 1935 – the League's handling of the Ethiopian imbroglio would be its last chance to prove its worth. Dawson, taking the most insular of views, was not optimistic. Quoting with approval '[his] plumber who didn't hold with the League of Nations because there were too many

---

* For Lothian's friends the 'true significance' was a function of the apparent contradiction between articles 16 and 19. The former article states unequivocally that should a member state resort to war 'it shall *ipso facto* be deemed to have committed an act of war against all other members of the League'. In which case, economic and financial sanctions would be implemented immediately, together with 'the prohibition of all intercourse . . . [with] the nationals of the covenant-breaking State'. Should these measures not suffice, it would be the duty of the Council to recommend military sanctions 'to be used to protect the Covenant of the League'. The latter clause called for 'the reconsideration . . . of treaties which have become inapplicable and the consideration of international conditions whose continuance might endanger the peace of the world'. The 'friends' placed great weight on all aspects of treaty revision. Redressing 'legitimate grievances' would lessen the likelihood of the League having to impose the sanctions article, an eventuality for which it was unprepared.

146 · *The Cliveden Set*

foreigners in it', he asked Nancy, why can't 'our statesmen develop a British point of view'? Nancy, who took her cue in foreign affairs from others, would in any case have agreed.[17]

But was there 'a British point of view'? In June, Anthony Eden arrived in Rome to put one interpretation of it to Mussolini. A package deal, it reduced the League to a secondary role and sought a way out of the impasse by buying off Italy with territorial concessions in the Ogaden region while compensating Ethiopia with a land corridor through British Somaliland to include the port of Zeila. Leaked to the press, the so-called Zeila proposals were, in any case, categorically rejected by Mussolini. Rejected but not discarded, the offer was a dummy run for the more sensational Hoare–Laval affair some six months later.[18]

Its failure led to another variant of British policy. In September, Sir Samuel Hoare put the case for collective security before the General Assembly of the League. His government, he asserted, would be 'second to none' in fulfilling its obligations under the Covenant. Afterwards, Hoare expressed 'amazement at the universal acclamation' his pledge had received. As one delegate put it, 'the British have decided to stop Mussolini, even if that means using force'. Nothing could have been further from the truth. The composition of the League determined that Britain would act as the sole guardian of international law and order, backed, perhaps, by an unreliable France. When, on 3 October, without any declaration of war, Italian troops crossed the Ethiopian border, the popular interpretation put on Hoare's rousing words rapidly faded. Elections, due in November, were held in the shadow of the Italian invasion. In tune with the vagaries of public opinion, Stanley Baldwin's spirited message to the country, 'all sanctions short of war', faithfully reflected the opinion of eleven and half million of his constituents, as revealed in a recent Peace Ballot.[19] Janus-like, British policy looked in two directions: towards backstairs Zeila-like deals, on the one hand; and on the other, maintaining its stance – albeit half-heartedly – as the guardian of public safety. It was the faint-heartedness of the latter position that upset the Lothian–Astor–Dawson fraternity.

During the autumn and winter of 1935 their mood turned distinctly anti-Italian. Dawson met the Italian ambassador at 4 St James's Square, Tom Jones and the Brands also being present. Over dinner Grandi 'held forth very well & pleasantly' about Ethiopia, but 'nothing new in it & it was not v convincing to me'; or to the others. Even in the privacy of his diaries, Dawson's style was subdued. Lothian was less inhibited. Moved by a report in the *Christian Science Monitor* that Mussolini, after absorbing Ethiopia, will 'create a black army to swallow Egypt', he proposed embarking on a hazardous game of brinkmanship. Play the 'decisive card', he advised Hoare, and 'cut communications between Italy and East Africa', assuming – or, rather, hoping – that British military and naval strength would be sufficient to fend off any Italian riposte. In this way, Mussolini, the 'worst of the dictators', would be forced to the conference table to settle 'the real issues which confront the world, migration, lower tariffs, open door, etc.' Apart from a thorough misreading of 'the real issues' which bothered the dictators, Lothian's proposal to block the Canal – in clear violation of the International Convention of 1888 – amounted to an act of war, and this at a time when Mussolini was threatening 'mad-dog' strikes in the Mediterranean. It was to be eyeball-to-eyeball confrontation. Should Mussolini blink first, Lothian would respond generously: an Italian mandate, or the partition of Ethiopia. Nothing was ruled out. In conclusion, he comforted Hoare by claiming that no less a figure than Palmerston 'would have taken [this] line'.[20]

Lothian was the most belligerent, and vociferous, of the group. The gravest of issues was at stake: the credibility of the Commonwealth as a force for world peace. Having taken 'responsibility', it must now take 'risks' in tackling Italy. Economic sanctions – in force since 18 November – should be augmented to include oil, the penultimate penalty, an act that would surely force Mussolini to his knees. But if all else failed, military action would undoubtedly bring him to his senses. Should Mussolini 'get away' with it, 'confidence in the Commonwealth as a defence of freedom and the reign of law . . . will be deeply, perhaps irretrievably, undermined'. There was a hysterical edge to Lothian's bravado: an 'all or nothing' state of mind.[21] But he was not alone. 'Shut the Suez Canal,' the Aga Khan, a satellite member of the fraternity, counselled Anthony Eden. 'Here is a case of open and inexcusable aggression, on condottieri lines.' The Khan never ceased reiterating that 'the real danger to the Empire is Italy'. One method of restraining this pariah state would be to sanction the *Anschluss*. Stationing German troops on the Brenner Pass would certainly slake Mussolini's thirst for foreign adventures, or so he thought.[22]

Others of the fraternity were less gung-ho. Ned Grigg, National Conservative member for Altrincham, thought his government had 'made a mess of things' – a phrase much in vogue. Hankering after old-fashioned 'spheres of interest', he held that an Anglo-French-Italian compact in North Africa would have diverted Mussolini's eyes from East Africa. Now it was too late: he would let Mussolini 'be top dog in Abyssinia'. Bob Brand too was less bellicose. Cool and practical, and only too aware of the League's weaknesses, he ruminated on Britain's predicament. He accepted as a given 'Mussolini's intolerable and defiant attitude', but he could offer no remedy, merely a counsel of despair. 'I have no solution for this hopeless dilemma,' he confessed to Dawson. About one point, however, he was absolutely clear: 'This damnable sanctions clause . . . is a delusion and a snare'. It was 'the biggest breeder of war'. Was Britain prepared to act as 'the universal policeman of the world', its fleet 'doing all the work'? Brand thought not. Like Lothian, he believed that the Dominions had failed to grasp the baleful ramifications of the sanctions clause. The Moot had always thought it 'impracticable'. Adhering to it religiously would destroy the unity of the Commonwealth, particularly as its advocates could easily, and irresponsibly, argue that it applied with equal justice to those revisionist nations that chose to resolve unilaterally the infinitely more menacing territorial disputes in central and eastern Europe. If only, Brand mused, it was possible to cut the Gordian knot and delete Article 16 from the Covenant.[23]

Sanctions – for Dawson, 'an odious word' – remained. Despite Lothian's militant mood – he was all for 'decisive sanctions' – even he knew that without unanimity of purpose, backed by a credible threat of war, it was a fanciful policy. After the Hoare–Laval *débâcle*,*[24] the immediate urgency of these speculations was swept away. All opposed this 'singularly maladroit and unfortunate act', as Lothian described it. He told the House of Lords: 'The whole world has read the recent peace offer as proof that we have gone soft and are unwilling to fight vehemently either for the League or ourselves.' Dawson led the press campaign against the plan, ridiculing it in a withering editorial, 'A Corridor for Camels'. His deputy editor, Robert Barrington-Ward, turned in disgust to his diary. 'I went to bed utterly humiliated and dispirited and ashamed of my country. The first time that a public event ever so worked on me. We have sacrificed honour and interest together.'[25] These prophetic words were to be repeated many times over almost three years later, in the context of the controversial Munich settlement. But on this occasion, those who then gave voice to

---

* The Hoare–Laval proposals were a rehash of the Zeila scheme, though more rewarding to Italy. They planned to give Ethiopia an outlet to the sea, either Zeila or Assab; the cession of some of the conquered areas in Tigre to Italy, and frontier rectifications in Italy's favour in the east and south-east, together with a large zone in the south and south-west in which Italy, acting under the League, would hold a monopoly for economic development. By this deal, approved by the Cabinet, roughly two-thirds of Ethiopia would fall under Italian control. It was further accepted that Britain and France were acting on behalf of the League, and it was for the League to ratify or reject the proposals.

In early December the two Foreign Secretaries met at the Quai d'Orsay to put together the final touches to this plan. No sooner had they finished than it was leaked by Laval's enemies to waiting journalists. Opinion in Parliament and the press took the high moral ground, protesting angrily at the government's abject capitulation to an aggressor state. Bewildered by this unexpected onslaught the government back-pedalled. Cabinet ministers, listening carefully to opinion in their constituencies, switched sides to repudiate the scheme. The unfortunate Hoare – bedridden from an ice-skating upset – found himself isolated. However, his duty was made clear to him – urged upon him also by Dawson – and he resigned forthwith. On 19 December Baldwin delivered the *coup de grâce*. Making 'one of his take-you-into-my-confidence speeches', he officially buried the Hoare–Laval agreement.

them were firmly opposed to the pro-German appeasement policies of the Lothians, Dawsons and Barrington-Wards. Firm against Italy, conciliatory towards Germany: for sound imperial reasons, the friends' order of priorities was clearly defined.

The Times' offensive against the government's policy of surrender to Mussolini received high praise, from some quarters. Cosmo Lang, Archbishop of Canterbury, thanked 'dear Geoffrey' for 'it expresses finely and calmly all that I feel', a sentiment echoed by Sir Horace Rumbold. Lionel Curtis also applauded loudly. In addition, he identified the author of this disgraceful fiasco. 'The root of this trouble was Vansittart,' he ruled. Dawson agreed wholeheartedly: 'As for Vansittart, I have always been clear that he is quite unsuited to his present position. He is really very lightweight, an admirable private secretary in his day, but not the stuff for the head of a great Department, or a mentor for any Government in difficulties.' Vansittart, with his anti-German and pro-Italian biases, coupled with his manifest lack of faith in the American option, emerges as one of the friends' chief bugbears. Later, when Vansittart had been elevated to the high-sounding, but hollow, post of Chief Diplomatic Adviser to the Government, Curtis credited Lothian for 'long and persistent efforts' that 'were largely responsible for the displacement of Vansittart'. What were these 'persistent efforts'? They have yet to come to light. Probably Lothian was whispering furiously to whoever would listen. But Eden and Chamberlain, the architects of Vansittart's demise, needed no convincing. They had long been determined to promote Vansittart into a position empty of any real influence. What is clear is that Vansittart – and the Foreign Office in general – regarded Lothian, with a mixture of scorn and alarm, as a well-meaning, innocent do-gooder, a dilettante toying with diplomacy while ruining British interests. Vansittart labelled Lothian as 'an incurably superficial Johnny-Know-All'.[26]

The repercussions of the Ethiopian imbroglio were not lost upon the Clivedenites; and they extended well beyond the confines of East Africa. First, the ability of the government to govern was called into question. One visitor to Cliveden, Mavis Tate (recently elected Conservative MP for Frome), scathingly pointed out that her Prime Minister's 'capacity for hiding his incapacity had grown from one premiership to another'. But not only Baldwin was at fault. The entire Cabinet had buckled under, cowardly shirking its responsibility, and in the most disgraceful and humiliating manner. Tom Jones, at least, came to Baldwin's defence: '[he] was not a trickster but the most honest PM of the century.' This rang false in Cliveden's ears. Neville Chamberlain, another regular guest, put the Clivedenites more at ease. 'Despite grave doubts, the Cabinet had decided to try out to the last extremity the possibilities of the League, only to find that its ultimate sanction must always be force. But quite frankly, as we all found out, the League's guns won't shoot.' Bravely admitting his role in the affair, Chamberlain made clear that he would have taken full responsibility for the fiasco. 'But', he told a responsive audience at a Cliveden weekend, 'I can tell you with some confidence, that [it] would not have transpired.'[27]

None of the friends denied that Britain – and France – had been severely humiliated.* Every option considered had been found seriously wanting. They had fallen between so many stools: the League and its sanctions policy; treaty revision; an unpredictable Commonwealth; the pipe dream of an Anglo-American *Pax*. All were at one, however, regarding the imperfections of the League and, in particular, over the self-evident shortcomings of a 'decisive sanctions' policy. With the United States, Germany and Japan pursuing their interests outside the League, and saddled with a time-serving France, Britain was too weak to put it into effect alone. This was the essence of Neville Chamberlain's message, and neither Bob Brand, Dawson, Lothian nor the Astors disagreed. Until Britain was strong enough, adequately rearmed, there must be no more acts of brinkmanship. Britain could not afford to play the game of who was bluffing whom. It was no longer a question of applying sanctions, but of how to avoid them altogether. Brand summed up this point: 'sanctions will not bring peace, but rather war, a war for which we are not prepared.'

Chamberlain's comments must have been sweet music to Dawson – and Lothian. To his way of thinking, Baldwin, unmethodical, slipshod in habit, had lost control of his Cabinet, allowing himself to be hoodwinked by bad counsellors, particularly Vansittart. Dawson damned the assumption that a pro-Italian policy would prevent Mussolini from falling into Hitler's arms: it was was pure nonsense, a typical piece of Foreign Office tomfoolery, a product of Vansittart's tortuous mind. As a result, Dawson argued, Britain's prestige had plummeted, its future bargaining position seriously undermined. His mind was now fixed firmly upon Germany. Recognizing Germany's legitimate grievances, Dawson reasoned that there was no substitute for a direct Anglo-German negotiation to rectify them. Convinced that Hitler would respond readily to the right kind of approach, he was no less confident that a satiated Germany would settle down as a good European neighbour.

If Lothian's views were on a par with Dawson's, Brand's were not.

---

* The miserable Ethiopian affair dragged on until the late spring of 1936. After Italy had brought into full play its military strength, including the use of air power and poison gas, Ethiopian resistance crumbled. On 5 May Italian forces entered Addis Ababa; four days later, Ethiopia was formally incorporated into the new Italian Empire.

True, time and again he voiced reservations regarding the effectiveness of the League, but regarding Germany his opinion was set hard. 'So long as Germany remains under a Nazi dictatorship, there is no chance of her becoming a good neighbour. The Hitlerite spirit – and this goes for Mussolini as well – will not allow it.' After one visit to Germany he told the following story, as if to justify his extreme convictions, perhaps agonizing over his indecision. As he recalled it, shortly after Hitler came to power he happened to be in Berlin on business, accompanied by a colleague from Lazard's, Erwin Schueller, an Austrian Jew. One evening they went to the Opera. In the box below sat Hitler and his entourage. Instinctively, Brand whispered to Schueller: 'If only I had a bomb now, we could finish the whole thing off.' Schueller, according to Brand, was shocked at the idea. So, no doubt, were those who heard this tale, for Brand's image as an international banker, restrained in character and discreet in conduct, was in stark contrast with an act of derring-do, particularly political assassination.

Lothian too had recently been within striking distance of Hitler, though no Brand-like thought crossed his mind. He brought back an entirely different message. Lothian harboured no doubts about the essential brutality and ruthlessness of the Nazi regime. In his own preferred phrase, it lacked 'any vestige of the Christian quality of mercy'. At the same time, the facts of international life could not be ignored. Hitler had stabilized and united Germany. By his inspired leadership, he had restored to Germany its national self-respect and international standing. Aware of this new reality, Lothian would cross-examine his friends: do we want a lasting European agreement or endless confrontation with Germany? No rational person would seek confrontation. But if an agreement, on what terms? Hitler's expansionist ambitions in Europe, it was widely feared, would drag Britain into another calamitous war. When they met in January 1935, Hitler told Lothian that 'Germany is determined not to have war'. The frontiers with France 'were settled'; the Polish question could be resolved 'by peaceful means'; and differences with Austria could be adjusted 'by a free plebiscite'. 'War', Hitler insisted, 'was a great madness, and the greatest madness of all was the war of 1914 between the two peoples – the English and German.' Having jointly recognized that war was out of the question, the British aristocrat and the German dictator hit upon another common cause. Spearheaded by an Anglo-German dialogue, they would aim at the pacification of Europe, confident that once Britain and Germany acted together all Europe would fall into line.

If sanctions were out and pacification in – and that was the general consensus among the 'friends' – what else remained? For Lothian the obvious answer was to construct a new European – even world – order based on a generous revision of the post-war treaties. Other outstanding problems, no less urgent, also needed to be resolved: the easing of discriminating immigration quotas, tariff reform, an open-door policy, a fair distribution of raw materials, perhaps even new colonial arrangements. 'The equation is simple,' Lothian judged. 'Treaty revision by pacific means, by negotiations between equals, adds up to no sanctions and no more embarrassing situations like the Hoare–Laval episode. Article 19 of the Covenant has to take precedence over Article 16. And all this could be more easily obtained if we took the initiative, not actually bypassing the League but presenting it – and the French – with a *fait accompli*.'

In every essential, the Dawson–Lothian axis had crystallized, with Waldorf and Nancy Astor and Lionel Curtis acting as its satellites. Waldorf, however, harboured certain reservations, not so much about policy towards Germany as about the state of Hitler's mind. Like Brand and Lothian, he too had experienced Hitler at first hand, as a member of a Christian Science delegation. 'Hitler dodged any discussion about our Church,' Waldorf explained later. 'He evinced no interest in it.' Instead, he turned his attention to less contentious matters. How can Anglo-German relations be improved, Hitler asked. By alleviating the plight of the Jews in Germany, Waldorf replied. Hitler reacted violently to Waldorf's bold response. It provoked one of his (staged?) tantrums, a 'convulsion' or 'spasm', as Waldorf diagnosed it. How can a man who behaved so irrationally govern so great a country, he wondered.

Only Brand took serious issue with the Dawson–Lothian line, considering it too sanguine by far. He had no faith that Germany under a Nazi dictatorship would ever adopt good-neighbourly policies. Its perverse doctrines, its unscrupulous leaders, the nihilistic spirit of its regime, were so profoundly at variance with every ideal, every value Britain stood for, that the two countries could never be fully reconciled. British foreign policy should have two main aims, he stated: to prevent German control over the Lowlands, and possibly Denmark; and to maintain our position in the Mediterranean. These goals can only be realized with French support. So that the key to British policy was not so much to activate an Anglo-German dialogue, but to rebuild the Anglo-French partnership, ruptured by the Hoare–Laval *débâcle*. Yet Brand too recognized that the question of treaty revision in central and eastern Europe was of paramount importance. 'If France is drawn into any conflict there,' he noted, 'and with her alliance system this is bound to happen, we can hardly stay out.'*

---

* Brand was referring to the French alliances with Poland (19 February 1921) and the Soviet Union (2 May 1935). France was also bound by the Czech–Soviet agreement (16 May 1935), a pact of mutual assistance that would come into operation only if France acted. There were also French links with the so-called Little Entente countries, Yugoslavia, Rumania and Czechoslovakia.

Brand probed further. How would all this affect the cohesion of the Empire? – for the friends always the most decisive of issues. Here was the rub. And it led Brand into deep water. Must we prevent the extension of Germany's influence eastwards at all costs, he pondered. Brand was honest enough to admit that there were no pat answers. 'I have come to believe, and I say this with the utmost reluctance, that such a development might be a lesser evil than a war by us to prevent it.' Lothian and Dawson held that it was feasible to groom Nazi Germany into playing a responsible European role. Brand held no such illusions. But like them, he was at this stage prepared to tolerate Germany's drive eastwards, naturally within the framework of treaty revision – and then what? Really, to hope for the best!

With respect to the failings of the League and the long-term aims of British policy, a general consensus emerged among the 'friends'. But it was one thing to define the problems confronting Britain and its Empire, it was quite another to devise a policy that would rescue them from their dilemma. Even Brand was floundering here. Lothian, however, had never been shy of assuming such a role. He was in touch with Smuts, that most distinguished of honorary Round Tablers. Now that sanctions had been lifted, Smuts brooded on the fall in prestige of the League. To his mind it affected also the status of the Commonwealth. 'The League has been a most powerful bond and support. We were bound together by the same great international treaty, and were allies together in war, or neutrals together in peace. If the Covenant goes this bond and support also goes, and very difficult constitutional questions may arise.'

Lothian was not entirely persuaded. The original Wilsonian Covenant was dead and could not be resurrected, he replied. That was the paramount lesson to be drawn from the Ethiopian crisis. To allow 'a broken League to be turned into a mere military alliance to maintain an outworn *status quo* in Europe at the dictation of Russia and France' would be the greatest of follies. A new and better system had to replace it, one that would grow 'from an informal cooperation between the British Commonwealth and the United States to control the oceans in this century as Great Britain alone controlled them in the last'. Such an accord would provide the impetus for a revived League 'which will have within itself both power and the possibility of growth'. But, he warned Smuts, this prescription will depend upon how the Dominions respond, 'and especially you yourself'.[28]

An Anglo–American compact was the hoariest of chestnuts. Undeterred, Lothian persisted in chasing his lodestar. Some years later, the trauma of Pearl Harbor gave it life – but by then Lothian was dead.

CHAPTER 7

Claud and 'The Week'

On 17 June 1936 a news-sheet named *The Week* published a piece entitled 'The Best People's Front'. It linked together Geoffrey Dawson and *The Times*, the government and its foreign policies and the Astor network – a top-drawer inner circle that had attained an 'extraordinary position of concentrated political power' and had become 'one of the most important supports of German influence' – concluding its exposé by noting how all 'rising young politicians' hankered after invitations to Cliveden weekends.[1] *The Week*'s editor, Claud Cockburn, was a gifted and highly original journalist. He would return to this theme time and again. But was it true or false? Had Cockburn 'discovered' or 'invented' an establishment conspiracy, a coterie that would eventually evolve into the so-called 'Cliveden Set'? Like so much else about Claud Cockburn's career, it is often exceedingly difficult to separate rumour from fact.[2]

Claud Cockburn (alias Frank Pitcairn) was born in Peking on 8 February 1904, the day the Japanese blew up the Russian flagship *Petropavlovsk*, anchored off Port Arthur. His family had a long tradition of imperial service. Lord Cockburn, his paternal grandfather, was a celebrated Scottish advocate who had lived for many years 'in oriental splendour' in India, a judge in the administration of the British Raj. When he finally returned home it was widely reported that he shone brightly 'in the Golden Age of Edinburgh society', though one visitor boldly asked whether it was not irksome, after his heavenly life in India, 'to exist in this state of indigent obscurity'. Claud's father, a member of the Eastern Consular Service, served for thirty years in the Far East. As 'Chinese Secretary', he was present at the siege of the Legation Quarter in Peking by the Boxers. From there he was posted to Seoul as Minister (later Consul-General) to Korea, where he spent the last years of his official career. Of a restless disposition, Claud's father, even after his retirement, could not resist occasional forays abroad. Once he was even co-opted on to an inter-allied financial mission to Hungary, although, as he disarmingly pointed out to his sponsors, he knew nothing of finance or of Hungary.

Much of Claud's childhood was spent following his father around. But in the manner of those of his background, he was formally educated in England. Berkhamsted was a minor public school. A venerable institution – founded in 1553 – it had fallen on hard times. But by the time Claud arrived it had recovered sufficiently to boast five hundred boys. Claud's father began to have second thoughts about the school when he learned of its motto, *Virtus laudata crescit* ('Virtue grows with praise'), a saying symbolizing, or so he inferred, a lax state of mind. Claud survived. Prevailing over the struggle between the 'Rugby Tradition' of Dr Arnold and the intimations of 'modernism', he later realized that one of the most valuable lessons this contest taught him was 'how to break other people's rules'. At Keble College, Oxford, he read Greats and at the same time began to dabble in journalism, editing *Isis* and occasionally contributing a column to an Oxford newspaper.

After graduating with first-class honours, and at a loss which career to follow, he spent the next two years in Europe on a travel scholarship from The Queen's College. He ruled out, absolutely and for ever, the Foreign Office. 'A wonderful opportunity for somebody – somebody else,' he chanted, echoing the refrain of a popular song. Perhaps *The Times*? It was not a suggestion he embraced with marked enthusiasm. Aware of the paper's elitist image, Claud wavered. 'Is indeed anyone, anywhere, truly worthy of *The Times*?' he asked impudently. Still, the idea of becoming a foreign correspondent held certain attractions. 'Think of William Russell! Think of George Morrison! Think of Wickham Steed!'

Unsure of his future, Claud found himself in Berlin in the mid-1920s. It was at the *Times* office, located in Unter den Linden, that he first met Norman Ebbutt, the paper's newly appointed correspondent in Germany. Without much ado and 'with extraordinary tact', Ebbutt pointed out that Claud would 'be doing him positively a favour by coming and "helping"'. Ebbutt's reputation as a reporter was without equal – in time, he would be elevated to almost legendary status in the history of contemporary journalism. Stockily built, his eyes concealed by thick, rimless spectacles, a compusive pipe-smoker, he presided every evening at his regular table in the Taverne public house, drinking, gossiping, swapping information with his fellow correspondents. So began Claud's association with *The Times*, as Ebbutt's apprentice. Fluent in German, Claud scanned the local newspapers, about thirty in number, and, guided by Ebbutt, expanded his range of contacts to include bankers, industrialists and Foreign Ministry officials, most notably Gustav Stresemann, the Foreign Minister himself, and a Prussian aristocrat, Wolfgang Gans Edler zu Putlitz.* But what of actual

* Later, Putlitz was transferred to the German embassy in London, where he was of

reporting? By tradition, *The Times* forbade novices from contributing to its paper. Ebbutt compromised. 'Of course,' he assured Claud, 'you will write for the paper, and we will get as many pieces of yours in as we can,' adding shrewdly, 'although naturally it will be necessary to pretend that I have sent them.'

For a while this ruse succeeded. Eventually, *The Times* accommodated itself to the reality of Claud's presence in its Berlin office, a concession eased by his noteworthy exposé of the vast media combine owned by Alfred Hugenberg, an extreme German nationalist who was to play a key role in Hitler's rise to power. His reputation on the rise, and his travel fellowship – and money – running out, Claud applied for a regular job on *The Times*, proposing that he serve in its New York bureau. Geoffrey Dawson's reply was most reassuring. 'Have no fear for tomorrow. Return at once. Job waiting.'

The Times chose its foreign correspondents with extreme care. Potential candidates were expected to prove their worth. Apprenticeship on a provincial newspaper was usually required, then some domestic reporting for *The Times*, and finally, assuming that performance was maintained, promotion to the Foreign Room. Even then, a foreign posting was by no means certain. More than one young hopeful had entered the Foreign Room never to leave it. Claud was determined to avoid this fate. That he did so was no doubt due to his own tenacity; but no less to an unknown benefactor, Sir Campbell Stuart, a powerful director of The Times Publishing Company and a close friend of Claud's uncle Frank. Sir Campbell had promised to keep a benevolent eye on Claud's interests.

Claud found the inhabitants of the Foreign Editorial Room at *The Times* much as he had anticipated. One was translating a passage from Plato's *Phaedo* into Chinese – for a wager! Another was investigating how to spell Kuala Lumpur, and discovered eleven correct ways: but which should receive the imprimatur of *The Times*? When Scott Moncrieff, the translator of Proust, was employed at Printing House Square the business of the office was often held up for half an hour or more while he and his colleagues sought the precise English word or phrase that would best convey the meaning and flavour of an excerpt from *A la recherche du temps perdu*. Claud remembered teatime as a serious affair. Seated around a large oval table, the juniors were separated from the seniors who barricaded themselves in with volumes of the *Encyclopaedia Britannica* so as to be able to take tea *and* 'get on with our work without being disturbed' by idle chatter. Once these learned gentlemen invented a competition – who could

considerable use to Claud. Holding genuine anti-Nazi views, he leaked information about the German government's intentions to various British sources. After the war, he turned up in East Berlin as an official of the German Democratic Republic's foreign service.[3]

compose the dullest headline. Claud won: 'Small earthquake in Chile. Not many dead.'

Delightful though these experiences were, embellishing the quaintly eccentric image of *The Times*, to say nothing of pumping up its employees' self-esteem, they were not sufficient to seduce Claud into becoming a permanent fixture at Printing House Square. He was bent on going to America. Ultimately, this would be decided by the editor, Geoffrey Dawson. But Dawson was a difficult man to pin down. 'It is impossible to argue with Dawson,' Bob Brand once said, 'he always agrees with you.'[4] Interviews with him tended to be affable but extremely vague in substance. He would greet you pleasantly enough, 'standing in front of his desk, poised always on the same mark on the carpet, both hands slightly outstretched . . . his whole attitude that of one who has been unable to prevent himself bounding from his chair and rushing forward to meet you'. Already impressed with this routine, his caller would be further overwhelmed by the voluble geniality of his conversation and the way he gently touched your arm as he manoeuvred you around the room. There you were, 'pacing the floor of the sanctum of the Editor-in-Chief of *The Times*', commanding his full attention 'while his secretary, you could imagine, told anxious Cabinet ministers and bishops over the telephone that the Editor was in conference'. The effect was mesmeric. In this 'state of partial hypnosis you were scarcely aware that with one arm across your shoulders the Editor was with the other hand opening the door at the far end of his office and pushing you gently into the corridor, bidding you a warm farewell after an interview which had lasted approximately eighty seconds'. What had been promised, what had been decided? Nothing. 'But for several hours you certainly felt that you had accomplished something or other.'

Claud's persistence and Sir Campbell's lobbying finally paid off. He was to go to New York as assistant to Louis Hinrichs, *The Times*' bureau chief. When Dawson invited him to a farewell dinner at his club, the Travellers', Claud expected to hear advice on how a correspondent of *The Times* should behave abroad, on his functions and responsibilities. But although they dined and drank well, the conversation was characteristically vague. Claud's future duties were left hanging in the air, open to interpretation. So, after a pleasant but indeterminate evening, the young cub reporter and the veteran editor went their different ways.*

Claud arrived in New York in July 1929. These were the days of the

---

* It needs to be stressed that Claud's charmingly impressionistic account of his meetings with Dawson – with whom his relations later deteriorated – could also be interpreted as sustaining the view of Dawson as an efficient, hard-working, no-nonsense editor of *The Times*, a judgement incidentally upheld by many.

great stocks and shares bonanza, the bullish market on a seemingly endless upswing. Hinrichs, Claud's senior, had personally suffered from the idiosyncrasies of the market. A Harvard graduate and a bon vivant, in his youth he had dabbled extensively on the stock exchange, profiting sufficiently to lead a leisurely existence until the repercussions of the San Francisco earthquake wiped out his fortune. He now specialized in economic and financial affairs. A familiar figure on Wall Street, he followed the speculative market with increasing pessimism. Together they witnessed the Great Crash on 'Black Thursday', 24 October. That day they interviewed Thomas Lamont, a senior partner of the leading banking firm J. P. Morgan, soliciting his comments on the *débâcle*. 'There has just been a little distress selling in the Stock Exchange,' he assured them. But even as he spoke, thirteen million shares were being unloaded.

Claud remained in the United States until the autumn of 1932, the early years of the Depression and the last years of Prohibition. In Chicago, he interviewed Al Capone at his headquarters in his suite at the Lexington Hotel. Gently frisked by a couple of 'bulging Sicilians', he was escorted into the mobster's presence. Their *tête-à-tête* was conducted in a civilized manner, even though Claud immediately spotted the barrel of a gun poking through the transom of a door behind Capone's desk – aimed, as it turned out, by Jack 'Machine Gun' McGurn, a notorious Capone hitman and a prime suspect in the St Valentine's Day massacre. 'Listen, don't get the idea I'm one of those goddamn radicals,' Capone snapped, every so often dipping his fingertips in the water of a silver rosebowl. 'Don't get the idea I'm knocking the American system. My rackets are run on strictly American lines. Capitalism, call it what you like, gives to each and every one of us a great opportunity if only we seize it with both hands and make the most of it.' Despite these profound insights, the interview was never filed. When asked why by John Walter, the minority owner of *The Times*, Claud replied that Capone's remarks were in essence identical with editorials of *The Times* itself, and he doubted whether the paper would be pleased to see itself in agreement with the most infamous racketeer in Chicago. After a moment's 'wry reflection', Walter agreed.

At the beginning of 1931 Claud began to reconsider his future. Not because *The Times* was disenchanted with his journalistic abilities. On the contrary, he had been offered the much prized Washington office. But he felt hemmed in by the stuffy procedures and underlying conservatism of *The Times*. Seeking other outlets for his energy and a more independent style of journalism, he began secretly 'bootlegging' articles to extreme left-wing American journals. In the summer of 1932 he decided finally to submit his resignation. Dawson replied, hoping to change Claud's mind. 'It was foolish', he maintained, 'to give up working for *The Times* simply on account of one's political views . . . *The Times* was a vehicle which could be used by people of the most varied opinions.' Dawson added solemnly: 'For myself, I have always regarded *The Times* as something of an organ of the Left,' appending in brackets the notable caveat: 'Though never, I hope, of the extreme Left.' Claud remained unconvinced. In New York, Dawson – who had come specially from Ottawa, where he had been covering the Imperial Economic Conference – tried again. Puzzled, he told Claud that 'It does seem rather bad luck that you of all people should "go red on us".' When, finally, Dawson referred to him as an 'ex-assistant', Claud knew that he had resigned at last.

By January 1933 Claud was back in Berlin, an eyewitness to the last days of the Weimar Republic. Among those he met were General Kurt von Schleicher, its last Chancellor, and Willi Münzenberg, a one-time 'Sparticist' and one of the founders of the German Communist Party. Whether he and Münzenberg ever met again remains unclear. But in an odd way their paths crossed, or at least ran along parallel lines. Fluent only in German and unable to write 'a coherent paragraph', Münzenberg was nonetheless a propagandist of genius. Adept in public relations, a fiery and irresistible public speaker, a gifted fund-raiser and a masterful organizer, he made converts from all sections of society, 'from English duchesses to American columnists to French savants'.

Dubbed as the 'Red Hearst', Münzenberg raised up media empires – the 'International Workers Aid' (also known as the 'Münzenberg Trust') and later the 'World Committee for the Relief of the Victims of German Fascism' – that encompassed a publishing house (Editions du Carrefour), book clubs, newspapers, magazines, and the financing of movies (including some of Eisenstein's) and plays. The branches of these organizations, run by 'highly respectable people' and supported by a galaxy of international celebrities, extended from Europe to the United States to Japan. As the *éminence grise* of the anti-fascist crusade, it was said, with little exaggeration, that Münzenberg invented the progressive fellow-traveller. Forced to flee Germany after Hitler came to power, Münzenberg, together with his assistant, Otto Katz, moved to Paris. From his headquarters at 83 Boulevard Montparnasse he directed the Comintern's West-European Agitprop Department. In Paris, his so-called 'paper mills' were forever in motion, grinding out sham organizations and causes and illusory enemies. He promoted Popular Fronts and staged international rallies, congresses and committees with the deft touch of a master showman. Ostensibly, all these activities were directed towards one particular purpose: to foster the anti-fascist campaign. Feeding off the controversies of the Spanish Civil War, Münzenberg sharpened the conflict to one between the reactionary, capitalist elite and the progressive intelligentsia in alliance with the working masses. Having attended the giant 'Amsterdam Peace Rally against War and Fascism', one of Münzenberg's creations, Claud had already been conscripted in the European anti-war movement. In time, he would enlist as a captain in what would be styled a European civil war.*[5]

By now Claud had determined on his future course. It had occurred to him while working in Washington. There he had been friendly with a fellow publicist who was engaged in a one-man battle against the all-powerful 'Radio Trust'. What captured Claud's imagination was the ingenious use made of 'the humble mimeograph machine'. Here was the great leveller, a handy functional tool in service to the muckraking tradition of American journalism. 'A mimeograph machine', Claud ruled at the time, 'is one of the few remaining weapons which still gives small and comparatively poor organizations a sporting chance in a scrap with large and wealthy ones.' This impression was reinforced in Berlin. Of all people, von Schleicher – one of Claud's contacts – also published a mimeographed paper, which was widely circulated among foreign embassies, legations and correspondents. Claud calculated that in terms of influence one reader of von Schleicher's sheet was equivalent to 'about five thousand readers of one daily newspaper'. But Claud's chief inspiration was the Parisian *Le Canard Enchaîné*, 'the best-informed publication in France', he claimed. True, many of its pieces were, 'thank God, in execrable taste', but he noted with immense pleasure that it carried no advertisements, received no subsidies, and still broke 'a little better than even'.

Claud's experience had demonstrated that a modern daily newspaper, catering for an infinite variety of people from diverse backgrounds and with different tastes, and corrupted by the advertising moguls, appealed to the lowest common denominator. Its superficiality attracted a mass readership, but left untapped a pool of serious readers. As he aimed at the 'Highest Common factor of reader-interest', this pool of top-level patrons would constitute Claud's clientele. He would not be intimidated by an editorial board or shareholders or advertising pressure. His news-sheet would express only one viewpoint – his own! With these thoughts fixed in his mind, Claud returned to London.

* In many ways Münzenberg survives as a shadowy figure. In 1938 he was summoned to Moscow, his party bosses alarmed at his individualism, the power he wielded, the influence he commanded, his exclusive control of funds, and the informal way he managed his – that is, their – affairs. Sooner than vanish into the Gulag or face the consequences of a show-trial, Münzenberg broke with the party. At the outbreak of war, he was interned by the French. Released with the advance of the German armies, he made his way to Switzerland – and then disappeared. Some days later his battered body was found hanging from a tree in a forest near Grenoble. Suicide or foul play – at the hands of Stalin's thugs? Like so much about Münzenberg's life, the precise circumstances of his death remain a mystery. Otto Katz, his chief aide, suffered a similar fate. Widely suspected of having been planted by his Moscow controllers to spy on Münzenberg, Katz survived until 1952. A victim of the Slansky trials, accused of being a British spy and a Zionist agent, Katz was duly sentenced to death and hanged.

First, he had to resolve the problem of lack of funds. To initiate such a venture, extravagant figures of £5–10,000 had been loosely mentioned. Claud settled for £40 – or so legend has it. His benefactor was an old Oxford acquaintance, a would-be novelist 'vegetating' somewhere in Berkshire and known simply as 'Ben'. Something of a dandy who sported a gold-rimmed monocle, Ben wished to return to London where he could 'meet people' and at the same time convince them that he was productively employed and not merely a social butterfly. No political animal, he was deputed to assist as Claud's business manager. Crystal, the wife of Archie Harding, another Oxford friend – with whom Claud happened to be lodging as a non-paying guest – also volunteered her services as an all-round assistant. A debutante-type – 'her idea of a major event in Home Affairs had been the exclusion of a friend from the Royal Enclosure at Ascot' – Crystal lacked all previous office experience. But she was 'pretty, energetic, intelligent and loyal', and her vivacious personality added to the smooth running of the office. This was crucial as Claud's administrative skills were negligible, a fact that was personified by his unkempt appearance and impatient disposition. Usually turning up in a shabby dark blue overcoat and a battered hat, he seemed to be in perpetual motion, resembling a rag doll whose elongated arms and legs flopped aimlessly all over the place. The staff was completed by a mysterious gentleman from Vancouver who drifted into the office. Forever floating bizarre money-making schemes, he suffered a nervous breakdown about a month after joining the staff. Finding him outside the Army and Navy Stores addressing the passers-by as 'Brothers in the Sun', Claud thoughtfully delivered him into the care of a nursing home.*

With his finances relatively secure, Claud hired a room from the Union of Democratic Control at 34 Victoria Street, within striking distance of Westminster and Whitehall. A tiny attic, it was approached by 'a dangerous looking cage', a lift that was usually out of action, or a gloomy staircase that terminated in a rickety ladder-like flight of stairs. Four chairs, two tables and a filing cabinet were installed, together with a duplicating machine bought on hire-purchase. Claud had already decided that he would call his news-sheet *The Week*. 'Perfect,' applauded his partner, Ben, clapping his hands. It would appear on buff-coloured foolscap paper, printed in a dark shade of brown ink. It would not be 'clean and dignified', but it would, Claud pointed out, be 'noticeable'.

Having settled the mechanics of producing *The Week*, Claud had now to make certain that he would indeed be tapping the pool of the 'Highest Common Denominator'. Were there any 'principles' involved in realizing

* All efforts to identify 'Ben' or the 'mysterious gentleman from Vancouver' have proved fruitless. They remain, sadly, enigmatic figures.

this aim? How would he ensure his journal's readability and guarantee its unique flavour? He was fond of quoting Thomas Barnes, the renowned mid-nineteenth-century editor of *The Times*.

> Newspaper writing, he said, is a thing *sui generis*; it is in literature what brandy is in beverages. John Bull, whose understanding is rather sluggish – I speak of the majority of readers – requires a strong stimulus. He consumes his beef and cannot digest it without a dram; he dozes composedly over his prejudices which his conceit calls opinions; and you must fire ten-pounders at his densely compact intellect before you can make it comprehend your meaning or care one farthing for your efforts.

What people said about *The Times* was immaterial to Barnes as long as they read it – and reading it had become 'a national habit' under his editorship. Newspaper stories, Barnes held, needed 'a little devil' in them. A 'born controversialist' and 'an egoist' (according to the historian of *The Times*), Barnes's variant of the paper was referred to as 'the "bloody old *Times*"'. All this was very much to Claud's liking.[6]

Kingsley Martin, editor of the *New Statesman and Nation*, once told Claud that many of the stories printed in *The Week* had already reached him in the 'form of rumour', but unable fully to confirm their veracity, he would not risk publishing them. Claud's outlook was quite different. He had absorbed from Wilmott Lewis, an American colleague, the notion that facts in themselves were of little value. What counted was how they were presented: it was all 'a question of style'. However you juggled them, facts always began with 'a point of view, a conception, and it is the point of view from which the facts are subsequently organized'. If editors refused to print anything that was not authenticated, very little of general interest would be published. Claud claimed to find this traditional caution arrogant and self-defeating. 'How can one tell truth from rumour in less than perhaps fifty years?' Fifty years! Far too long for a weekly paper to wait.

Claud developed this theme in an extreme and provocative form – and it did him, as he admitted, much harm. He was wont to proclaim that 'rumours were just as important, just as significant, just as – in the last analysis – "valid" as "facts"'. In fact, he meant that there were occasions when the essence of a particular rumour was as meaningful and worthy of mention as a proven fact. The speculations, even the gossip, of informed people deserved to be reported. Claud came to regard this as a vital principle of modern journalism. One friend, less certain, and overwhelmed by Claud's weekly exposure of multifarious forms of domestic and international skulduggeries, asked him: 'Are you really as sure as you sound that this is actually going to happen?' 'I am not at all sure that it is going to happen,' Claud replied, 'but I am entirely sure that if we don't publish it it will certainly happen.' In this way, Claud devised his theory of 'preventive journalism' – as he tolerantly put it. Some found intoxicating this delicious mixture of rumour spiced with fact. Cyril Connolly, for one, rejoiced that 'motive was peeled from motive, betrayal found under betrayal, bribe upon bribe, and always in the august and persuasive language of *The Times* . . . His victims literally could not believe their eyes.' This was to take a very liberal attitude. Claud's dividing line between rumour and fact was dangerously thin and carelessly delineated. At times he would stray across it, and then elegantly wander back. If the casualties of his meanderings could not 'believe their eyes', they often had sound reason to do so.

John Wheeler-Bennett, a historian and a leading figure at Chatham House, told Claud that very soon he would be 'either quite famous or in gaol'. Claud responded that 'lots of people have been both'. Despite his bravado, Claud's 'creative' or 'preventive' journalism was a high-risk business. Libel actions and heavy fines were one danger; infringing the Official Secrets Act, an offence that carried a prison sentence, another. What saved Claud was his ignorance of the law and the poverty of his estate. He refused, on principle, to seek legal advice about potentially libellous pieces, thereby neutralizing the temptation to omit or tone down any of his compilations of rumour-cum-fact that, if published, might land him in court. When threatened with a lawsuit, which happened quite often, he would impress upon the aggrieved party the virtual insolvency of his organization. In any case, a trial was always a hazardous undertaking. Was the effort and expense worthwhile? Any rational calculation of Claud's assets normally persuaded the claimant of the futility of seeking justice in a court of law. Nor, again on principle, would Claud make a public apology. But, by way of compensation, he would offer to print another story on the same subject if the accused cared to add any new facts to show that the offending article had been baseless. Thwarted, the budding plaintiff usually caved in. No lawsuit was ever filed against *The Week*. Neither did the government seek to curtail its activities – at least in peacetime – however much it suspected *The Week* of engaging in espionage or of winkling out state secrets from public servants.

Claud faced other pitfalls. By exposing satanic plots on a weekly basis he was fulfilling a salutary public service. But what if they were nipped in the bud by the authorities and failed to happen? Or even worse, what if his numerous enemies were setting him up, plying him with specious information in order to unmask him as a liar, as a fabricator of sinister events? How many times could he cry 'Wolf!' without losing his credibility? These were inbuilt gambles. Claud took the risk. Given reasonable intelligence, energy and general alertness, he reckoned that it 'ought to be possible to avoid most of the dangers most of the time'. And with growing experience, he developed – or so he maintained – a sixth sense in these matters. Not that Claud successfully evaded these pitfalls at all times. But he considered it pusillanimous to be inhibited by them. 'Surely', he would say to anxious friends, 'it is a lot better to make a public goat of myself twice running than to let those sons of bitches get away with anything, even one time in three.' Claud would not have quarrelled with Lady Bracknell's assertion: 'I never travel without my diary. One should always have something sensational to read in the train.'

The first issue of *The Week* appeared on Wednesday, 29 March 1933. It was preceded by scenes of great editorial confusion. The actual production of the paper was left until Wednesday morning in order, Claud argued, to pre-empt the existing weeklies with as much hot news as possible. Claud wrote the entire issue – a modest three pages of foolscap – and cut the stencils, touching up the material as he progressed, a routine that excluded any prospect of efficiency. An added complication was that none of Claud's associates had ever used a duplicating machine. As they experimented, 'stencils cracked like sails in a gale', bespattering the attic with a viscous brown ink. Nor did the presence of Crystal's Pekinese dog, 'Pig', help. Perhaps bored, or perhaps agitated by the commotion, 'Pig', whose bearing suggested that he was surrounded by 'a lot of loonies', attacked the reserve tubes of ink, chewing them up, covering himself with sticky ink and ruining piles of stationery in the process. Eventually, some sort of order was restored, and *The Week* finally emerged in what would would become its distinctive format, smudgy in appearance, lively in content. Its leading story told of a 'Black-Brown-Fascist plan', of 'plots and counterplots' in the European capitals over a Mussolini-sponsored four-power arrangement to regulate the affairs of Europe. Dramatically, it revealed that a definite proposal had been forwarded to London and Warsaw that envisaged granting concessions to Germany in the Polish Corridor while compensating Poland with a 'slice of Russian Ukraine'.*[7] Entirely satisfied with his

* During Ramsay MacDonald's visit to Rome in mid-March 1933, Mussolini had presented him with the draft of a four-power pact. A latter-day revival of the Concert of Europe, it called for the powers – Britain, Italy, Germany and France – to coordinate their policies, first in Europe, to carry through 'peaceful revision' of the post-war treaties, but also in all 'extra-European questions'. The pact was initialled that June. All along France had expressed great unease at the prospect of treaty revision, mindful that it might disrupt its eastern system. When Germany bolted from the League and the Disarmament Conference in October 1933, the French retaliated by scotching the Pact. It was never ratified. However, at the time the fear of German expansion in the East to recover its 'lost territories' was a given in European diplomatic and political circles. It was a theme enlarged upon regularly in *The Week*, where it was defined as the 'One Way Gun' syndrome. In the short run Polish–German relations were settled in an eye-catching manner by a ten-year non-

finished product, Claud and his helpers retired to the Café Royal to celebrate over bottles of champagne. The proprietors 'know me quite well', he assured his nervous aides, 'they will put the champagne on the slate'.

To sustain the degree of 'sensationalism' required, Claud relied on a formidable network of informants. It centred on a group of foreign correspondents based in London. Chief among them were Negley Farson of the *Chicago Daily News*, Frederick Kuh of the United Press, Stefan Litauer of the Polish News Agency, and Paul Scheffer of the *Berliner Tageblatt*, together with 'a varying group' of French journalists. Nourished by feelings of camaraderie, these gentlemen of the fourth estate cultivated Claud in the sure knowledge that he would float stories in *The Week* that their more scrupulous papers hesitated to publish – until they were confirmed. Two or three times a week they would meet at Farson's office in Bush House – identified as the 'lie factory' or 'devil's cauldron' – or around one of the marble-topped tables at the Café Royal to pool their information. Claud's range of sources widened. Dissident Conservative MPs, members of the Labour Party, City of London luminaries, visiting diplomats, contacts at the French, Italian, German and Soviet embassies – including Ivan Maisky, the Russian ambassador – landed in his web. A frequent visitor to the Continent, he maintained his previous contacts in Amsterdam, Brussels and Paris. In Berlin, Franz von Papen's *chef de cabinet*, Herbert von Bose, was a regular source until he was gunned down at his desk by Hitler's executioners, a victim of the 'Night of the Long Knives' of 30 June 1934.

Of particular importance was an old friend of Claud's, Vladimir Poliakoff. An experienced journalist, one-time diplomatic correspondent of *The Times*, later reporting for the *New York Times* (as the columnist 'Augur') and the *Evening Standard*, he was considered to be an authority on foreign affairs. Of Russian origin, Poliakoff was violently anti-German and – unlike Claud – fiercely anti-Communist. Extraordinarily well informed, he found his sources mainly in the anti-appeasement factions of the Foreign Office and the Quai d'Orsay, but also among senior officials of the Italian foreign service. His contacts operated at the very highest level. In London, he was on familiar terms with Rex Leeper, head of the News Department at the Foreign Office, and more importantly he found a line to Sir Robert Vansittart, its Permanent Under-Secretary. Both of these officials were anti-appeasers, and both, whenever it suited their purpose, leaked intelligence that reached Poliakoff, and usually Claud.[8] Like

aggression pact signed in January 1934. Nonetheless, *The Week*'s opening lead story eventually took concrete shape. During the German–Polish negotiations in the autumn and winter of 1938–9 Germany offered the above deal, only to have it 'flicked' aside by the Polish Foreign Minister, Colonel Beck.

Vansittart, Poliakoff aimed to split Fascist Italy from Nazi Germany in the hope of isolating Hitler, thereby strengthening the European anti-German front – a ploy that came to an ignominious finale with the abortive Hoare–Laval pact of December 1935. This was definitely not Claud's view, who regarded both these right-wing dictatorships with uncompromising hostility. Poliakoff, such was his enthusiasm for placating Italy, was accused by his enemies of being a hired agent of Mussolini. Once Claud, writing in the *Daily Worker*,* had dared to suggest that he had been the go-between in a backstairs intrigue involving the Italian government and Neville Chamberlain, a charge that led Poliakoff to issue a libel suit against the offending parties – unsuccessfully as it turned out.

This was a passing storm. It did not disrupt their intimacy. For Claud, Poliakoff 'strode and occasionally tiptoed around and about the diplomatic world of the twenties and thirties like a panther'. They would often meet at Poliakoff's small house in South Kensington, where, over a glass of lemon tea or vodka, or while exercising his two Afghan dogs in his garden, Poliakoff would impart to Claud in his 'harsh Slavonic accent' the latest political gossip he had garnered from his infinite variety of contacts. They were stories that appealed to Claud, for they had that particular 'zip and zang which you get from official sources only when a savage intra-mural departmental fight is going on'.

Precise circulation figures regarding *The Week* are difficult to come by. Claud originally relied on a readers' list numbering some 1,200 names. Kindly offered by the Union of Democratic Control, it consisted of one-time subscribers to its defunct journal, *Foreign Affairs*. This proved to be a complete dud. It brought in seven subscriptions, stabilizing at thirty-six. Some weeks later Claud was accidentally rescued from this potentially fatal setback by the unlikely figure of Ramsay MacDonald. The Prime Minister was acting President of a World Economic Conference then convening at the Geological Museum in South Kensington – a combination of topic and venue that presented the wits with a field day. *The Week* had reported on this event in dismal terms, casting grave doubts on its chances of success, remarking that the 'only spade at work on the Conference was the grave-digger's'. MacDonald decided to hold an off-the-record press conference

---

* In the mid-thirties Harry Pollit, leader of the British Communist Party, had asked Claud to report for the *Daily Worker* and to write a book about the Spanish Civil War, naturally from the Party's standpoint. Claud agreed. Adopting the *nom de plume* Frank Pitcairn, he doubled as the *Worker*'s assistant editor. Too free a spirit ever to submit fully to the Party's dictates, he nevertheless joined it, swept up by the general fervour that prompted so many of the European Left to champion Popular Fronts and other progressive causes that were openly battling the forces of reaction. Like so many of his contemporaries, he too placed the Communist Party in the vanguard of this epic struggle. No dogmatic Marxist, however, Claud quit the Party soon after the Second World War.

to dispose of these pessimistic forecasts. Foreign and diplomatic correspondents from all round the world made their way down into the crypt of the Museum, where, surrounded by its fossils, they waited to hear MacDonald put the record straight. Evil influences were everywhere, the Prime Minister railed, plotting and conspiring to sabotage his efforts to resolve the economic crisis. Suddenly he produced a document. Waving it at his audience, he cried: 'This, this is where you will find all this sort of thing coming from.' The impious document was the latest copy of *The Week*, from which MacDonald then proceeded to quote in order to prove his point. Before long the Economic Conference joined the other fossils in the Museum, laid to rest by a string of self-righteous platitudes. But MacDonald's revelation had provided Claud with his first major scoop. *The Week*'s future was secure.

After these disclosures *The Week*'s circulation rose steadily. Claud would take subscriptions in cash over his table at the Café Royal, using it as 'a nearly free place' as it charged only three shillings for a good bottle of wine. On one occasion Professor Joad came to his aid, declaring that no patron of the Café Royal could claim to have 'any idea upon what was going on unless he were a subscriber to *The Week*'. In time, Claud boasted that it was one of the half-dozen British publications most often quoted in the world press. According to its publisher–editor–chief correspondent, its subscribers included the

Foreign Ministers of eleven nations, all the embassies and legations in London, all diplomatic correspondents of the principal newspapers stationed in London, the leading banking and brokerage houses in London, Paris, Amsterdam, and New York, a dozen members of the United States Senate, twenty or thirty members of the House of Representatives, about fifty members of the House of Commons and a hundred or so in the House of Lords, King Edward VIII, the secretaries of most of the leading Trade Unions, Charlie Chaplin and the Nizam of Hyderabad.

Léon Blum and Joseph Goebbels read it; as did an inscrutable warlord in China. The Republican Senator William Borah, isolationist in outlook and Chairman of the Senate Committee for Foreign Affairs, cited it repeatedly; while Joachim Ribbentrop, Hitler's ambassador in London, called for its suppression, holding it to be the fount of all anti-Nazi evil.

There were other news-sheets that aimed at providing inside information.* None challenged *The Week*'s notoriety. Claud had every reason to

---

* Frederick August Voigt, the prominent journalist, edited *The Arrow*; Sir Joseph Ball, Director of the Conservative Research Department, brought out *Truth* (to serve Neville Chamberlain's interests); Gordon-Lennox printed his *Whitehall Letter*; and Commander Stephen King-Hall published the *King-Hall Newsletter*. A distinguished lawyer circulated a

rejoice, even if one friendly critic noted that *The Week* had 'achieved the remarkable feat of being 70 per cent right and 100 per cent wrong' – and that just for the events of 1939! One authority has put *The Week*'s circulation as high as 40,000. It had proved successful beyond Claud's wildest expectations. 'Not merely noticeable,' as he remarked, 'it was unquestionably the nastiest-looking bit of work that ever dropped on to a breakfast table.'

Broadsheet, while an Anglo-Catholic ecclesiastic produced *Father Desmond's Views*. It was also possible to subscribe to *In Plain English*, *Fleet Street News Letter*, and imperial news-sheets such as *Hong-Kong News Letter* and *Considerations*. Only King-Hall's paper matched *The Week*'s appeal.

CHAPTER 8

The Cliveden Set – Discovered or Invented?

The weekend of 23 October 1937 was typically autumnal – blustery, cloudy, with occasional showers but mild temperatures. At Cliveden it was full house: thirty to lunch. Among the house guests were the Anthony Edens – generally regarded as the prize catch – Sir Nevile Henderson (recently appointed Ambassador to Berlin), Sir Alexander Cadogan (soon to replace Vansittart as Permanent Under-Secretary at the Foreign Office), the Rt. Hon. Edward Algernon Fitzroy (Speaker of the Commons), Lady Alexandra Metcalfe and Lady Mary Ravensdale (Lord Curzon's daughters), John Walter Nicholls (Second Secretary at the Foreign Office), Robert Bernays (Liberal MP for Bristol North), Katherine Elliot, Tom Jones, and the regular contingent, Dawson, Lothian, Curtis and Bob Brand.[1]

The company was fond of playing an intellectual version of musical chairs: remaking the Cabinet, or assuming the responsibilities of the Prime Minister or the Foreign Secretary. One actual reshuffle that certainly pleased a majority of those present was the assumption of the premiership by Neville Chamberlain, replacing Baldwin. It signalled firmer direction at the top. Chamberlain would lead from the front, particularly in foreign affairs. And as he worked in tandem with Halifax, it was held that the Lord Privy Seal's fortunes were on the rise: this to the detriment of Eden's position. Considered by many who knew him well as 'a lightweight', Eden did not inspire all-out confidence among his colleagues. Perhaps all this put him under extra strain. Never in the best of health, he had 'aged' and looked 'dog-tired'. Eden did not stint his criticism of the Cabinet of which he, as Foreign Secretary, was a key player. 'Very weak,' he noted, revealing that the rearmament programme was 'far in arrears', and claiming that 'we can't do business with Germany until we are re-armed – say in 1940.'

No doubt, the Germany question dominated the conversation. New initiatives were in the air. This was much to Lothian's liking. He had been deeply influenced by two recent events: Hitler's sudden – though not unforeseen – coup of March 1936, when German troops had reoccupied the Rhineland, shattering the Locarno treaties; and the occasion, not quite six months past, of his second encounter with Hitler. His mood was pessimistic. For one thing, the Abyssinian *débâcle* and the Rhineland coup had killed the League. 'It was a noble ideal, but it is effectively over,' he concluded. But more to the point, parochial national interest – a Cliveden fixation – had triumphed over enlightened world government, their all-conquering panacea for international anarchy.

Lothian drew the obvious conclusion. Hitler had recovered, unilaterally, full sovereignty for Germany, taking the same measures to defend Germany as are claimed by every other independent country. In Berlin last May, he had found Goering in pugnacious mood and Hitler far from amiable, despite assurances about the inviolability of the Franco-German frontier and a pledge that 'no difficulties would arise from the German side in regard to eastern Europe'. Both Hitler and Goering had stressed the perilous state of the German minorities: Memel swallowed up by the Lithuanians; Danzig choked by the Poles; and the Sudeten Germans persecuted by the Czechs. Regarding Austria, although relations had improved of late, neither had ruled out the *Anschluss* at some future date. Their language, Lothian felt, conveyed a sinister threat of force. Hitler had bluntly stated that Germany 'would stand no nonsense next time'. Everywhere, they insisted, Britain stood in the way of legitimate German ambitions, national self-determination or the return of colonies. And everywhere, they persisted, the French were meddling in eastern Europe, blocking any reasonable settlement. Was this a repeat of the encirclement policy we knew from pre-war years, Lothian asked himself, recognizing all too well what it had led to in 1914.

These first-hand confrontations with the Nazi leadership had made a strong impression on Lothian. Time was running out. More than anything an Anglo-German dialogue must be revived. Here was the key to an overall European settlement. Lothian took Anthony Eden's Leamington speech as a starting point. Addressing his constituents on 20 November 1936, Eden had listed Britain's 'definite obligations', those in defence of which Britain would resort to arms: to preserve the integrity of the British Commonwealth; to defend France and Belgium against unprovoked aggression, in accordance with existing commitments; and to honour the treaties with Iraq and Egypt. Eden's declaration did not entirely satisfy Lothian. He wished to define what Britain would *not* fight for. Certainly not for the League, a broken vessel; nor to honour the obligations of others. As he had explained to the Nazi leaders, 'Britain had no primary interests in eastern Europe,' areas that fell within 'Germany's sphere'. To be be dragged into a conflict not of Britain's making and not in defence of its vital interests would bedevil relations with the Dominions, fatal for the unity of the Empire. For the Clivedenites, this was always the bottom line.

But how to lure Germany into an agreement? What was to be the bait? Naturally, sweeping colonial concessions were out of the question; some minor adjustments might be made in West Africa, although this issue was not of overriding concern to Hitler. Eastern Europe was the sticking point. In effect, Lothian was prepared to turn central and eastern Europe over to Germany, presenting Hitler with an 'Ottawa-like economic Mittel-Eur-opa'. When Lothian had remarked that nationalism was 'a basic factor in the modern world', Hitler pounced: what about the claims of ethnic Germans in Czechoslovakia, Memel, Austria, Danzig, he wanted to know. Ominously, Hitler added that if the persecution of these minorities continued the German frontier would have to lie 'much further east than its present position'. It was to circumvent such an eventuality that Lothian favoured abolishing the *status quo* by 'positive diplomacy'. Reined in by a French-inspired 'encirclement', Germany should be actively manoeuvred to 'a position of balance in Europe'. Why then, Lothian queried, oppose the *Anschluss*, or a settlement in Germany's favour of the Czech–Danzig –Memel crises?

Lothian set only one condition: that Germany should not 'destroy the independence of other non-German races in eastern Europe'. But what did this mean in practice when Lothian had made clear to Hitler that eastern Europe lay well within its orbit? That Hitler was an unsavoury, unscrupulous politician was not in question. But it was necessary to face reality, not evade it. Hitler ruled Germany with a popular mandate. Behind him stood more extremist groups, reckless, arrogant, brutal in character, pushing him forward. Given these bitter truths, Lothian argued that his guidelines constituted the 'optimal solution' to Germany's problems – and also, by definition, to Europe's. Was all this being unduly optimistic, self-deluding? Repeatedly, Hitler had extended an olive branch. Regretting 'the blunder of 1900' – when negotiations for an Anglo–German agreement had run into a dead end – and the disaster of 1914 for both Germany and Britain, he enticed Lothian with the exciting prospect of a meaningful Anglo–German dialogue. Lothian built much on these assurances. So confident was he that he conveyed his ideas to the Cabinet, and to the dominion prime ministers, who had gathered in London in May 1937 for the Imperial Conference.

Nancy, at any rate, would have found no fault in Lothian's reasoning. 'In twenty years', she was fond of saying, 'I've never known Philip to be wrong on foreign politics.' She might well have added a flourish of her own, pointing out that 'Germany should rearm, given that it is surrounded by hostile Roman Catholic Powers.' Waldorf too was firm for Lothian. 'Colonies for Germany is a matter of status,' he noted. 'Without them we

deny to Germany full equality of rights, its rehabilitation in its own eyes
after the humiliation of Versailles, a psychological factor of immense
importance.' Turning to central Europe, he did not propose dismembering
Czechoslovakia. But he broached a series of pertinent questions. 'Would
we send our menfolk across Europe to lay down their lives to preserve
Czechoslovakia? Would it be so terrible to see an extension of German
influence in the heartland of Europe? Is a strong Germany there a greater
danger to our Empire than a powerful Roman Empire dominating the
Mediterranean and Red Sea?'

There was no need to convince Dawson. In late October *The Times*
published a leader, 'The Claim to Colonies', that faithfully mirrored
Lothian's opinions. Dawson was strongly in favour of a direct Anglo-
German dialogue, unimpeded by extraneous players, including the League.
Then, having played its part in orchestrating a European settlement,
Britain should distance itself from irrelevant conflicts in eastern Europe.
Time was of the essence. Dawson knew this to be also Chamberlain's view
because Tom Jones, who was present at Cliveden that weekend, had told
the company so. 'We have spurned [Hitler's] repeated offers time and
again,' Jones said, echoing the Prime Minister's thoughts. 'They will not
be kept open indefinitely. His price will mount.' Hitler will surprise us
again, Jones believed. 'We cannot count on him taking no dramatic step in
the meantime.'

Nevile Henderson, another guest, agreed. As ambassador to Berlin his
views carried the stamp of authority, particularly at Cliveden. Not,
however, at the Foreign Office. Considered too weak, too vain, too shallow,
Henderson was regarded by most of his professional colleagues as being
excessively susceptible to Nazi pressure. Now he fully endorsed Lothian's
ideas.* Nor was he above raising the stakes if the company warranted it,
often giving the impression that he was acting as the Prime Minister's

* The Foreign Office saw Lothian as Henderson's *alter ego*, and in this case rightly so.
There can be no doubt that Henderson was swayed by Lothian's assessment of his talks with
the Nazi leaders. He parroted Lothian's opinions, point by point. The officials pounced
upon the unmistakable similarities between their respective memoranda. Vansittart was
particularly scornful. He thought Henderson's paper of 10 May 1937 (*DBFP*, Series 2, vol.
XIX, no. 53, 98–105, and FO371/20736/7232) 'ill-thought out and above all contrary to
the policy of H.M.G. ... [and] so crude a piece of work that it was not worthy of
circulation'. Other officials followed suit: 'This is the German doctrine'; 'This is Lord
Lothian'; 'This is again full acceptance of the German attitude'; 'Lord Lothian again, & in
full.' Lothian's own account of his visit (GD40/17/203, and *DBFP*, Series 2, vol. XVIII,
no. 480, 731 n9) provoked Vansittart's definition of him as 'a very amiably incurable
amateur' who proposed, 'to be quite precise, the conquest of Austria & Czechoslovakia & the
*re*conquest of Danzig and Memel; followed by the reduction of the other states to the
condition of satellites – *military* satellites – when required ... [this] is quite incompatible
with our interests.'

personal agent, hinting broadly that he was taking his instructions from 10 Downing Street and not the Foreign Office. 'Neville has outlined to me his thoughts on a German-European settlement,' Henderson revealed, promising, 'I can discharge this policy faithfully and with the utmost ease as it corresponds so closely with my private conceptions.'*[2]

Only Brand took exception to this general consensus. Agreement with Germany was possible, he assented, but not at the expense of 'breaking with France'. Theoretically, Brand's proviso was sound. But would it hold true when put to the test? In any case, having gone on record as saying that the extension of German influence eastwards might be 'a lesser evil' than going to war to prevent it, Brand had carelessly compromised himself.

The parameters of Cliveden's 'foreign policy' were clear-cut. As the League was now moribund, Britain must undertake foreign policy initiatives alone: first with Germany, and then gradually drawing in France and Italy. In this way, the Concert of Europe, in its classic nineteenth-century form, would be revived. There would be no concessions, no treaty revision, except within the framework of an overall European context – and this would have to include a reduction of arms and a solid commitment by the four powers to preserve the peace. There must be no policy of bluff, no sabre-rattling. Britain should never threaten war unless it intended to carry out the threat, even if Germany used force to revise Versailles, as over the Rhineland, for example. All were agreed that until an agreement was reached, Britain must continue to rearm and to institute some form of national service.

Lothian, forever fertile in thought, floated other options should this scenario not materialize. Following Dawson, he suggested that Britain could always revert to its traditional policy of 'detachment', of distancing itself from Europe. Backed by the Dominions, and if possible in company with the United States, Britain could create 'an oceanic group', an Anglo-American-Commonwealth naval *Pax* that would maintain world peace, just as the British fleet did in the nineteenth century. Perhaps unable to cope with the cruel realities of the twentieth century, Lothian looked back nostalgically to a once glorious, but no longer existent, past.

*

* There is no contemporary evidence that Henderson had a direct line to 10 Downing Street. In his memoirs he recorded one meeting with Chamberlain, sometime in April 1937, before he took up his post in Berlin, when there occurred, apparently, a congenial meeting of minds. Later, an acquaintance of Henderson's, Professor T. P. Conwell-Evans, who lectured in English literature at the University of Königsberg (and who had translated for Lothian at his interview with Hitler), recalled Henderson confessing to having received 'instructions constantly' from 10 Downing Street. Perhaps; but, equally, perhaps not. In any case, this entire crew – from the Cliveden group to Halifax (himself an honorary member), Henderson and Chamberlain – held similar, though not identical, views regarding an eventual Anglo-German agreement.

It would not be too fanciful to suggest that whatever political talk took place at Cliveden that weekend followed these general lines. Neither in substance nor in its personal make-up did this gathering differ from countless others. No sinister plots were hatched – at least not in the formal sense. The mood was certainly more buoyant, mainly because Neville Chamberlain, decisive and vigorous, had assumed the premiership and was known to be hostile to what was quaintly labelled the 'secular' view of the Foreign Office, intending, as he put it, 'to stir it up with a long pole'.[3] Yet as a result of this inoffensive get-together the myth of the 'Cliveden Set' was launched. It caught on like wildfire, beguiling a worldwide audience. No name was too improbable to be listed among its members, no intrigue too preposterous to be counted among its schemes.

It began with a newspaper scoop. On 9 November 1937 a report appeared in the *Evening Standard* that Lord Halifax, Master of the Middleton Hounds, had been invited to attend an International Hunting Exhibition in Berlin; but also that, as Lord President of the Council, he would conduct talks with the Nazi leaders. Three days later the government officially confirmed the visit. The following day the *Evening Standard* revealed the gist of a likely deal: 'Hitler is ready, if he receives the slightest encouragement, to offer to Great Britain a ten-year "truce" in the colonial issue ... In return ... Hitler would expect the British Government to leave him a free hand in Central Europe.'[4]

On 17 November, the day that Halifax arrived in Berlin, Claud Cockburn's *The Week* exposed the 'sensational' but 'true facts' of this 'sinister affair'. It claimed that the *Evening Standard*'s reports were correct in all essentials but one: the deal, as a concrete proposal, was first moulded 'into usable diplomatic shape' on 23–24 October by 'the queer Anglo-American gathering' at Cliveden that for years has 'exercised so powerful an influence on the course of "British" policy'. Beavering away at the heart of this intrigue was 'that little knot of expatriate Americans and "super-nationally" minded Englishmen', the Astors, Lothian, and the masters of Printing House Square, Dawson and Barrington-Ward. Pressure was exerted and Cabinet approval gained. Eden resisted the idea, but his opinion was taken for what it was worth, 'exactly nothing'. As a result, he tendered his resignation (on 8 November), but later withdrew it, turning it, like so many of Eden's 'nervous gestures', into 'a political event without consequences'. *The Week* failed to explain why Eden, the alleged victim of the plot, had been present at Cliveden that weekend, and Halifax, its instrument, had been absent.

Halifax's absence would not have bothered Cockburn. A Clivedenite himself, Halifax could be relied upon to play his part in the plot. As for Eden's presence, *The Week* cleared up that complication a week later. His charm masking his naivety, Eden had been invited to the 'fateful meeting' for a special purpose 'which it seems he did not understand': he was asked 'in order to "associate" him with the intrigue'. At Cliveden, Eden, apparently, had violently opposed the 'whole perilous business'; but to no avail. The Cabinet, behind his back – at the time he was in Brussels attending a conference – decided to go ahead with the Halifax mission. More names were added to the alleged conspiracy: Henderson, obviously; Lord Londonderry, notoriously pro-German in outlook; and the Aga Khan, an intimate of the Clivedenites who subscribed fully to their revisionist convictions. 'Aga was in grand form,' Dawson once noted, '& surveyed the European situation . . . with amazing knowledge and good sense. He is all of my mind on the subject of Germany.' Lothian, 'as usual', was hovering ominously in the background, serving as 'the main link with Cliveden and "The Times"'.*[5]

These revelations about bypassing Eden and the Foreign Office had been inspired by a variety of sources. The Foreign Office had known about the proposed visit for some time; indeed, rumours of it had been in the air since April 1936. On 14 October – ten days before the fateful gathering at Cliveden – Halifax, in Churchill's presence, had informed Eden that he had been invited to Berlin by Goering, that he would certainly see Hitler, that the Prime Minister approved, and that therefore he had accepted. Eden evinced little enthusiasm at this news, but he saw no sound reason to oppose Halifax's trip. Feelings ran higher among his officials. According to the well-known journalist Frederick Augustus Voigt, Vladimir Poliakoff, who had originally scooped the story in the *Evening Standard*, had been briefed by 'a high official in the F.O. . . . so that it would receive stunt publicity and be denied by the Germans'. Poliakoff's exposé did indeed generate a fierce protest from the Germans, but not to the point of cancelling the visit. Who had leaked the information? Most probably Rex Leeper, Head of the Foreign Office News Department, prompted by his chief, Vansittart. Vansittart, whose relations with both Eden and Chamberlain were at the lowest of premiums, was especially hostile, as his minutes vividly show. A desperate ploy on Vansittart's part, it sealed his fate. By December he had been effectively neutralized. Given no option, he accepted the title of Chief Diplomatic Adviser to the Government, a post devoid of real power and influence. Long considered by the Clivedenites as their *bête noire*, Vansittart's fall was greeted by them with cries of joy; they even – though mistakenly – claimed some credit for it. Nevertheless, according to at least one source, the Vansittart–Poliakoff–Cockburn combination continued to operate against them.[6]

---

* Londonderry, a member of the Anglo-German Fellowship, had himself visited Germany for talks with the Nazi leaders, including Hitler. He also claimed responsibility for 'putting the idea into Halifax's head' of a meeting with Hitler.

So far, these two issues of *The Week*, feeding its readers with alleged insider information on the Halifax visit, had hardly created a stir. In Claud Cockburn's words: 'Absolutely nothing happened. It made about as loud a bang as a crumpet falling on a carpet.' Other Cockburn 'crumpets' had fallen equally silently in the past. Since the spring of 1936, he had pinpointed the Cliveden group as among those who were pointing a 'one way gun', with Hitler's finger on the trigger, eastwards. The Astors, *The Week* had established, were among the 'most important supporters of German influence here', commanding an 'extraordinary position of concentrated political power'. And as for 'rising young politicians', invitations to Cliveden were more important to them 'than the fact that the end of all these lovely editorials, dinners and garden parties will be war'. These suggestive particulars, though irksome and unwelcome, were deemed by the Astor group as being of small consequence. Typical of the lack of journalistic standards flaunted by *The Week*, they made little general impact.[7]

All this changed from 22 December 1937. In this issue *The Week* intensified its assault on Cliveden, 'the Halifax coup' once again providing its main story, but now identifying 'the Cliveden Set' as the villain of the piece. It had already disclosed (24 November) that Halifax – pigeon-holed as 'the representative of Cliveden and Printing House Square rather than of more official quarters' – had raised the questions of Austria and Czechoslovakia with Hitler. Any 'military aims', judged *The Week*, will be camouflaged by so much hot air about 'plebiscites and self-determination of minorities', more 'soothing syrup' for the British public. Unexpectedly, the plotters had suffered a setback. Chamberlain's 'studiously vague references' in the Commons amounted to 'a deadlock' in the negotiations; in effect it signified a 'resounding defeat of "the Cliveden Set" and "Printing House Square"'. Checked momentarily, 'the "friends" of the Third Reich' would not yield. 'A new push' was anticipated. 'Exposed to the demands of the Astor family', Chamberlain was highly vulnerable to the 'vast influences emanating from Cliveden', Britain's 'other Foreign Office'. An even more dangerous 'putsch', to be orchestrated by the 'Set', was confidently predicted.[8]

One point should be stressed immediately. No plot was concocted at Cliveden that weekend. There was no need to. At the most, there emerged the usual coincidence of opinions. Lothian, Dawson and the Astors were all strongly in favour, under certain conditions, of earmarking eastern Europe as a sphere of German influence. Curtis was more cautious. He had faulted Lothian's stand over the Rhineland, fearing that his 'dearest friend' was encouraging German aggression. But he too did not rule out new arrangements in eastern Europe, granting Germany 'special economic privileges' there; or of breaking up Czechoslovakia into autonomous cantons, mainly to appease the *Sudetendeutsche*. Nor was Brand, the most anti-Nazi of the group, quite so firm as might be supposed. Highly critical of Lothian's pro-appeasement views, and ready to fight to preserve western Europe, he would, albeit reluctantly, consider allowing Germany 'a free hand' in central and eastern Europe.[9]

This coincidence of opinion extended to Halifax and Neville Chamberlain. Chamberlain viewed the Berlin visit as 'a great success', having paved the way for negotiations with Germany about 'the practical questions involved in a European settlement'. Even Eden stood up to be counted, swinging behind his chief's point of view, at least on paper. After 'a very satisfactory talk' they found themselves 'in absolute agreement about Germany'. Later, Eden informed the Prime Minister: 'As you know, I entirely agree that we must make every effort to come to terms with Germany.' Eden, as Foreign Minister, knew that for some years now his Ministry had been engaged in a search for a German agreement, though without success. Experience had left a majority of its officials extremely doubtful whether anything of substance could be squeezed out of Germany; but they could offer no convincing reason not to make another effort. This state of mind was more broadly based, reflecting a wide spectrum of so-called informed public opinion. Cockburn's 'Cliveden Set' – or certain members of it – broke this general consensus only by the intensity of their conviction that a German agreement *had* to be reached.[10]

Hidden beneath *The Week*'s farrago of creative journalism there were some grains of truth. In one important particular *The Week* had got it right. Halifax, armed with Foreign Office memoranda – including Henderson's, but also a less compromising one by William Strang, Head of the Central Department – had spoken to Hitler about a negotiated extension of German influence in eastern Europe, along the same lines that Lothian and Company had been advocating for some time. 'Britain has no primary interests in Eastern Europe,' Lothian had told Hitler (4 May 1937), offering him these areas as a special, indeed exclusive, German sphere of interest. 'On all these matters [Danzig, Austria, Czechoslovakia],' Halifax had told Hitler (17 November 1937), 'we were not necessarily concerned to stand for the *status quo* as today . . . If reasonable settlements could be reached with . . . those primarily concerned we certainly had no desire to block.' This was not quite *The Week*'s 'one way gun'. Halifax had not declared 'open season' on eastern Europe. But what had registered with the Germans was the fact that Halifax, of his own accord, had raised the question of 'certain changes in the European system', specifically to ease the plight of German minorities in central and eastern Europe.[11]

Two weeks prior to Halifax's arrival, Hitler had addressed a closed circle of Germany's military chiefs – with von Neurath, the Foreign Minister, also in attendance – on the goals of German policy. To secure, preserve and enlarge 'the racial community', Hitler had lectured them, it was necessary to acquire additional *Lebensraum* in the East, an aim that could be realized only 'by means of force', warning that this was never without 'attendant risks'. Specifically, he outlined scenarios whereby Czechoslovakia and Austria would be overrun. And although he now identified Britain as a 'hate-inspired antagonist', he also maintained that Britain had written off the Czechs. No decision for war had been taken, but Hitler had clearly raised his sights, targeting his long-standing goal of expansion eastwards. In this way, Halifax's visit – to say nothing of Lothian's incessant lobbying – confirming Britain's indifference in areas so vital to Germany's future could only have reassured Hitler. Given these broad hints, Hitler would surely draw the conclusion – not extravagant in the circumstances – that Britain was open to diplomatic extortion, if shrewdly applied. Accordingly, as 1938 progressed and Hitler gobbled up Austria and dismembered Czechoslovakia – with apparent British acquiescence, or at least with no fierce response – *The Week*'s piquant revelations were lent added credibility.[12]

The term 'Cliveden Group' or 'Clique', a chic, elitist coterie that convened frequently at Cliveden, had been a commonplace item in the political and gossip columns for some time. It precipitated no great stir. But 'The Cliveden Set' had about it a more sophisticated, mysterious ring. The phrase first appeared on 28 November 1937 in the *Reynolds News*, a Labour-oriented Sunday that ran substantially the same story as *The Week* about pro-German shenanigans at Cliveden. Almost a month later the term was picked up by *The Week*. Featuring 'The Cliveden Set' as its main story, it assured its readers that this conniving and disloyal gang of top-drawer Englishmen and expatriate Americans had a set agenda of further putsches. Within weeks the machinations of 'The Cliveden Set' had become a topic for worldwide speculation.

If Claud Cockburn did not actually coin the term, he most certainly benefited from it. 'The consequences', he recalled, 'astounded me.' *The Week*'s tiny office became a mecca for journalists the world over anxious to cash in on the latest sensation. Once set in motion, the catchphrase 'went marching on, round and round the world'. Cockburn continued to snipe at Cliveden. Naturally, he assumed that Vansittart's so-called promotion was the work of '*les Cagoulards*' (the 'Hooded Ones'), as he now dubbed the Astor–Lothian circle. This was a damning smear. In the autumn of 1937, *les Cagoulards*, an extreme right-wing faction in France, had conspired to overthrow the Third Republic: their plot had been uncovered, but not before bombs had exploded near the Etoile. 'Schloss Cliveden' rose above the Thames – with, no doubt, Nancy as its reigning Queen, and Lothian its Crown Prince. At the same time, David Low, the *Evening Standard*'s brilliant cartoonist, conceived his 'Shiver Sisters' series, catching Nancy, Lothian and Dawson holding high the slogan 'Any Sort of Peace at Any Sort of Price'; or, choreographed by a gleeful Goebbels, ballet dancing (or goose-stepping?) to the tune of a Nazi 'Foreign Policy' gramophone record. The 'Shiver Sisters' also attained star billing in *Babes in the Wood – the Panto with a Political Point*, a pantomime produced by the Communist-run Unity Theatre. According to the *Daily Worker* it played to full houses throughout the winter of 1938–9.[13]

No British publication, from the *Manchester Guardian* to *Lilliput*, overlooked the 'Set's' delinquent behaviour. In particular, the left-wing press had a field day. Commenting on the stony 'Germanic Astor heart', *Reynolds News* incarcerated Chamberlain 'in protective custody at Cliveden', spotlighting the 'Men – and the women – behind the Cabinet crises and Great Britain's surrender to Fascist blackmail'. The *News Chronicle*, *Tribune* and the *Daily Worker* reported in similar fashion, detecting 'treachery' at every step, naming Berlin as Nancy's 'spiritual home'. The Communist Party soon discovered another long-expected coup. It alleged that at a weekend party at Cliveden in January 1938 the 'Set' had engineered the campaign that led eventually to Eden's resignation as Foreign Secretary and his replacement by Halifax. Having already pulled down Vansittart, the 'Set' had now toppled Eden.* These wild stories made superb copy. Covered in detail in the Dominions, they amused and thrilled readers throughout the world. From Vancouver to Tokyo, via New York and Berlin, the presumed machinations of 'The Cliveden Set' titillated vast audiences.[14]

The circle of conspirators expanded to fantastic dimensions. Everyone who was anyone was included, or so it seemed. Apart from the regulars, it was confidently reported that the Londonderrys, Sir John Simon (Chancellor of the Exchequer), Sir Samuel Hoare (Home Secretary), Sir Montagu Norman (Governor of the Bank of England), Lady Honor Guinness (Channon), Sir Henri Deterding (Director-General of Royal Dutch Shell), Sir Harry McGowen (Chairman of Imperial Chemical Industries), Sir Josiah Stamp (a prominent statistician and economist), and many others were among the Cliveden activists. Here were the guilty ones, all highly placed, who were deliberately manipulating British foreign policy. Thirty years after these events, Claud Cockburn, the chief propagator of these tales, finally admitted that many of his aspiring plotters

---

* This putsch went unrecorded in the columns of *The Week*, perhaps because Cockburn knew that Cliveden had been closed throughout January: the Astors were visiting the United States and Lothian was touring India. It is quite possible that Cockburn placed the 'scoop' in the *Daily Worker*, where he was doubling up as a correspondent.

'would not have known a plot if you had put it under their noses and quite simply had gone to Cliveden for a good dinner' – or, he should have added, had not gone there at all!¹⁵

As the Astors ran a London establishment, that too was kept under close observation. Prompted by Cockburn, 1930s-style paparazzi loitered by the entrance of 4 St James's Square, hoping to snap the conspirators in the act. They succeeded. 'Come on, Geoffrey, we're compromised. Better pose nicely,' instructed Nancy. 'Awful things they've said about us . . . [they] think we're spies or something.' Dawson played the game. 'Who are you?' asked one unschooled photographer. 'Ribbentrop,' he replied blithely. Halifax appeared. Walking 'stiffly' towards the paparazzi he brushed past them, looking a little astonished, and enquired with a smile: 'What's going on here?' Tom Jones lacked his friends' sense of humour. When he realized that he had been ambushed, he panicked. Covering his head in his raincoat like a wanted criminal, he bolted up the steps and disappeared into the house to partake of his harmless lunch. As reported, the conduct of 'Lady Astor's Gang' was highly suspicious.¹⁶

A month later the goings-on in St James's Square led to some heated exchanges in the Commons. Nancy had invited Neville Chamberlain to yet another of her luncheon parties, this time to meet a group of North American journalists. The Prime Minister had been remarkably indiscreet, revealing the background to Eden's resignation, particularly as it related to Anglo-American relations. He also left them with the strong impression that he favoured concessions to the dictator states within the framework of a German–Italian–Franco–British pact to be aimed, eventually, at the Soviet Union. At least, this was the gist of his remarks as reported in their newspapers. Explanations were called for. Why, enraged MPs asked, was the Prime Minister briefing American reporters when he should be making his foreign policy statements 'to the representatives of the people in this House'. 'Not a word of truth in it,' interjected Nancy. No interview had taken place. The object of the luncheon was solely to enable Chamberlain to meet the journalists 'privately and informally'. The angry MPs remained unconvinced. Nothing, apparently, could expunge the damaging image of Nancy's house parties. Later, a horrified Eden reported from America that 'Nancy and her Cliveden set has done much damage, and 90 per cent of the US is firmly persuaded that you [Baldwin] and I are the only Tories who are not fascists in disguise.' Even when Nancy protested at the occupation of Prague she was met with cries of 'Cliveden', 'Why don't you have another lunch?'¹⁷

Much of the criticism of the 'Set' was focused on Nancy. Her flamboyant, provocative style aroused antipathy on all sides, even though in some ways she was the least culpable of the group, certainly when compared to the hard-liners, Dawson and Lothian. 'The harm which these silly hostesses do is really immense,' grumbled Harold Nicolson. 'They convey to foreign envoys the impression that policy is decided in their own drawing-rooms . . . I should be most unhappy if I were Lady Astor. She must realize that her parrot cries have done much damage to what (to do her justice) she must dimly realize is the essence of her adopted class and country.'[18]

Denounced from the soapboxes at Hyde Park Corner, Nancy and her Clivedenites were attacked from all quarters. Sir Stafford Cripps (Labour MP for East Bristol and advocate of a Popular Front against fascism) weighed in, as did Willie Gallacher (Communist MP for West Fife), to name but two of the more articulate. From across the Atlantic, similar voices were heard. Upton Sinclair, the radical American writer, lent his considerable skills to dealing further blows to Cliveden's tottering reputation.[19]

Naturally, the 'friends' felt compelled to defend their reputations. Nancy, in typical fashion, inveighed against 'all this mischievous rubbish', the source of which was 'a false and stupid story published in a Communist rag'. She proclaimed her faith in 'Democracy and in Parliamentary government', while registering her opposition 'to all forms of dictatorship, whether Fascist, Nazi or Communist'. Waldorf was more restrained: 'The whole conception of a "Cliveden Set" is a myth from beginning to end,' he cautioned the readers of *The Times*. In Glasgow, at a meeting of Scottish Liberals, Lothian fobbed off the whole affair as 'a complete mare's nest'. Dawson was as discreet as ever. After being caught 'red-handed' by the paparazzi, he confined his protest to his diaries, tamely remarking that 'The "Cliveden Gang" business is becoming tiresome.' The Astors eventually found a champion in George Bernard Shaw, who no doubt accounted himself a paid-up member of the 'Set'. 'I could prove that Cliveden is a nest of Bolshevism, or indeed of any other bee in the world's bonnet,' he asserted, concluding that 'Never has a more senseless fable got into the headlines.' But Shaw's somewhat condescending style probably did his friends more harm than good. At any rate, his contribution to the debate provoked another riposte from Upton Sinclair. If nothing else, controversy raged.[20]

No matter how vehemently, and cogently, the Astors and Company proclaimed their innocence, their denials failed to carry conviction. There was no end to the amount of calumny heaped upon them, in particular upon Nancy. Hate mail of the crudest type began to arrive. Addressed to 'Mrs Judas', it read: 'Nancy had a Fancy Boy named Hitler. When's the baby arriving?' Or, 'You blasted American whore of a chorus-girl. Go back to your own country!' Scarcely veiled threats were also delivered: 'When

you reach our shores again . . . you will get what is coming to you.'
'Resign!' demanded one ill-wisher. 'Pro-Germans are not wanted in a
British Parliament.'

Some criticism was more dignified but no less telling. At the height of
the Munich crisis Nancy received a forceful reminder of how treacherous
her – and her cronies' – behaviour appeared to outsiders:

> I hope you now realize how scandalous has been the conduct of the pro-Nazi
> element in our National life as represented by yourself, various members of yr
> family and certain aristocrats who have apparently dictated our foreign policy
> since Chamberlain took over . . . [you] should shamefacedly retire from public
> life . . . No National unity can be obtained with our present traitorous Premier
> who has fooled the electors long enough, and whose anti-Red bias has led to
> the surrender of our honour and perhaps even of our Empire . . . I should
> certainly not like to be a Londonderry or an Astor if a war starts as all those
> who have hitherto toadied to Hitler will incur inevitably public odium – as I
> think, fully deserved.'[21]

From Nancy's perspective all this was a carefully orchestrated smear
campaign: its instigator, the corrupt Claud Cockburn. When John
Strachey finally introduced them in the lobby of the House of Commons,
Nancy, instead of shaking hands, made as if to spit at him.[22]

One other aspect of Nancy's behaviour gave rise to much hostile
comment. Her all too frequent outbursts against the Jews – so easily
interpreted as an indication of anti-Semitism – did nothing to repair her
tattered reputation. Here was another link that tied her to Hitler – and
perhaps, by association, also her friends. Was it a result of the increasing
strain she was under, or her perpetually loose tongue, or her inbred
prejudices? Probably, a combination of all three. It began in New York in
the summer of 1937. About to sail for Europe, she complained to reporters
of 'the appalling anti-German propaganda here'. 'If the Jews are behind
[it],' she warned, 'they've gone too far. And it will react on them.' The
American Jewish Congress (Women's Division) responded spiritedly.
'Dear Lady Astor,' wrote Louise Wise, its president,

> If Jews in America are against Nazi Germany, it is because they conceive it to
> be their duty as Americans to battle for civilization and humanity and therefore
> to stand against the crimes of Hitlerism . . . to render their country the service
> of making it aware of that monstrous iniquity – imperiling all that men hold
> dear in the political and spiritual world – of Nazism or Hitlerism.

Nancy protested. Her intention had been 'to help the Jews as anyone else',
claiming, in an astonishing rewriting of history, that 'The Zionist

Movement [had] started in this House.' In fact, Nancy had no doubt of the Jews' ultimate responsibility, writing confidently to Lothian some time later of 'this Jewish Communistic propaganda'.[23]

Matters got out of hand after a stormy meeting of the Foreign Affairs Committee in the House on 28 February 1938. Harold Nicolson witnessed the scene.

> In the corridor a friend of mine called Alan Graham (Conservative MP for the Wirral Division of Cheshire) came up to Nancy and said, 'I do not think you behaved very well.' She turned upon him and said, 'Only a Jew like you would *dare* to be rude to me.' He replied, 'I should much like to smack your face.' I think she is a little mad.[24]

This ugly incident was widely reported in the press. So was another. Guests at a private dinner of the English Speaking Union noted that Nancy's 'emotions about the Jews' had overcome 'her sense of fitness'. 'Is not this lady's spiritual home in Berlin?' asked the *News Chronicle*. Nancy refuted these charges: they have 'caused pain not only to me but to many of my friends who are themselves Jews'. But her denials lacked conviction. Denounced as 'fanatically anti-Jewish', Nancy's reputation would not survive these accusations.[25]

There was, however, another side to her much publicized anti-Jewish bigotry. Some years earlier Nancy had responded favourably to appeals from Lewis Namier and 'Baffy' Dugdale to help place German Jewish academics, refugees from Nazi persecution, in British universities. The fate of German Jewish women and children also moved her, and she cooperated in funding a special appeal to alleviate their desperate plight. This was the giving side of her character. In March 1938, Felix Frankfurter, a major figure in American jurisprudence, soon to be appointed as a Supreme Court judge, turned to Nancy for help. His uncle, Dr Solomon Frankfurter, an elderly scholar resident in Vienna, had been rounded up by the Nazis in the days immediately after the *Anschluss*: could Nancy help? Without a second thought, she intervened – and in characteristic style. As she put it, she spoke to the German ambassador in London 'in no uncertain terms'. Demanding the immediate release of Frankfurter's unfortunate relative, she warned the German diplomat that unless her petition was fulfilled she would go to Vienna herself – hinting at an international scandal. Dr Solomon Frankfurter was released on 28 March.

Nancy informed Frankfurter of the good news. But at the same time she defended Cliveden's good name against the foul accusations fabricated by 'a Communist Sheet', discounting them as a transparent attempt 'to create suspicion and a class war'. 'I am very much surprised', she went on, 'that you knowing me and having visited Cliveden should have swallowed all this propaganda.' Frankfurter made clear that it was not the 'gossip-mongering' that upset him, but the 'political philosophy' that Cliveden had come to represent, of acquiescence 'in the series of violent measures taken by Hitler and the general undermining of international law and order and the decencies of civilization'. But he was equally candid about Nancy's more outrageous statements about the Jews. The American press was not controlled by the Jews, he remarked, correcting one of Nancy's wilder allegations. Anti-Semitism '[is] an essential aspect of Nazism', he reminded her, and to persist in this vein would lead people to 'infer a sympathy on your part with Hitler's anti-Semitism' which, Frankfurter added, 'I know to be untrue'. Nancy listened; but there is no evidence that she heeded Frankfurter's wise advice.[26]

It was a familiar syndrome. Nancy could relate to, respect, even like, Jews, or Catholics, on an individual level, but would inevitably suspect the worst of them as a collective entity. During the First World War, Chaim Weizmann, the Zionist leader, attended an Astor dinner party. Apropos of nothing, Nancy told her guests that before she had met Weizmann 'she had disliked Jews'. In her inimitable way, she alerted her guests. 'Don't believe him!' she exclaimed, glaring at Weizmann. 'He's a great charmer. He will convert you to his point of view. He is the only decent Jew I have ever met.' Stunned into dead silence, the embarrassed guests looked down at their plates, at a loss how to react. It was a pattern to be repeated many times in the future.[27]

CHAPTER 9

Rethinking

The furore levelled at the 'Cliveden Set' never slackened, even though as war approached the views of its members underwent perceptible changes. During the winter of 1937–8 a sort of 'brains trust' on foreign affairs functioned at All Souls College. Dubbed by Lionel Curtis as 'Salter's Soviet', it took its nickname from the Gladstone Professor of Political Theory and Institutions at Oxford, Sir Arthur Salter, the main driving force behind the group. As Curtis had been largely responsible for Salter's appointment, it was only natural that he should be invited to join the team. For some years now Curtis had maintained a relatively low profile in public affairs. His main concern had been to complete his masterwork, *Civitas Dei*, the third volume of which had appeared in October 1937. Its contemporary political message echoed clearly the nuances of the pro-appeasement school, reflecting majority opinion among the Round Tablers: an attack on the onerous and humiliating terms of the Versailles treaty; a blank condemnation of French policy as vindictive and short-sighted; extreme alarm at the inflated number of sovereign states, a phenomenon he deplored as it increased the likelihood of war; and lastly, and logically, no faith in the League as an instrument of world peace.

But *Civitas Dei* was also, indeed primarily, a blueprint for the future. It envisaged a new global system, one free of the selfish, predatory nationalism that in the past had wrecked all hope of international cooperation and a world commonwealth. Instead, it would unite mankind, rendering 'all men obedient to laws common to all in things which affect them'. Its kernel would be Curtis's vision of the British (or English-speaking) Commonwealth, a creation he saw as the nearest representation to the Kingdom of God on earth. Only when human society had attained this sacred goal would it realize its full potential. Curtis's *magnum opus* was greeted coolly. At All Souls, the criticism (of the first volume) had been 'shattering'. T. E. Lawrence referred to this 'puzzling, awkward book', but thought also that it displayed 'courage and common sense, as well as wisdom', qualities that will cause 'the public to spit on it'. Still, he added generously, 'great swordsmen' shouldn't care. On imperial federation, the essential first stage in Curtis's grand design, the Moot split: Brand and Grigg against, Lothian and Curtis for. But even Lothian cautioned against any explicit endorsement of Curtis's writings, a plain sign of Curtis's blossoming reputation as a crank.[1]

'Salter's Soviet' was composed of a mixed bunch. Vigorous critics of the government's foreign policy, Harold Nicolson or A. L. Rowse, rubbed shoulders with its loyal defenders, Lord Allen of Hurtwood or Arnold Toynbee, or even Curtis himself. Other members included Harold Macmillan, Basil Liddell Hart, H. A. L. Fisher and Geoffrey Hudson; while figures such as Dawson, Brand, Lothian and Amery remained on its fringes, available for consultation when necessary. In some ways it was a perfect framework for Curtis, a natural-born proselytizer. But on this occasion he failed to batter his colleagues into submission. The young firebrands on the 'Soviet', Rowse and Hudson, frustrated him, particularly as Curtis detected in them the same 'streak of fanaticism' that had moved him at their age. Rowse in particular was viewed as an incorrigible troublemaker. Having recently clashed with Lothian in a public and acrimonious debate in the correspondence columns of The Times, Rowse readily identified Lothian as Britain's 'public enemy number one'. Although not maligned in the same manner, Curtis was damned guilty by association. His advocacy of more favourable arrangements for Germany, 'special economic privileges' in eastern Europe, or the cantonization of Czechoslovakia to resolve the injustices done to the Sudeten Germans, failed to convince the 'Soviet'. Curtis had set out with the premise that 'twenty years of peace were worth any price', but came away thwarted, appalled by Nicolson's 'anti-German stance'. The split between 'the realists and the moralists', as Nicolson put it, was complete. After several months the 'Soviet' dispersed without reaching an agreed statement of intent, differing on everything except the need for more efficient air defence precautions, a measure backed vigorously by Curtis. Still, in some circles Curtis's image as the pre-eminent wheeler-dealer continued to flourish. In one flight of fancy, the diarist of Time and Tide renamed the 'Cliveden Set' the 'Curtis Set'.[2]

The first German move into central Europe, the absorption of Austria in March 1938, sharpened the differences among the core members of the 'Set'. Brand, its principal dissident, took issue with Dawson, forever indulgent to German claims. For some time now The Times, in everything but name, had been advocating the Anschluss. In one leader it had referred to the 'crude blunder' of Versailles in forbidding it. 'The gravitational pull of a nation of 70 million cannot be denied,' it pontificated, asserting that 'It would be as easy to divert the Gulf Stream.' Other editorials in the same vein followed, noted with much alarm by the Foreign Office and the Czechs, and 'with much satisfaction' in Berlin. You are too 'pro-German', Brand told Dawson. Why does *The Times* keep harping on the theme that 'Austria should have been included in Germany at the Peace Treaty', he asked. 'Do we consider it desirable to hand over a still relatively cultivated and civilized state to be Nazified?' Dawson denied these charges, but not to Brand's satisfaction. In executing the *Anschluss* Hitler had wielded the 'mailed fist in the most brutal form', Brand retorted. One day we shall have to oppose him and 'the result will be war'.[3]

If Dawson, or *The Times* (the two were considered synonymous), advocated the *Anschluss* to settle a long-standing grievance, Lothian regarded the demise of Austria by the 'mailed fist' with some satisfaction. By ending the hegemony of the League of Nation powers, a 'disastrous period' that had driven the Germans to National Socialism 'as the one method by which they could recover their unity and their natural rights', it offered a favourable opportunity to rebuild Europe on a new and more equitable basis. The outstanding issues in Europe, those of the German minorities, could now be resolved, of course by consent. Lothian tempered his ardour by insisting on a display of physical strength – some form of national service – sufficient to convince the fascist powers that war would be the alternative to agreed revision. As 'substantial international (though not internal) justice at last exists in Europe', he thought it was possible to make this demand. After the brutal destruction of Austria as an independent state, Lothian's public consistency of purpose takes on a surrealistic dimension. But Lothian was never wholly consistent. Privately, he was already airing reservations. 'We have now got so much nearer to a position of collective justice for Germany that the problem of preventing Germany going beyond what is legitimate may soon become urgent,' he wrote to Allen of Hurtwood. What was legitimate? Primarily to neutralize French influence in eastern Europe where Germany would then be allowed to establish 'a proper economic foundation for her life'. Eastern Europe was still the sticking point: he would not countenance an automatic British commitment there.[4]

No sooner had the immediate shock of the *Anschluss* died down than 'the League of Nation powers' geared themselves up to meet the long anticipated Czech crisis. 'It seems to me', Smuts wrote to Lothian, expressing a general view, '[that] with Austria in his possession, Hitler has unlocked the door to South Eastern Europe.' His conclusions were more contentious. Lothian was lectured on the 'inevitability' of Germany overrunning, 'politically and commercially', the whole of south-eastern Europe. This prospect did not faze Smuts. No vital British – or imperial – interest was at stake. And if only Britain pursued the right course, it did not necessarily mean war. 'Why should Germany fight if she can achieve

188 · *The Cliveden Set*

her ends by peaceful penetration and the spread of Nazism?' So, Smuts argued to an attentive Lothian, while Germany becomes master of the Continent, Britain 'may have to confine herself to the position of . . . an interested spectator and no more'. Smuts admitted that it was an 'ugly picture' and smacked of 'defeatism'. But was there a realistic alternative, he asked. However controversial, Smuts's views were perceived in some circles as being entirely rational and perceptive; and his massive reputation as a shrewd, responsible statesman lent added weight to his judgements.[5]

The Czech crisis did not overtake western statesmen unawares. In some ways, it had been on the European agenda since the Versailles settlement. It now simmered menacingly for the next six months. However tackled, it presented a problem of considerable complexity, one not given to foolproof solutions. Guided by Thomas Masaryk and Eduard Beneš, Czechoslovakia promised to be the one country in central and eastern Europe where liberal, democratic institutions would flourish, a stable element in an unsettled area. Yet its problems were formidable. Involved in border disputes with its neighbours, it was rent internally by national and religious discord. Bound by treaties to France and the Soviet Union, Czechoslovakia was a vital link in the so-called encirclement of Germany, a notion anathema to the Clivedenites. Beneš, the Czech president, though a skilful politician and diplomat, was burdened by a high-handed, overbearing reputation. But worst of all, as Lothian never tired of telling his friends, Beneš was guilty of acting as an instrument of French policy. Jan Masaryk, the Czech minister in London, struck back. Protesting at yet another 'unjust attack on Beneš', he suggested that Lothian cease 'parcelling out pieces of Europe'. Lothian gave away nothing in return. Fully determined to acknowledge 'the legitimate claims of Germany' by annulling 'the fundamental errors of the Versailles Settlement', he claimed to be advancing 'the cause of peace'.[6]

Many, probably a majority of Englishmen conversant with European affairs, were troubled at the Czech government's treatment of its ethnic minorities. The plight of the Sudeten Germans, in particular, received much sympathetic coverage, generating widespread feeling in favour of some sort of autonomy for the Sudetenland, or at least a lessening of its ties to the central government in Prague. Much of the credit for this was due to Konrad Henlein, the leader of the Sudeten German Party, a paid agent of the Germans who had been instructed by Hitler always to pitch his demands too high for the Czechs to accept. Henlein visited London on three occasions. Presenting himself as a moderate hemmed in by extremists, his carefully staged performances were sufficiently compelling to convince even the most implacable of anti-Nazis, Vansittart or Churchill, for example, who found him 'moderate' and 'amenable'. Henlein's public relations campaign yielded rich dividends. He lectured to sympathetic audiences at Chatham House and met leading politicians and officials. It was hardly surprising that the Clivedenites felt in tune with his litany of complaints. Even Brand, the strong man among them, was in favour of substantial concessions to the Sudeten Germans – but not to the point of any erosion of Czech sovereignty; and certainly not to the use of force to extinguish it.[7]

The key events of September 1938 are all too familiar: Hitler's Nuremberg speech; Neville Chamberlain's flights to Germany; the western powers' representations to the Czechs; and the final crisis-laden days, leading to the well-timed appeal by Mussolini (and Roosevelt) for a conference at Munich where the concluding humiliating scene was enacted, Sudeten German regions being ceded to Germany. Throughout these weeks Lothian and Curtis were in Sydney, Australia, attending the second British Commonwealth Relations Conference. Other members of the 'Set' remained in England. Dawson was on holiday at Langcliffe, his estate in Yorkshire. He returned to London on 6 September. That evening he helped rewrite a leader that, as he put it, 'ventilated rather crudely the idea which we had often raised before, of a secession of the Sudeten fringe'. As he anticipated, it triggered off a great 'hubbub'. It was all too readily assumed that *The Times* represented official opinion, an impression denied immediately by the government, though with little effect. 'A sinister blow' aimed at a peaceful conclusion to the crisis, the *Daily Telegraph* called it. The Foreign Office 'went up through the roof', but its chief, Halifax, was less agitated. Over lunch at the Travellers', he admitted to Dawson that he was 'as much in the dark as anyone else as to what is likely to happen next'.

Had the government already decided to destroy Czechoslovakia? *The Week* speculated that it had. At a gathering at 'Schloss Cliveden' on the weekend of 26 March, with Chamberlain in attendance, and between playing charades, it reported that a decision had been taken to abandon Czechoslovakia to its fate. By mid-August, so Claud Cockburn ruminated, the 'Cliveden Set' wished only that the 'Czechs would hurry up and get it over with'. A month later he presumed that Dawson's notorious leader had been 'a carefully arranged signal deliberately set off by the British "*Cagoulards*" in arrangement with the German government and especially with Herr von Ribbentrop'. These were extravagant conjectures. In fact, Dawson could claim, with justice, that his 'mild suggestion' echoed many other voices. He could, for example, point to the left-wing weekly, the *New Statesman and Nation*. It had pre-empted *The Times*, arguing that 'the question of frontier revision, difficult though it is, should at once be tackled. The strategical value of the Bohemian frontier should not be made the occasion of a world war. We should not guarantee the *status quo*.' No one could accuse its radical editor, Kingsley Martin, of being pro-Nazi.

Yet his remarks could just as easily have been uttered at 'Schloss Cliveden'. Much later, Martin deeply regretted his 'lapse'. But this odd encounter of editorial views between *The Times* and the *New Statesman* demonstrates how widespread was the sympathy among informed public opinion to border adjustments on 'the Sudeten fringe'.[8]

In Australia, Lothian and Curtis watched as the crisis unfolded. Before he left London, Lothian had telephoned Jan Masaryk and told him that he had ceased to be a Germanophile. But it remains a moot point whether or not he had ceased to be unduly sensitive to what he called legitimate German grievances. Opposed to revision by violence, he was still prepared to press strongly 'for changes which are just or overdue'. Lothian was corresponding regularly with the Astors, receiving 'most useful cables' from Waldorf. Hitler's first meeting with Chamberlain at Berchtesgaden 'alarmed' Lothian: 'heroic & courageous', certainly, but 'terribly likely to lead to another Hoare–Laval plan'. Facing an intransigent Hitler, 'Neville will be forced to offer a compromise'. 'It's a horrible dilemma,' he confessed, but 'rather than split the country and democratic world by immediate concessions we ought to say that if Hitler invades Czecho-Slovakia it means war.'

Perhaps, unwittingly, Lothian had moved into the Churchill–Vansittart camp. He soon vacated it. After the breakdown of the second round of talks at Godesberg, when war seemed imminent, he concluded that Hitler had called the democracies' bluff. Neither France not Britain would assist Czechoslovakia if attacked. 'Whichever way I look at it Hitler is master of Central Europe & we & the democracies are bang up against it unless we unite & arm.' Nancy urged him to come home. But then came 'the marvellous news . . . of the success of the Munich Conference'. Lothian was delighted. Unlike the Quai d'Orsay and Lord Robert Cecil, the 'real war minds in Europe today', Chamberlain had pulled off a masterly coup. 'Nobody else could have done the trick & I've no doubt prayer helped the result. He'll be the darling of the Western world – a most unexpected position – for a while.' Lothian predicted 'some nasty moments as the Germans march into the Sudeten territory & the worthless Czechs & Social Democrats flee before them'. He reminded the Astors: if 'the Nazis are difficult, [it is] because we and the French have steadily taught them that nothing but force would count'.

Time and again Lothian stressed that 'we must complete our armaments so as to go on convincing him [Hitler] that there is now no way forward for them by means of European war.' But who was the true warmonger? Lothian condemned Czech policy tooth and nail. 'Beneš has been the Quai d'Orsay's powerful tool in Europe since 1920 & if Czecho-Slovakia is saved it's not because of Beneš. His policy led inevitably to world war in which

Czecho-Slovakia would have been far more deeply mutilated or destroyed altogether.' For the Astors' benefit, Lothian summed up his position:

> My own impression is that Europe, including the Nazis, have now turned their back on world war, if only because a general war means letting Russia loose in Europe, and trust a final settlement, including disarmament, may be possible if Neville's lead is followed up. He is the only person who steadfastly refused to accept the view that Hitler & the Nazis were incorrigible & would understand nothing but the thick stick.[9]

Lothian's views, however breathlessly put, were not exceptional. When Duff Cooper resigned from the Cabinet in protest at the Munich agreement, the only minister to do so, Nancy saw 'the hand of God; he hasn't drawn a sober breath for three months!' Disenchanted with an impotent League of Nations, denouncing the 'secret lobbying' of the French, condemning the Franco-Czech military alliance that had threatened 'the security and independence of Germany', Nancy had no quarrel with the settlement. On the other hand, Waldorf was not entirely satisfied. But dealing with Czechoslovakia, he denied its existence 'in the sense of [its] being one people united by race'. It was a 'festering sore in the middle of Europe', he told a public meeting in Plymouth, adding: 'because I said that, I was called a Nazi and you have heard a lot of nonsense about the Cliveden set.' Only the timely intervention of Neville Chamberlain, he went on, had saved 'the real Czech State'. Curtis made no direct reference to the crisis, but in view of his resolute advocacy of the cantonization of Czechoslovakia there is no reason to believe that he differed in any meaningful way from the position of his friends. In any case, within a year he was off on one of his 'stunts', chasing the cause of world union with renewed vigour.[10]

Only Bob Brand inveighed against the Munich settlement. Government statements defending the settlement left him cold: he found nothing in them 'to bite on at all'. Chamberlain was 'very "naife"'. It is going to be difficult for him to ask the country to do all it must *do*, with that wretched piece of paper which he got Hitler to sign.' He wrote in the same vein to Geoffrey Dawson, the most intractable of the Municheers, arraigning the Nazi regime, its leader, and its practices. Dawson too disapproved strongly of the Nazi tyranny; nor had he been particularly impressed with the Chamberlain–Hitler declaration. But, he insisted, the Nazi regime, our 'creation', would have been immensely strengthened by a war. Privy to official government documents, he outlined the weaknesses of any potential anti-German coalition: the Russians, busy murdering their 'leading generals and admirals', were 'immobilized'; while the French were 'positively squealing to be saved by any means from their obligations to the

Czechs'. Dawson's mind was locked, unable to grasp why, as he put it, Brand's was so 'consistently negative'. For Brand's benefit, he pointed to the only way ahead. 'I feel more certain than ever that the proper policy for this country is (1) to continue to lend a hand in removing recognized legitimate international grievances before they come to a head, and (2) to use our opportunity to get on with our own defensive preparations.'[11]

And what of the unity of the Commonwealth, a factor that weighed so heavily with the Round Tablers? To what extent could Canada, Australia, South Africa be relied upon to back Britain in the event of a European war? Malcolm MacDonald, the Dominions (later Colonial) Secretary, thought not at all. He even hinted that should such an emergency arise the Commonwealth was in danger of breaking up. Throughout the crisis, Dawson was in close contact with the dominion high commissioners in London. Responsive to their anxieties, he passed on to the government, usually through Halifax, their misgivings. Dawson believed that Munich was a 'great achievement'. Dominion leaders were equally gladdened by the agreement. Messages arrived at Printing House Square from South Africa and Australia expressing the 'warmest congratulations' at the government's proficient handling of the crisis and 'immense relief' at its outcome. (William Lyon) MacKenzie King, Prime Minister of Canada, wrote on a more personal note: 'Canada is rejoicing tonight at the success which has crowned your unremitting efforts for peace.' Dawson was positive that he had preserved the integrity of the Empire. No doubt other, more formidable challenges lay ahead. But thanks to his persistent lobbying the Empire would face them united.[12]

The general euphoria that had swept the country after Munich soon faded. A noticeable backlash set in. As for the 'friends', apart from Brand it was not so much the terms of the settlement that troubled them as the manner in which it had been forced upon the government. No one would have dared to emulate *The Week*'s irreverent description of Chamberlain as having 'turned all four cheeks' to Hitler. But Hitler's strong-arm tactics caused much unease among those who began to see them as evidence of a lawless, untameable regime. As usual, it was Lothian who took the lead, a reflection of his quicksilver character, finely tuned to reflect the ups and downs of a volatile world.

The winter of 1938–9 saw him in the United States. His 'notorious' past pursued him. 'The Cliveden Set yarn is still going strong everywhere here,' he reported to Nancy from Chicago. 'It symbolizes the impression spread by the left and acceptable to the average American that aristocrats and financiers are selling out democracy in Spain and Czechoslovakia because they want to preserve their own property and privileges . . . [and] Chamberlain is their tool.' He met Felix Frankfurter. 'I had a most intimate talk with Lothian,' Frankfurter briefed Roosevelt, '[he] is *now* as hot against Hitler as any of us, and said that Chamberlain now knows that his "appeasement" policy is a complete flop as to Hitler.' Some days later Lothian conferred with Roosevelt himself, impressing upon the President that he had 'completely abandoned his former belief that Hitler could be dealt with as a semi-reasonable human being'. For a thousand years Britain had been the guardian of Anglo-Saxon civilization, he went on. Now, lacking the resources to match its worldwide commitments, Britain was no longer able to fulfil its destiny. The United States must take up 'the sceptre': only Roosevelt 'could save the world'. But Roosevelt would not be drawn. In fact, he 'got mad clear through'. 'I wish the British would stop this "We who are about to die, salute thee" attitude,' he wrote to Roger Merriman, the Master of Eliot House at Harvard. 'What [they] need today is a good stiff grog, inducing not only a desire to save civilization but the continued belief that they can do it. In such an event they will have a lot more support from their American cousins.'[13]

Soon after Lothian's return from America his attitude towards Germany stiffened. Nancy Astor, excessively susceptible to his changing moods, gloomily remarked, 'I have come to the conclusion that Philip does not understand Hitler as well as he thought he did.' Perhaps war was unavoidable, Nancy conceded, 'but I at least remain convinced that the main reason we have reached this impossible predicament is the existence of widespread material injustice and that the only way to avoid war is to achieve spiritual justice.' She failed to elaborate.

Much had happened in the meantime to account for this shift in attitude.[14] On 10 March Sir Samuel Hoare, addressing his Chelsea constituents, predicted the approach of a new Golden Age. Five days later Hitler's troops occupied Prague and seized Bohemia and Moravia, tearing up the much vaunted Munich agreement. Public opinion in England was outraged. In much the same way that the Munich settlement had generated a euphoric mood of 'peace for our time', Prague sparked off an angry counter-reaction. Nancy too was swept up by the general sense of outrage. At question time in the House of Commons, she asked Neville Chamberlain, 'Will the Prime Minister lose no time in letting the German Government know with what horror the whole of this country regards Germany's actions?' Without waiting for Chamberlain's reply, Vyvyan Adams, a Conservative member, rose and said: 'You caused it yourself.'

A week later Hitler annexed Memel. At the same time, sweeping German demands on Poland were revived, particularly with regard to the future status of Danzig and the Polish Corridor. Not to be upstaged, an irate Mussolini had seized Albania on 7 April, extending his New Roman Empire across the Adriatic. These events constituted the grimmest of denouements to years of Clivedenite lobbying, speechifying and campaigning to obtain an overall European settlement, one that in particular would appease Hitler's resurgent Germany. Prague and Albania had finally put paid – at least in the minds of most observers – to that sanguine hope.

Even Neville Chamberlain succumbed – at least in public. Could Hitler's word ever be trusted again? Speaking at Birmingham, he warned that 'any attempt to dominate the world by force was one which the Democracies must resist'. Public sentiment hardened perceptibly against Nazi Germany. Those who had enthusiastically supported the government's Munich-oriented line now seriously questioned the wisdom of such policies. Perhaps to shed the burden of their own guilt for this unhappy state of affairs, they sought to lay the blame elsewhere. If people were indeed searching for a high-profile scapegoat, the 'Cliveden Set', by definition, was the most natural of targets. 'How terrible has been the influence of the Clivedon Set,' chorused Anthony Eden and Harold Nicolson. 'A defeatist, pampered group,' went on Nicolson, that 'prevented us from taking a strong line while it could have made for peace.'[15] At any rate, criticism of the 'Set' never slackened, its image as a bunch of Nazi fellow-travellers never faded – even if by now its so-called intrigues no longer warranted star-billing in *The Week*.

Lothian, Cliveden's high priest, had also changed his tune. He had condoned Munich because it had avoided war, but equally because it had quashed one of the most glaring follies of Versailles and rectified a situation that many thought intolerable. Horrified by the dicatators' coups, he had read, for the first time, the unexpurgated edition of *Mein Kampf*.[16] Judging from his words, he underwent a cathartic experience. 'Hitler is in effect a fanatical gangster who will stop at nothing to beat down all possibility of resistance anywhere to his will,' he wrote to an American friend.

For Dawson, Munich, even in retrospect, remained the best of all options. To the last he proclaimed himself an impenitent Municheer. Even at this late stage, he was not entirely convinced that it was too late to separate Hitler from his extremists – as he was wont to put it – and still reach a reasonable agreement over Poland. Nor was he wholly persuaded that the country would reject such a settlement out of hand. Is Danzig worth another war, he would repeatedly ask.

Brand harboured no such doubts. He had reached the conclusion, long before Lothian's awakening, that the Nazis were 'a set of gangsters' and not to be trusted. Now, confronting Dawson, he feared another Munich over Poland. As he had recently heard Chamberlain 'sing a paean of praise' lauding that scandalous agreement, he felt that the Prime Minister would not balk at another unsavoury deal. Nor, he suspected, would Halifax, who had told the Lords that he hoped 'the German people' hadn't written off all hope of an agreement with Britain. Brand was adamant. Britain must stand by its guarantees, boldly and without equivocation;* otherwise, the

* On 31 March 1939, Britain and France extended a guarantee of aid to Poland in the

government would lose all credibility. He badgered Dawson. Any surrender to Germany over Danzig should be an immediate cause for war. Would *The Times* also take this view? 'Lately', he wrote to Dawson, 'I have had an uncomfortable feeling that *The Times* hates to face these facts.'

The feverish events of the past few weeks fired up Brand. The government lacked backbone, he charged. 'With precious few exceptions the present cabinet consists either of career men or hopeless mugwumps, like Simon [Chancellor of the Exchequer], for example.' He lent his voice to the swelling chorus that called for the reconstruction of the government. He wanted a genuine National Government, by which he meant the inclusion of Churchill – a dramatic move, certainly, but it would show the world that Britain meant business. Without it, he feared that the Russian negotiations would peter out, leaving Britain empty-handed in eastern Europe. And then, Brand concluded, the Polish guarantee would be worthless should Hitler decide to march eastwards.

Brand had never been more outspoken. But neither too had Lothian. His current position constituted a remarkable volte-face from the views he had previously held. But Lothian, fearful that war would break out by the end of the summer, sounded determined enough. He now referred to Hitler's use of 'ruthless power' to remake the world as set out in *Mein Kampf*. Remaking the world? Only at the expense of the British Empire, Lothian decided. To deter Hitler (and Mussolini) the powers had to stage an emphatic demonstration of diplomatic unity – one that would include the support of the United States – backed, if necessary, by the employment of superior force. From this game plan, it was but a short step for Lothian to endorse Churchill's arguments in favour of a Grand Alliance with the Soviet Union. The balance of forces among the Clivedenites shifted. A Brand–Lothian axis evolved. Echoed in varying degrees by the Astors and Curtis, it ranged itself against the still 'impenitent' Dawson.

Lothian's *mea culpa* was all the more convincing because he, above all others, had come to symbolize Cliveden's pro-appeasement spirit. No one had championed it more fervently, or campaigned more strenuously on its behalf. But in one particular, his views had not changed. Tried before a packed jury and sentenced by a hanging judge, Germany, he still held, had been grievously wronged at Versailles. Lothian had wished, as befitted a humane, liberal person, to redress the glaring injustices of that prejudiced treaty. Was there ever a more noble cause? But by obliterating Czech independence, by tearing up freely negotiated treaties, Hitler had placed

---

event of aggression; a week later it was augmented into a mutual pact of assistance. Similar guarantees were given to Greece and Rumania (13 April); and on 12 May, Britain signed a mutual assistance pact with Turkey. At the same time, the first tentative moves were taken to conclude an agreement with the Soviet Union.

himself well beyond the pale. There would be no more unilateral concessions, no more surrendering to blackmail. If Hitler genuinely wanted a peaceful solution, he had to show it by deeds not words. If ever that stage was reached, Lothian was prepared to put every issue on the table, no matter how controversial: colonies, *Lebensraum*, raw materials, trade barriers, disarmament. Until then, Britain's prime task was to resist every threat of aggression. Only vigorous action would ensure that Hitler would not trample all over Europe.

Lothian's argument that Hitler was reversing the whole trend of modern civilization towards national self-government would not have held much appeal to Lionel Curtis. He might, perhaps, have counter-claimed that the current crisis was decisive proof that national sovereignty was the root of all international evil: that nationalism, by its very nature, was a destructive force. Opposed to any government reshuffle, Curtis was ready to support Chamberlain in every step he took to resist aggression. Improved air defences would be a positive first move. Some form of national service would be another. Regarding these matters he had approached Ernest Bevin, hoping that organized labour would add its voice to those who advocated no surrender over Danzig.

Yet typically, while others were agonizing over the impasse in eastern Europe, Curtis's eyes were raised upwards, towards the Kingdom of God. Recently, an American, Clarence Streit, had restated the case for world government. Reinvigorated by Streit's treatise, *Union Now*, Curtis resumed his quest. He organized 'a gathering of enthusiasts at Blickling', Lothian's estate in Norfolk: he spoke in Boston and lectured at Chatham House on 'World Order': he thought in terms of yet another worldwide movement to advance his cherished, but elusive, goal. He would lead, but who would follow? At first, Lothian took up the call, encouraging Curtis to set up a British Federal Union Society. Always wavering, he soon backtracked, quoting with approval Smuts, who saw in Streit's work, not a blueprint for action, but 'a dialogue of Plato'. Brand would add, *sotto voce*, that the whole idea was 'so much nonsense'. And Lord Robert Cecil would ensure that the League of Nations Union would not associate itself with 'the kind of nonsense Lionel Curtis and his friends may be talking'. Never undone by criticism, Curtis brushed aside these aspersions. He would battle on, alone, misunderstood, but unbowed.

Despite Dawson's stubborn defence of Neville Chamberlain, the 'friends' were clearly uneasy about the quality of the Prime Minister's leadership. Waldorf Astor, normally the coolest of men, would no longer countenance words and resolutions unless supported by action. He told the House of Lords: 'I think we should be big enough to admit that during the past year or two each of us and all of us as individuals and as parties have probably made some mistakes. I do not think it would be possible to find anybody whose record, whose forecast had been completely correct.' The Axis can be broken, he contended, but only by the application of overwhelming force. Incensed at Mussolini's sack of Albania, he saw it as a *casus belli*. To resist the naked power politics of the dictators, he called for increased rearmament and the total mobilization of civil resources: manpower, industry, the country's wealth. How, Waldorf asked, did Chamberlain intend to put Britain's new commitments in eastern Europe into effect? Why would he not commit himself to a Soviet connection? Chamberlain was dithering. The British people were waiting for a message, an appeal to energize, to rouse the country. Was Chamberlain capable of providing the inspiration the country needed? Waldorf left the question unanswered.[17]

By the summer of 1939 the 'Cliveden Set', trailing after public opinion, had in effect reversed its position. Dawson was the odd man out. 'Dawson is just naturally pro-German,' Northcliffe once noted, 'he can't help it.'[18] On 1 April 1939 *The Times* ran a contentious leader. Differentiating between 'independence' and 'integrity', it appeared to weaken Britain's recent guarantee to Poland. 'Integrity', it explained, 'might have meant an unconditional guarantee of all existing Polish frontiers', implying that this should not be an aim of British policy. As Dawson noted ruefully, his leader sparked off much 'self-righteous comment' and 'malignant abuse', a great 'to-do'. Churchill detected 'sinister' motives. It was fiercely attacked in the Commons. Was the Printing House Square 'gang' up to its old tricks again, parcelling out other people's territories to Nazi Germany? Dawson protested. But his apologias rang false: his reputation as an appeaser was too solid. Brand, calling for a more assertive National Government, endeavoured to fortify Dawson's resolve. Strengthened by Churchill's presence, it would be able to take 'a firm stand'. In any event, the government must abide by its guarantee to Poland. 'If we have another Munich, then no one in the world will follow us.' Brand was adamant: no surrender to German demands on Danzig; any German move into the Polish Corridor should be 'an immediate cause for war'. 'I do hope *The Times* will take this line,' wrote Brand, uneasy at Dawson's refusal to face reality. Lothian was equally steadfast. Advocating 'action – not speeches' to avert 'another Munich', he begged Dawson to dispel 'the widespread suspicion that *The Times* [is] ready to surrender Danzig'. There is no evidence that Dawson followed Brand's or Lothian's advice. 'The Danzig liability' still bothered Chamberlain, as it did Dawson.[19]

A weekend gathering of 2–4 June at Cliveden was the last of its kind before the outbreak of hostilities. Present was Adam von Trott zu Solz, David Astor's Oxford friend. Von Trott, unknown to his hosts, was treading a delicate line. A resolute anti-Nazi and a functionary of the German Foreign Ministry, though in an unofficial capacity, he came to England as the agent of certain of his superiors who were desperate to avoid a war that could only be disastrous for Germany. Apparently a package deal had been worked out by von Trott's chiefs: on the one hand, to restore a semblance of independence to Bohemia and Moravia; on the other, to compensate Germany in the Polish Corridor. Von Trott was to seek out those circles in Britain most likely to further this scheme. Cliveden was the obvious address – and his friendship with the Astors assured him easy access to this clique which, that weekend, included Lothian, Halifax, Dawson, Brand, Tom Jones and Sir Thomas Inskip (Secretary of State for the Dominions) among the thirty-odd guests. He was listened to politely. His official record to the German Foreign Ministry, phrased prudently to demonstrate his credentials as a dyed-in-the-wool Nazi, noted in particular Lothian's views, 'undoubtedly the cleverest and most supple politician among them'. 'If Germany *led*, but did not dominate, Central and Eastern Europe,' he reported Lothian as saying, 'the Western European nations could then feel reassured about their political independence. England–America (which Lothian naturally likes to regard as one!) and Germany, as the only real Great Powers, could then jointly shape and guarantee the future of world politics.' This sounds like authentic Lothianism.

But von Trott's programme, however moderately promoted, still reflected extreme nationalist ideas, unacceptable to the burgeoning anti-appeasement circles in Britain, including most Clivedenites. To sanction it would be tantamount to allowing Germany to plunder Poland as it had sacked Czechoslovakia. In any case, it was too late for such concessions. Prague had fundamentally changed things in a way perhaps unsuspected by von Trott and his masters. Lothian told him that Hitler must accept 'the principle of the inviolability of weaker nations'. Neville Chamberlain, whom von Trott met later in London, spoke in a mood of 'great excitement'. 'The British people too were "passionately stirred",' he said, 'and . . . would fight if another independent nation were "destroyed".' Not that Chamberlain was opposed to 'a peaceful settlement'. But first Germany must take concrete measures to rebuild international confidence. He needed an unmistakable signal that Germany was no longer bent on 'the destruction of other nations'. Von Trott's visit had no significant effect on British (or German) policy – perhaps a fitting finale to Clivedenite politicking.[20]

The drift to war continued, brought to a head by the Nazi–Soviet Pact of 22 August 1939. When, on the Sunday morning of 3 September, Chamberlain broadcast to the nation confessing that 'his long struggle to win peace has failed' and that, 'Consequently, this country is now at war with Germany,' Nancy remarked: 'I cannot believe that it has happened.'[21] The 'Cliveden Set' dissolved by force of circumstances. Its image as a fifth column, however, lingered on, and on.

CHAPTER 10

Full Circle

Lord Lothian was offered the Washington embassy in August 1938. It was not a popular choice at the Foreign Office. Ever since his days as private secretary to Lloyd George senior officials had considered him an irredeemable busybody; and his diplomatic forays in the 1930s only hardened their opinion. When a report of his ill-starred interview with Roosevelt – who had 'got mad clear through' with Lothian – reached their desks, they worked to quash the proposal. 'This is, of course, just typical of the line that conceited ass (and the whole Cliveden set) takes . . . I hope and pray this fortunate letter will kill the appointment.' But Halifax favoured Lothian, as did Dawson, who lobbied vigorously on his friend's behalf. Finally, Chamberlain agreed. And Roosevelt, when asked, replied: 'Look here, there can be no possible difficulty about his *agrément* [approval] or anything of that sort.' Exactly a year later Lothian took up his duties as ambassador to the United States.[1]

Lothian expected 'to swing public opinion' in America to support Britain's war effort. In contrast to his previous interview with Roosevelt, he now emphasized British self-reliance. He managed his press conferences with 'consummate ease'.[2] Appealing for American aid, he balanced his ardour for a firm Anglo-American accord with his duties as the mouthpiece of British policy. Despite their grave differences in the 1930s, Lothian was enthusiastic for Churchill's wartime leadership; indeed he had canvassed for his inclusion in the government in the summer of 1939. However, his high regard for Churchill did not prevent him from adding his voice to those who were advocating a compromise peace with Germany in the days after Dunkirk. Lothian 'telephones wildy from Washington', noted a worried Harold Nicolson, 'begging Halifax not to say anything . . . which might close the door to peace. [He] claims that he knows the German peace terms and that they are most satisfactory.'*[3]

* It is not clear what precisely Lothian knew, or how. On 19 July 1940 Hitler had

On the whole, Lothian's public relations campaign in America 'to win friends and influence people' succeeded, as did his endeavours regarding more tangible issues. The 'destroyers for bases' deal and the transition from the 'cash and carry' policy to the Lend-Lease Act owed much to his forceful canvassing. Gradually, he earned the trust of the American administration and the respect of Whitehall. 'Lothian is doing magnificently in Washington,' the Foreign Office learned. 'The President likes him and was always pleased to see him, which was rare as he found most people bores . . .'

In November 1940 Lothian came to England on leave. He spent a weekend at Cliveden with his oldest friends, the Astors, Brand, Dawson and Curtis. Expounding upon the 'mutual recognition of the interdependence of the USA and the British Commonwealth', he proposed a 'kind of Amphictyonic Council [a feature of a league of states in ancient Greece]' that would thrash out a common policy. More was not practicable, he cautioned. It was his last message to the Moot. In declining health – he was wont to doze off at meetings – he returned to Washington. On 12 December 1940 he died, at the age of fifty-eight, from a kidney disorder. The circumstances were tragic. True to his religious beliefs he refused qualified medical aid and, instead, sought solace from a Christian Science male nurse.

The eulogies were generous. Oliver Harvey, an outspoken opponent of his at the Foreign Office, wrote: 'In spite of all our misgivings L. proved himself a very great Ambassador and he will be very hard indeed to replace.' Churchill told Roosevelt that he was 'deeply grieved at loss of Lothian who was our greatest Ambassador to the United States . . . We have lost a good friend and high Interpreter.' His friends, naturally, were devastated. Nancy had lost one of the cornerstones of her life; Curtis, his most devoted – though, at times, fickle – ally. At All Souls, Curtis, in a moment of frankness, confided to Leslie Rowse: 'Philip died in the knowledge that he had been wrong.' The Lothian family motto counselled *Sero sed Serio* (Late but in Earnest), an apposite epitaph for the final phase of his career.[4]

Geoffrey Dawson tendered his resignation as editor of *The Times* in April

addressed the Reichstag appealing 'once more to reason and commonsense in Great Britain': he saw 'no reason why this war must go on'. After Germany's stunning military victories in western Europe (and earlier in Poland), Hitler assumed that Britain, now standing alone, without a European ally, would seek some form of settlement. For his part, Hitler was prepared to guarantee the British Empire while Britain in return would have to return the German colonies and concede German primacy in Europe. At the end of May, as the troops were being evacuated from Dunkirk, the British Cabinet toyed with the idea of a deal with Germany. It was soon cast aside.

1939. Reluctant 'to sink slowly in ability', he wished to bring in 'new blood at the highest level', and so he recommended Robert Barrington-Ward, his deputy for the last twelve years, to succeed him. No precise date was set for his retirement. As war broke out five months later, he soldiered on until the summer of 1941.[5]

Dawson never tired of repeating that he remained an unrepentant champion of the Munich policy. His loyalty to Chamberlain was touching. 'Amiable in language & voice,' he commented, impressed by the Prime Minister's proclamation of war. By the spring of 1940, with the Norwegian crisis coming to a head, Dawson became increasingly critical of the way the government functioned. His complaints were not directed at Chamberlain himself. On the contrary, Dawson praised Chamberlain's 'vigour, courage, and despatch of business'. But as the government was 'too cumbrous for rapid and vigorous initiative', *The Times* called for greater delegation of authority to relieve the intolerable strain imposed upon its senior ministers. Dawson made it quite clear that there was an overriding need to strengthen the government by including Labour, to make it 'representative of the full strength of Parliament and the country'. Chamberlain was 'peeved' by Dawson's candour. But in any case, his days as Prime Minister were numbered. When the Commons debated the botched Norwegian campaign, his government scraped home with a severely reduced majority of eighty-one, tantamount to a vote of no-confidence. 'It meant', Dawson realized at once, 'a reconstruction.' Two days later, on 10 May, Winston Churchill kissed hands to become Prime Minister. 'A *very* tiring day,' Dawson sombrely recorded, noting that Churchill's new appointments were '*not* too well chosen ... Too many friends.'[6]

Dawson regarded Churchill as something of a political gadfly. They had clashed constantly in the past. Would Churchill, capricious by nature, fulfil his duties as a responsible Prime Minister? Despite his initial reservations, Dawson finally came to acknowledge Churchill's charismatic leadership. 'Like no one else in sight he has the courage, the imagination, the power of leadership which are the attributes of a great War Minister. England is fortunate ... in having produced the man to fit the emergency.' So far as any man can, he determined, Churchill had earned that much-abused title 'indispensable'. The sting was concealed in his summing-up: 'the problem of his ultimate successor should never be far from the mind of the far-sighted leader.' It was the last editorial Dawson composed for *The Times*.[7]

Dawson's resignation took effect from 1 October 1941. He retired to Langcliffe – now providing board for several evacuees as well as members of his own family. Never idle, he occupied himself with voluntary work. A governor of three schools, Eton, Giggleswick (the local grammar school) and Cheltenham, he also resumed editing *The Round Table*. There were frequent trips to London where he would dine with friends at the

Travellers' or Grillion's; and of course regular visits to Oxford, drawn back to All Souls and Rhodes House, those institutions where he felt most at ease and which had done so much to shape him.

Dawson's political heritage was never in doubt. Neville Chamberlain died of cancer in November 1940. Probably the last letter that he received was from Geoffrey Dawson.

> My dear Neville [he began], I shall always be an impenitent supporter of what is called the 'Munich policy'. No one who sat in this place, as I did during the autumn of '38, with almost daily visitations from eminent Canadians and Australians, could fail to realize that war with Germany at that time would have been misunderstood and resented from end to end of the Empire. Even in this country there would have been no unity behind it. We now know that it was inevitable sooner or later; but we owe it all to you that it was later rather than sooner and that we are assuredly going to win it . . . Bless you for all you have done for this country.[8]

How fitting that this defence of 'appeasement', highlighting the need to preserve imperial unity, should be Dawson's political swansong.

Dawson's last two years at Printing House Square, the strain of managing a great newspaper in wartime conditions, had left him physically run-down. He suffered from sciatica and failing eyesight. In February 1942 he survived a serious heart attack. Weakened as he was, the country pursuits he so much enjoyed, shooting or long country walks, were now beyond him. His vitality slowly ebbing away, Geoffrey Dawson died on 7 November 1944 at the age of seventy.

In April 1939 Nancy Astor prayed that 'nothing will happen' to Chamberlain, a forceful leader who dominated the Commons and commanded the support of a united country. Two months after the outbreak of war she was more circumspect. At a 1922 Club dinner in London, Chamberlain had sneered at the Labour Party. 'We were better off without them,' he scoffed. Nancy reported to Lothian. 'The whole thing was so completely lacking in statesmanship, uplift or vision of any kind, it really got one down for the moment . . . I am sure he meant it as a fighting speech, but its effect on me was to make me wish that Winston were PM. This was only momentary, and I knew it was wrong, but that was my reaction.' Her criticism mounted. In April 1940, she bluntly told Chamberlain that 'you have to get rid of your "duds".' Even those who trust the Prime Minister, Nancy informed the Commons, 'feel that he is not a wise selector of men'. On 7 May, Dawson, dining at 4 St James's Square, found 'a very discontented party'. The following day Nancy, perhaps unwittingly, helped to ensure that Churchill became Prime Minister. Responding to the Norwegian *débâcle*, forty members who normally supported the government joined forces with Labour to vote against it. Nancy was among them. Not given to retrospection, she had no qualms about collaborating with the Conservative rebels. 'No man did better for peace' than Chamberlain, Nancy reasoned, '[but] he was hopeless for war.'[9]

'I am naturally a headliner,' Nancy once said. 'Smart sayings flash into my mind, and before I know it they flash out and they are really not so smart as all that, and seldom important ... from this I have often suffered.' Apparently, embarrassing statements continued to flash in and out. While civilians at home were being 'blitzed and bombed', the British army in the Middle East was 'basking in the sun'; or Englishwomen preferred to marry soldiers from the Dominions because Englishmen 'were such cowards'. Shouldn't troops returning home from Middle East Command wear 'yellow bands on their arms' because they are 'all [venereally] diseased', she asked. Finally, the troops serving in Italy were maligned as 'D Day Dodgers'. They responded cheerfully enough:

> Dear Lady Astor you think you're pretty hot,
> Standing on the platform talking bloody rot ...
> We're the D Day Dodgers, out in Italy;
> Always on the vino, always on the spree.

Nancy vehemently denied the authorship of these slanderous remarks. She put it all down to 'subtle enemy propaganda', designed to undermine the fighting spirit of the army. There is no evidence to sustain this charge; equally, there is little direct evidence linking Nancy with these gibes. Unfortunately for her, they were treated as fact, not fiction. Nancy's public image was such that it proved impossible to kill these rumours.[10]

Nor did Nancy's parliamentary reputation improve. There had been a steady decline in her performance since the late 1920s – even if punctuated by occasional moments of brilliance. Harold Nicolson thought that debating with her was 'like playing squash racquets with a dish of scrambled eggs'. When Nancy expounded on the future of Germany after the war she was told that 'the views of the Noble Lady have been almost inevitably wrong', a sign that the 'Cliveden Set' mystique died hard, if at all. There were routine 'dust-ups' with other members. Spotting Geoffrey Lloyd (a Conservative MP) out of uniform, she snapped: 'You ought to be ashamed of yourself.' At times she was harshly treated, regardless of her undoubted gift for repartee. Aneurin Bevan wished to gauge public opinion in 'every club, pub and household'. Nancy interjected: 'We do not go to pubs.' Bevan: 'No, that is why the Noble Lady is so ignorant. She need not worry, Plymouth will deal with her all right.'

Despite Bevan's put-down, Nancy dealt with Plymouth in her own way. She fraternized easily, and her constituents willingly reciprocated. Together with Waldorf – by then Plymouth's Lord Mayor – she organized public dances on The Hoe, where photographers caught her waltzing with servicemen and others. During the war Plymouth was heavily blitzed. In all, eleven hundred people were killed, many thousands injured, and large areas of the city laid to waste. The most devastating raids occurred in the spring of 1941. Setting an example by their fortitude, the Astors remained in the city throughout these terrible days. Looking at the blazing fires that swept through Plymouth, Nancy's eyes 'filled with tears'. Pushing back her steel helmet, she said: 'There goes thirty years of our lives, but we'll build it again.' Jointly, the Astors engaged in relief work. Waldorf, anticipating the future, initiated the planning of a new city centre. If Waldorf laboured endlessly behind the scenes, Nancy sustained public morale in a visible manner, more in keeping with her high-profile character. It was probably her greatest contribution to the war effort.[11]

By the end of the war it was apparent to everyone that Nancy must retire from the House of Commons – to everyone, that is, except Nancy. Determined to prevent her probable humiliation at the polls, Waldorf, upheld by the family, insisted. Nancy vacillated, but eventually yielded to the pressure. As compensation, she lobbied for a peerage. Churchill refused her petition, responding to it with 'an embarrassingly long silence followed by an angry grunt', a signal that their ongoing feud was by no means over. Nancy never came to terms with her changed fortunes. She paced the terrace at Cliveden, 'tears streaming down her eyes'. 'I'll miss the House,' she admitted, '[but] the House won't miss me. It never misses anybody.'[12]

Nancy blamed Waldorf for having manoeuvred her out of active politics. Her resentment never abated. It was compounded by a family struggle over the future of the *Observer*. Waldorf had forced Garvin's resignation in February 1942, proposing eventually to seat his son David in the editor's chair. Nancy hotly opposed Waldorf's choice. David had embraced radical left-wing beliefs, she held, and would turn the *Observer* into a subversive organ propagating ultra-socialist views. For Nancy, no prospect could be more appalling. Waldorf noted that she 'must begin the day with a hymn of hate against the Socialists'. Jakie took a broader view of it. Given to 'accumulating dragons to slay', his mother's current foes were 'Socialism, Roman Catholicism, Psychiatry, the Jews, the Latins and the *Observer*'. But once again Waldorf prevailed. In 1948, David succeeded as editor of the *Observer*. It proved to be an admirable appointment in every way. Under his skilful editorship the *Observer* reinforced its reputation as a quality newspaper, distinguished by a liberal style and investigative reporting techniques, attaining almost a cult status in some circles. Nancy, however, remained unreconciled to Waldorf's ruling and indifferent to David's achievements.

These incidents generated such tension that Nancy distanced herself from Waldorf. In effect, their marriage broke down. As Waldorf put it, their 'earlier harmonious collaboration' had vanished. 'What's wrong with this family,' said Nora when she visited Cliveden after the war, 'there's no love in it.' Living apart as much as together, Waldorf spent most of his time at Cliveden or at David's house at Sutton Courtney, Nancy at Rest Harrow or at Hasely Court, Oxfordshire, the home of her niece Nancy Lancaster. Nancy also tended to holiday alone and visit the United States without him.

Other, more tangible, aspects of the Astors' lives changed. During the war Cliveden's extensive facilities were again utilized as a hospital by the Canadian army. In 1942, Waldorf decided to turn Cliveden over to the National Trust, with the proviso that his heirs be allowed to lease the house should they wish to do so. This was a perfectly respectable way of coping with the burden of death duties. But it was not only a money-saving device. In offering the property Waldorf wished to share the amenities of Cliveden with the general public; but no less he desired to preserve it as a place 'where men and women of all types, Ministers, MPs, businessmen, trade unionists, educationalists, civil servants' would continue to gather as they had done in the past.[13] Having secured Cliveden's future, Waldorf sold his London mansion at 4 St James's Square, purchasing a more modest residence at 35 Hill Street, Mayfair.

Waldorf died in September 1952 at Cliveden. Never physically robust, his health had been deteriorating for some time. He had suffered a minor stroke in 1942, and a more serious one in 1950. Of late, unable to walk more than a few steps, he had been confined to a wheelchair. Overshadowed by Nancy's dominating nature, Waldorf cut a lacklustre figure. But the image belied the reality. A natural modesty should not be confused with a lack of ability or strength of character. Churchill offered him a post at the Ministry of Agriculture in his wartime administration. Troubled by his failing strength, but also aware of his responsibilities in Plymouth, Waldorf reluctantly turned it down. Although Waldorf followed his friends down a political cul-de-sac in the 1930s – as did countless others – in other ways his instinct proved sound. Acting as Nancy's political agent, he saved her from many gaffes, polishing his skills in damage control. Waldorf was 'the real ruler, not Nancy', concluded one intimate of the family. Towards the end, Nancy went to him. 'We had forty happy years together,' she mourned. 'No two people ever worked more happily than we did. These last seven years have been heart-breaking – but thank God he was like his old self the last ten days and oh how it makes me grieve of the years wasted!'[14]

After her forced retirement from Parliament, Nancy found herself in a state of limbo. Deprived of constructive occupation, she sought recompense elsewhere; but in vain. Angry at the world, and still full of fight, Nancy had only her fading reputation to sustain her. Her behaviour became increasingly cranky, old prejudices bubbling. She would insult David in public, scolding him for putting 'so many black men on the front page', furious at the liberal stand the *Observer* took over apartheid or independence for the emerging states of Africa.[15]

While estranged from Waldorf, Nancy had attempted to take her friend George Bernard Shaw under her wing. But Shaw, whose wife Charlotte had recently died, kept Nancy at a long arm's length. 'Keep Off, Keep Off, Keep Off, Keep Off,' he urged her.

My dear Nancy [he wrote], If you will not let me manage my work and my household in my own way you must not come at all . . . All this nonsense about my having to be looked after, and the job bequeathed to you by Charlotte, is a worn-out joke which you are beginning to believe in yourself. Let me hear no more of it. You need looking after far more than I do . . .

'Upset your own household not mine,' he suggested; 'in this house what I say, goes.' Slighted, but not put off, Nancy persevered. At Shaw's funeral, another mourner, impressed by Nancy's excellent performance, caught her acting 'as if she was the widow'.[16]

The 'Cliveden Set' controversy generated a backlash that never abated. It put Nancy perpetually on the defensive. When she discovered that the Gestapo had included her name on its 'Black List', she reacted with a cry of delight. Here was the 'complete answer to the terrible lie that the so-called "Cliveden Set" was pro-Fascist', Nancy exclaimed excitedly. Anti-fascist *and* anti-Communist, she aired her liberal principles in her customary manner. Meeting the junior senator for Wisconsin, Joe McCarthy, glass in hand, she asked him: 'What's that you're drinking?' 'Whisky,' the notorious witch-hunter replied. 'I wish it was poison,' Nancy struck back.[17] Her fascination with politics endured. The Astor interest in Parliament remained impressive: three of her sons, Bill, Michael and Jakie, at various times, took their seats in the Commons. But, with no other choice open to her, Nancy's interest in politics could manifest itself only in the form of a compulsive hobby.

In 1958 Nancy moved into a spacious apartment at 100 Eaton Square. Bob Brand, husband of her late and much loved sister Phyllis, and who did much to comfort her during these difficult years, took some of its rooms. Nancy remained a devout Christian Scientist. But she became more flexible in her drinking habits. A fanatical advocate of temperance, she was now spotted taking a glass of Dubonnet once in a while – claiming it to be a substitute for Ribena – and even, on occasion, an egg-nog.

In the early sixties, a different sort of 'Cliveden Set' captured the headlines of the world press. A public greedy for salacious detail learned of foxy call-girls and their high-society pimp, of drug-dealers and sex orgies, of brutal rent racketeers, of a government minister who not only shared his mistress with a Soviet agent but shamelessly committed the ultimate sin of lying to Parliament about it. Cliveden featured prominently in these lurid tales, as did Nancy's eldest son, Bill, the 3rd Viscount Astor. Nancy, always prudish in matters of sex, was shielded by her friends and family from the fall-out of the so-called Profumo affair. Eventually, she unearthed the truth. Together with David and her maid, Rose Harrison, she decided to go to Cliveden to rally round Bill. On arrival, her companions found that she had (fortunately) forgotten the intended purpose of her journey, such was the condition of her failing memory. It was her last recorded visit to Cliveden.

Less than a year later, while staying at the Ancasters' family house, Grimsthorpe, Nancy suffered a stroke. Medical aid was called and the ever-loyal Rose Harrison was summoned to her bedside. Weak, and her speech impaired, Nancy still showed sporadic flashes of her old spirit, her fabled irreverence. Michael Astor witnessed one scene. 'The nurse bent down to pick up something that had fallen off the bedside table. Mother extended a frail arm and gave the posterior a little slap.' Slowly, Nancy drifted off into a coma. 'A lot of the time she is back in Virginia,' Michael noted. Towards the end, Nancy raised her hands and called out, 'Waldorf.' She died early the following morning, on 2 May 1964, aged eighty-five.

Nancy once said, 'In spite of my six children, I feel a stranger in a strange land.' At her funeral service her casket of ashes was covered by a Confederate flag, a memento from the Civil War. Together with Waldorf's, the casket was interred in the chapel at Cliveden.[18]

In May 1940, as the German Panzer divisions were driving deep into northern France towards the Channel ports, Lionel Curtis's mood was tolerably gung-ho. He boosted Halifax's fighting spirit. Should Britain and France be overwhelmed, 'the conquered nations' should retire to Canada to continue the struggle. From the New World Britain would maintain its command of the seas. Eventually, the United States would intervene and the 'ultimate victory of right over wrong' would be guaranteed. Two months later, after the capitulation of France, his tune changed. Like others, he contemplated a compromise peace. Britain, the Dominions and her European allies would constitute one bloc; Nazi Germany and her satellites, the other. We should not 'interfere with the internal affairs of

Germany', he suggested, 'nor with any state which wishes of its own free will to join with Hitler's system'. Halifax, who had recently been tempted to open negotiations with Nazi Germany, now rejected these ideas out of hand. Any future worldwide order would come into being only 'when liberties, now destroyed, are restored', he countered.[19]

Future world orders were Curtis's bread and butter. At this time, Curtis was enthusiastic for Clarence Streit's *Union Now*, a blueprint for world federal union. Curtis was a pillar of its British section. Based in London, at 44 Gordon Square, it boasted 10,000 disciples in the capital and an equal number in the provinces. Aware of its activities, a highly sceptical Foreign Office advised issuing a government statement indicating 'the utopian character of its ideas'. Others, far more intimate with Curtis, took the same line. The Moot was split, Curtis, virtually a lone voice, versus the rest. 'Everyone was against him,' Brand wrote to Nancy, 'but that makes no difference to him. He really sometimes is quite monstrous . . . His scheme is *absolutely fantastic*. It doesn't belong to the real world at all . . .' Typically, these criticisms served only to stimulate Curtis. He took to the offensive. From Oxford, he sharpened his polemical skills, composing booklets and pamphlets championing the goal of organic federal union. One of them, *Decision* (1941), sold out within weeks, prompting the *Times Literary Supplement* to remark cheekily on 'The return of Achilles to the battlefield of Troy'. Barely two years after his best-seller, Curtis revised his position. Brand, a true friend but a harsh critic, reported that 'Lionel is no longer interested in "Union Now"', but had returned to his first love, 'the Federation of the British Commonwealth'. And, Brand added later, Curtis 'would be extraordinarily angry if anyone said he had ever abandoned it'. Curtis had turned full circle.[20]

After the war, the Round Table circle, Chatham House gatherings, and the select society at All Souls remained the centres of Curtis's life. His association with Oxford was long-standing, his loyalty to its institutions and traditions absolute. Appointed to a research fellowship at All Souls from 1921, he acted as sub-Warden of the College during the latter years of the war. Few would claim that Curtis was an outstanding historian. Rigid as he was in his ideas, his historical memory, although far-reaching, seemed to many to be highly selective, tailored to fit a preconceived thesis. *Civitas Dei*, his *magnum opus*, was faulted by historians and theologians alike. But his inner fire and the sincerity of his writings carried him beyond reach of their censure. Oxford honoured him, perhaps more for his public service than for his contribution to original scholarship. At an encaenia the Public Orator doffed his hat when he mentioned Curtis's name. 'You take your hat off when you mention the name of the Almighty or a very godly person,' he explained, justifying his flattering gesture.[21]

Forever the optimist, the post-1945 years brought renewed hope for

Curtis. Hiroshima and Nagasaki, he thought, made a future war between the powers, an atomic war, inconceivable. The prospect of the entire destruction of mankind was simply too frightful to contemplate. By its internal dynamics, so to speak, the atomic age would inaugurate an era of world federal government. Curtis was partly right: no global nuclear war broke out. But localized conventional conflicts erupted aplenty, stoked all too often by a militant nationalism, Curtis's particular bugbear. Nor, to Curtis's regret, was there a significant movement towards world union. Instead, the atomic bomb spawned the 'balance of terror'. It precipitated the Cold War, one bloc diametrically opposed to the other, the threat of a cataclysmic war always alarmingly imminent. Small wonder that some months after the Cuban crisis Brand commented on how Curtis's 'great visions have been smashed by the actual course of history'.[22]

Despite the 'actual course of history', Curtis never lost sight of his guiding star. Active in the United Europe movement, he perceived it as a precursor of greater things. Waldorf, in his capacity as chairman of Chatham House Council, proposed that the Nobel peace prize for 1947 be awarded to Curtis. Throughout this century, Waldorf explained, Curtis's 'sole aim has been to promote by practical means the friendship of nations and peoples'. He did so by shunning fame, by toiling indefatigably behind the scenes, by manipulating constantly his extensive network of highly placed contacts. These arguments failed to convince the committee in Oslo.[23]

Curtis died at his home at Kidlington, Oxford, in November 1955. In one of the last interviews he gave, he reviewed the rationale of his life's work.

> The only way to win the peace is, as we won the war, by creating forces by land, sea and air that no aggressor would dare to challenge. To do this free nations must merge their national sovereignties into an international sovereignty with a government confined to one function, the prevention of war.

If the 'The fox knows many things – the hedgehog one *big* one,' then Curtis was most definitely a hedgehog.[24]

On the outbreak of the Second World War Bob Brand's career picked up from where he had left it in the First: he returned to America on government service. Brand's expertise in international economic and financial matters, together with his intimate contacts at the highest levels of American society, were two invaluable assets. This combination, it was felt, would enable him to contribute significantly to the British war effort. He headed the British Food Mission in Washington until May 1944, also doubling as the senior member of the British–American Combined Food Board. Brand's guiding hand helped to guarantee a steady flow of foodstuffs at stable prices, while his urbane personality damped down personal jealousies, a key factor in securing a more equitable rationing system between the often conflicting interests of the powers concerned. For a further two years Brand acted as the Treasury's representative in the American capital. In this capacity he was heavily involved in the repercussions brought on by the abrupt termination of Lend-Lease, and, eventually, in the securing of the life-saving American and Canadian loans. At the same time, at Bretton Woods and Savannah, Brand participated in the setting up of a new international financial system, one that pegged exchange rates to the US dollar and launched the International Bank for Reconstruction and Development and the International Monetary Fund. These were years of intense activity. Drained physically, yet conscious of his accomplishments, Brand returned home in May 1946, having once again fully realized the faith put in him by his chiefs.

In 1946, in recognition of his wartime services, Brand was created 1st Baron Brand of Eydon. He accepted the peerage as much in sorrow as in joy. While his son was alive he had refused the honour, not wishing to saddle him with a peerage. But James, a lieutenant and tank commander in the Coldstream Guards, had been killed in action in the last days of the war, and Brand now felt free to accept the award. He divided his time between Lazard's – and the boards of other companies and banks – All Souls, and the House of Lords; or increasingly at his country home, Eydon Hall, near Rugby. A president of the Royal Economic Society, Brand retired from Lazard's in 1960.

The immediate post-war years saw a reckoning with British policy in the 1930s. Historians, led by Sir Lewis Namier and Sir John Wheeler-Bennett, scrutinized Baldwin's and Neville Chamberlain's 'appeasement' policies to telling effect. 'The Unnecessary War', Churchill called it, 'unnecessary' because if the British government, naive and faint-hearted, had adopted a more rigorous policy towards Nazi Germany war could have been avoided.[25] From the early 1960s this conventional wisdom – one certainly upheld by Brand – came under gradual, but continual, fire. 'Appeasement' was now to be seen in a wider context. There were no more Children of Light battling the Children of Darkness, no more heroes or villains. Instead, we find working politicians, morally upright, diligent, harassed, picking their way through a minefield of economic, social, political, international and psychological constraints. Their foreign policy options restricted, they had little, if any, room for manoeuvre. Brand found himself caught up in this debate. Would the ghosts of Cliveden ever be laid to rest?

In 1962 an American professor of history at Georgetown University, Carroll Quigley, consulted Brand about a piece of research he was conducting. His thesis, briefly, told of a 'secret society' founded by Cecil Rhodes and 'his principal trustee', Milner. Devoted to the preservation and expansion of the British Empire, it still functioned. Known variously as Milner's Kindergarten, or the Round Table group, or the 'Cliveden Set', they met 'secretly' (*sic*) at All Souls, Blickling and Cliveden. Among its leaders he named Lothian and Brand. Quigley crowed that he had revealed 'one of the most important historical facts of the twentieth century', for this group had been 'the unknown force guiding [Chamberlain's] government', the 'hidden factor' responsible for its policy. Here was a 'conspiracy theory' that even Claud Cockburn would have envied. Brand's cool mind had no time for this kind of nonsense. 'Astounded' at Quigley's conclusions, Brand dismissed his conjectures as 'absolute moonshine' and 'entirely without foundation'. Summing up, he told Quigley: 'Your ideas on this subject are a mare's nest based on an illusion' – as indeed they were.[26]

Brand's received ideas were put to a far more formidable test by Donald Cameron Watt, a senior lecturer in International History at the London School of Economics. Watt – in time, the most distinguished diplomatic historian of his generation – had submitted an article, 'Appeasement Reconsidered', to *The Round Table* for publication. It challenged the prevailing orthodoxy in no uncertain manner. Watt argued that the assumption, hitherto unquestioned, that Britain possessed 'the military and economic strength and the will-power' to oppose aggression, whether acting alone or through a collective coalition under the League, was without foundation. In fact, it ran 'directly contrary . . . to the trend of advice given to the British Government by its military and economic advisers, and to the whole trend of British opinion throughout the 1920s and 1930s'. It was this grim reality, Watt concluded, that made Chamberlain's policy 'the only one possible in the circumstances'.

Brand reviewed Watt's provocative piece in advance. It puzzled him. The quality of Watt's scholarship could not be faulted, but the cogency of his arguments disconcerted Brand. Unable to dismiss Watt's case, he thought it 'subject to correction'. But his corrections, when examined, amounted to another counter-indictment. He blamed Baldwin – who 'had done nothing' – more than Chamberlain. What should Baldwin have done? Initiate conscription, rearmament, 'and take all measures to meet the attack which was almost certainly coming from Hitler'. Brand was most irritated by Watt's assumption that 'any government' would have followed the path of masterly inactivity mapped out by Baldwin. Given the right leadership, given dynamic inspiration from the top, it could have been different. The author, Brand noted sharply, minimizes 'the efforts of men like Winston Churchill and Amery'. 'I do not know what *The Round Table* should do with this article,' Brand confessed. 'It is terribly long, and personally I think it misleads the reader, not intentionally, but by its thesis that really no Government could earlier have convinced the people of the enormous dangers they were running after Hitler's seizure of power'. Echoing positions he had first voiced in the 1930s, it was Brand's final word on the 'appeasement' debate.[27]

Brand died at the Old Vicarage, Firle, East Sussex, the home of his daughter, Dinah, in August 1963. He was eighty-four years old, a highly respected figure, known for his wisdom and slightly austere common sense. His obituaries invariably referred to his modesty and self-deprecating manner, as well as his open-minded, inquiring mind. Felix Frankfurter described him 'as one of the sweetest natures it was my good fortune ever to know'.[28] After all, in South Africa he had been 'the most outstanding of a very able team'.

Epilogue

They were, as the saying goes, children of their time. Their lives spanned the rise and fall of the Victorian British Empire. Born to a class and generation that was expected to serve Britain's growing imperial power, they set out to redeem their birthright. Their experiences in South Africa as Milner's *Kinder* marked them for life. Young men from a privileged background, elitist by definition, stamped by a sense of duty, against enormous odds they had orchestrated a stunning coup: the unification of South Africa. In their eyes it constituted a model that defined the future of the British Empire. For some, at least, it was also a harbinger of greater things to come, of world union no less. Shrouded in a mystique they did not disown, they returned to England saddled by a reputation and a mission that would remain with them for the rest of their lives.

At the turn of the century, many upper-class Englishmen sensed Britain's declining status as a great power. Imperial Germany was the most immediate cause for concern. But from across the Atlantic they noted with equal disquiet America's first bid for an overseas Empire. Churchill, in 1896, had pictured America 'as a great lusty youth' conducting its affairs 'with a good-hearted freshness which may well be the envy of older nations of the earth'. Should its 'good-hearted freshness' extend to furthering its interests abroad, it would do so at Britain's expense; and as 'lusty youths' were difficult to control, some sort of reckoning had to be made – more on the British side than the American. 'I would never quarrel with the Americans if I could possibly avoid it,' wrote Lord Selborne, First Lord of the Admiralty, fearing an Anglo–American naval race that Britain could not win.[1] In the light of American drive, power and ambition, the prospect of confrontation was daunting, of war inconceivable. British policy-makers sensibly opted for an Anglo–American rapprochement.

The Round Tablers' instinctive response to Britain's changing fortunes was twofold: to prevent the break-up of the British Empire, and to foster the so-called 'special relationship'. It focused on a bonding of the Anglo-Saxon Brotherhood – a notion replete with racial overtones. From this sprang their obsession with federal or organic union of the Empire – they often wavered between one and the other. Some viewed the future Commonwealth as a rewarding 'white man's burden'. Following their mentors, Rhodes and Milner, they openly patronized the native peoples, their attitudes frequently tinged with racism. There was hardly a trace of self-consiousness or embarrassment in their convictions. What would be regarded as outright racism to the modern eye was viewed by their generation as the natural order of things. White, western cultures *were* superior to natives ones, and it was the duty of the more advanced civilizations to nurture the less fortunate ones to political maturity, economic proficiency and social improvement.[2] One would write of 'child races' and the 'lower civilizations as the chief menace to the peace of the world'. Even Brand announced his intention that 'the white man shall always be top dog', though he wondered whether 'this is consonant with mutual citizenship in a Commonwealth'.[3] Of course, nurturing the 'special relationship' between the two great Anglo-Saxon peoples was a given. Curtis, always tempted by extravagant ideas, went much further. Regarding America as a kind of prodigal son, he ruminated on its eventual return to the fold.

In retrospect, it can be seen that their programme, whatever its pretensions, was an admission of weakness. It reflected a widespread premonition that Britain was falling behind in the great power race. Anxious to keep up with the future giants, Germany and the United States, their projects were designed to preserve a status that was fast disappearing – as it happened, for ever. On every count, their game plan was doomed to failure. And the signs were there to see. Dominion nationalism was on the rise, as Lothian, at least, recognized when he visited Canada in 1909. Nor would it fade away. On the contrary, it flowered, leading the Commonwealth down a different road from that intended by Curtis and his followers. Nor were the Americans particularly enthralled by the British version of the 'special relationship'. Except in a vague, sentimental, but politically meaningless way, it meant little to most American politicians. In the final analysis, it was the American century, and they would not share it with a decrepit British Empire. Nor would they allow Britain to sustain its former greatness by clinging to their coattails.

There was something anachronistic about these friends, particularly Curtis. The group's fixation with Empire politics and the 'special relationship' left it with a lopsided view of world affairs, marginalizing Europe. Chasing history, they failed to catch up with it, hard as they tried.

*

The Bible says, 'They have sown the wind, and they shall reap the whirlwind' (Hosea 8:7). In this case, Claud Cockburn sowed, but others reaped.* Millions of ordinary people around the world gave credence to the stories he circulated about the machinations of the 'Cliveden Set'. And not only common folk: world leaders too succumbed to these tales, if it suited their purpose. The Germans, in particular, were intrigued, as Ribbentrop's intemperate courting of the 'Set' showed; and likewise, in a quite different context, Adam von Trott's mission. Pro-Russian circles and the Soviet hierarchy were also ready to swallow these stories: they slotted in neatly with a more wide-ranging conspiracy theory, one predicated on a bellicose capitalist-fascist world scheming incessantly to bring about the destruction of the Soviet Union.

Ironically, and more to the point given the importance of the 'special relationship' to the 'Set', Roosevelt, briefing the press, uncovered 'the Cliveden Set of Washington', a 'fifth column' that manipulated a 'sixth column' to carry out its shabby work. His 'Washington Set' centred on those American monied, conservative interests with whom the architects of the New Deal were in perpetual conflict. Have you seen this 'miserable reference to the "Cliveden Set"?' Walter Lippmann asked Brand. Roosevelt was implying that both 'Sets' were bent on undermining the true interests of their respective countries. There were visible links between Cliveden and Washington: perhaps the Astors, but most certainly Joseph Kennedy, the United States ambassador to London, who was reported to be consorting with the Clivedenites, and whose support for appeasement was well known. *The Week* pounced in its usual manner, writing of Kennedy as 'defeatist' and 'anti-Rooseveltian'. Roosevelt's policy was no more than 'a Jewish production', Kennedy was revealed as saying, as he forecast that the President would fall in the forthcoming November 1940 elections.[5]

Here was another conspiracy theory – American-style. But as with so much else about Roosevelt, it is impossible to say with certainty what he actually thought. In all probability he was exploiting the notoriety of the 'Set' as a convenient stick to beat his enemies – never lacking on Capitol Hill and in Wall Street. Still, his denigratory comments gave a new twist to Cockburn's creative journalism.

* Cockburn, however, eventually reaped his own whirlwind. In January 1941 Herbert Morrison, the Home Secretary, shut down the *Daily Worker* and *The Week* on the same day, maintaining that the papers' 'slavish obedience to the Moscow line was a negation of freedom of the printed word'. The CID men went first to the offices of the *Daily Worker*, where they found Cockburn at work. In a comic scene, the inspector-in-charge, who apparently was hard pressed for time, suggested that they drive together across town in a police car to *The Week*'s premises in Victoria Street so that the closure notice could be delivered in person to Cockburn, the owner of the about-to-be suppressed journal at its place of business, as required by law. Cockburn gladly accepted this civilized offer.

Michael Astor accepted 'the notional idea of a "set"', though he hesitated from 'defining too precisely what the word implies'. Its chief victim, Vansittart, denied 'the existence of any conscious or organized body', but thought that 'all sorts of pies were fingered' by the Clivedenites as they talked too much 'of that which they knew not'. Was it possible to give the 'Set' a precise definition? One can say with absolute certainty that it was not a mafia-like conspiracy. There might have been a 'Prophet' but there was no 'Godfather'. As one observer remarked, with a touch of exaggeration, 'The so-called "Group" had as much unity as the passengers in a railway train.'[6]

For the general public, however, the 'Set' assumed a symbolic significance. A Clivedenite was taken as a handy code-name for anyone rich or politically powerful who was actively furthering policies beneficial to Nazi Germany. Their alleged wheeler-dealing behind the scenes had about it an authentic ring enhanced by their exclusive social standing, their highly placed political contacts, and the splendour of their country estates.* They were top-notch people, the cream of society, weaving the most elaborate of designs. Such material made for dramatic, glamorous copy, for a conspiracy theory of quality. It fed an inquisitive, star-struck public hungry for such feasts.

The 'Cliveden Set' was entrapped in a time warp of its own making. It held that treaty revision in agreement with Germany was a noble, morally correct cause, legitimate in both its European and international contexts, and one that best served British interests. It was, they would argue, infinitely preferable to Hitler grabbing what he coveted: surprising the West with a series of *faits accomplis*. And, they went on, it was most certainly preferable to going to war over matters that were, in their estimation, of marginal importance to Britain. Their state of mind lasted until the spring of 1939. Brand, a regular visitor to Hitler's Germany, was the notable exception, but his Cassandra-like warnings fell for the most part on deaf ears. His was a lone voice, unsettling the other regulars of the so-called 'Cliveden Set'.

'My mother', David Astor suggested, 'never really understood the "Cliveden Set" image of her simply because she was convinced that it was absolutely false. But it did her reputation tremendous damage, and also that of our family. All that people remember today about the Astors is the "Cliveden Set" and the "Profumo Set". Both stories were inventions, but it appears that they'll be with us for ever.'[7]

* The 1930s have been confidently defined as 'the swan-song of country-house life' (see Lawrence and Jeanne C. Fawtier Stone, *An Open Elite? England 1540–1880* [OUP, 1984], 425). It was, however, an extended 'swan-song' that in one way or another stretched well into the post-war era. Nor did the so-called decline in 'country-house life' detract from the glamour invested in it by those doomed to observe it from the outside.

So the myth of the 'Cliveden Set' persists. The stigma attached to its image continues to stain the reputation of its members. It even makes occasional appearances in respectable history books. Claud Cockburn, who cultivated the term and created the legend, knew better. Recalling Thomas Lamont's – the American financier's – tongue-in-cheek denial of a Power Trust, he applied it with more relevance to his creation: 'There was no ['Set'] – just people interested in the same objectives standing around in a co-operative frame of mind.'[8]

As for Cliveden itself, the grounds remain as beautiful as ever, tended by the National Trust, littered with the Roman sculpture purchased and placed by the 1st Viscount Astor. The house, however, underwent a metamorphosis. It survived in its original form until the death of the 3rd Viscount, William ('Bill') Astor, in 1966. Stanford University then leased it as a centre for its English schools. In this casual manner it met, in a roundabout way, Waldorf's wish to preserve it as a place 'where men and women of all types' would continue to gather. After almost twenty years of hosting American students, the house was taken over by Cliveden Hotel Ltd in 1985. Following thorough restoration, conversion and redecoration it was opened to the public as a luxury hotel, its rooms named and appointed in the old style, so that a fortunate couple can reserve the 'Lady Astor Full Double Suite' or 'Lord Astor's Superior Double' – or even 'Garibaldi's Standard Double'. Thankfully, three rooms are kept open to the public, the old French Dining Room, the Library and the Great Hall, a tantalizing reminder of Cliveden's halcyon days.*

---

* In the late 1990s Cliveden Hotel Ltd was acquired by 'Destination Hotels and Resorts', a company in which Bill Gates has a 10 per cent interest.

Acknowledgements

Realizing a project of this kind depends upon the goodwill and encouragement of many individuals. My search for information led me to intrude upon the privacy of friends, colleagues and strangers alike, taxing their patience, often picking their brains in what appeared to them, no doubt, as little more than casual conversations. To all I am indebted. For their forbearance, frankness and hospitality I wish to thank: Mr David Astor; Mr Timothy Garton Ash; Mr and Mrs William Bell; the late Lord Beloff; the late Sir Isaiah Berlin; Mr Michael Bott; Dr Piers Brenden; Lord Bullock; the late Lady Ford; Sir Edward Ford; Mr James Fox; Sir Martin Gilbert; Professor Ellis Joffe; Professor Wm. Roger Louis; Dr Alex May; Dr Inbal Rose; Professor Sasson Sofer; Mr Martin Tyson; Professor Donald Cameron Watt; and the late Charles Wenden.

My thanks are also extended to the staffs of the numerous Archives, Libraries and Institutions that generously extended their facilities to me: the Archives and Manuscripts Division at the University of Reading; the Bodleian Library, Oxford (in particular the staff in Room 132, its Modern Papers Reading Room); the British Library and its Newspaper Collection at Colindale; the British Library of Political and Economic Science at the London School of Economics; the British Council Library, Jerusalem; the Corrington Library, All Souls College, Oxford; the Institute for Historical Research, Senate House, London; the Library for Humanities and Social Sciences and the National Library at The Hebrew University, Jerusalem; the Library at St Antony's College, Oxford; the Doe Memorial Library at the University of California, Berkeley; the Library at Rhodes House, Oxford; the Search Room at Churchill Archives Centre, Churchill College, Cambridge; the Scottish Record Office, National Archives of Scotland, Edinburgh; the Public Record Office, Kew; *The Times* Archives, London; The Royal Commission on Historical Manuscripts, Chancery Lane, London.

Copyright material at the Public Record Office is reproduced by kind permission of the Controller of Her Majesty's Stationery Office. I am grateful to other institutions for permission to quote material of which they hold the copyright: the Archives and Manuscripts Division at the University of Reading; the Bodleian Library, Oxford; the British Library of Political and Economic Science at the London School of Economics; the British Library and its

Newspaper Collection at Colindale; and the Scottish Record Office, National Archives of Scotland. I also wish to acknowledge those authors and publishers (listed in the Bibliography or mentioned in the Notes) for quotations I have used from works of which they hold the copyright. Allow me to express in advance my apologies for those cases that I have inadvertently overlooked.

Special thanks are due to the University of California at Berkeley for inviting me to spend a year with them. The staff and students at the Department of History received me most warmly and ensured that my stay there was a congenial and fruitful one. It was in these agreeable and stimulating surroundings that I began research on this book. I must also thank the Warden and Fellows and Staff of St Antony's College, Oxford, for allowing me to spend much time in their company, exploiting their hospitality and the facilities of the College.

I am grateful to Mr Martin Lubowski and Dr Inbal Rose for pursuing various enquiries on my behalf. Dr Rose and Mr David Astor read the manuscript, either in whole or in part. For their informed comments I remain greatly in their debt.

To Andrew Lownie, the most patient, optimistic and supportive of literary agents, I owe much. Many thanks are also due to the staff at Jonathan Cape, in particular to my editor, Will Sulkin, together with Jörg Hensgen and their staff, for their skill and professionalism in guiding this project to its conclusion.

Authorship is the loneliest of occupations, and perhaps only those who have experienced it first-hand can appreciate the need to be helped at all times by encouragement and support. So, finally, I wish to record my deepest thanks and admiration to my wife and daughter, Tslilla and Inbal, for their patience and understanding in sustaining me throughout this demanding, yet rewarding, task.

Notes

Prologue

1 Lord Riddell, *Intimate Diary of the Peace Conference and After* (1933), 330.

2 Quoted in Alex May, *The Round Table, 1910–66* (unpublished D.Phil. thesis, Oxford, 1995), 7.

3 Entry for 15 August 1917, Hankey Diaries, 1/3, Churchill College, Cambridge; also Stephen Roskill, *Hankey: Man of Secrets* (1970), i, 422–3.

4 May, 62.

5 Walter Nimocks, *Milner's Young Men: The 'Kindergarten' in Edwardian Imperial Affairs* (1970), ix.

6 John E. Kendle, *The Round Table Movement and Imperial Union* (University of Toronto Press, 1975), 281.

7 See May, 12, and Kendle, 293. As 'a disaster . . .', see Carroll Quigley, *The Anglo-American Establishment: From Rhodes to Cliveden* (New York, 1981), xi. For some reason, Quigley, an American historian, developed a pathological dislike for the chief shareholders of 'God's Truth Ltd'.

8 Quoted in A. M. Gollin, *Proconsul in Politics: A Study of Lord Milner in Power and Opposition* (1964), 41.

9 From the first issue of *The Round Table* (November 1910); also Kendle, 46–73, and May, 1.

10 May, 241.

11 See Donald Watt's 'Foreword' in *Chatham House and British Foreign Policy, 1919–1945* (Lothian Foundation Press, 1994), i.

12 The memberships of the *Kindergarten* and the London Moot may be found in May, 1–2, and Appendix E, 456–68. For the London Moot, some sixty names are listed.

13 See in particular *Tribune*, 25 March 1938. Other quotations from newspaper clippings relating to the 'Set' in the Astor Papers, MS1416/1/1588, deposited at Reading University. Most of those named by *Tribune* and other journals can by no measure be counted as members of the 'Cliveden Set', although most of them had been guests at Cliveden. The 'Set', as dealt with here, consisted of those core members mentioned above.

14 See Michael Astor's acceptance of 'the notional idea of a "set"', *Tribal Feeling* (1964), 138.

15 For Henry Fairlie's article see the *Spectator* (September 1955); see also Walter Ellis, 'The Twilight of the Establishment', *Sunday Times* (17 September 1995). Also Peter Hennessy, *The Great and the Good* (Policy Studies Institute, March 1986); and Hugh Thomas (ed.), *The Establishment: A Symposium* (1959).

16 Quoted in May, 24.

17 See Donald Cameron Watt, 'The Nature of the Foreign-Policy-Making Elite in Britain', in *Personalities and Policies: Studies in the Formulation of British Foreign Policy in the Twentieth Century* (Greenwood Press, Westport, Connecticut, 1965) ; also William Wallace, *Foreign Policy and the Political Process* (1971), 9.

18 See Norman Rose, *Vansittart: Study of a Diplomat* (1978), 196; for other comments by Vansittart see PRO FO371/18824/C785, 4 February 1935, and FO371/20735/C3621, 18 and 29 May 1937.

19 John Grigg, *Nancy Astor: Portrait of a Pioneer* (1980), 105; and Grigg, 'Woman About the House', *Times Magazine* (27 January 1996).

Chapter 1: Cliveden

1 Quoted in *Cliveden* (The National Trust, 1994), 5. Unless stated otherwise, the following section is based on: *Cliveden*, op. cit.; H. B. Wheatley (ed.), *The Diary of Samuel Pepys* (Bell, London, 1928–35); Leonard Wallace Cowie, *Hanoverian England* (1967); Joan Walters, *The Royal Griffon* (1972); Hester Chapman, *Great Villiers* (1949); Christopher Hibbert, *Garibaldi and His Enemies* (Penguin Books, 1987); Gervas Huxley, *Victorian Duke* (1967); Eric Richards, *The Leviathan of Wealth: The Sutherland Fortune in the Industrial Revolution* (1973); David Cannadine, *The Decline and Fall of the British Aristocracy* (Picador, Pan Books, 1992); Philip Magnus, *Gladstone* (John Murray, London, 1963); Banister Fletcher, *A History of Architecture on the Comparative Method* (Athlone Press, 1961, 7th edn).

2 Unless stated otherwise, the section on the Astors is based on: G. Myers, *History of the Great American Fortunes* (Chicago, 1910), 3 vols.; K. H. Porter, *John Jacob Astor, Business man* (Cambridge, Mass., 1931), 2 vols.; Maurice Collis, *Nancy Astor: An Informal Biography* (1960); A. M. Gollin, *The Observer and J. L. Garvin, 1908–1914* (1960); Michael Astor, *Tribal Feeling* (1964); Christopher Sykes, *Nancy: The Life of Lady Astor* (New York, 1972); Kenneth Young (ed.), *The Diaries of Sir Robert Bruce Lockhart* (1973–80); Elizabeth Langhorne, *Nancy Astor and her Friends* (1974); John Grigg, *Nancy Astor: Portrait of a Pioneer* (1980); Stephen Koss, *The Rise and Fall of the Political Press in Britain* (University of North Carolina Press, 1984), vol. 2; Derek Wilson, *The Astors: The Life and Times of the Astor Dynasty, 1763–1992* (1993); *International Historical Statistics: The Americas, 1750–1988* (Stockton Press, 1993, 2nd edn).

3 Quoted in Wilson, 109.

4 See D. T. Lynch, *'Boss' Tweed* (1927).

5 Victoria Glendinning, *Vita* (Penguin Books, 1980), 32.

6 See Wilson, 164, and Robert Blake, *The Unknown Prime Minister: The Life and Times of Andrew Bonar Law, 1858–1923* (1955), 101. Stephen Koss, *The Rise and Fall of the Political Press in Britain*, 199–200, also records this conversation, but names Waldorf Astor, William's son, as the petitioner. This cannot have been the case as Waldorf opposed a hereditary peerage for the family, seeing it as a hindrance to his own political career.

7 Details in MS1416/1/6/8; Rosina Harrison, *Rose: My Life in Service* (Viking Press, New York, 1975), 46–7; and Collis, 37, 40.

Chapter 2: Waldorf and Nancy

1 Michael Astor, 42.

2 See Halifax, *Fullness of Days* (1957).

3 From the recollections of Percy Lubbock, *Shades of Eton*, quoted in Birkenhead, *Halifax*, 51; and Jonathan Gathorne-Hardy, *The Public School Phenomenon* (Penguin Books, 1979), 103.

4 Sir H. C. Maxwell Lyte, *A History of Eton College* (4th edn, 1911), 562.

5 Quotations in Michael Astor, 43, 44.

6 Wilson, 136.

7 Welldon, quoted in Correlli Barnett, *The Collapse of British Power* (1972), 28; for Churchill's recollection, see Randolph S. Churchill, *Winston S. Churchill* (1966), i, 113.

8 See *Eton Calendars* and *Eton College Chronicle* for this period; and Correlli Barnett, 28.

9 Quotations in Morris, 117, 135.

10 See Waldorf's obituary in *The Times*, 3 October 1952.

11 See Michael Astor, 44–5. For 'daring reverse', see Joyce Grenfell, *Requests the Pleasure* (Futura Books, 1991), 34.

12 See Christopher Sykes, *Nancy: The Life of Lady Astor* (New York, 1972), 84.

13 Sykes, 69.

14 For this passage, see Lady Astor's draft autobiography (hereafter, NDA), in the Astor Papers, MS1416/1/6/87.

15 Robert Rhodes James, *Victor Cazalet: A Portrait* (1976), 142.

16 See Rosina Harrison, *Rose: My Life in Service* (New York, 1975), 61–3; A. L. Rowse, *Memories of Men and Women* (1980), 66; and the painting of her by John Singer Sargent, that now hangs in the Great Hall at Cliveden.

17 Quoted in Sykes, 18.

18 Collis, 13; Sykes, 43, 150; and Harrison, 60.

19 Quoted in Maurice Collis, *Nancy Astor: An Informal Biography* (1960), 158.

20 See Michael Astor, 29–30; and Collis, 20.

21 See James M. McPherson, *Battle Cry of Freedom* (OUP, New York, 1988), 686.

22 Quotations from NDA; also Sykes, 56–7.

23 Quotations in Rowse, 28; Harrison, 98; and Grigg, 55.

24 NDA; Sykes, 61–2, 66.
25 Harrison, 91.
26 Quoted in Michael Astor, 41.
27 Quoted by John Grigg in *Dictionary of National Biography, 1961–70.*
28 See Keith Middlemas (ed.), *Thomas Jones: Whitehall Diary* (1969), ii, 125; and Nigel Nicolson (ed.), *Harold Nicolson, Diaries and Letters, 1930–39* (Fontana Books, 1969), 260.
29 Quoted in Wilson, 153.
30 NDA.
31 Keith Middlemas (ed.), *Thomas Jones: Whitehall Diary* (1969), i, 261.
32 See Grigg, 105–6, and Sykes, 96.
33 See Michael Astor, 76; Collis, 41; and Joyce Grenfell, *In Pleasant Places* (1979), 198, and *'Darling Ma': Letters to her Mother, 1932–1944* (1988), 18; and Harrison, 100–1.
34 Collis, 46.
35 For Churchill sulking, see Harrison, 112; Kitchener as collector, Collis, 46; for literary and other figures, Collis, 47, 49, Nancy invariably addressed Strachey as 'Dear Author', see Michael Holroyd, *Lytton Strachey: A Biography* (Penguin Books, 1980), 828.
36 See Collis, 45, and Sykes, 177–8.
37 Nicolson Diaries, ii, 469.
38 See Harrison, 89, 127, 169; A. L. Rowse, *Memories of Men and Women* (1980), 47; Michael Astor, 55; Sykes, 167.
39 See Notes of Mary Baker Eddy Biography, MSS Brand 182; NDA; Michael Astor, 51–3; and Sykes, 42, 138–9.
40 NDA; and Rowse, 38.
41 Michael Astor, 50, 57.
42 Martin Gilbert (ed.), *Winston S. Churchill. Companion Volume V, part 2, The Wilderness Years, 1929–1935* (1981), 300–1 (hereafter, *CV/5*, etc.).
43 Rowse, 38.
44 Interview in *Sunday Express*, 23 February 1936 (MS1416/1/7/75), and *Dictionary of National Biography, 1961–1970.* For 'punch-ups', see Noel Annan, *Our Age* (HarperCollins, 1995), 266.
45 Michael Astor, 47.
46 Michael Astor, 49; Harrison, 156.
47 See *CV/2, part 2*, 1053, 1084–5.
48 For support of Insurance Bill, see his comments in *P.D.*, Commons, vol. 26, cols. 320–7; vol. 27, cols. 566, 1121; vol. 39, col. 1189; vol. 41, col. 1631; for Lloyd George singing, see Collis, 68–9; Nancy's admission, Autobiographical sketch, 1951 (Sykes, 96); and as misfits, John Vincent (ed.), *The Crawford Papers: The Journals of David Lindsay, twenty-seventh Earl of Crawford and tenth Earl of Balcarres, 1892–1940* (Manchester University Press, 1984), 539.
49 See Prologue, pp. 1–4 above, and Chapter 3, p. 52–5.
50 This was Robert Brand's considered opinion. Quoted in Sykes, 125–6.
51 Waldorf to Nancy, 28 September 1931, Astor Papers, 1066/1/9/4; quoted in Wilson, 261.

Chapter 3: The Kinder

1 Quoted in Birkenhead, *Halifax* (1965), 56.
2 See A. M. Gollin, *Proconsul in Politics: A Study of Lord Milner in Opposition and in Power* (1964), *passim*; and James Morris, *Farewell the Trumpets* (Penguin edn, 1980), 115–24.
3 Quoted in Jan Morris, *Oxford* (OUP Paperback, 1979), 47.
4 Quotations attributed to Thomas Gaisford, Dean of Christ Church, and Mandell Creighton, Bishop of London.
5 Morris, 243–4.
6 Matthew Arnold, from *Thyrsis* and *Essays in Criticism* (First Series, 1865, preface).
7 Quotations in J. R. M. Butler, *Lord Lothian (Philip Kerr), 1882–1940* (1960), 21, 41; Lord Brand, 'Philip Kerr: Some Personal Memories', *The Round Table* (June 1960); and A. L. Rowse, *All Souls and Appeasement* (1961), 32.
8 For the passage, and quotations, on Kerr's religious restlessness, see Michael Astor, 139–40; Butler, 3–10; Lord Brand, 'Philip Kerr: Some Personal Memories', *The Round Table* (June 1960); *Dictionary of National Biography, 1931–1940* (entry by Lord Brand); *The Times*, 13 December 1940 (Obituary, Edward Grigg).
9 See David Lloyd George, *The Truth About the Peace Treaties* (1938), i, 263–5; for Churchill, John Colville, *The Fringes of Power: Downing Street Diaries, 1939–1955* (1985), 312; also Winston S. Churchill, *The Second World War* (1949), ii, 354, 490.
10 Quotations in Butler, 17, 18.
11 The Report (1908), is in PRO CO293/41. Quotations in Butler, 25–7.
12 Quotations in Butler, 30, and Deborah Lavin, *From Empire to International Commonwealth: A Biography of Lionel Curtis* (Clarendon Press, Oxford, 1995), 36, 81.
13 Quotations in Butler, 37–40. No references are given, particularly for Kerr to Brand, 1 November 1909, but see also Kerr's (undated) memorandum recording his impressions of his Canadian trip, GD40/17/11 (Lothian Papers).
14 May, 54, and Lavin, 106.
15 May, 44.
16 See his articles: 'Anglo–German Rivalry', *The Round Table* (November 1910); 'The Anglo-Japanese Alliance', *The Round Table* (February 1911); 'The New Problem of Imperial Defence', 'The Emigration Question in Japan', *The Round Table* (May 1911); 'Britain, France and Germany', *The Round Table* (December 1911); and 'The Grand Alliance Against Aggression', *The Round Table* (June 1939).
17 Quoted in Butler, 49.
18 Butler, 88; and Kerr to Curtis, 28 May 1922, Butler, 91–2.
19 See Brand Memoir, 'Memories and Thoughts about Nancy Astor' (I am grateful to Mr James Fox for making this paper available to me); A. J. P. Taylor (ed.), *Lloyd George: The Diaries of Frances Stevenson* (1971), 214; Michael Astor, 54; and A. L. Rowse, *Memories of Men and Women* (1980), 28.

20 See, for example, Nancy Astor to Lothian, 24 September 1937, MS1415/1/ 4/56 (Lothian Papers).
21 Butler, 44–5; and Stephen Koss, *The Rise and Fall of the Political Press in Britain: The Twentieth Century* (1984), 199.
22 Private information.
23 Quotations in Lavin, *From Empire to Commonwealth: A Biography of Lionel Curtis* (OUP, 1995), 9, 13.
24 From Curtis's diary of his travels as a tramp, in MSS Curtis 140.
25 Quoted in Rowse, 'Lionel Curtis: "The Prophet"', in *Glimpses of the Great* (1985), 76. Rowse, himself homosexual, wonders whether or not there was 'an unconscious homo-eroticism among Milner's Young Men'. So far, there is no evidence for this supposition; or at least none has yet come to light.
26 See Chapter 2, pp. 8–9.
27 See L. S. Amery, *My Political Life* (1953), i, 57.
28 Lavin, 32–4.
29 Quoted in David Watt, 'The Foundation of the Round Table', *The Round Table* (November 1970), no. 240.
30 Butler, 23.
31 Michael Astor, 79.
32 Lavin, 40.
33 See MSS Brand 182, 1 January 1910; and Lavin, 36, 51, 106, 111, 319.
34 See W. K. Hancock, *Smuts: The Sanguine Years, 1870–1919* (Cambridge University Press, 1962), 29–30, 126 (also 121, 203, 246); and for his 'Slim' reputation, 274–5. Also David Watt's illuminating articles, 'The Men of the Round Table', *The Round Table* (July 1969), no. 235, and 'The Foundation of the Round Table', *The Round Table* (November 1970), no. 240. And Lavin, 99.
35 See pp. 54–5; also David Watt, 'The Foundation of the Round Table'; Walter Nimocks, *Milner's Young Men* (1968), 134–6; Lavin, 108–9; Richard Jebb, *Studies in Colonial Nationalism* (1905); and May, 39–42.
36 Quotations in Butler, 37–40, and David Watt, 'The Foundation of the Round Table'.
37 See the *Green Memorandum* (1910), known later as the 'Annotated Memorandum', and finally as 'Round Table Studies, First Series'. These papers are discussed fully in Kendle, 76–80, and Lavin, 111–12. Similar 'Eggs' followed: *The Form of an Organic Union of the Empire* (1911), *The Commonwealth of Nations* (1916) and *The Problem of Commonwealth* (1916).
38 Quoted in Hancock, *Smuts*, i, 351.
39 Curtis was not the originator of the term 'Commonwealth', despite his success in laying claim to the expression. See Deborah Lavin, 'Lionel Curtis and the Idea of Commonwealth', 97, in *Oxford and the Idea of Commonwealth* (1982), eds. F. Madden and D. K. Fieldhouse. Quotation in Lavin, 'Lionel Curtis . . .', 107–8.
40 Quotations in Lavin, *From Empire to Commonwealth: A Biography of Lionel Curtis*, 231, and Lavin, 'Lionel Curtis and the Idea of Commonwealth'.
41 See Sykes, 126, 183, and Lavin, 117, 164, 170.
42 See Curtis to Nancy Astor, 1 October 1912, MS100 /1/ (Astor Papers);

Norman Rose, *Churchill: An Unruly Life* (1994), 90; Sykes, 126–7; and Lavin, 121.

43 Quoted in Lavin, 121.

44 Robert Boothby, *New Statesman and Nation*, 10 December 1955, in his review of John Evelyn Wrench's biography of Dawson.

45 Quotations in Richard Meinertzhagen, *Middle East Diary, 1917–1956* (1959), x; John Betjeman's blank-verse autobiography, *Summoned by Bells* (1960), 94; *The Times*, 8 November 1944; and Wrench, 29.

46 L. S. Amery, *My Political Life* (1953), i, 62–3.

47 See Charles W. Brodribb, *Government by Mallardy: A Study in Political Ornitholgy* (1932), quoted in Nimocks, 51; and A. L. Rowse, 'Lionel Curtis: "The Prophet"'.

48 For the mores of All Souls, see quotations in Morris, 194–5; Nimocks, 50; and L. S. Amery, *My Political Life* (1953), i, 321.

49 Quotion in Wrench, 34. For the Robinson (Dawson) relationship with Perry, see Nimocks, 28.

50 Quotations from correspondence with his family, in Wrench, 38, 39, 41.

51 For Milner's attitude towards Chinese labour, see Gollin, 61–74.

52 Quotations in Wrench, 40, 42.

53 For Dawson's appointment, see Gollin, 161–2; also Wrench, 44.

54 See Beatrice Webb, *Our Partnership* (1948), 312; and Gollin, 103.

55 Quotations in *The History of the Times: The Twentieth Century Test, 1884–1912* (1947), iii, 769, and *The History of the Times: The 150th Anniversary and Beyond, 1912–1948* (1952), iv, Part 1, 462; also Francis Williams, *Dangerous Estate: The Anatomy of Newspapers* (1957), 274.

56 See Gollin, 129.

57 *The Times*, 27 July 1925.

58 See Wrench, 56–7, and Nimocks, 67, 89.

59 See Amery, *My Political Life*, i, 338–9, and Gollin, 161–2. For the Amery and Milner connection, see Wm. Roger Louis, *In the Name of God, Go! Leo Amery and the British Empire in the Age of Churchill* (New York, 1992), 39–40.

60 See *The History of The Times*, iii, 742.

61 Quotations in *The History of The Times*, iv, Part 1, 1–2, 34, 170.

62 See *The History of The Times*, iii, 574, 583, 584, 742, and Wrench, 64, 66.

63 *The History of The Times*, iii, 770.

64 See *The History of The Times*, iii, 770, and iv, Part 1, 152–4.

65 Quotation in Beaverbrook, *Politicians and the War*, i, 99; see also R. C. K. Ensor, *England, 1870–1914* (1st edn, 1936; OUP, 1960), 312, 446.

66 Quotations in *The History of The Times*, iv, Part 2, 1109; Wrench, 51, 57, 88, 94–5; and Gollin, 221.

67 See *The History of The Times*, iv, Part 2, 543, 546.

68 Brand, 'Memories and Thoughts about Nancy Astor'.

69 These appraisals in W. K. Hancock, *Smuts* (1962), i, 261; Donald McLachlan, *In the Chair: Barrington Ward of The Times, 1927–1948* (1971), 37; and *The Times*, 24 August 1963.

70 From R. H. Brand, 'Philip Kerr: Some Personal Memories', *The Round Table* (June 1960).

71 *Summoned by Bells*, 67.

72 Quotations in Jonathan Gathorne-Hardy, *The Public School Phenomenon* (Penguin Books, 1979), 136, 325, 345; and Correlli Barnett, *The Collapse of British Power* (1972), 32, 35.

73 Betjeman, 104.

74 See H. A. L. Fisher, *A History of Europe* (1957 edn), v; and Richard Crossman, *The Charm of Politics* (1958), 6.

75 Quotions in Nimocks, 40, 41.

76 For Brand's attitude to Milner see his article 'Lord Milner and General Smuts', *Listener*, 15 October 1953; ; the observer was Frederic Eggleston, a member of the Australian delegation to the Imperial War Conference, 1917, quoted in Kendle, 219. Opposed to 'metaphysics' in John Buchan, 'Ordeal by Marriage', quoted in May, 57.

77 From Brand, 'Memories and Thoughts About Nancy Astor'.

78 For bachelordom and its merits, see Lavin, 64; and for picnicking with nice English girls, Brand to Lady Hampden, 5 January 1909, Brand Papers, File 185.

79 Quotations in Lavin, 84, 85, and Brand, 'Lord Milner and General Smuts'.

80 Brand to Lady Hampden, 9 May 1909, Brand Papers, File 185.

81 For Brand's role in preparing the constitution and his co-operation with Smuts, see L. M. Thompson, *The Unification of South Africa* (Clarendon Press, 1960), 133–4; W. K. Hancock, *Smuts*, i, 261, 262; Nimocks, 105–6; and David Watt's entry on Brand in the *Dictionary of National Biography, 1961–1970*.

82 *Listener*, 15 October 1953.

83 See Lavin, 60; D. A. Low, 'What Happened to Milner's Young Men: What of Their Successors?', *The Round Table* (1990); and *The Round Table* (1970).

84 Quotations in Brand, *The Union of South Africa* (1909), 47–8, 98, 100–4, 110–11, 118.

85 Nimocks, 179.

86 See p. 66.

87 For the results of the group's discussions, see Curtis, *The Form of an Organic Union of the Empire* (privately printed, revised 23 March 1911), quoted in May, 87. For Canada and 'men of influence', see D. A. Low, 'What Happened to Milner's Young Men: What of Their Successors?', *The Round Table* (1990), 315.

88 Quotations from *The Round Table* (November 1910), 64–7, the first issue of the journal. See also Jasper Ridley to Brand, 9 April 1914, Brand Papers, File 26/2.

89 These details in Brand, 'Memories and Thoughts . . .'

90 Quotations from Brand, 'Memories and Thoughts . . .'

91 See 'Lombard Street and War', *The Round Table* (March 1912), and 'War and Financial Exhaustion', *The Round Table* (December 1914).

Chapter 4: War Games – and Peacemaking

1 See Butler, 56, and Sykes, 153–4.
2 See Lavin, 124–5.
3 Wrench, 89.
4 This passage is based on the following pieces that appeared in *The Round Table*: 'War in Europe' (September 1914); 'Four Months' War' (December 1914); 'Burden of Victory' (June 1915); 'National Duty in War' (September 1915); 'Harvest of War' (December 1915); 'War for Public Right' (March 1916); issue of June 1916, in particular 'Principle of Peace'; 'War Aims' (September 1916); 'The Making of Peace' (December 1916).
5 Martin Gilbert, *Churchill: Companion Volume III, part 2* (1972), 985–6.
6 See *History of The Times* (1952), iv, part 2, 271 n2; Gollin, 268–9; Wrench, 123, for the Lloyd George–Milner meeting; and Peter Clarke, *Hope and Glory: Britain 1900–1990* (1996), 75–6.
7 This passage based on: L. S. Amery, *My Political Life* (1953), ii, 81–2; Gollin, 323–4; Christopher Addison, *Four and A Half Years* i, 201; John Turner, *British Politics and the Great War* (1992), 113–14; and for Garvin, Stephen Koss, *The Rise and Fall of the Political Press in Britain: The Twentieth Century* (1984), 280, 287, also *DNB, 1941–50*. Also Dawson Diaries for 1916.
8 Quotations from *The History of The Times* (1952), iv, part 1, 297–8.
9 Hankey Diaries, 1/1, 11 January 1917; Gollin, 375–6.
10 For Kerr's influence and Nancy's pushing, see Keith Middlemas (ed.), *Thomas Jones: Whitehall Diary* (1969), i, 31, 40.
11 See Brand, 'Memories and Thoughts . . .'.
12 For Curtis's ideas on dyarchy, see his book *Dyarchy* (1920); also Lavin, 135–57, and for quotations.
13 For these developments, see Kendle, 218–19, and D. A. Low, 'What Happened to Milner's Young Men', *The Round Table* (1990), no. 315.
14 From NDA, Astor Papers, MS1416/1/6/87.
15 Lord Riddell, *Intimate Diary of the Peace Conference and After, 1918–1923* (1933), 148.
16 From NDA.
17 See Collis, 91, 156–7; Sykes, 304–5; Robert Rhodes James (ed.), *'Chips': The Diaries of Sir Henry Channon* (Penguin edn, 1970), 98; and Brand, 'Memories and Thoughts . . .'.
18 See Curtis's articles, 'Windows of Freedom', *The Round Table* (December 1918), no. 33, and 'Price of Liberty', *The Round Table* (September 1919). no. 36. Also Lavin, 158–61, 171.
19 Lavin, 163, and Kendle, 259.
20 See Harold Nicolson, *Peacemaking* (Methuen, University Paperback, 1964), 352–3; Donald Cameron Watt, 'Introduction', and Deborah Lavin, 'Lionel Curtis and the Founding of Chatham House', in Andrea Bosco and Cornelia Navari (eds.), *Chatham House and British Foreign Policy, 1919–1945* (Lothian Foundation Press, 1994), i–vii, 61–9; Lavin, *Curtis*, 165–8, 172. For Abe Bailey and £150,000, see A. L. Rowse, 'Lionel Curtis: "The Prophet"', in

230 · *The Cliveden Set*

Glimpses of the Great (1985), 72. Deborah Lavin puts the sum at a more modest £100,000, see Bosco and Navari, 68.

21 Curtis's Irish period can be followed in Keith Middlemas (ed.), *Thomas Jones: Whitehall Diary* (1969), i, 200, 206, 211, 269, 271, 274, 277, and Lavin, 180–225.
22 A. L. Rowse, 'Lionel Curtis: "The Prophet"'; and Lavin, 258.
23 See *The History of The Times, 1912–1948* (1952), part 1, 454–5, 461–4, 468–9, 472–3, 480; Oliver Woods and James Bishop, *The Story of The Times* (1985), 224–6; Wrench, 173–91; and S. J. Taylor, *The Great Outsider* (Phoenix paperback, 1996), 212.
24 Wrench, 146 n1, 200, 202.
25 Wrench, 192–3.
26 See *The History of The Times*, iv, part 2, 766. Walter had put up another £100,000.
27 Dawson's memorandum of 18 November 1922, MSS Dawson 69; extracts printed in *The History of The Times* (1952), iv. part 2, 779–81. On 'Uncle John', Michael Astor, 146; and Churchill to Dawson, 29 January 1923, MSS Dawson 69.
28 Brand to Altschul, 8 April 1919, Brand Papers, File 18.
29 See Brand's 'Notes [to Cecil] on General Economic Position', 5 April 1919, Brand Papers, File 18; also his articles, 'Finance and Reparations', 'International Financial Co-operation', and 'The Future of Reparations and Inter-Allied Debts' in *The Round Table* (June 1919, March 1920, March 1923 respectively); and Kerr's article, 'The Peace of Versailles', *The Round Table* (June 1919).
30 David Lloyd George, *The Truth About the Peace Treaties* (1938), 9; and Nicolson, *Peacemaking*, 119, 242.
31 Brand to Grigg, 20 April 1922, quoted in May, 334.
32 Vansittart, *Lessons of My Life* (1944), 21; and Ben Pimlott, *The Political Diary of Hugh Dalton* (1986), 149.
33 Brand, 'Memories and Thoughts . . .'; Michael Astor, 144.
34 Quotations for this passage, unless stated otherwise, from Kerr's articles, 'War Aims', 'The Making of Peace', 'The Peace of Versailles' and 'The Harvest of Victory' in *The Round Table* (September 1916, December 1916, June 1919 and September 1919 respectively).
35 For Kerr's opposition to treaty revision; as 'a weathervane', see Butler, 77, 242; and as 'a pendulum', Brand, 'Memories and Thoughts . . .'.
36 Butler, 78.
37 See Hankey Diaries (Churchill College, Cambridge), 1/1, 1/3, entries for 6 February and 6 December 1917.
38 Lloyd George, *The Truth*. . . , i, 9, 263; Butler, 71; and Riddell, 282.
39 For Kerr's drafting of the clause, see Hankey to Butler (Kerr's biographer), 25 August 1958, Hankey Papers (Churchill College, Cambridge), 4/50; Butler, 72–3; and Riddell, 34. No less culpable was Smuts, the Round Tablers' friend, who had shrewdly urged that war pensions were a legitimate civil damage, thereby considerably inflating the final bill. See Hancock, *Smuts*, i, 540–2. See also Butler, 72–3; Riddell, 34; and Fox, 303.

40 Lloyd George, *The Truth...*, i, 404–16, 416–20, 422; also Frank Owen, *Tempestuous Journey* (1954), 537–8. For Smuts's alleged presence at Fontainebleau, see Hancock, *Smuts*, i, 514.

41 See L. F. Fitzhardinge, 'W. M. Hughes and the Treaty of Versailles, 1919', *Journal of Commonwealth and Political Studies* (July 1967), V, no. 2.

42 Kerr, 'The Victory That Will End War', *The Round Table* (March 1918), quoted in May, 187–8.

Chapter 5: Back to Normality

1 From Strachey's letter to Dora Carrington, quoted in Michael Holroyd, *Lytton Strachey: A Biography* (Penguin edn, 1993), 835–6.

2 See Middlemas (ed.), *Whitehall Diary*, i, 23; Rose Harrison, *My Life...* 112, 114–15; Joyce Grenfell, *Darling Ma: Letters to Her Mother* (1944), 10–11, and Norman Rose (ed.), *'Baffy': The Diaries of Blanche Dugdale, 1936–1947* (1973), 9.

3 Grenfell, 12, 39.

4 *Nicolson Diaries*, i, 50–1, 152, 204, 238, 407–8; *Channon Diaries*, 31, 51; *Alan Clark Diaries* (Phoenix Paperback, 1996), 23 n2.

5 See *Channon Diaries*, 43, 48; *Nicolson Diaries*, i, 255; and *Dugdale Diaries*, 34 n155.

6 See Anne de Courcy, *Circe: The Life of Edith, Marchioness of Londonderry* (1992), 146–7, 198, 280; David Marquand, *Ramsay MacDonald* (1977), 688; Sykes, 379; interview with David Astor, 10 October 1997.

7 See Rose Harrison, 44–5ff. (50, 53, 64–7, 80, 83–7, 92–5, 98, 100, 109, 134, 144, 153); for Lee's notice, see Michael Astor, 63; 'present room' in Grenfell, *In Pleasant Places*, 192.

8 Interview with David Astor, 10 October 1997; Thomas Jones, *A Diary with Letters, 1931–1950* (OUP, 1969), 151, 193; Hankey Diaries (Churchill College, Cambridge), 1/5, entry for 15 February 1920.

9 See *Nicolson Diaries* (Fontana edn, 1969), i, 57–8, 389–90, and *Channon Diaries* (Penguin edn, 1970), 286, 382.

10 Quotations from Walter Elliot's memoir (1955) on Cliveden and the Astors, in Sykes, 244–7. Also *Dugdale Diaries*, 141; and Joyce Grenfell, *Requests the Pleasure*, 100, and *Darling Ma*, 60.

11 See Sykes, 244; Dawson Diaries, 21 July 1934, MSS Dawson 38, 23 October 1937, MSS Dawson 41, and 6 August 1938, MSS Dawson 42.

12 *Nicolson Diaries*, i, 57–8, 260; and *Channon Diaries*, 201.

13 For this passage, see Michael Astor, 60–82; Middlemas, *Whitehall Diaries*, ii, 125–7; Joyce Grenfell, *In Pleasant Places* (1979), 190–8; Rose Harrison, 104–5; Walter Elliot's memoir, Sykes, 244–7.

14 For the above passage, see Curtis and Kerr, *The Prevention of War* (1924), and Curtis, *The Capital Question of China* (1932); also Lavin, 171, 179, 227–52; Kendle, 277; Butler, 108. I am also grateful to Professor Ellis Joffe for information on the Shanghai Settlement and the situation in China in general.

15 The following passage on Brand is based on: Brand, 'The Future of

Reparations . . . ', his tract, *Why I am Not a Socialist* (1923), and Brand to Kerr, 5 December 1929, quoted in Robert Skidelsky, *Politicians and the Slump* (1967), 156. Also entry for Brand in *DNB*, 1961–70, and obituary notice in *The Times*, 24 August 1963; Lord D'Abernon, *Ambassador of Peace* (1929), ii, 122–3, 126–9; Robert Skidelsky, *John Maynard Keynes* (1983), i, 337, and ii (Penguin edn, 1995), 22–3, 118–20, 123–4, 186, 265–7, 345–62; May, 231, 335; Charles Loch Mowatt, *Britain Between the Wars, 1918–1940* (1968), 261–2; F. P. Walters, *A History of The League of Nations* (OUP, 1969), 89, 112; Middlemas, *Whitehall Diaries*, ii, 176; and Fox, 356.

16 Kerr to Brand, 24 April 1923, Brand Papers, File 182.

17 See Kerr, 'The Locarno Treaties', *The Round Table* (December 1925); for Smuts, *The Times*, 11 November 1925; and for Dawson, *The History of The Times*, iv, part 2, 801–4.

18 For Chamberlain, see his statement to the House of Commons, *Parliamentary Debates*, 5th series, Commons, vol. 188, 429, 520–1, and Ritchie Ovendale, 'Britain, the Dominions and the Coming of the Second World War, 1933–9', in Wolfgang J. Mommsen and Lothar Kettenacker (eds.), *The Fascist Challenge and the Policy of Appeasement* (1983); and for Hertzog, *The Times*, 13 and 14 December 1926.

19 See Lavin, 225; *The History of The Times*, iv, Part 2, 804, 879–80; and Butler, 115, 132.

20 For the insinuations against *The Times*, see Stephen Koss, *The Rise and Fall of the Political Press in Britain*, ii, *The Twentieth Century* (1984), 480; and Kerr quoted in May, 336.

21 See Brand, *Memories and Thoughts* . . . 58–9; Dan Laurence (ed.), *Bernard Shaw: Collected Letters, 1926–1950* (1988), 142; and Wilson, 245.

22 For this passage, see Harrison, 162; Brand, *Memories and Thoughts*. . . ; Grenfell, *Darling Ma*. . . , 42; Sykes, 317–20, 326–7, 351; Wilson, 249–53, 398.

23 Michael Astor, 121–2.

24 For the passage on the Astors' visit to the Soviet Union, see Waldorf Astor's diary of the trip, Astor Papers; interview with David Astor, 10 October 1997; Sykes, 329–43; Collis, 161–8; Wilson, 236–7; Butler, 164; Holroyd, 234–48; Winston Churchill, *Great Contemporaries* (1949), 38–9; and Fox, 429.

Chapter 6: Regional Distractions

1 Quotations are taken from Brigitte Granzow's illuminating study, *A Mirror of Nazism: British Opinion and the Emergence of Hitler, 1929–1933* (1964), 56–7, 95, 107, 109, 135, 138, 170–1, 183–4, 198–9, 221; and Robert Graves and Alan Hodge, *The Long Week-End* (Penguin edn, 1971), 436.

2 See Norman Rose, *Churchill*, 188, and Bernard Crick's 'Introduction' to Granzow, *A Mirror of Nazism*.

3 For Churchill, see Norman Rose, *Churchill*, 219; for Rumbold, Martin Gilbert, *Sir Horace Rumbold: Portrait of a Diplomat, 1869–1941* (1973), ch. 16:

and for Vansittart, FO371/14350, C3358/3358/62, 'An Aspect of International Relations in 1930'; CAB24/227, CP4(32), 'The United Kingdom and Europe', 1 January 1932; Vansittart Papers (at Churchill College, Cambridge), 2/1, 2/3–5; and FO371/18852, C8852/55/14, Minutes of 1 December 1935; also Norman Rose, *Vansittart: Study of a Diplomat* (1978), 47–8, and ch. VI.

4 Quotations in *The History of The Times*, iv, part 2, 795–6.

5 For Lothian, see *The Times*, 22 April 1937; Lothian to Smuts, 16 March 1937, GD40/17/333 (Lothian Papers, Scottish Record Office); and 'The League in Crisis', *The Round Table* (December 1935). Also Dawson to Brand, 2 October 1938, *The Times* Archives, London.

6 See Christopher Thorne, 'The Shanghai Crisis of 1931: The Basis of British Policy', *American Historical Review* (1970), v.75.

7 For failed Anglo-American naval talks, see D. C. Watt, *Personalities and Policies* (1965: Greenwood Press, Connecticut, 1975 edn), 91–5; and Ann Trotter, *Britain and East Asia* (Cambridge University Press, 1975), ch. 6. See also Minutes of DRC, CAB16/109–12; Fisher to Hankey, 12 February 1934, CAB16/109; Vansittart's minutes of 5 February 1934, FO371/17593, and Vansittart to Sir Ronald Lindsay (ambassador at Washington), 24 September 1934, Royal Archives, GV/M2433/3. Also Norman Rose, *Vansittart*, 126–7, and Keith Feiling, *The Life of Neville Chamberlain* (1947), 253.

8 Chamberlain's paper, sent first to Sir John Simon, underwent some revision owing to Foreign Office reservations, and was eventually submitted to the Cabinet as a joint memorandum on 16 October 1934, CP223 (34), CAB27/596. The final draft spoke of a non-aggression pact 'with *both* the United States *and* the British Empire – preferably in a single instrument'. See also a memorandum by Fisher, 19 April 1934, CAB29/148; Feiling, 253–4; Iain Macleod, *Neville Chamberlain* (1962), 178; and Trotter, 98–9.

9 See Smuts, 'The Present International Outlook', *International Affairs* (January 1935), and Lothian, 'The Crisis in the Pacific', *International Affairs* (March 1935).

10 Butler, 201, 209, and Lothian, 'The Crisis in the Pacific'.

11 For Lothian's lobbying see his lecture to a Chatham House audience on 5 June 1934, printed as 'The Place of Britain in the Collective System', *International Affairs* (September 1934); his memorandum of 11 October 1934, GD40/17/198, and Lothian to Ramsay MacDonald, 12 November 1934, GD40/17/199 (Lothian Papers); also his articles, 'Navies and the Pacific' and 'Power Politics in the Pacific', *The Round Table* (September and December 1934). See also Vansittart's minute of 9 February 1935, FO371/18160/F7373; *The Times*, 12 November 1934; Smuts, 'The Present International Outlook'; Watt, *Personalities. . .*, 97 and n2; and Hancock, *Smuts*, ii, 268.

12 Smuts to Lothian, 14 December 1934, GD40/17/200; Norman Davis to Roosevelt, 27 November 1934, *Foreign Relations of the United States* (*FRUS*) 1934, i, 358–9, quoted in Watt, 98–9; and Christopher Thorne, *The Limits of Foreign Policy: The West, the League and the Far Eastern Crisis of 1931–1933* (1972), 391, 401–2.

13 See Joseph Grew, *Ten Years in Japan* (New York, 1944), 141–2; and Smuts to Lothian, 14 December 1934. For more detailed surveys of this episode, see

234 · *The Cliveden Set*

Trotter, *Britain and East Asia*; Watt, *Personalities. . .* , essay 4; Wm. Roger Louis, *British Strategy in the Far East, 1919–1939* (OUP, 1971), ch. VII; Stephen Endicott, *Diplomacy and Enterprise* (1975); Peter Lowe, *Great Britain and the Origins of the Pacific War: A Study of British Policy in East Asia, 1937–41* (OUP, 1977), and *Britain in the Far East: A Survey from 1819 to the Present* (1981); and Ian Nish, 'Japan's Policy Towards Britain', in James Morley (ed.), *Japan's Foreign Policy, 1868–1941* (New York, 1974).

14 See Lothian's articles, 'The League in Crisis' and 'World Crisis', *The Round Table* (December 1935 and June 1936).

15 See Wrench, 247; Rose, *Churchill*, 236; and H. V. Hodson (editor of *The Round Table*) to Lothian, 16 August 1935, GD40/17/304. Also May, 343–4.

16 See Philip Kerr, 'The British Empire, the League of Nations and the United States', *The Round Table* (March 1920); and May, 187–9.

17 Dawson to Nancy Astor, 16 March 1936, MS1461/1/4/82; interview with Nancy Astor in *Sunday Express*, 23 February 1936 (see MS1416/1/7/75).

18 For the Zeila episode, see FO371/19913, J1459, 2435/1/1; and for Eden in Rome, Avon, *Facing the Dictators* (1962), 220–9, and Mario Toscano, 'Eden's Mission to Rome on the Eve of the Italo-Ethiopian Conflict', in *Studies in Diplomatic History and Historiography in Honour of G. P. Gooch* (1961), ed. A. O. Sarkissian.

19 For Baldwin see Keith Middlemas and John Barnes, *Baldwin: A Biography* (1969), 865–9, and Koss, 540.

20 Dawson Diaries, 19 September 1935, MSS Dawson 39; and Lothian to Hoare, 18 October 1935, GD40/17/301.

21 See Lothian to Hoare, 18 October 1935; Lothian, 'Europe, the League and Abyssinia'; 'The League in Crisis'; 'World Crisis'; 'World Crisis of 1936', *The Round Table* (September 1935; December 1935; June 1936; October 1936); and his speeches to the House of Lords, 23 October 1935, *P.D.*, Lords, vol. 98, cols. 1162–7; 19 December 1935, *P. D.*, Lords, vol. 99, cols. 296–304; 8 April and 7 May 1936, *P.D.*, Lords, vol. 100, cols. 526–33, 884–98.

22 Aga Khan, *The Memoirs of Aga Khan* (1954), 258, and a Memorandum by the Aga Khan, 29 May 1936, GD40/17/317.

23 See Brand to Dawson, 2 September 1935, MSS Brand 198, and his two memoranda on 'British Foreign Policy', September and November 1935, drawn up for the Moot's consideration, MSS Brand 135. Also Kenneth Young (ed.), *The Diaries of Sir Robert Bruce Lockhart, 1915–1938* (1973), 330.

24 See minutes of the crucial Cabinet meetings of 2 and 9 December 1935, in CAB23/82; for precise details of the Hoare–Laval plan, CP235(35), CAB24/257; for an overview of the negotiations, see Rose, *Vansittart*, 157–79.

25 For Dawson, see his diaries for December 1935, MSS Dawson 39, *The Times*, 16 December 1935, and *The History of The Times*, iv, Part 2, 897–8; for Lothian, 'World Crisis', and *P.D.*, Lords, vol. 99, col. 301; and for Barrington-Ward, Donald MacLachlan, *In the Chair: Barrington-Ward of The Times, 1891–1948* (1971), 164.

26 Correspondence between Curtis and Dawson, 17 and 18 December 1935, in MSS Curtis 10, and Curtis to Dawson, 24 June 1938, MSS Curtis 12; also Wrench, 327, and Rose, *Vansittart*, 196–210.

27 For general sources for the following passage, see Thomas Jones, *A Diary with Letters* (1969 edn), 160–1, 170–2, 175; Templewood, *Nine Troubled Years* (1954), 183–8; and Avon, *Facing the Dictators*, 298. For Chamberlain, Keith Feiling, *The Life of Neville Chamberlain* (1947), 273–6, and Chamberlain's speech in Commons, 19 December 1935. For Dawson, Wrench, 324–7, and Dawson Diaries for December 1935, MSS Dawson 39, also *The History of The Times*, iv, Part 2, 897–8, 913. For Brand, Brand to Hoare, 2 September 1935, MSS Brand 198, his memoranda of September and November 1935, and a memorandum by H. V. Hodson, 1 May 1936, MSS Brand 135. For Lothian, see note of his meeting with Hitler 29 January 1935, GD40/17/201 (also printed in Butler, appendix III), Lothian to Sir John Simon, 30 January 1935, GD40/17/201, Smuts to Lothian, 20 February 1935, GD40/17/296, Lothian to Ribbentrop, 20 March 1935, GD40/17/202; *P.D.*, Lords, vol. 99, col. 296–304; Lothian's two articles in *The Times*, 31 January and 1 February 1935; and Lothian's Burge Memorial Lecture, 28 May 1935, printed as *Pacifism is not enough (nor Patriotism either)* (OUP, 1935), 296–304. See June 1935 issue of *The Round Table* for treaty revision in general. The exact date of Waldorf Astor's interview with Hitler is not clear. It took place some time in the spring–summer of 1933. See Dawson Diaries, 3 October 1933, MSS Dawson 37; and interview with David Astor, 18 September 1996.

28 Correspondence between Smuts and Lothian of 22 June and 8 July 1936 in GD40/17/323; see also Butler, 210–11, and 'World Crisis', *The Round Table* (June 1936).

Chapter 7: Claud and 'The Week'

1 *The Week*, 17 June 1936.
2 This chapter relies on Claud Cockburn's volumes of autobiography, *In Time of Trouble* (1956) and *Crossing the Line* (New York, 1960), and that of his wife, Patricia Cockburn, *The Years of The Week* (1968). These memoirs make colourful and lively reading, but are not entirely accurate regarding some historical details. However, they provide a useful and authentic background to the events here told, and are often surprisingly dependable as a source. But they should be read with caution, perhaps bearing in mind Claud's theory of 'preventive journalism'. More specifically, for quotations about Cockburn's career, unless stated otherwise, see *In Time of Trouble*, 19–20, 28, 37–8, 87–8, 97, 105, 127–8, 222, 226, 227, 234–5; *Crossing the Line*, 17–19; and *The Years of The Week*, 6, 12, 41–4, 88–9, 231–2, 263.

For additional, and supporting, references see Franklin Reid Gannon, *The British Press and Journalism, 1936–1939* (OUP, 1971), 132–5; Norman Rose, *Vansittart: Study of a Diplomat* (1978), 206–7; Richard Cockett, *Twilight of Truth: Chamberlain, Appeasement and the Manipulation of the Press* (1989), 29–30, 37; Oliver Woods and James Bishop, *The Story of The Times* (1985), 293; Robert Graves and Alan Hodge, *The Long Week-End* (Penguin edn, 1971), 421–2; Donald Cameron Watt, 'The Week That Was' and 'Those Were The Weeks That Were', *Encounter* (May 1972, May 1986); Aaron L.

Goldman, 'Claud Cockburn, *The Week* and the "Cliveden Set"', *Journalism Quarterly* (1972), vol. 49, no. 4.

3 Wolfgang zu Putlitz, *The Putlitz Dossier* (1957).

4 Quoted in Donald MacLachlan, *In the Chair: Barrington-Ward of The Times, 1927–1948* (1971), 218.

5 Arthur Koestler, who worked for Münzenberg's organization in the early thirties, wrote perceptively about him in *Invisible Writing* (The Beacon Press, Boston, 1955), 198–212, 313–14. See also Rolf Surmann, *Münzenberg – Legende* (Koln, 1983); Harald Wessel, *Münzenberg Ende* (Berlin, 1991); Robert Conquest, *The Great Terror* (Pelican edn, 1981), 578; and David Cesarani, *Arthur Koestler: The Homeless Mind* (Vintage Books, 1999), 98, 101–6, 110–11, 120–2, 148–9, 152–3, 168. Also Donald Cameron Watt, 'The European Civil War' in Wolfgang J. Mommsen and Lothar Ketternacker (eds.), *The Fascist Challenge and the Policy of Appeasement* (1983), and Watt, 'The Week that Was' and 'Those Were the Weeks That Were', *Encounter* (May 1972, May 1986).

6 See Claud Cockburn, *Crossing the Line* (New York, 1960), 21, and *The History of The Times* (1951), iii, 15.

7 See *The Week*, 29 March 1933.

8 But not only to Claud. Vansittart and Leeper also fed information to another broadsheet, the *Whitehall Letter*, edited by Victor Gordon-Lennox, diplomatic correspondent of the anti-appeasement *Daily Telegraph*. MI5, noting the accuracy of the *Letter*'s reports, placed it under observation, an honour also accorded to *The Week*. See Donald Cameron Watt, 'Chamberlain's Ambassadors' in *Diplomacy and World Power: Studies in British Foreign Policy, 1890–1950*, eds. Michael Dockrill and Brian McKercher (Cambridge University Press, 1996), 159.

Chapter 8: The Cliveden Set – Discovered or Invented?

1 For the following passage: in general, Visitors' Book, Astor Papers; *The Times*, 23 October 1937; Thomas Jones, *A Diary. . .* , 193, 215, 369–70.

For Lothian: accounts of his discussions with Hitler and other Nazi leaders in GD40/17/203, 4 May 1937; *DBFP*, Series 2, vol. XVIII, no. 480, 727–31, Henderson to Vansittart, 10 May 1937, reporting Lothian meetings; also Butler, appendix III, 337. Lothian's paper of 4 May (GD40/17/203) was brought to the knowledge of Cabinet ministers and circulated among dominion Prime Ministers who had gathered in London in May for the Imperial Conference. Also Lothian to Halifax, 9 June 1936, GD40/17/320; Lothian to Smuts, 8 July 1936, GD40/17/317; Lothian to Smuts, 16 March 1937, GD40/17/333; Lothian to Nevile Henderson, 13 September 1937, GD40/17/344; Nancy Astor to Brand, 10 February 1938, MS1416/1/3/13. And *P.D.*, Lords, vol. 100, col. 526–33, debate on 'European Situation', 8 April 1936, and vol. 104, col. 391–403, debate on 'Foreign Affairs', 2 March 1937. See also Lothian's articles, 'The Locarno Treaties', *The Round Table* (December 1925); 'The World Crisis', *The Round Table* (June 1936); 'The

World Crisis of 1936', *Foreign Affairs* (October 1936); 'The Problem of Germany', *The Round Table* (June 1937); 'The New World Situation', *The Round Table* (September 1937); 'Germany and the Peace of Europe', *International Affairs* (November 1937). Lothian's remark to Flandin quoted in Winston Churchill, *The Second World War*, i, *The Gathering Storm*, 153.

For Dawson: see *The Times*, 28 October 1937; *The History of The Times*, iv, part 2, 905 n1; and *Documents of International Affairs, 1938* (OUP, 1942), part 1, 59. And Brand: Thomas Jones, *A Diary* . . . , 193.

For Waldorf Astor: see his article, 'Causes of Dangers and Unrest in Europe', *Western Morning News and Daily Gazette*, 5 February 1937, and his letter to *The Times*, 13 October 1937; Waldorf to Garvin, 26 April 1936, Astor Papers, quoted in Wilson, 264; and Waldorf's memorandum of his visit to Austria, April 1936, FO371/20361, R2723/21/3. And Nancy Astor: Nancy to Lothian, 17 December 1937, MS1416/1/4/56; Jones, *A Diary* . . . , 215; Sykes, 381; and Grigg, *Nancy Astor*, 145.

For Nevile Henderson: see Henderson to Sir Orme Sargent, 20 July 1937, enclosing his memorandum of 10 May 1937, *DBFP*, Series 2, vol. XIX, no. 53, 98–105; also Waldorf Astor to Garvin, 26 October 1937, Garvin Papers, quoted in Richard Cockett, 29. Also Nevile Henderson, *Failure of a Mission* (1940), 16–17, and T. P. Conwell-Evans, *None So Blind* (privately printed, 1947), 72. And D. C. Watt, 'Chamberlain's Ambassadors . . .', in Michael Dockerill and Brian McKercher (eds.), *Diplomacy and World Power: Studies in British Foreign Policy* (CUP, 1996).

For Eden: Jones, *A Diary* . . . , 369–70; John Harvey (ed.), *The Diplomatic Diaries of Oliver Harvey, 1937–1940* (1970), entry for 23 April 1937, 41; and Rose, *Churchill*, 195, 234–5, 246.

2 See Nevile Henderson, *Failure of a Mission* (1940), 16–17; T. P. Conwell-Evans, *None So Blind*, 72; and Donald Cameron Watt, 'Chamberlain's Ambassadors', in *Diplomacy and World Power* . . .

3 Neville Chamberlain to Hilda Chamberlain, 24 October 1937, NCP19/1/1025 (Chamberlain Papers, University of Birmingham); also his memorandum of 2 April 1937, FP(36), FO371/20735, C2618/270/18, outlining his ideas for a European settlement.

4 Quoted in Gannon, 129.

5 *The Week*, 17 and 24 November 1937.

6 For above paragraph: FO371/20737, C8293/270/18, containing Vansittart's comments on Henderson's despatch on the eve of Halifax's visit: it summarized the ambassador's conversations with German leaders and suggested autonomy for German minorities in eastern Europe. Also Dawson Diaries, entry for 22 April 1936, MSS Dawson 40; Avon, *Facing the Dictators* (1962), 509; Churchill, *The Second World War*, i, 194–5; Rose, *Vansittart*, 206; Harvey Diaries, 57; Voigt to Crozier, 17 November 1937, quoted in Franklin Reid Gannon, *The British Press and Germany, 1936–1939* (OUP, 1971), 130–1; and Patricia Cockburn, *The Years of The Week* (1968), 232.

7 See *The Week*, 25 March and 17 June 1936, and 17 and 24 November 1937; and Claud Cockburn, *Crossing the Line* (New York, 1960), 19.

8 Quotations in *The Week*, 24 November and 22 December 1937.

9 See Curtis to Brand, 20 December 1937, MSS Curtis 11, and Curtis to Dawson, 17 January 1938, MSS Curtis 12; and Lavin, 278. Also Brand to Dawson, 17 July 1936, MSS Brand 198, and Brand memorandum on 'British Foreign Policy' (Spring, 1936), MSS Brand 135.

10 See Feiling, *Neville Chamberlain*, 332–3, diary entry for 26 November 1937; Harvey Diaries, entry for 7 December 1937, 63; Avon, 547; Eden to Chamberlain, 31 January 1938, PREM1/276; Norman Rose, 'The Resignation of Anthony Eden', *Historical Journal*, 25, 4 (1982); W. N. Medlicott, 'Britain and Germany: The Search for Agreement, 1930–1937' (The Creighton Lecture, Athlone Press, 1969); and a Foreign Office Paper (January 1938) on negotiations with Germany, CAB27/626.

11 Halifax's account of talks, *DBFP*, Series 2, vol. XIX, 545; German account of talks, *DGFP*, Series D, vol. 1, nos. 31, 33, p. 6. Also Avon, 513, Cockett, 28, Butler, 341.

12 Minutes of the so-called Hossbach conference in *DGFP*, Series D, vol. 1, no. 19. The significance of this event has aroused much controversy. For the most balanced interpretation, see Alan Bullock, *Hitler: A Study in Tyranny* (Penguin edn, 1969), 367–71; but also A. J. P. Taylor, *The Origins of the Second World War* (Penguin edn, 1980), 20–2, 169–71.

13 See *Discord of Trumpets*, 261–2; *The Week*, 5 January and 30 March 1938; Cockburn's more polished exposé in *Current History* (February 1938); and *Evening Standard*, December 1937–January 1938. Also *Daily Worker*, 11 March 1939.

14 See *Reynolds News*, 27 February 1938, 3 and 6 March 1938, 3 April 1938; *News Chronicle*, 22 March 1938; *Daily Worker*, 30 March 1938; also *Sidelights on the Cliveden Set: Hitler's Friends in Britain* (March–April 1938), published in two editions (20,000 copies) by the Communist Party. Newspaper clippings in Astor Papers, MS1461/1/1/1585, 1587, 1588, and MS1461/1/7, 75–80.

15 See 'Who's Who in the Cliveden Baronage', *Tribune*, 25 March 1938, and *Greenwich Time* (Connecticut), 24 October 1938, in MS1461/1/1/1590; also Cockburn, *A Discord of Trumpets*, 261.

16 See *Daily Express*, 2 April 1938, and *The Week*, 6 and 20 July 1938; also Patricia Cockburn, *The Years of The Week*, 230.

17 American newspaper reports in MS1416/1/1/1587, 1588. Also *PD*, Commons, 5th series, vol. 337, cols. 956–8, 21, 27 June 1938, and vol. 345, col. 615, 16 March 1939; *New York Times*, 17 March 1939; and Sykes, 391–2. Eden quoted in David Carlton, *Anthony Eden* (Unwin Paperback, 1986), 147.

18 *Nicolson Diaries*, i, entry for 10 April 1939.

19 See *Manchester Guardian*, 28 March 1938; *New York Times*, 28 February and 10 November 1938; *Sidelights on The Cliveden Set . . .*; for Gallacher, *P.D.*, Commons, vol. 333, col. 116; and Upton Sinclair's broadside, 'We Have Traitors In Our Midst', *Tribune*, 25 March 1938.

20 See 'Lady Astor Interviews Herself', *Saturday Evening Post*, 4 March 1939, and *Daily Herald*, 5 May 1938; also, 'I Abominate Fascism', *Tribune*, 23 December 1938; 'Munich and the Cliveden Set', *Sunday Chronicle*, 12 March 1939; and NDA and 'The Cliveden Set', MS1416/1/6/87. For Waldorf: *The Times*, 5 May 1938; for Lothian: *Northern Despatch*, 27 April 1938; for

Dawson: MSS Dawson 42, 1 April 1938. Also George Bernard Shaw, 'GBS Hits Out in Defence of Lady Astor', *Sunday Graphic*, 5 March 1939, and 'Bernard Shaw Answers Frederick L. Collins About Lady Astor', *Liberty*, 11 March 1939; also Upton Sinclair, 'An Open Letter to George Bernard Shaw About Lady Astor', *Liberty*, 22 April 1939.

21 Hatemail in letters and postcards in MS1461/1/1/1583, 1587; C. Lodge (?) to Nancy Astor, 26 September 1938, MS1461/1/1/1583.
22 Interview with David Astor; also John Grigg, *Nancy Astor*, 149.
23 See *New York Times*, 1 July 1937; Louise Wise to Nancy Astor, 6 July 1937, MS1416/1/1/1498; and Nancy Astor to Lothian, 12 January 1939, MS1416/1/4/58.
24 *Nicolson Diaries*, i. 320.
25 *News Chronicle*, 21 and 23 March 1938; and *Nicolson Diaries*, i, 320.
26 Papers regarding the placement of German Jewish academics in MS1416/1/1236. The Nancy Astor–Felix Frankfurter correspondence in MS1416/1/1/1586, and Max Freedman (ed.), *Roosevelt and Frankfurter: Their Correspondence, 1928–1945* (Boston, 1967), 473–5.
27 Quoted in Norman Rose, *Chaim Weizmann: A Biography* (New York, 1986), 149, and Vera Weizmann, *The Impossible Takes Longer* (1967), 68.

Chapter 9: Rethinking

1 See *Civitas Dei*, ii, 381–4, iii, 72–5, 80–1, 127; David Garnett (ed.), *The Letters of T. E. Lawrence* (1938), 808; Lavin, 261, 268–74; and May, 357.
2 For passage on 'Salter's Soviet', see Curtis to Brand, 20 December 1937, MSS Curtis 11; to Dawson, 17 January 1938, and to Allen, 28 February 1938, MSS Curtis 12; and to Halifax and Lothian, 10 and 17 March 1938, GD40/17/353. For the Lothian–Rowse clash, see *The Times*, 26 August and 10 September 1937, and *Time and Tide*, 16 April 1938. Also Charles Wenden, 'Appeasement and All Souls' (unpublished) for forthcoming *History of All Souls*; Sidney Astor, '"Salter's Soviet": Another View of All Souls and Appeasement', in *Power, Personalities and Policies: Essays in Honour of Donald Cameron Watt* (1992), (ed.) Michael Fry; Martin Gilbert (ed.), *Plowing My Own Furrow: The Life of Lord Allen of Hurtwood*.
3 See FO371/21132, R8010/188/12; *The Times*, 29 November 1937; and Brand to Dawson, 17 and 22 February 1938, Dawson to Brand, 17 February 1938, Times Archives.
4 See Lothian's letter to *The Times*, 14 March 1938; and Lothian to Lord Allen, 8 March 1938, to Aga Khan, 31 March 1938, GD40/17/352; and to Nevile Henderson, 14 April 1938, GD40/17/362. Also *P.D.*, Lords, vol. 108, cols. 133–9, Lothian's speech of 16 March 1938.
5 See Smuts to Lothian, 20 May 1938, GD40/17/367.
6 See Masaryk to Lothian, 28 February 1939, and Lothian to Masaryk, 4 March 1938, GD40/17/356; also *P.D.*, Lords, vol. 108, cols. 133–9, Lothian's speech of 16 March 1938.
7 See unsigned memo, 8 June 1938, MSS Brand 135, and Wenden, 14–15.

Record of Henlein's May 1938 visit in *BDFP*, series 3, vol. i, 633–5, and appendix II; also, *Nicolson Diaries*, i, 333–4. For Henlein in general, see R. M. Smelser, *The Sudeten Problem, 1933–38: Volkstumpolitik and the Formulation of Nazi Foreign Policy* (Folkestone, 1975), and Keith Robbins, 'Konrad Henlein and the Sudeten Question and British Foreign Policy', *Historical Journal* (1969), 12, 4. For Churchill's position, see Martin Gilbert (ed.), *Winston S. Churchill: Companion Volume V, Part 3*, 1018, 1025, 1112; for Vansittart's, see Rose, *Vansittart*, 222–6.

8 See *The Times*, 7 September 1938; Dawson Diaries, 6–8 September 1938, MSS Dawson 42; *Daily Telegraph*, 8 September 1938; *The Week*, 30 March, 6 April, 17 August, 14 September and 21 September 1938; and *New Statesman and Nation*, 27 August 1938, and Kingsley Martin, *Editor* (1968), 255–7. For Masaryk's protest to the Foreign Office at *The Times* leader and government denial, FO371/21764, C9356/4770/18.

9 Lothian to Waldorf and Nancy Astor, 14, 16, 23 and 30 September 1938, and 4 October 1938, in MS1416/1/4/57. Also Butler, 225, 237 nt.

10 For Nancy, see Grenfell, *Darling Ma*, 57, and the *Evening Herald*, 10 October 1938; for Waldorf, *Western Independent*, 9 October 1938; also Lavin, 282–3.

11 See Dawson to Brand, 2 October 1938, *The Times* Archives, and Brand to Nancy Astor, 7 October 1938, MS1416/1/3/14.

12 See meeting of Foreign Policy Committee of Cabinet, 18 March 1938, CAB27/623, and Cabinet Minutes for 22 March 1938, CAB23/93. Also Dawson Diaries for 25 and 30 September 1938, MSS Dawson 42. Correspondence with James Barry Munnik Herzog, Prime Minister of South Africa, Joseph Aloysius Lyons, Prime Minister of Australia, and MacKenzie King, 30 September 1938, in MSS Dawson 93. For this question in general, see D. C. Watt, 'The Commonwealth and the Munich Crisis', *Personalities and Policies* (Greenwood Press, Westport, Connecticut, 1975), and Ritchie Ovendale, *'Appeasement' and the English Speaking World* (Cardiff, 1975).

13 See Lothian to Nancy Astor, 5 January 1939, MS1416/1/1/58. Other quotations in Max Freedman (ed.), *Roosevelt and Frankfurter: Their Correspondence, 1928–1945* (Boston, 1967), 472; David Reynolds, 'Lord Lothian and Anglo-American Relations, 1939–40', *Transactions of the American Philosophical Society* (1983), vol. 73; and *The Week*, 5 October 1938.

14 For the following passage, see:

For Lothian: *P.D.*, Lords, vol. 112, cols. 616–23, 13 April 1939; Lothian to T. W. Lamont, 29 March 1939, GD40/17/377; Lothian to Patrick Duncan, 5 April 1939, GD40/17/381; to Felix Frankfurter, 10 May 1939, GD40/17/382; to Vansittart, 11 May 1939, GD40/17/387; to T. C. Catchpool, 15 May 1939, GD40/17/389; to Halifax, 5 June 1939, GD40/17/390; to Dawson, 28 June 1939, MSS Dawson 82; and his article, 'Grand Alliance', *The Round Table* (June 1939).

For Brand: Brand to Dawson, 18 February 1938 and 16 March 1939, *The Times* Archives; Brand to Dawson, 28 June 1939, MSS Dawson 82, and 15 May 1939, MSS Brand 116; and Brand to A. L. Kennedy, 11 May 1939; Brand to Coupland, 8 December 1939, MSS Brand 153; Brand to Nancy Astor, 6 October 1940, MS1416/1/3/14.

For Dawson: Dawson to John Astor, 4 April 1939, MSS Dawson 82; Dawson Diaries, January to August 1939, in particular 3 and 12 April, MSS Dawson 43; Dawson to Neville Chamberlain, 9 October 1940, MSS Dawson 81.

For Curtis: Smuts to Lothian, 27 March 1939, GD40/17/377; Curtis to Lothian, 4, 6, 24 April 1939, MSS Curtis 15; Curtis to Halifax and Bevin, 18 June 1939, MSS Curtis 17; correspondence for May 1939, MSS Curtis 16; Curtis to Halifax, 15 July 1939, MSS Curtis 18; speech to Chatham House, 21 Febrary 1939, MSS Curtis 22 (later published in *International Affairs*); Clarence Streight, *Union Now* (English edn, October 1939); and Donald S. Birn, *The League of Nations Union, 1918–1945* (OUP, 1981), 205–6.

For Nancy Astor, FO371/24036, W10544, which includes extracts from her address to the International Women's Congress, Copenhagen, 10 July 1939; and Nancy Astor to Bob Brand, 5 April 1939, MS1416/1/3/14.

For Waldorf Astor: *P.D.*, Lords, vol. 110, cols. 1470–3, 5 October 1938, and vol. 112, cols. 624–8, 13 April 1939; also FO371/23078, C8400/3778/18 – reports on 'Cliveden Set Reverses Self' from *Chicago Daily News*, 10 May 1939. Also Halifax's speech of 8 June 1939, *P.D.*, Lords, vol. 113, cols. 350–64.

15 *Nicolson Diaries*, i, entries for 19 and 23 September 1938 and 10 April 1939.

16 *Mein Kampf* was published in an unexpurgated English edition by Hurst and Blackett in 1939.

17 See also, for Lothian: Lothian to Felix Frankfurter, 10 May, GD40/17/382; to Vansittart, 11 May, GD40/17/387; and to T. C. Catchpool, 15 May, GD40/17/389. For the Astors, see Nancy Astor to Brand, 5 April 1939, MS1416/1/3/14, and Dawson Diaries, 12 April 1939, MSS Dawson 43. For Curtis, see MSS Curtis 13–17 and 22 (these boxes are full of Curtis's obsession), and Lothian to Frank Aydelotte (President of Swarthmore College), 6 March 1939, GD40/17/369. For Brand, see Dawson Diaries, 31 January 1939, MSS Dawson 43, and Brand to Dawson, 16 March 1939, The Times Archives.

18 Quoted in Reginald Pound and Geoffry Harmsworth, *Northcliffe* (New York, 1960), 827.

19 For *The Times* leader, see *The Times*, 1 April 1939; *P.D.*, 5th series, Commons, vol. 345, cols. 2579–80; and *The History of The Times*, iv, part 2, 962–3. For Brand's messages see Brand to A. L. Kennedy, 11 May 1939, and to Dawson, 15 May 1939, MSS Brand 116; also Brand to Dawson, 28 June 1939, MSS Dawson 81; and Lothian to Dawson. 28 June 1939, MSS Dawson 81. For 'Danzig liability' see Dawson Diaries, 6 July 1939, MSS Dawson 43.

20 Von Trott's report on his 'Fact-Finding Visit to Britain' in *DGFP*, Series D, vol. vi, 674–84. Also Klemens von Klemperer, 'Adam von Trott zu Solz and British Foreign Policy', *Central European History* (1981), 14; Christopher Sykes, *Troubled Loyalty* (1968), ch. 10; David Astor, 'Why the revolt against Hitler was ignored', *Encounter* (1969); and Watt, *How War Came*, 391–4.

21 Quoted in Sykes, 414.

242 · *The Cliveden Set*

Chapter 10: Full Circle

1 For Lothian's appointment, see Halifax to Lothian, 11 August 1938, GD40/ 17/369; Foreign Office opposition, *Harvey Diaries*, 258–9, and *Cadogan Diaries*, 90, 130, 154, and Wrench, 39. Roosevelt quoted in David Reynolds, 'Lord Lothian and Anglo-American Relations, 1939–40'.

2 *Nicolson Diaries*, ii, entries for 22 July and 22 October 1940.

3 *Nicolson Diaries*, ii, 101, entry for 22 July 1940.

4 For this passage see Lothian to Garvin, 5 July 1939, GD40/17/390; Dawson to Halifax, 13 December 1940, *The Times* Archives; *The American Speeches of Lord Lothian* (1941), ed. Lionel Curtis; Ronald Steel, *Walter Lippmann and the American Century* (Boston, 1980), 384; Warren Kimball, *Churchill and Roosevelt: The Complete Correspondence* (Princeton, 1984), i, 54, 65, 66–7, 112; Reynolds, 'Lord Lothian and Anglo-American Relations', 15 n48, 58; Rowse, *All Souls and Appeasement*, 32; Butler, 257 *passim*.

5 See Dawson to John Astor, 4 April 1939, and John Astor to Dawson, 15 August 1941, MSS Dawson 82.

6 See *The Times*, 16 April and 6 May 1940; and Dawson Diaries, 17 April, 5 May, 8 May, 13 May 1940.

7 *The Times*, 8 September 1941.

8 Dawson to Chamberlain, 8 November 1940, MSS Dawson 81 and 9 October 1940.

9 See Nancy to Brand, 5 April 1939, MS1416/1/3/14; Nancy to Lothian, 22 November 1939, GD40/17/394; *P.D.*, Commons, vol. 359, cols. 760–2; Dawson Diaries, 7 May 1940, MSS Dawson 44; and Nancy to Lothian, 28 May 1940, MS1416/1/2/478.

10 See an interview with Nancy, 21 December 1938, MS1416/1/1/1591; newspaper clippings relating to her indiscretions in MS1416/1/1/1573, in particular *Daily Mirror*, 9 February 1945; also *The Times*, 28 April 1995.

11 German quote in connection with Vansittart's *Black Record* controversy, *P.D.*, Commons, vol. 368, cols. 417–8; for 'dust-up', *Channon Diaries*, 382; 'scrambled eggs' in James Lees-Milne, *Harold Nicolson: A Biography* (1980–1), ii, 159; Bevan's quip, *P.D.*, 5th series, Commons, vol. 392, col. 309, 23 September 1940. For the Astors in Plymouth, see Sykes, 432–7, 458–9; Collis, 196–201; Grigg, 155–61; and Wilson, 325–7.

12 Quoted in Sykes, 477, and Fox, 526.

13 Quotations in Wilson, 328, 342, and Fox, 515, 523.

14 Quotations in Rowse, *Memories of Men and Women*, 62, and Sykes, 508.

15 Fox, 542.

16 Quotations in Holroyd, 472, and Laurence (ed.), *Bernard Shaw: Collected Letters, 1929–1950* (1988), 848, 514.

17 See Note in MS1461/1/1/1590, and Sykes, 511.

18 See Rose Harrison, 235–6, Sykes, 523–4, and Wilson, 397.

19 Curtis to Halifax, 18 May and 18 July 1940, and Halifax to Curtis, 24 July 1940, MSS Curtis 22.

20 See FO371/24363, C3910/267/62 (undated notes, but Spring 1940); Brand to Nancy, 6 October 1940, MS1416/1/3/14, also Brand to Coupland, 8

December 1939, MSS Brand 153; Curtis to Hailey, 8 September 1941, MSS Brand 153; Brand to Nancy, 30 November 1943, MSS Brand 197, and Brand to Halifax, 4 April 1945, MSS Brand 197. Also Lavin, 293–4.
21 Quoted in Lavin, 319.
22 See Brand to Sir William Haley (editor of *The Times*), 2 May 1963, MSS Brand 20, and Lavin, 301–2.
23 See Lavin, 305.
24 See *The Listener*, 8 May 1952. 'The fox . . .', from Archilochus (an early Greek soldier-poet), and the theme of the late Sir Isaiah Berlin's celebrated essay, *The Hedgehog and the Fox: An Essay on Tolstoy's View of History* (New York, 1957).
25 Churchill, *The Second World War: The Gathering Storm* (1948), i, viii.
26 See Brand to Quigley (undated but 17 December 1962), MSS Brand 200. Quigley's work was eventually published as *The Anglo-American Establishment* (New York, Books in Focus, 1982). Unable to find a publisher, Quigley waited almost twenty years for his book to see the light of day.
27 From Brand's 'Notes' of 26 June 1963, MSS Brand 200. Watt's article, 'Appeasement Reconsidered', was eventually printed in *The Round Table* (September 1963). Unusually, the editor prefaced it with a note that incorporated Brand's caveats. See also Watt, 'Appeasement: the Rise of a Revisionist School?', *Political Quarterly* (April–June 1965), in which he elaborates on his earlier paper. It would not be an exaggeration to say that today most scholars accept the basic tenets of Watt's thesis.
28 See Joseph P. Lash (ed.), *From the Diaries of Felix Frankfurter* (New York, 1975), 189.

Epilogue

1 Quotations in *CV/1*, i, 597–600, and G. W. Monger, *The End of Isolation* (1963), 72 nl.
2 On this topic see Michael Howard, 'Empire, Race and War in pre-1914 Britain', *The Lessons of History* (OUP, 1993).
3 Quotations in Lavin, 116.
4 See Cockburn, *Crossing the Line*, 64–5, and Koss, i, 604.
5 See Walter Lippmann to Brand, 23 June 1942, MSS Brand 197; Franklin D. Roosevelt, *Complete Presidential Press Conferences of Franklin D. Roosevelt* (New York, De Capo Press, 1972), vol. 19, 149, 231–2 (I am grateful to Professor Warren Kimball and Mr Fred Pollock for tracing this reference for me); I. Maisky, *Who Helped Hitler?* (1965), 119–23; and *How War Came*, 127–8, 229. For Kennedy, see *The Week*, 5 July 1939, and Dawson Diaries, MSS Dawson 42, 23 September 1938; also Watt, *How War Came*, 132.
6 See Michael Astor, *Tribal Feeling*, 138; Lord Vansittart, *The Mist Procession* (1958), 482–3; Thomas Jones, *A Diary with Letters, 1931–1950*, 403; and Cockburn, *The Devil's Decade* (1970), 229.
7 Interview with David Astor, 20 February 1996.
8 *The Week*, 30 March 1938.

Bibliography

The papers of Waldorf and Nancy Astor (classified as MS) are located at Reading University; and those of Philip Kerr/Lord Lothian (GD40), at the Scottish Record Office, Edinburgh. The papers of Lionel Curtis, Geoffrey Dawson (including his Diaries) and Robert Brand are at the Bodleian Library, Oxford. All CAB, FO, CO and PREM citations are to be found at the Public Record Office, Kew. References to other collections of private papers may be found in the Notes.

I have also made use of *Hansard: Parliamentary Debates, Commons and Lords*, 4th and 5th series; *Documents on German Foreign Policy*, Series D, vol. VI; *Foreign Relations of the United States*; and *Documents on British Foreign Policy, 1918–39*. I found the Newspaper Cuttings Files at the Astor Archives particularly useful. Other newspapers consulted included *The Week*; *Daily Telegraph*; *The Times*; and *New York Times*.

Books

Unless stated otherwise, the place of publication is London.

Aigner, Dietrich, *Das Ringen um Deutschland* (Frankfurt, 1969)
Amery, L. S., *Lionel Curtis, 1872–1952* (7 March 1952, typescript at Chatham House)
Anon., *The History of The Times*, vol. iv, parts 1 and 2 (1952)
Atholl, Duchess, *Working Partnership* (1958)
Astor, Michael, *Tribal Feelings* (1963)
Avon, Earl, *Facing the Dictators* (1961)
Ayerst, David, *Garvin of the Observer* (1985)
Barnes, John, and Nicholson, David, *The Leo Amery Diaries*, 2 vols (1980; 1988)
Beaverbrook, Lord, *Politicians and the War, 1914–1916*, 2 vols (1928; n.d)
Belloc, Hilaire, *Complete Verse* (1970)
Beloff, Max, *Imperial Sunset. Britain's Liberal Empire*, vol. 1 (1969)
Birkenhead, Lord, *Halifax* (1965)
Birn, Donald S., *The League of Nations Union, 1918–1945* (Oxford, 1981)
Bloch, Michael, *The Duke of Windsor's War* (1982)

—— *The Secret File of the Duke of Windsor* (1988)

Boothby, Robert, *I Fight to Live* (1947)

—— *My Yesterday, Your Tomorrow* (1962)

Bosco, Andrea, and Navari, Cornelia (eds.), *Chatham House and British Foreign Policy, 1919–1945* (Lothian Foundation Press, 1994)

Brand, Robert, *Why I am not a Socialist* (1923)

Branson, Noreen, and Heinemann, Margot, *Britain in the Nineteen Thirties* (1970)

Buchan, John, *Pilgrim's Way: An Essay in Recollection* (Cambridge, Mass., 1940)

—— *Memory, Hold-the-Door* (1940)

Butler, R. A., *The Art of the Possible* (1971)

—— *The Art of Memory* (1982)

Butler, J. R. M., *Lord Lothian* (1960)

Cannadine, David, *The Decline and Fall of the British Aristocracy (1992)*

Cantril, H., and Strunk, M., *Public Opinion, 1935–46* (Princeton, 1951)

Carlton, David, *Anthony Eden* (1986)

'Cato', *Guilty Men* (1940)

Ceadel, Martin, *Pacifism in Britain, 1914–45: The Defining of a Faith* (Oxford, 1980)

Cockburn, Claud, *In Time of Trouble* (1956)

—— *Crossing the Line* (New York, 1960)

—— *View From the West* (1961)

—— *The Devil's Decade* (1973)

Cockburn, Patricia, *The Years of 'The Week'* (1968)

Cockett, Richard, *Twilight of Truth: Chamberlain, Appeasement and the Manipulation of the Press* (1989)

Cockett, Richard (ed.), *My Dear Max: The Letters of Brendan Bracken to Lord Beaverbrook, 1924–58* (1990)

Collis, Maurice, *Nancy Astor* (1960)

Communist Party of Great Britain, *Hitler's Friends in Britain: Sidelights on the Cliveden Set* (March 1938)

Cooper, Artemis, *A Durable Fire: The Letters of Duff and Diana Cooper* (1983)

Coote, Colin, *Editorial* (1965)

Cowles, Virginia, *The Astors* (New York, 1979)

Cowling, Maurice, *The Impact of Hitler* (Cambridge, 1975)

Cross, Colin, *The Fascists in Britain* (1961)

Cross, J. A., *Sir Samuel Hoare* (1977)

De Courcey, Anne, *Circe: The Life of Edith, Marchioness of Londonderry* (1992)

Dilks, David (ed.), *The Diaries of Sir Alexander Cadogan* (1971)

Dodd, W. E. (ed.), *Diaries of William Dodd, 1933–1938* (New York, 1941)

Donaldson, Frances, *Edward VIII* (1974)

Feiling, Sir Keith, *The Life of Neville Chamberlain* (1946)

Fox, James, *The Langhorne Sisters* (1998)

Gannon, Frank, *The British Press and Germany, 1936–1939* (Oxford, 1971)

Garnett, David (ed.), *The Letters of T. E. Lawrence* (1938)

Gathorne-Hardy, G. M., *Lionel Curtis, 1872–1955: An Appreciation* (1955)

Gilbert, Martin, *Plough My Own Furrow: The Life of Lord Allen of Hurtwood* (1965)

—— *The Roots of Appeasement* (1966)

Gilbert, Martin, and Gott, Richard, *The Appeasers* (1963)

Gollin, A. M., *Proconsul in Politics: A Study of Lord Milner in Power and Opposition* (1964)

Granzow, Brigitte, *A Mirror of Nazism: British Opinion and the Emergence of Hitler, 1929–1933* (1964)

Graves, Robert, and Hodges, Alan, *The Long Week-End: A Social History of Great Britain, 1918–1939* (New York, 1941)

Grenfell, Joyce, *Requests the Pleasure* (Futura Books, 1991)

—— *In Pleasant Places* (1979)

—— *Darling Ma: Letters to her Mother, 1932–1944* (1988)

Griffith, Richard, *Fellow Travellers of the Right* (Oxford, 1983)

Grigg, Edward, *The Faith of an Englishman* (1936)

—— *Britain Looks to Germany* (1938)

—— *American Speeches of Lord Lothian, 'Preface'* (1941)

Grigg, John, *Nancy Astor: Portrait of a Pioneer* (1980)

Hamilton, Alastair, *The Appeal of Fascism* (1971)

Harrison, Rose, *Rose: My Life in Service* (New York, 1975)

Harrison, Tom, and Madge, Charles, *Britain by Mass-Observation* (1986)

Harvey, John (ed.), *The Diplomatic Diaries of Oliver Harvey, 1937–40* (1970)

Henderson, Sir Nevile, *Failure of a Mission* (1940)

—— *Water Under the Bridges* (1945)

Heuston, R. F. V., *Lives of the Lord Chancellors* (Oxford, 1964)

Hoare, Sir Samuel (Templewood), *Nine Troubled Years* (1954)

Holroyd, Michael, *George Bernard Shaw*, 3 vols (1988–1991)

—— *Lytton Strachey: A Biography* (1980)

Howard, Michael, *War and the Liberal Conscience* (Rutgers University Press, 1978)

James, Robert Rhodes (ed.), *'Chips': The Diaries of Sir Henry Channon* (1967)

—— *Memoirs of a Conservative: J. C. C. Davidson's Memoirs and Papers, 1910–37* (1969)

—— *Victor Cazalet: A Portrait* (1976)

—— *Anthony Eden* (1986)

Jones, Thomas, *Diary with Letters* (1954)

Kendle, John E., *The Round Table Movement and Imperial Union* (Toronto, 1975)

Kerr, Philip, and Curtis, Lionel, *The Prevention of War* (New Haven, 1923)

Khan, Aga, *Memoirs: World Enough and Time* (1954)

Kingsmill, Hugh, and Muggeridge, Malcolm, *1938: A Preview of Next Year's News* (1937)

Klemperer, Klemens von (ed.), *A Noble Combat: The Letters of Sheila Grant Duff and Adam von Trott zu Solz, 1932–1939* (Oxford, 1988)

—— *German Resistance Against Hitler: The Search for Allies Abroad, 1938–1945* (Oxford, 1992)

Koss, Stephen, *The Rise and Fall of the Political Press in Britain*, 2 vols (1981; 1984)

Langhorne, Elizabeth, *Nancy Astor* (1974)

Lavin, Deborah, *From Empire to International Commonwealth: A Biography of Lionel Curtis* (Oxford, 1995)

Londonderry, Lord, *Ourselves and Germany* (1938)

Lothian, Lord, *Pacifism is not Enough, nor Patriotism Either* (Burges Memorial Lecture, Oxford, 1935)

Louis, Wm. Roger, *In the Name of God, Go!* (New York, 1992)

MacKenzie, Norman and Jeanne (eds.), *The Diary of Beatrice Webb, 1924–1943*, vol. 4 (1985)

MacLachlan, Donald, *In the Chair: Biography of Robert Barrington-Ward* (1970)

McNeile, Cyril ('Sapper'), *Bulldog Drummond at Bay* (1935)

Magubane, Bernard, *The Round Table Movement: Its Influence on the Historiography of Imperialism* (Sapes Books, 1994)

Maiski, Ivan, *Who Helped Hitler?* (1964)

Margach, James, *The Anatomy of Power: The War between the Media from Lloyd George to Callaghan* (1978)

Martin, Kingsley, *Editor: A Volume of Autobiography, 1931–35* (1968)

Marwick, Arthur, *Clifford Allen: The Open Conspirator* (1964)

Masters, Anthony, *Nancy Astor: A Life* (1981)

Middlemass, Keith (ed.), *Whitehall Diary*, 2 vols (Oxford, 1969)

—— *Diplomacy of Illusion* (1972)

Middlemass, Keith, and Barnes, John, *Baldwin: A Biography* (1989)

Minney, R. J., *The Private Papers of Hore-Belisha* (1960)

Mitford, Jessica, *Hons and Rebels* (1960)

Mosley, Nicholas, *Rules of the Game. Beyond the Pale: Memoirs of Sir Oswald Mosley and Family* (Dalkey Archive Press, Illinois, 1991)

Mosley, Sir Oswald, *My Life* (1968)

Muggeridge, Malcolm, *The Thirties* (1940)

Mullally, Frederic, *Fascism inside England* (1946)

Newton, Scott, *The Profits of Power* (Oxford, 1996)

Nicolson, Nigel (ed.), *Sir Harold Nicolson. Diaries and Letters*, 2 vols (1966; 1967)

Nimocks, Walter, *Milner's Young Men: The 'Kindergarten' in Edwardian Imperial Affairs* (1970)

Ovendale, Ritchie, *Appeasement and the English-Speaking World: Britain, the United States, the Dominions, and the Policy of 'Appeasement'* (Cardiff, 1975)

Pakenham, Lord, *Born to Believe* (1953)

Pimlott, Ben (ed.), *The Political Diary of Hugh Dalton, 1918–40* (1986)

Pryce-Jones, David, *Unity Mitford: A Quest* (1976)

Quigley, Carroll, *The Anglo-American Establishment: From Rhodes to Cliveden* (New York, 1982)

Ramsden, John, *A History of the Conservative Party: The Age of Balfour and Baldwin, 1902–1940* (1978)

Ribbentrop, Joachim, *The Ribbentrop Memoirs* (1954)

Rogger, Hans, and Weber, E. (eds.), *The European Right: A Historical Profile* (1965)

Rose, Norman (ed.), *'Baffy'. The Diaries of Blanche Dugdale, 1936–1947* (1973)

—— *Vansittart: Study of a Diplomat* (1978)

—— *Churchill: An Unruly Life* (1994)

Rowse, A. L., *The English Past* (1952)
—— *All Souls and Appeasement* (1961)
—— *Friends and Contemporaries* (1989)
—— *Memories of Men and Women* (1980)
—— *Glimpses of the Great* (1985)
Royal Institute of International Affairs, *Germany's Claim to Colonies* (May 1938)
Salter, Sir Arthur, *Memoirs of a Public Servant* (1961)
Schmidt, Paul, *Hitler's Interpreter* (1951)
Seymour-Ure, Colin, *The Political Impact of Mass Media* (1973)
Shirer, William, *Berlin Diaries, 1934–41* (New York, 1961)
Sinclair, David, *Dynasty: The Astors and their Times* (1983)
Skidelsky, Robert, *Oswald Mosley* (1975)
Smith, Patricia Anne, *Lord Lothian and British Foreign Policy* (unpublished dissertation, Carleton University, 1968)
Steed, Wickham, *The Press* 1938)
Streit, Clarence, *Union Now* (1939)
Stuart, James, *Within the Fringe* (1967)
Stuart, Charles (ed.), *The Reith Diaries* (1975)
Sykes, Christopher, *Nancy: The Life of Lady Astor* (1972)
—— *Troubled Loyalty: A Biography of Adam von Trott* (1968)
Taylor, A. J. P. (ed.), *Lloyd George: A Diary by Frances Stevenson* (1971)
—— *Beaverbrook* (1972)
Taylor, S. J., *The Great Outsider* (1996)
Thompson, Neville, *The Anti-Appeasers* (1971)
Thornton, A. P., *The Imperial Idea and Its Enemies* (1959)
Trevelyan Scholarship Project, *The British Union of Fascists in Yorkshire, 1934–1940* (1960)
Tritton, F. J., *Carl Heath: Apostle of Peace* (1951)
Turner, John (ed.), *The Larger Idea: Lord Lothian and the Problem of National Sovereignty* (1988)
Vincent, John (ed.), *The Crawford Papers: The Journals of David Lindsay, 27th Earl of Crawford and 10th Earl of Balcarres, During the Years 1892–1940* (1984)
Von Klemperer, Klemen, *German Resistance Against Hitler* (Oxford, 1992)
Waley, Daniel, *British Public Opinion and the Abyssinian War* (1975)
Watkins, K. W., *Britain Divided: The Effect of the Spanish Civil War on British Public Opinion* (1963)
Watt, Donald Cameron, *Personalities and Policies: Studies in the Formulation of British Foreign Policy in the Twentieth Century* (Greenwood Press, Connecticut, 1975)
—— *How War Came* (1989)
Weinberg, Gerhard L., *The Foreign Policy of Hitler's Germany*, 2 vols (1970)
Wendt, B. J., *Economic Appeasement* (Frankfurt, 1971)
West, Rebecca, *The Meaning of Treason* (1949)
Williams, Francis, *Dangerous Estate* (1957)
Williamson, Philip (ed.), *The Modernisation of Conservative Politics: The Diaries and Letters of William Bridgeman, 1904–1935* (1988)
Wilson, Derek, *The Astors* (1993)

Winn, Alice, *Always a Virginian* (n.d.)
Woolf, Stuart (ed.), *European Fascism* (1968)
Wrench, Sir Evelyn, *Geoffrey Dawson and Our Times* (1955)
Young, Kenneth (ed.), *The Diaries of Sir Robert Bruce Lockhart, 1915–1938; 1939–65*, 2 vols (1973; 1980)
Zeman, Z. A. B., *Nazi Propaganda* (1964)

Articles

Adamthwaite, Anthony, 'The British Government and the Media, 1937–1938', *Journal of Contemporary History* (April 1983)
Angell, Norman, 'Clivedonism', *Time and Tide* (2 April 1938)
Anon., 'The Problem of Germany', *The Round Table* (June 1937)
Anon., 'Czechoslovakia and Its Minorities', *The Round Table* (June 1937)
Anon., 'Lionel Curtis: Prophet of Organic Union', *The Round Table* (December 1955)
Anon., 'Dougal Orme Malcolm', *The Round Table* (December 1955)
Anon., 'An Editor and His Times: Geoffrey Dawson and the National Government', *The Round Table* (June 1956)
Aronsfeld, C. C., 'The London *Times* and Hitler', *Midstream* (April 1985)
Astor, Nancy, 'I Hate Fascism', *The Forum* (April 1939)
—— 'Lady Astor Interviews Herself', *Saturday Evening Post* (4 March 1939)
Ball, Stuart, 'The Politics of Appeasement: The Fall of the Duchess of Atholl and the Kinross and West Perth By-election, December 1938', *The Scottish Historical Review* (April 1990)
Barrington-Ward, R. M., 'James Louis Garvin', *DNB* (hereafter *DNB*) (1941–1950)
Bosco, Andrea, 'National Sovereignty and Peace: Lord Lothian's Federalist Thought', in John Turner (ed.), *The Larger Idea: Lord Lothian and the Problem of National Sovereignty* (1988)
Bosworth, R. J. B., 'The British Press, the Conservatives, and Mussolini, 1920–34', *Journal of Contemporary History*, vol. 5, no. 2 (1970)
Brand, Lord, 'Philip Kerr', *DNB* (1931–40)
—— 'Edward, Lord Altrincham', *The Round Table* (March 1956)
—— 'Philip Kerr: Some Personal Memories', *The Round Table* (June 1960)
—— 'Lionel George Curtis', *DNB* (1951–1960)
Calvert, Henri, 'L'action politique d'un grand journaliste', *Revue d'Histoire* (July 1957)
Cline, Catherine Ann, 'British Historians and the Treaty of Versailles', *Albion* (Spring, 1988)
Cockett, Richard, 'Communication: Ball, Chamberlain and *Truth*', *Historical Journal*, vol. 33, no. 1 (1990)
Curtis, Lionel, 'World Order', *International Affairs* (March 1939)
Donnelly, M. S. 'J. W. Defoe and Lionel Curtis – Two Concepts of the Commonwealth', *Political Studies*, vol. 8 (1960)

Edwards, P. G., 'The Foreign Office and Fascism, 1924–1929', *Journal of Contemporary History*, vol. 5, no. 2 (1970)

Feetham, Richard, 'Sir Patrick Duncan', *DNB* (1940–1950)

Garton Ash, Timothy, 'The Round Table and Nazi Germany Before the Outbreak of European War' (unpublished essay, Oxford)

Goldman, Aaron, 'Claud Cockburn, *The Week* and the "Cliveden Set" ', *Journalism Quarterly*, vol. 49, no. 4 (1972)

—— 'The Link and the Anglo-German Review', *South Atlantic Quarterly* (Summer, 1972)

Grigg, Edward, 'Merits and Defects of the Locarno Treaty', *International Affairs* (March 1935)

—— 'Lionel (William) Hitchen', *DNB* (1931–40)

Grigg, John, 'Nancy Witcher Astor', *DNB* (1961–1970)

Hodson, H. V., 'John Dove', *DNB* (1931–40)

—— 'The Round Table, 1910–1981', *The Round Table* (October 1981)

Howard, Michael, 'All Souls College and the Round Table', *All Souls College* (Oxford)

Inglis, Brian, 'The Influence of *The Times*', *Historical Studies*

Jeffrey-Jones, Rhodri, 'Lord Lothian and American Democracy: An Illusion in Pursuit of an Illusion', *Canadian Review of American Studies*, vol. 17, no. 4 (1986)

Kerr, Philip, see Lothian, Lord

Lavin, Deborah, 'Lionel Curtis and the Idea of Commonwealth', in F. Madden and D. K. Fieldhouse (eds.), *Oxford and the Idea of Commonwealth* (1982)

Le May, G. H. L., 'Richard Feetham', *DNB* (1961–70)

Lothian, Lord, 'Anglo-German Rivalry', *The Round Table* (November 1910)

—— 'The Foundations of Peace', *The Round Table* (June 1915)

—— 'War Aims', *The Round Table* (September 1916)

—— 'The Commonwealth and the World', *The Round Table* (March 1935)

—— 'The Crisis in the Pacific', *International Affairs* (March 1935)

—— 'Germany Rearmed', *The Round Table* (June 1935)

—— 'Europe, the League, and Abyssinia', *The Round Table* (September 1935)

—— 'The League in Crisis', *The Round Table* (December 1935)

—— 'Root of Our Present Discontent', *The Round Table* (March 1936)

—— 'The World Crisis', *The Round Table* (June 1936)

—— 'The World Crisis of 1936', *Foreign Affairs* (October 1936)

—— 'From Agadir to Nuremberg', *The Round Table* (December 1936)

—— 'Power Politics and the Imperial Conference', *The Round Table* (March 1937)

—— 'Problem of Germany', *The Round Table* (June 1937)

—— 'The New World Situation', *The Round Table* (September 1937)

—— 'The Imperial Conference', *The Round Table* (September 1937)

—— 'Germany and the Peace of Europe', *International Affairs* (November 1937)

—— 'Politics and Currencies', *The Round Table* (March 1938)

—— 'Issues in British Foreign Policy', *International Affairs* (May 1938)

—— 'The Crisis and the Future', *The Round Table* (December 1938)

—— 'The United States and Europe', *International Affairs* (May, 1939)

—— 'The Grand Alliance Against Aggression', *The Round Table* (June 1939)

Low, D. A., 'What Happened to Milner's Young Men: What of Their Successors?', *The Round Table* (1990)

Luo Xu, 'Kelaifuden Jikuan He Yinggua Suijing Zhengee' (The Cliveden Set and the British Policy of Appeasement), *Lishi Yanjui* 5 (1986)

Malcolm, Dougal O., 'Geoffrey Dawson', *DNB* (1941–1950)

McDonough, Frank, '*The Times*, Norman Ebbutt and the Nazis, 1927–37', *Journal of Contemporary History* (July 1992)

Middleton, J. S., 'Reginald Clifford Allen', *DNB* (1931–1940)

Monroe, Elizabeth, 'The Round Table and the Middle Eastern Peace Settlement, 1917–1922', *The Round Table* (November 1970)

Morison, Stanley, 'Robert McGowan Barrington-Ward', *DNB* (1941–1950)

Morrah, Dermot, 'Sir Dougal Orme Malcolm', *DNB* (1951–1960)

Nimocks, Walter, 'The Kindergarten and the Origins of the Round Table Movement', *South Atlantic Quarterly*, vol. 63 (1964)

Pinder, John, 'Prophet Not Without Honour: Lothian and the Federal Idea', *The Round Table* (1983)

Rich, Paul, 'Elite and Popular Culture: "Patriotism and the British Intellectuals", 1886–1945', *History of European Ideas*, vol. 2 (1989)

Rose, Kenneth, 'Edward William MacLeay Grigg', *DNB* (1951–1960)

Rose, Norman, 'The Resignation of Anthony Eden', *The Historical Journal*, vol. 25, no. 4 (1982)

Rowse, A. L., 'Lionel Curtis: The Prophet', in *Glimpses of the Great/Memories and Glimpses* (1985/1986)

Schiller, Kathleen, 'Lionel Curtis – the Man', *Freedom and Union: Journal of the World Republic* (October 1949)

Smuts, Jan, 'The Present International Outlook', *International Affairs* (1935)

Startt, James D., 'Into the Thirties with J. L. Garvin: Private Thoughts of a Great Publicist', *Library Chronicle of University of Texas*, 10 (1978)

Taylor, A. J. P., 'Review article of The History of The Times, vol. 4', *New Statesman and Nation* (26 Aprial 1952)

—— 'Review of *Dawson*', *Observer* (26 October 1955)

—— 'The Chinese Cracker of Cliveden', *Times Literary Supplement* (20 October 1972)

Thomas, B. B., 'Thomas Jones', *DNB* (1951–1960)

Toynbee, Arnold, 'After Munich: The World Outlook', *International Affairs* (January 1939)

—— 'Lionel Curtis', in *Acquaintances* (Oxford, 1967)

Tyack, Geoffrey, 'Service on the Cliveden Estate Between the Wars', *Oral History Review*, 1 (1977)

Veith, Jane Karoline, 'J. P. Kennedy and British Appeasement', in Paul Kennedy (ed.), *United States Diplomats in Europe* (Santa Barbara, 1981)

Watt, David, 'Robert Henry Brand', *DNB* (1961–1970)

—— 'The Foundation of The Round Table: Idealism, Confusion, Construction', *The Round Table* (November 1970)

Watt, Donald Cameron, 'The Week That Was', *Encounter* (May 1972)

—— 'Those Were the Weeks that Were', *Encounter* (May 1986)

Wenden, Charles, 'Appeasement and All Souls', *All Souls College* (Oxford)

Woods, Oliver, 'Waldorf Astor', *DNB* (1951–1960)

Index

200
Cliveden 120
Cliveden Set 194
Nancy Astor 204
'Salter's Soviet' 186
1922 Club dinner 203
Nobel peace prize (1947) 210
Norman, Sir Montagu Norman 179
North Africa, Anglo–French–Italian compact 147
North West Company 14
Northcliffe, Lord 19, 77–9, 93, 106
  Asquith's dilatory ways 96
  British Mission to Washington 97
  Daily Mail 105
  relationship with Dawson 105–6
  The Times 105–7, 197, 105–6
Norway, crisis 202, 204
Nourmahal ('Light of the Harem') (yacht) 16

Observer 19–20, 43, 133
  David Astor as editor 205–6
  Far Eastern situation 143
  Hitler 136–7
  Milner's praises 94
  Waldorf Astor ownership 96
oceanic group 173
Official Secrets Act 163
Ogaden region 146
Oliver, Frederick Scott 62, 956
  Alexander Hamilton: An Essay on American Union (1906) 55,62
  Plas Newydd weekend Moot 54–5, 87
Oliver (lobbyist) 97
organic union 63, 65–6, 93–4
Orkney, Earl of 10, 21
Oslo, Nobel peace prize (1947) 210
Ottawa, Canada 140
  Imperial Economic Conference 159
  Imperial Munitions Board 62, 89–90, 97
Outwoods near Derby 59
Oxford
  All Souls 47, 59, 61, 70–3, 78, 82, 107, 212
  Curtis 59, 105, 123, 201, 209
  Dawson 70–2, 105–7, 203
  'Salter's Soviet' (wartime brains trust) 185–6
Balliol College 47, 49
Beit lectureship in colonial history 67
Christ Church 46–7
Curtis, Lionel George 67
gardens 28
Gladstone Professor of Political Theory and Institutions 185
graduate colleges 70
Historic Buildings Fund 87
Keble College 155
Kinder 46
Magdalen College 47, 70
New College 28–9, 47, 51, 57, 60–1, 82, 88
Newman Society 51
Radcliffe Square 71
Rhodes House 203
Trinity College curate 60–1
University 46
University Parks 107

Pacific Fur Companies 14
Page, Walter 59
Palestine 144
Pall Mall Gazette 19, 43, 74, 96
Palmerston, Lord Henry John Temple 147
Papacy 39–40
Paraguay, 'Chaco war' 145
Paris
  Hotel Majestic 103–4, 106
  Le Canard Enchaîné 160
  Peace Conference *see* Versailles Peace Conference
  Popular Fronts 159–60
  Ritz Hotel 88
  Waldorf and Nancy wedding trip 35
Park Hotel, New York (later Astor House) 14
Parliament, party for State opening 116
Parliament Bill 19–20, 44
Paxton, Sir Joseph 12
Pearl Harbor 153
Pember, Warden 105
Perham, Margery 124
Perry, John Frederick (Peter) 47, 53, 61–2, 72, 82
Petropavlovsk (Russian flagship) 154
Phillips, Lionel 74